Mystic Christianity

Mystic Christianity

H. Spencer Lewis

CONTENTS

Introduction

"The Kingdom of God is within you." – Luke 17:21

Christianity, for many, has become a hollow ritual—a religion of external authority, inherited guilt, and institutional control. But buried beneath centuries of dogma lies a radiant core of mystical truth: the direct realization of divinity within the human soul.

This collection, Mystic Christianity, is a revival of that hidden tradition.

For those disillusioned with rigid theology or seeking a deeper, more transformative understanding of Christ, this volume offers a way inward. It restores Christ not only as a historical figure, but as a symbol of inner alchemy—a bridge between the material and the spiritual, the human and the divine.

Each work in this compilation illuminates a different facet of this forgotten wisdom.

Rudolf Steiner, in Christianity as Mystical Fact, challenges us to see the Gospels not merely as historical documents but as initiatory texts—embedded with archetypal meaning and links to the ancient mysteries of Egypt, Greece, and Persia. His philosophical lens reminds us that Christianity was not born in a vacuum but emerged from a lineage of spiritual awakening across cultures.

H. Spencer Lewis, in The Mystical Life of Jesus, goes beyond the canonical story to uncover the secret teachings, hidden travels, and initiatic knowledge of Christ. Drawing from Rosicrucian sources, he paints a picture of a man whose life was a sacred mission not just to die, but to awaken humanity to a divine inheritance.

Carey and Perry, in God-Man: The Word Made Flesh, take this even further—unveiling a startling synthesis of scripture, anatomy, and esoteric science. To them, the body is the temple, the Christos is a literal internal force, and the path to salvation is not belief—but biology harmonized with spirit.

Together, these works demolish the wall between religion and spirituality. They offer not blind faith, but gnosis—direct knowledge of God through personal experience.

This book is not for the complacent. It's for the seekers. The wanderers. The ones who know there's more to the story than sermons and stained glass. It's for those ready to reclaim the mystical Christ—and awaken the divine light within.

Publisher

CHRISTIANITY AS MYSTICAL FACT

CHRISTIANITY AS MYSTICAL FACT AND THE MYSTERIES OF ANTIQUITY

BY
DR. RUDOLF STEINER

First published in 1902, Christianity as Mystical Fact is a groundbreaking work that reframes Christianity not as a break from the ancient mystery traditions—but as their evolutionary fulfillment. With the clarity of a philosopher and the insight of a mystic, Rudolf Steiner reveals that beneath the surface of the Gospel stories lies a spiritual science—a path of initiation designed to awaken the inner self.

Steiner, the founder of Anthroposophy, explores how the mysteries of Isis, Dionysus, and other ancient initiatory figures find their culmination in the Christ impulse. For Steiner, Jesus is not merely a historical man, but a cosmic being whose incarnation was the pivotal event in human spiritual development. His crucifixion and resurrection are not only symbolic but metaphysical realities, playing out on the grand stage of soul evolution.

This book invites readers to see Christ not through dogma, but through the lens of myth, symbol, and spiritual archetype. It connects the dots between ancient wisdom and modern spiritual awakening, offering a view of Christianity that transcends literalism without discarding the power of the story.

It's a dense, illuminating work—best read slowly, and pondered deeply.

As the opening to this Mystic Christianity compilation, Christianity as Mystical Fact lays the metaphysical foundation for everything that follows. If you've ever sensed that Christianity had deeper roots or a higher purpose than what modern religion offers, Steiner provides the key.

Preface

Christianity as Mystical Fact was the title given by the author to this work, when, eight years ago, he gathered into it the substance of lectures delivered by him in 1902. The title indicated the special character of the book. In it the attempt was made, not merely to represent historically the mystical content of Christianity, but to describe the origin of Christianity from the standpoint of mystical contemplation. Underlying this intention was the thought that at the genesis of Christianity mystical facts were at work which can only be perceived by such contemplation.

It is only the book itself which can make clear that by "mystical" its author does not imply a conception which relies more on vague feelings than on "strictly scientific statements." It is true that "mysticism" is at present widely understood in the former [iv]sense, and hence it is declared by many to be a sphere of the human soul-life with which "true science" can have nothing to do. In this book the word "mysticism" is used in the sense of the representation of a spiritual fact, which can only be recognised in its true nature when the knowledge of it is derived from the sources of spiritual life itself. If the kind of knowledge drawn from such sources is rejected, the reader will not be in a position to judge of the contents of this book. Only one who allows that the same clearness may exist in mysticism as in a true representation of the facts of natural science, will be ready to admit that the content of Christianity as mysticism may also be mystically described. For it is not only a question of the contents of the book, but first and foremost of the methods of knowledge by means of which the statements in it are made.

Many there are in the present day who have a most violent dislike to such methods, which are regarded as conflicting with the ways of true science. And this is not only the case with those willing to admit other [v]interpretations of the world than their own, on the ground of "genuine knowledge of natural science," but also with those who as believers wish to study the nature of Christianity.

The author of this book stands on the ground of a conception which sees that the achievements of natural science in our age must lead up into true mysticism. In fact, any other attitude as regards knowledge actually contradicts everything presented by the achievements of natural science. The facts of natural science itself indeed cannot be comprehended by means of those methods of knowledge which so many people would like to employ to the exclusion of others, under the illusion that they stand on the firm ground of natural science. It is only when we are prepared to admit that a full appreciation of our present admirable knowledge of nature is compatible with genuine mysticism, that we can take the contents of this book into consideration.

The author's intention is to show, by means of what is here called "mystical knowledge," how the source of Christianity prepared its [vi]own ground in the mysteries of pre-Christian times. In this pre-Christian mysticism we find the soil in which Christianity throve, as a germ of quite independent nature. This point of view makes it possible to understand Christianity in its independent being, even though its evolution is traced from pre-Christian mysticism. If this point of view be overlooked, it is very possible to misunderstand that independent character, and to think that Christianity was merely a further development of what already existed in pre-Christian mysticism. Many people of the present day have fallen into this error, comparing the content of Christianity with pre-Christian conceptions, and then thinking that Christian ideas were only a continuation of the former. The following pages are intended to show that Christianity presupposes the earlier mysticism just as a seed must have its soil. It is intended to emphasise the peculiar character of the essence of Christianity, through the knowledge of its evolution, but not to extinguish it.

It is with deep satisfaction that the author is able to mention that this account of the [vii]nature of Christianity has found acceptance with a writer who has enriched the culture of our time in the highest sense of the word, by his important works on the spiritual life of humanity. Edouard Schuré, author of Les Grands Initiés,[1] is so far in accord with the attitude of this book that he undertook to translate it into French, under the title, Le mystère chrétien et les mystères antiques. It may be mentioned by the way, and as a symptom of the existence at the present time of a longing to understand the nature of Christianity as presented in this work, that the first edition was translated into other European languages besides French.

The author has not found occasion to alter anything essential in the preparation of this second edition. On the other hand, what was written eight years ago has been enlarged, and the endeavour has been made to express many things more exactly and circumstantially than was then possible. Unfortunately [viii]the author was obliged, through stress of work, to let a long period elapse between the time when the first edition was exhausted, and the appearance of the second.

Rudolf Steiner.

May, 1910.

POINTS OF VIEW

Natural Science has deeply influenced modern thought. It is becoming more and more impossible to speak of spiritual needs and the life of the soul, without taking into consideration the achievements and methods of this science. It must be admitted, however, that many people satisfy these needs, without letting themselves be troubled by its influence. But those who feel the beating of the pulse of the age must take this influence into consideration. With increasing swiftness do ideas derived from natural science take possession of our [2]brains, and, unwillingly though it may be, our hearts follow, often in dejection and dismay. It is not a question only of the number thus won over, but of the fact that there is a force within the method of natural science, which convinces the attentive observer that that method contains something which cannot be neglected, and is one by which any modern conception of the universe must be profoundly affected. Many of the outgrowths of this method compel a justifiable rejection. But such rejection is not sufficient in an age in which very many resort to this way of thinking, and are attracted to it as if by magic. The case is in no way altered because some people see that true science long ago passed, by its own initiative, beyond the shallow doctrines of force and matter taught by materialists. It would be better, apparently, to listen to those who boldly declare that the ideas of natural science will form the basis of a new religion. If these ideas also appear shallow and superficial to one who knows the deeper spiritual needs of humanity, he must nevertheless take note of them, for it is to them that attention is now turned, [3]and there is reason to think they will claim more and more notice in the near future.

Another class of people have also to be taken into account, those whose hearts have lagged behind their heads. With their reason they cannot but accept the ideas of natural science. The burden of proof is too much for them. But those ideas cannot satisfy the religious needs of their souls,—the perspective offered is too dreary. Is the human soul to rise on the wings of enthusiasm to the heights of beauty, truth, and goodness, only for each individual to be swept away in the end like a bubble blown by the material brain? This is a feeling which oppresses many minds like a nightmare. But scientific concepts oppress them also, coming as they do come with the mighty force of authority. As long as they can, these people remain blind to the discord in their souls. Indeed they console themselves by saying that full clearness in these matters is denied to the human soul. They think in accordance with natural science so long as the experience of their senses and the logic of their intellect demand it, but they keep to the religious [4]sentiments in which they have been educated, and prefer to remain in darkness as to these matters,—a darkness which clouds their understanding. They have not the courage to battle through to the light.

There can be no doubt whatever that the habit of thought derived from natural science is the greatest force in modern intellectual life, and it must not be passed by heedlessly by any one concerned with the spiritual interests of humanity. But it is none the less true that the way in which it sets about satisfying spiritual needs is superficial and shallow. If this were the right way, the outlook would indeed be dreary. Would it not be depressing to be obliged to agree with those who say: "Thought is a form of force. We walk by means of the same force by which we think. Man is an organism which transforms various forms of force into thought-force, an organism the activity of which we maintain by what we call 'food,' and with which we produce what we call 'thought.' What a marvellous chemical process it is which could change a certain quantity of food into the divine tragedy of [5]Hamlet." This is quoted from a pamphlet of Robert G. Ingersoll, bearing the title, Modern Twilight of the Gods. It matters little if such thoughts find but scanty acceptance in the outside world. The point is that innumerable people find themselves compelled by the system of natural science to take up with regard to world-processes an attitude in conformity with the above, even when they think they are not doing so.

It would certainly be a dreary outlook if natural science itself compelled us to accept the creed proclaimed by many of its modern prophets. Most dreary of all for one who has gained, from the content of natural science, the conviction that in its own sphere its mode of thought holds good and its methods are unassailable. For he is driven to make the admission that, however much people may dispute about individual questions, though volume after volume may be written, and thousands of observations accumulated about the struggle for existence and its insignificance, about the omnipotence or powerlessness of natural selection, natural science itself is moving in a direction which, [6]within certain limits, must find acceptance in an ever-increasing degree.

But are the demands made by natural science really such as they are described by some of its representatives? That they are not so is proved by the method employed by these representatives themselves. The method they use in their own sphere is not such as is often described, and claimed for other spheres of thought. Would Darwin and Ernst Haeckel ever have made their great discoveries about the evolution of life if, instead of observing life and the structure of living beings, they had shut themselves up in a laboratory and there made chemical experiments with tissue cut out of an organism? Would Lyell have been able to describe the development of the crust of the earth if, instead of examining strata and their contents, he had scrutinised the chemical qualities of innumerable rocks? Let us really follow in the footsteps of these investigators who tower like giants in the domain of modern science. We shall then apply to the higher regions of spiritual life the methods they have used in the study of nature. We [7]shall not then believe we have understood the nature of the "divine" tragedy of Hamlet by saying that a wonderful chemical process transformed a certain quantity of food into that tragedy. We shall believe it as little as an investigator of nature could seriously believe that he has understood the mission of heat in the evolution of the earth, when he has studied the action of heat on sulphur in a retort. Neither does he attempt to understand the construction of the human brain by examining the effect of liquid potash on a fragment of it, but rather by inquiring how the brain has, in the course of evolution, been developed out of the organs of lower organisms.

It is therefore quite true that one who is investigating the nature of spirit can do nothing better than learn from natural science. He need only do as science does, but he must not allow himself to be misled by what individual representatives of natural science would dictate to him. He must investigate in the spiritual as they do in the physical domain, but he need not adopt the opinions they entertain about the spiritual [8]world, confused as they are by their exclusive contemplation of physical phenomena.

We shall only be acting in the spirit of natural science if we study the spiritual development of man as impartially as the naturalist observes the sense-world. We shall then certainly be led, in the domain of spiritual life, to a kind of contemplation which differs from that of the naturalist as geology differs from pure physics and biology from chemistry. We shall be led up to higher methods, which cannot, it is true, be those of natural science, though quite conformable with the spirit of it. Such methods alone are able to bring us to the heart of spiritual developments, such as that of Christianity, or other worlds of religious conceptions. Any one applying these methods may arouse the opposition of many who believe they are thinking scientifically, but he will know himself, for all that, to be in full accord with a genuinely scientific method of thought.

An investigator of this kind must also go beyond a merely historical examination of the documents relating to spiritual life. This is necessary just on account of the attitude [9]he has acquired from his study of natural history. When a chemical law is explained, it is of small use to describe the retorts, dishes, and pincers which have led to the discovery of the law. And it is just as useless, when explaining the origin of Christianity, to ascertain the historical sources drawn upon by the Evangelist St. Luke, or those from which the "hidden revelation" of St. John is compiled. History can in this case be only the outer court to research proper. It is not by tracing the historical origin of documents that we shall discover anything about the dominant ideas in the writings of Moses or in the traditions of the Greek mystics. These documents are only the outer expression for the ideas. Nor does the naturalist who is investigating the nature of man trouble about the origin of the word "man," or the way in which it has developed in a language. He keeps to the thing, not to the word in which it finds expression. And in studying spiritual life we must likewise abide by the spirit and not by outer documents.

THE MYSTERIES AND THEIR WISDOM

A kind of mysterious veil hangs over the manner in which spiritual needs were satisfied during the older civilisations by those who sought a deeper religious life and fuller knowledge than the popular religions offered. If we inquire how these needs were satisfied, we find ourselves led into the dim twilight of the mysteries, and the individual seeking them disappears for a time from our observation. We see how it is that the popular religions cannot give him what his heart desires. He acknowledges the existence of the gods, but knows that the ordinary ideas about them do not solve the great problems of existence. He seeks a wisdom which is jealously guarded by a community of priest-sages. His aspiring soul seeks a refuge in this community. If he is found by the sages [11]to be sufficiently prepared, he is led up by them, step by step, to higher knowledge, in places hidden from the eyes of outward observers. What then happens to him is concealed from the uninitiated. He seems for a time to be entirely removed from earthly life and to be transported into a hidden world.

When he reappears in the light of day a different, quite transformed person is before us. We see a man who cannot find words sublime enough to express the momentous experience through which he has passed. Not merely metaphorically but in a most real sense does he seem to have gone through the gate of death and to have awakened to a new and higher life. He is, moreover, quite certain that no one who has not had a similar experience can understand his words.

This was what happened to those who were initiated into the Mysteries, into that secret wisdom withheld from the people and which threw light on the greatest questions. This "secret" religion of the elect existed side by side with the popular religion. Its origin vanishes, as far as history is concerned, into the obscurity in which the origin of nations [12]is lost. We find this secret religion everywhere amongst the ancients as far as we know anything concerning them; and we hear their sages speak of the Mysteries with the greatest reverence. What was it that was concealed in them? And what did they unveil to the initiate?

The enigma becomes still more puzzling when we discover that the ancients looked upon the Mysteries as something dangerous. The way leading to the secrets of existence passed through a world of terrors, and woe to him who tried to gain them unworthily. There was no greater crime than the "betrayal" of secrets to the uninitiated. The "traitor" was punished with death and the confiscation of his property. We know that the poet Æschylus was accused of having reproduced on the stage something from the Mysteries. He was only able to escape death by fleeing to the altar of Dionysos and by legally proving that he had never been initiated.

What the ancients say about these secrets is significant, but at the same time ambiguous. The initiate is convinced that it would [13]be a sin to tell what he knows and also that it would be sinful for the uninitiated to listen. Plutarch speaks of the terror of those about to be initiated, and compares their state of mind to preparation for death. A special mode of life had to precede initiation, tending to give the spirit the mastery over the senses. Fasting, solitude, mortifications, and certain exercises for the soul were the means employed. The things to which man clings in ordinary life were to lose all their value for him. The whole trend of his life of sensation and feeling was to be changed.

There can be no doubt as to the meaning of such exercises and tests. The wisdom which was to be offered to the candidate for initiation could only produce the right effect upon his soul if he had previously purified the lower life of his sensibility. He was introduced to the life of the spirit. He was to behold a higher world, but he could not enter into relations with that world without previous exercises and tests. The relations thus gained were the condition of initiation.

In order to obtain a correct idea on this matter, it is necessary to gain experience of [14]the intimate facts of the growth of knowledge. We must feel that there are two widely divergent attitudes towards that which the highest knowledge gives. The world surrounding us is to us at first the real one. We feel, hear, and see what goes on in it, and because we thus perceive things with our senses, we call them real. And we reflect about events, in order to get an insight into their connections. On the other hand, what wells up in our soul is at first not real to us in the same sense. It is "merely" thoughts and ideas. At the most we see in them only images of reality. They themselves have no reality, for we cannot touch, see, or hear them.

There is another way of being connected with things. A person who clings to the kind of reality described above will hardly understand it, but it comes to certain people at some moment in their lives. To them the whole connection with the world is completely reversed. They then call the images which well up in the spiritual life of their souls actually real, and they assign only a lower kind of reality to what the senses hear, touch, [15]feel, and see. They know that they cannot prove what they say, that they can only relate their new experiences, and that when relating them to others they are in the position of a man who can see and who imparts his visual impressions to one born blind. They venture to impart their inner experiences, trusting that there are others round them whose spiritual eyes, though as yet closed, may be opened by the power of what they hear. For they have faith in humanity and want to give it spiritual sight. They can only lay before it the fruits which their spirit has gathered. Whether another sees them, depends on his spiritual eyes being opened or not.

There is something in man which at first prevents him from seeing with the eyes of the spirit. He is not there for that purpose. He is what his senses are, and his intellect is only the interpreter and judge of them. The senses would ill fulfil their mission if they did not insist upon the truth and infallibility of their evidence. An eye must, from its own point of view, uphold the absolute reality of its perceptions. The eye is right as far as it goes, [16]and is not deprived of its due by the eye of the spirit. The latter only allows us to see the things of sense in a higher light. Nothing seen by the eye of sense is denied, but a new brightness, hitherto unseen, radiates from what is seen. And then we know that what we first saw was only a lower reality. We see that still, but it is immersed in something higher, which is spirit. It is now a question of whether we realise and feel what we see. One who lives only in the sensations and feelings of the senses will look upon impressions of higher things as a Fata Morgana, or mere play of fancy. His feelings are entirely directed towards the things of sense. He grasps emptiness when he tries to lay hold of spirit forms. They withdraw from him when he gropes after them. They are just "mere" thoughts. He thinks them, but does not live in them. They are images, less real to him than fleeting dreams. They rise up like bubbles while he is standing in his reality; they disappear before the massive, solidly built reality of which his senses tell him.

It is otherwise with one whose perceptions and feelings with regard to reality have [17]changed. For him that reality has lost its absolute stability and value. His senses and feelings need not become numbed, but they begin to be doubtful of their absolute authority. They leave room for something else. The world of the spirit begins to animate the space left.

At this point a possibility comes in which may prove terrible. A man may lose his sensations and feelings of outer reality without finding any new reality opening up before him. He then feels himself as if suspended in the void. He feels as if he were dead. The old values have disappeared and no new ones have arisen in their place. The world and man no longer exist for him. This, however, is by no means a mere possibility. It happens at some time or other to every one who is seeking for higher knowledge. He comes to a point at which the spirit represents all life to him as death. He is then no longer in the world, but under it,—in the nether world. He is passing through Hades. Well for him if he sink not! Happy if a new world open up before him! Either he dwindles away or he appears to himself transfigured. In the [18]latter case he beholds a new sun and a new earth. The whole world has been born again for him out of spiritual fire.

It is thus that the initiates describe the effect of the Mysteries upon them. Menippus relates that he journeyed to Babylon in order to be taken to Hades and to be brought back again by the successors of Zarathustra. He says that he swam across the great water on his wanderings, and that he passed through fire and ice. We hear that the Mystics were terrified by a flashing sword, and that blood flowed. We understand this when we know from experience the point of transition from lower to higher knowledge. We then feel as if all solid matter and things of sense had dissolved into water, and as if the ground were cut away from under our feet. Everything is dead which we felt before to be alive. The spirit has passed through the life of the senses, as a sword pierces a warm body; we have seen the blood of sense-nature flow. But a new life has appeared. We have risen from the nether-world. The orator Aristides relates this: "I thought I touched the god and felt him draw near, and I was then between [19]waking and sleeping. My spirit was so light that no one who is not initiated can speak of or understand it." This new existence is not subject to the laws of lower life. Growth and decay no longer affect it. One may say much about the Eternal, but words of one who has not been through Hades are "mere sound and smoke." The initiates have a new conception of life and death. Now for the first time do they feel they have the right to speak about immortality. They know that one who speaks of it without having been initiated talks of something which he does not understand. The uninitiated attribute immortality only to something which is subject to the laws of growth and decay. The Mystics, however, did not merely desire to gain the conviction that the kernel of life is eternal. According to the view of the Mysteries, such a conviction would be quite valueless, for this view holds that the Eternal is not present as a living reality in the uninitiated. If such an one spoke of the Eternal, he would be speaking of something non-existent. It is rather the Eternal itself that the Mystics are [20]seeking. They have first to awaken the Eternal within them, then they can speak of it. Hence the hard saying of Plato is quite real to them, that the uninitiated sinks into the mire, and that only one who has passed through the mystical life enters eternity. It is only in this sense that the words in the fragment of Sophocles can be understood: "Thrice-blessed are the initiated who come to the realm of the shades. They alone have life there. For others there is only misery and hardship."

Is one therefore not describing dangers when speaking of the Mysteries? Is it not robbing a man of happiness and of the best part of his life to take him to the portals of the nether-world? Terrible is the responsibility incurred by such an act. And yet ought we to refuse that responsibility? These were the questions which the initiate had to put to himself. He was of opinion that his knowledge bore the same relation to the soul of the people as light does to darkness. But innocent happiness dwells in that darkness, and the Mystics were of opinion that that happiness should not be sacrilegiously interfered with. [21]For what would have happened in the first place if the Mystic had betrayed his secret? He would have uttered words and only words. The feelings and emotions which would have evoked the spirit from the words would have been absent. To do this preparation, exercises, tests, and a complete change in the life of sense were necessary. Without this the hearer would have been hurled into emptiness and nothingness. He would have been deprived of what constituted his happiness, without receiving anything in exchange. One may also say that one could take nothing away from him, for mere words would change nothing in his life of feeling. He would only have been able to feel and experience reality through his senses. Nothing but a terrible misgiving, fatal to life, would be given him. This could only be construed as a crime.

The wisdom of the Mysteries is like a hothouse plant, which must be cultivated and fostered in seclusion. Any one bringing it into the atmosphere of everyday ideas brings it into air in which it cannot flourish. It withers away to nothing before the caustic verdict of modern science and logic. Let us [22]therefore divest ourselves for a time of the education we gained through the microscope and telescope and the habit of thought derived from natural science, and let us cleanse our clumsy hands, which have been too busy with dissecting and experimenting, in order that we may enter the pure temple of the Mysteries. For this a candid and unbiassed attitude of mind is necessary.

The important point for the Mystic is at first the frame of mind in which he approaches that which to him is the highest, the answers to the riddles of existence. Just in our day, when only gross physical science is recognised as containing truth, it is difficult to believe that in the highest things we depend upon the key-note of the soul. Knowledge thereby becomes an intimate personal concern. But this is what it really is to the Mystic. Tell some one the solution of the riddle of the universe! Give it him ready-made! The Mystic will find it to be nothing but empty sound, if the personality does not meet the solution half-way in the right manner. The solution in itself is nothing; it vanishes if the necessary feeling is not kindled at its contact. [23]A divinity approaches you. It is either everything or nothing. Nothing, if you meet it in the frame of mind with which you confront everyday matters. Everything, if you are prepared, and attuned to the meeting. What the Divinity is in itself is a matter which does not affect you; the important point for you is whether it leaves you as it found you or makes another man of you. But this depends entirely on yourself. You must have been prepared by a special education, by a development of the inmost forces of your personality for the work of kindling and releasing what a divinity is able to kindle and release in you. What is brought to you depends on the reception you give to it.

Plutarch has told us about this education, and of the greeting which the Mystic offers the divinity approaching him; "For the god, as it were, greets each one who approaches him, with the words, 'Know thyself,' which is surely no worse than the ordinary greeting, 'Welcome.' Then we answer the divinity in the words, 'Thou art,' and thus we affirm that the true, primordial, [24]and only adequate greeting for him is to declare that he is. In that existence we really have no part here, for every mortal being, situated between birth and destruction, merely manifests an appearance, a feeble and uncertain image of itself. If we try to grasp it with our understanding, it is as when water is tightly compressed and runs over merely through the pressure, spoiling what it touches. For the understanding, pursuing a too definite conception of each being that is subject to accidents and change, loses its way, now in the origin of the being, now in its destruction, and is unable to apprehend anything lasting or really existing. For, as Heraclitus says, we cannot swim twice in the same wave, neither can we lay hold of a mortal being twice in the same state, for, through the violence and rapidity of movement, it is destroyed and recomposed; it comes into being and again decays; it comes and goes. Therefore, that which is becoming can neither attain real existence, because growth neither ceases nor pauses. Change begins in the germ, and forms an embryo; then there appears a child, then a youth, a man, and an [25]old man; the first beginnings and successive ages are continually annulled by the ensuing ones. Hence it is ridiculous to fear one death, when we have already died in so many ways, and are still dying. For, as Heraclitus says, not only is the death of fire the birth of air, and the death of air the birth of water, but the same change may be still more plainly seen in man. The strong man dies when he becomes old, the youth when he becomes a man, the boy on becoming a youth, and the child on becoming a boy. What existed yesterday dies to-day, what is here to-day will die to-morrow. Nothing endures or is a unity, but we become many things, whilst matter wanders around one image, one common form. For if we were always the same, how could we take pleasure in things which formerly did not please us, how could we love and hate, admire and blame opposite things, how could we speak differently and give ourselves up to different passions, unless we were endowed with a different shape, form, and different senses? For no one can rightly come into a different state without change, and one who is changed is no longer [26]the same; but if he is not the same, he no longer exists and is changed from what he was, becoming something else. Sense-perception only led us astray, because we do not know real being, and mistook for it that which is only an appearance."[2]

Plutarch often describes himself as an initiate. What he portrays here is a condition of the life of the Mystic. Man acquires a kind of wisdom by means of which his spirit sees through the illusive character of sense-life. What the senses regard as being, or reality, is plunged into the stream of "becoming"; and man is subject to the same conditions in this respect as all other things in the world. Before the eyes of his spirit he himself dissolves, the sum-total of his being is broken up into parts, into fleeting phenomena. Birth and death lose their distinctive meaning, and become moments of appearing and disappearing, just as much as any other happenings in the world. The Highest cannot be found in the connection between development and decay. It can only be [27]sought in what is really abiding, in what looks back to the past and forward to the future.

To find that which looks (i.e. the spirit) backwards and forwards is the first stage of knowledge. This is the spirit, which is manifesting in and through the physical. It has nothing to do with physical growth. It does not come into being and again decay as do sense-phenomena. One who lives entirely in the world of sense carries the spirit latent within him. One who has pierced through the illusion of the world of sense has the spirit within him as a manifest reality. The man who attains to this insight has developed a new principle within him. Something has happened within him as in a plant when it adds a coloured flower to its green leaves. It is true the forces causing the flower to grow were already latent in the plant before the blossom appeared, but they only became effective when this took place. Divine, spiritual forces are latent in the man who lives merely through his senses, but they only become a manifest reality in the initiate. Such is the transformation which takes place in the Mystic. By his development [28]he has added a new element to the world. The world of sense made him a human being endowed with senses, and then left him to himself. Nature had thus fulfilled her mission. What she is able to do with the powers operative in man is exhausted; not so the forces themselves. They lie as though spellbound in the merely natural man and await their release. They cannot release themselves. They fade away to nothing unless man seizes upon them and develops them, unless he calls into actual being what is latent within him.

Nature evolves from the imperfect to the perfect. She leads beings, through a long series of stages, from inanimate matter, through all living forms up to physical man. Man looks around and finds himself a changing being with physical reality, but he also perceives within him the forces from which the physical reality arose. These forces are not what change, for they have given birth to the changing world. They are within man as a sign that there is more life within him than he can physically perceive. What they may make man is not yet there. He feels [29]something flash up within him which created everything, including himself, and he feels that this will inspire him to higher creative activity. This something is within him, it existed before his manifestation in the flesh, and will exist afterwards. By means of it he became, but he may lay hold of it and take part in its creative activity.

Such are the feelings animating the Mystic after initiation. He feels the Eternal and Divine. His activity is to become a part of that divine creative activity. He may say to himself: "I have discovered a higher ego within me, but that ego extends beyond the bounds of my sense-existence. It existed before my birth and will exist after my death. This ego has created from all eternity, it will go on creating in all eternity. My physical personality is a creation of this ego. But it has incorporated me within it, it works within me, I am a part of it. What I henceforth create will be higher than the physical. My personality is only a means for this creative power, for this Divine is within me." Thus did the Mystic experience his birth into the Divine.

[30]The Mystic called the power that flashed up within him a daimon. He was himself the product of this daimon. It seemed to him as though another being had entered him and taken possession of his organs, a being standing between his physical personality and the all-ruling cosmic power, the divinity.

The Mystic sought this—his daimon. He said to himself: "I have become a human being in mighty Nature, but Nature did not complete her task. This completion I must take in hand myself. But I cannot accomplish it in the gross kingdom of nature to which my physical personality belongs. What it is possible to develop in that realm has already been developed. Therefore I must leave this kingdom and take up the building in the realm of the spirit at the point where nature left off. I must create an atmosphere of life not to be found in outer nature."

This atmosphere of life was prepared for the Mystic in the Mystery temples. There the forces slumbering within him were awakened, there he was changed into a higher creative spirit-nature. This transformation [31]was a delicate process. It could not bear the untempered atmosphere of everyday life. But when once it was completed, its result was that the initiate stood as a rock, rising from the eternal and able to defy all storms. But it was impossible for him to reveal his experiences to any one unprepared to receive them.

Plutarch says that the Mysteries gave deep understanding of the true nature of the daimons. And Cicero tells us that from the Mysteries, "When they are explained and traced back to their meaning, we learn the nature of things rather than that of the gods."[3] From such statements we see clearly that there were higher revelations for the Mystics about the nature of things than that which popular religion was able to impart. Indeed we see that the daimons, i.e., spiritual beings, and the gods themselves, needed explaining. Therefore initiates went back to beings of a higher nature than daimons or gods, and this was characteristic of the essence of the wisdom of the Mysteries.

[32]The people represented the gods and daimons in images borrowed from the world of sense-reality. Would not one who had penetrated into the nature of the Eternal doubt about the eternal nature of such gods as these? How could the Zeus of popular imagination be eternal if he bore within him the qualities of a perishable being? One thing was clear to the Mystics, that man arrives at a conception of the gods in a different way from the conception of other things. An object belonging to the outer world compels us to form a very definite idea of it. In contrast to this, we form our conception of the gods in a freer and somewhat arbitrary manner. The control of the outer world is absent. Reflection teaches us that what we conceive as gods is not subject to outer control. This places us in logical uncertainty; we begin to feel that we ourselves are the creators of our gods. Indeed, we ask ourselves how we have arrived at a conception of the universe that goes beyond physical reality. The initiate was obliged to ask himself such questions; his doubts were justified. "Look at all representations of the [33]gods," he might think to himself. "Are they not like the beings we meet in the world of sense? Did not man create them for himself, by giving or withholding from them, in his thought, some quality belonging to beings of the sense-world? The savage lover of the chase creates a heaven in which the gods themselves take part in glorious hunting, and the Greek peopled his Olympus with divine beings whose models were taken from his own surroundings."

The philosopher Xenophanes (B.C. 575-480) drew attention to this fact with a crude logic. We know that the older Greek philosophers were entirely dependent on the wisdom of the Mysteries. We will afterwards prove this in detail, beginning with Heraclitus. What Xenophanes says may at once be taken as the conviction of a Mystic. It runs thus:

"Men who picture the gods as created in their own human forms, give them human senses, voices, and bodies. But if cattle and lions had hands, and knew how to use them, like men, in painting and working, they would paint the forms of the gods and [34]shape their bodies as their own bodies were constituted. Horses would create gods in horse-form, and cattle would make gods like bulls."

Through insight of this kind, man may begin to doubt the existence of anything divine. He may reject all mythology, and only recognise as reality what is forced upon him by his sense-perception. But the Mystic did not become a doubter of this kind. He saw that the doubter would be like a plant were it to say: "My crimson flowers are null and futile, because I am complete within my green leaves. What I may add to them is only adding illusive appearance." Just as little could the Mystic rest content with gods thus created, the gods of the people. If the plant could think, it would understand that the forces which created its green leaves are also destined to create crimson flowers, and it would not rest till it had investigated those forces and come face to face with them. This was the attitude of the Mystic towards the gods of the people. He did not deny them, or say they were illusion; but he knew they had been created by man. The same [35]forces, the same divine element, which are at work in nature, are at work in the Mystic. They create within him images of the gods. He wishes to see the force that creates the gods; it comes from a higher source than these gods. Xenophanes alludes to it thus: "There is one god greater than all gods and men. His form is not like that of mortals, his thoughts are not their thoughts."

This god was also the God of the Mysteries. He might have been called a "hidden God," for man could never find him with his senses only. Look at outer things around you, you will find nothing divine. Exert your reason, you may be able to detect the laws by which things appear and disappear, but even your reason will not show you anything divine. Saturate your imagination with religious feeling, and you may be able to create images which you may take to be gods, but your reason will pull them to pieces, for it will prove to you that you created them yourself, and borrowed the material from the sense-world. So long as you look at outer things in your quality of simply a reasonable being, you must deny the existence of God; for God [36]is hidden from the senses, and from that reason of yours which explains sense-perceptions.

God lies hidden spellbound in the world, and you need His own power to find Him. You must awaken that power in yourself. These are the teachings which were given to the candidate for initiation.

And now there began for him the great cosmic drama with which his life was bound up. The action of the drama meant nothing less than the deliverance of the spellbound god. Where is God? This was the question asked by the soul of the Mystic. God is not existent, but nature exists. And in nature He must be found. There He has found an enchanted grave. It was in a higher sense that the Mystic understood the words "God is love." For God has exalted that love to its climax, He has sacrificed Himself in infinite love, He has poured Himself out, fallen into number in the manifold of nature. Things in nature live and He does not live. He slumbers within them. We are able to awaken Him; if we are to give Him existence, we must deliver Him by the creative power within us.

[37]The candidate now looks unto himself. As latent creative power as yet without existence, the Divine is living in his soul. In the soul is a sacred place where the spellbound god may wake to liberty. The soul is the mother who is able to conceive the god by nature. If the soul allows herself to be impregnated by nature, she will give birth to the divine. God is born from the marriage of the soul with nature,—no longer a "hidden," but a manifest god. He has life, a perceptible life, wandering amongst men. He is the god freed from enchantment, the offspring of the God who was hidden by a spell. He is not the great God, who was and is and is to come, but yet he may be taken, in a certain

sense, as the revelation of Him. The Father remains at rest in the unseen; the Son is born to man out of his own soul. Mystical knowledge is thus an actual event in the cosmic process. It is the birth of the Divine. It is an event as real as any natural event, only enacted upon a higher plane.

The great secret of the Mystic is that he himself creates his god, but that he first prepares himself to recognise the god created [38]by him. The uninitiated man has no feeling for the father of that god, for that Father slumbers under a spell. The Son appears to be born of a virgin, the soul having seemingly given birth to him without impregnation. All her other children are conceived by the sense-world. Their father may be seen and touched, having the life of sense. The Divine Son alone is begotten of the hidden, eternal, Divine, Father Himself.

FOOTNOTES:
[2]Plutarch's Moral Works, On the Inscription EJ at Delphi, pp. 17-18.
[3]Plutarch, On the Decline of the Oracles; Cicero On the Nature of the Gods.

THE GREEK SAGES

THE GREEK SAGES BEFORE PLATO IN THE
LIGHT OF THE WISDOM OF THE MYSTERIES

Numerous facts combine to show us that the philosophical wisdom of the Greeks rested on the same mental basis as mystical knowledge. We only understand the great philosophers when we approach them with feelings gained through study of the Mysteries. With what veneration does Plato speak of the "secret doctrines" in the Phædo. "And it almost seems," says he, "as though those who have appointed the initiations for us are not at all ordinary people, but that for a long time they have been enjoining upon us that any one who reaches Hades without being initiated and sanctified falls into the mire; but that he who is purified and consecrated when he arrives, dwells with the gods. For those who have to do with [40]initiations say that there are many thyrsus-bearers, but few really inspired. These latter are, in my opinion, none other than those who have devoted themselves in the right way to wisdom. I myself have not missed the opportunity of becoming one of these, as far as I was able, but have striven after it in every way."

It is only a man who is putting his own search for wisdom entirely at the disposal of the condition of soul created by initiation who could thus speak of the Mysteries. And there is no doubt that a flood of light is poured on the words of the great Greek philosophers, when we illustrate them from the Mysteries.

The relation of Heraclitus of Ephesus (535-475 B.C.) to the Mysteries is plainly given us in a saying about him, to the effect that his thoughts "were an impassable road," and that any one, entering upon them without being initiated, found only "dimness and darkness," but that, on the other hand, they were "brighter than the sun" for any one introduced to them by a Mystic. And when it is said of his book, that he deposited it in [41]the temple of Artemis, this only means that initiates alone could understand him. (Edmund Pfleiderer has already collected the historical evidence for the relation of Heraclitus to the Mysteries. Cf. his book Die Philosophie des Heraklit von Ephesus im Lichte der Mysterienidee. Berlin, 1886.) Heraclitus was called "The Obscure," because it was only through the Mysteries that light could be thrown on his intuitive views.

Heraclitus comes before us as a man who took life with the greatest earnestness. We see plainly from his features, if we know how to reconstruct them, that he bore within him intimate knowledge which he knew that words could only indicate, not express. Out of such a temper of mind arose his celebrated utterance, "All things fleet away," which Plutarch explains thus: "We do not dip twice into the same wave, nor can we touch twice the same mortal being. For through abruptness and speed it disperses and brings together, not in succession but simultaneously."

A man who thus thinks has penetrated the nature of transitory things, for he has felt [42]compelled to characterise the essence of transitoriness itself in the clearest terms. Such a description as this could not be given, unless the transitory were being measured by the eternal, and in particular it could not be extended to man without having seen his inner nature. Heraclitus has extended his characterisation to man. "Life and death, waking and sleeping, youth and age are the same; this in changing is that, and that again this." In this sentence there is expressed full knowledge of the illusionary nature of the lower personality. He says still more forcibly, "Life and death are found in our living even as in our dying." What does this mean but that it is only a transient point of view when we value life more than death? Dying is to perish, in order to make way for new life, but the eternal is living in the new life, as in the old. The same eternal appears in transitory life as in death. When we grasp this eternal, we look upon life and death with the same feeling. Life only has a special value when we have not been able to awaken the eternal within us. The saying, "All things fleet away," might be repeated a [43]thousand times, but unless said in this feeling, it is an empty sound. The knowledge of eternal growth is valueless if it does not detach us from temporal growth. It is the turning away from that love of life which impels towards the transitory, which Heraclitus indicates in his utterance, "How can we say about our daily life, 'We are,' when from the standpoint of the eternal we know that 'We are and are not?'" (Cf. Fragments of Heraclitus, No. 81.) "Hades and Dionysos are one and the same," says one of the Fragments. Dionysos, the god of joy in life, of germination and growth, to whom the Dionysiac festivals are dedicated is, for Heraclitus, the same as Hades, the god of destruction and annihilation. Only one who sees death in life and life in death, and in both the eternal, high above life and death, can view the merits and demerits of existence in the right light. Then even imperfections become justified, for in them too lives the eternal. What they are from the standpoint of the limited lower life, they are only in appearance,—"The gratification of men's wishes is not necessarily a happiness for them. Illness [44]makes health sweet and good, hunger makes food appreciated, and toil rest." "The sea contains the purest and impurest water, drinkable and wholesome for fishes, it is undrinkable and injurious to human beings." Here Heraclitus is not primarily drawing attention to the transitoriness of earthly things, but to the splendour and majesty of the eternal.

Heraclitus speaks vehemently against Homer and Hesiod, and the learned men of his day. He wished to show up their way of thinking, which clings to the transitory only. He did not desire gods endowed with qualities taken from a perishable world, and he could not regard as a supreme science, that science which investigates the growth and decay of things. For him, the eternal speaks out of the perishable, and for this eternal he has a profound symbol. "The harmony of the world returns upon itself, like that of the lyre and the bow." What depths are hidden in this image! By the pressing asunder of forces, and again by the harmonising of these divergent forces, unity is attained. How one sound contradicts another, and yet, together, [45]they produce harmony. If we apply this to the Spiritual world, we have the thought of Heraclitus, "Immortals are mortal, mortals immortal, living the death of mortals, dying the life of the Immortals."

It is man's original fault to direct his cognition to the transitory. Thereby he turns away from the eternal, and life becomes a danger to him. What happens to him, comes to him through life, but its events lose their sting if he ceases to set unconditioned value on life. In that case his innocence is restored to him. It is as though he were from the so-called seriousness of life able to return to his childhood. The adult takes many things seriously with which a child merely plays, but one who really knows, becomes like a child. "Serious" values lose their value, looked at from the standpoint of eternity. Life then seems like a play. On this account does Heraclitus say, "Eternity is a child at play, it is the reign of a child." Where does the original fault lie? In taking with the utmost seriousness what does not deserve to be so taken. God has poured Himself into the universe of things. If we take these [46]things and leave God unheeded, we take them in earnest as "the tombs of God." We should play with them like a child, and should earnestly strive to awaken forth from them God, who sleeps spellbound within them.

Contemplation of the eternal acts like a consuming fire on ordinary illusions about the nature of things. The spirit breaks up thoughts which come through the senses, it fuses them. This is the higher meaning of the Heraclitean thought, that fire is the primary element of all things. This thought is certainly to be taken at first as an ordinary physical explanation of the phenomena of the universe. But no one understands Heraclitus who does not think of him in the same way as Philo, living in the early days of Christianity, thought of the laws of the Bible. "There are people," he says, "who take the written laws merely as symbols of spiritual teaching, who diligently search for the latter, but despise the laws themselves. I can only blame such, for they should pay heed to both, to knowledge of the hidden meaning and to observing the obvious one." If the question is discussed whether Heraclitus meant by [47]"fire" physical fire, or whether fire for him was only a symbol of eternal spirit which dissolves and reconstitutes all things, this is putting a wrong construction upon his thought. He meant both and neither of these things. For spirit was also alive, for him, in ordinary fire, and the force which is physically active in fire lives on a higher plane in the human soul, which melts in its crucible mere sense-knowledge, so that out of this the contemplation of the eternal may arise.

It is very easy to misunderstand Heraclitus. He makes Strife the "Father of things," but only of "things," not of the eternal. If there were no contradictions in the world, if the most multifarious interests were not opposing each other, the world of becoming, of transitory things, would not exist. But what is revealed in this antagonism, what is poured forth into it, is not strife but harmony. Just because there is strife in all things, the spirit of the wise should pass over them like a breath of fire, and change them into harmony.

At this point there shines forth one of the [48]great thoughts of Heraclitean wisdom. What is man as a personal being? From the above point of view Heraclitus is able to answer. Man is composed of the conflicting elements into which divinity has poured itself. In this state he finds himself, and beyond this becomes aware of the spirit within him,—the spirit which is rooted in the eternal. But the spirit itself is born, for man, out of the conflict of elements, and it is the first which has to calm them. In man, Nature surpasses her natural limits. It is indeed the same universal force which created antagonism and the mixture of elements which is afterwards, by its wisdom, to do away with the conflict. Here we arrive at the eternal dualism which lives in man, the perpetual antagonism between the temporal and the eternal. Through the eternal he has become something quite definite, and out of this, he is to create something higher. He is both dependent and independent. He can only participate in the eternal Spirit whom he contemplates, in the measure of the compound of elements which that eternal Spirit has effected within him. And it is just on [49]this account that he is called upon to fashion the eternal out of the temporal. The spirit works within him, but works in a special way. It works out of the temporal. It is the peculiarity of the human soul that a temporal thing should be able to work like an eternal one, should grow and increase in power like an eternal thing. This is why the soul is at once like a god and a worm. Man, owing to this, stands in a mid-position between God and animals. The growing and increasing force within him is his daimonic element,—that within him which pushes out beyond himself.

"Man's daimon is his destiny." Thus strikingly does Heraclitus make reference to this fact. He extends man's vital essence far beyond the personal. The personality is the vehicle of the daimon, which is not confined within the limit of the personality, and for which the birth and death of the personality are of no importance. What is the relation of the daimonic element to the personality which comes and goes? The personality is only a form for the manifestation of the daimon.

[50]One who has arrived at this knowledge looks beyond himself, backwards and forwards. The daimonic experiences through which he has passed are enough to prove to him his own immortality. And he can no longer limit his daimon to the one function of occupying his personality, for the latter can only be one of the forms in which the daimon is manifested. The daimon cannot be shut up within one personality, he has power to animate many. He is able to transform himself from one personality into another. The great thought of reincarnation springs as a matter of course from the Heraclitean premises, and not only the thought but the experience of the fact. The thought only paves the way for the experience. One who becomes conscious of the daimonic element within him does not recognise it as innocent and in its first stage. He finds that it has qualities. Whence do they come? Why have I certain natural aptitudes? Because others have already worked upon my daimon. And what becomes of the work which I accomplish in the daimon if I am not to assume that its task ends with my [51]personality? I am working for a future personality. Between me and the Spirit of the Universe, something interposes which reaches beyond me, but is not yet the same as divinity. This something is my daimon. My to-day is only the product of yesterday, my to-morrow will be the product of to-day; in the same way my life is the result of a former and will be the foundation of a future one. Just as mortal man looks back to innumerable yesterdays and forward to many to-morrows, so does the soul of the sage look upon many lives in his past and many in the future. The thoughts and aptitudes I acquired yesterday I am using to-day. Is it not the same with life? Do not people enter upon the horizon of existence with the most diverse capacities? Whence this difference? Does it proceed from nothing?

Our natural sciences take much credit to themselves for having banished miracle from our views of organic life. David Frederick Strauss, in his Alter und Neuer Glaube, considers it a great achievement of our day that we no longer think that a perfect organic being is a miracle issuing from [52]nothing. We understand its perfection when we are able to explain it as a development from imperfection. The structure of an ape is no longer a miracle if we assume its ancestors to have been primitive fishes which have been gradually transformed. Let us at least submit to accept as reasonable in the domain of spirit what seems to us to be right in the domain of nature. Is the perfect spirit to have the same antecedents as the imperfect one? Does a Goethe have the same antecedents as any Hottentot? The antecedents of an ape are as unlike those of a fish as are the antecedents of Goethe's mind unlike those of a savage. The spiritual ancestry of Goethe's soul is a different one from that of the savage soul. The soul has grown as well as the body. The daimon in Goethe has more progenitors than the one in a savage. Let us take the doctrine of reincarnation in this sense, and we shall no longer find it unscientific. We shall be able to explain in the right way what we find in our souls, and we shall not take what we find as if created by a miracle. If I can write, it is owing to the fact that I learned to write. No [53]one who has a pen in his hand for the first time can sit down and write off-hand. But one who has come into the world with "the stamp of genius," must he owe it to a miracle? No, even the "stamp of genius" must be acquired. It must have been learned. And when it appears in a person, we call it a daimon. This daimon too must have been to school; it acquired in a former life what it puts into force in a later one.

In this form, and this form only, did the thought of eternity pass before the mind of Heraclitus and other Greek sages. There was no question with them of a continuance of the immediate personality after death. Compare some verses of Empedocles (B.C. 490-430). He says of those who accept the data of experience as miracles:

Foolish and ignorant they, and do not reach far with their thinking,
Who suppose that what has not existed can come into being,
Or that something may die away wholly and vanish completely;
Impossible is it that any beginning can come from Not-Being,
Quite impossible also that being can fade into nothing;
[54]
For wherever a being is driven, there will it continue to be.
Never will any believe, who has been in these matters instructed,
That spirits of men only live while what is called life here endures,
That only so long do they live, receiving their joys and their sorrows,
But that ere they were born here and when they are dead, they are nothing.

The Greek sage did not even raise the question whether there was an eternal part in man, but only enquired in what this eternal element consisted and how man can nourish and cherish it in himself. For from the outset it was clear to him that man is an intermediate creation between the earthly and the divine. It was not a question of a divine being outside and beyond the world. The divine lives in man but lives in him only in a human way. It is the force urging man to make himself ever more and more divine. Only one who thinks thus can say with Empedocles:

When leaving thy body behind thee, thou soarest into the ether,
[55]
Then thou becomest a god, immortal, not subject to death.

What may be done for a human life from this point of view? It may be introduced into the magic circle of the eternal. For in man there must be forces which merely natural life does not develop. And the life might pass away unused if the forces remained idle. To open them up, thereby to make man like the divine,—this was the task of the Mysteries. And this was also the mission which the

Greek sages set before themselves. In this way we can understand Plato's utterance, that "he who passes unsanctified and uninitiated into the world below will lie in a slough, but that he who arrives there after initiation and purification will dwell with the gods." We have to do here with a conception of immortality, the significance of which lies bound up within the universe. Everything which man undertakes in order to awaken the eternal within him, he does in order to raise the value of the world's existence. The fresh knowledge he [56]gains does not make him an idle spectator of the universe, forming images for himself of what would be there just as much if he did not exist. The force of his knowledge is a higher one, it is one of the creative forces of nature. What flashes up within him spiritually is something divine which was previously under a spell, and which, failing the knowledge he has gained, must have lain fallow and waited for some other exorcist. Thus a human personality does not live in and for itself, but for the world. Life extends far beyond individual existence when looked at in this way. From within such a point of view we can understand utterances like that of Pindar giving a vista of the eternal: "Happy is he who has seen the Mysteries and then descends under the hollow earth. He knows the end of life, and he knows the beginning promised by Zeus."

We understand the proud traits and solitary nature of sages such as Heraclitus. They were able to say proudly of themselves that much had been revealed to them, for they did not attribute their knowledge to their transitory personality, but to the [57]eternal daimon within them. Their pride had as a necessary adjunct the stamp of humility and modesty, expressed in the words, "All knowledge of perishable things is in perpetual flux like the things themselves." Heraclitus calls the eternal universe a play, he could also call it the most serious of realities. But the word "earnest" has lost its force through being applied to earthly experiences. On the other hand, the realisation of "the play of the eternal" leaves man that security in life of which he is deprived by that earnest which has come out of transitory things.

A different conception of the universe from that of Heraclitus grew up, on the basis of the Mysteries, in the community founded by Pythagoras in the 6th century B.C. in Southern Italy. The Pythagoreans saw the basis of things in the numbers and geometrical figures of which they investigated the laws by means of mathematics. Aristotle says of them: "They first studied mathematics, and, quite engrossed in them, they considered the elements of mathematics to be the elements of all things. Now as numbers are naturally the first thing in [58]mathematics, and they thought they saw many resemblances in numbers to things and to development, and certainly more in numbers than in fire, earth, and water, in this way one quality of numbers came to mean for them justice, another, the soul and spirit, another, time, and so on with all the rest. Moreover they found in numbers the qualities and connections of harmony; and thus everything else, in accordance with its whole nature, seemed to be an image of numbers, and numbers seemed to be the first thing in nature."

The mathematical and scientific study of natural phenomena must always lead to a certain Pythagorean habit of thought. When a string of a certain length is struck, a particular sound is produced. If the string is shortened in certain numeric proportions, other sounds will be produced. The pitch of the sounds may be expressed in figures. Physics also expresses colour-relations in figures. When two bodies combine into one substance, it always happens that a certain definite quantity of the one body, expressible in numbers, combines with a certain definite [59]quantity of the other. The Pythagoreans' sense of observation was directed to such arrangements of measures and numbers in nature. Geometrical figures also play a similar rôle. Astronomy, for instance, is mathematics applied to the heavenly bodies. One fact became important to the thought-life of the Pythagoreans. This was that man, quite alone and purely through his mental activity, discovers the laws of numbers and figures, and yet, that when he looks abroad into nature, he finds that things are obeying the same laws which he has ascertained for himself in his own mind. Man forms the idea of an ellipse, and ascertains the laws of ellipses. And the heavenly bodies move according to the laws which he has established. (It is not, of course, a question here of the astronomical views of the Pythagoreans. What may be said about these may equally be said of Copernican views in the connection now being dealt with.) Hence it follows as a direct consequence that the achievements of the human soul are not an activity apart from the rest of the world, but that in those achievements the cosmic laws are expressed. [60] The Pythagoreans said: "The senses show man physical phenomena, but they do not show the harmonious order which these things follow." The human mind must first find that harmonious order within itself, if it wishes to behold it in the outer world. The deeper meaning of the world, that which bears sway within it as an eternal, law-obeying necessity, this makes its appearance in the human soul and becomes a present reality there. THE MEANING OF THE UNIVERSE IS REVEALED in the soul. This meaning is not to be found in what we see, hear, and touch, but in what the soul brings up to the light from its own unseen depths. The eternal laws are thus hidden in the depths of the soul. If we descend there, we shall find the Eternal. God, the eternal harmony of the world, is in the human soul. The soul-element is not limited to the bodily substance which is enclosed within the skin, for what is born in the soul is nothing less than the laws by which worlds revolve in celestial space. The soul is not in the personality. The personality only serves as the organ through which the order which pervades cosmic space [61] may express itself. There is something of the spirit of Pythagoras in what one of the Fathers, Gregory of Nyssa, said: "It is said that human nature is something small and limited, and that God is infinite, and it is asked how the finite can embrace the infinite. But who dares to say that the infinity of the Godhead is limited by the boundary of the flesh, as though by a vessel? For not even during our lifetime is the spiritual nature confined within the boundaries of the flesh. The mass of the body, it is true, is limited by neighbouring parts, but the soul reaches out freely into the whole of creation by the movements of thought."

The soul is not the personality, the soul belongs to infinity. From such a point of view the Pythagoreans must have considered that only fools could imagine the soul-force to be exhausted with the personality.

For them, too, as for Heraclitus, the essential point was the awakening of the eternal in the personal. Knowledge for them meant intercourse with the eternal. The more man brought the eternal element within him into existence, the greater must he [62] necessarily seem to the Pythagoreans. Life in their community consisted in holding intercourse with the eternal. The object of the Pythagorean education was to lead the members of the community to that intercourse. The education was therefore a philosophical initiation, and the Pythagoreans might well say that by their manner of life they were aiming at a goal similar to that of the cults of the Mysteries.

PLATO AS A MYSTIC

The importance of the Mysteries to the spiritual life of the Greeks may be realised from Plato's conception of the universe. There is only one way of understanding him thoroughly. It is to place him in the light which streams forth from the Mysteries.

Plato's later disciples, the Neo-Platonists, credit him with a secret doctrine which he imparted only to those who were worthy, and which he conveyed under the "seal of secrecy." His teaching was looked upon as mysterious in the same sense as the wisdom of the Mysteries. Even if the seventh Platonic letter is not from his hand, as is alleged, it does not signify for our present purpose, for it does not matter whether it was he or another who gave utterance to the [64]view expressed in this letter. This view is of the essence of Plato's philosophy. In the letter we read as follows: "This much I may say about all those who have written or may hereafter write as if they knew the aim of my work,—that no credence is to be attached to their words, whether they obtained their information from me, or from others, or invented it themselves. I have written nothing on this subject, nor would anything be allowed to appear. This kind of thing cannot be expressed in words like other teaching, but needs a long study of the subject and a making oneself one with it. Then it is as though a spark leaped up and kindled a light in the soul which thereafter is able to keep itself alight." This utterance might only indicate the writer's powerlessness to express his meaning in words,—a mere personal weakness,—if the idea of the Mysteries were not to be found in them. The subject on which Plato had not written and would never write, must be something about which all writing would be futile. It must be a feeling, a sentiment, an experience, which is not gained by [65]instantaneous communication, but by making oneself one with it, in heart and soul. The reference is to the inner education which Plato was able to give those he selected. For them, fire flashed forth from his words, for others, only thoughts.

The manner of our approach to Plato's Dialogues is not a matter of indifference. They will mean more or less to us, according to our spiritual condition. Much more passed from Plato to his disciples than the literal meaning of his words. The place where he taught his listeners thrilled in the atmosphere of the Mysteries. His words awoke overtones in higher regions, which vibrated with them, but these overtones needed the atmosphere of the Mysteries, or they died away without having been heard.

In the centre of the world of the Platonic Dialogues stands the personality of Socrates. We need not here touch upon the historical aspect of that personality. It is a question of the character of Socrates as it appears in Plato. Socrates is a person consecrated by his dying for truth. He died as only an initiate can die, as one to whom death is [66]merely a moment of life like other moments.

He approaches death as he would any other event in existence. His attitude towards it was such that even in his friends the feelings usual on such an occasion were not aroused. Phædo says this in the Dialogue on the Immortality of the Soul: "Truly I found myself in the strangest state of mind. I had no compassion for him, as is usual at the death of a dear friend. So happy did the man appear to me in his demeanour and speech, so steadfast and noble was his end, that I was confident that he was not going to Hades without a divine mission, and that even there it would be as well with him as it is with any one anywhere. No tender-hearted emotion overcame me, as might have been expected at such a mournful event, nor on the other hand was I in a cheerful mood, as is usual during philosophical pursuits, and although our conversation was of this nature; but I found myself in a wondrous state of mind and in an unwonted blending of joy and grief when I reflected that this man was about to die." The dying Socrates instructs his disciples about immortality. His personality, [67]which had learned by experience the worthlessness of life, furnishes a kind of proof quite different from logic and arguments founded on reason. It seems as if it were not a man speaking, for this man was passing away, but as if it were the voice of eternal truth itself, which had taken up its abode in a perishable personality. Where a mortal being is dissolving into nothing, there seems to be a breath of the air in which it is possible for eternal harmonies to resound.

We hear no logical proofs of immortality. The whole discourse is designed to lead the friends where they may behold the eternal. Then they will need no proofs. Would it be necessary to prove that a rose is red, to one who has one before him? Why should it be necessary to prove that spirit is eternal, to one whose eyes we have opened to behold spirit? Experiences, inner events, Socrates points to them, and first of all to the experience of wisdom itself.

What does he desire who aspires after wisdom? He wishes to free himself from what the senses offer him in every-day perception. He seeks for the spirit in the [68]sense-world. Is not this a fact which may be compared with dying? "For," according to Socrates, "those who occupy themselves with philosophy in the right way are really striving after nothing else than to die and to be dead, without this being perceived by others. If this is true, it would be strange if, after having aimed at this all through life, when death itself comes they should be indignant at that which they have so long striven after and taken pains about." To corroborate this, Socrates asks one of his friends: "Does it seem to you befitting a philosopher to take trouble about so-called fleshly pleasures, such as eating and drinking? or about sexual pleasures? And do you think that such a man pays much heed to other bodily needs? To have fine clothes, shoes, and other bodily adornments,—do you think he considers or scorns this more than utmost necessity demands? Does it not seem to you that it should be such a man's whole preoccupation not to turn his thoughts to the body, but as much as possible away from it and towards the soul? Therefore this is the first mark of the philosopher, that [69]he, more than all other men, relieves his soul of association with the body."

On this subject Socrates has something more to say, i.e., that aspiration after wisdom has this much in common with dying, that it turns man away from the physical. But whither does he turn? Towards the spiritual. But can he desire the same from spirit as from the senses? Socrates thus expresses himself on this point: "But how is it with reasonable knowledge itself? Is the body a hindrance or not, if we take it as a companion in our search for knowledge? I mean, do sight and hearing procure man any truth? Or is what the poets sing meaningless, that we see and hear nothing clearly?... When does the soul catch sight of truth? For when it tries to examine something with the help of the body, it is manifestly deceived by the latter."

Everything of which we are cognisant by means of our bodily senses appears and disappears. And it is this appearing and disappearing which is the cause of our being deceived. But when with our reasonable intelligence we look deeper into things, the [70]eternal element in them is revealed to us. Thus the senses do not offer us the eternal in its true form. The moment we trust them implicitly they deceive us. They cease to deceive us if we confront them with our thinking insight and submit what they tell us to its examination.

But how could our thinking insight sit in judgment on the declarations of the senses, unless there were something living within it which transcends sense-perception? Therefore the truth or falsity in things is decided by something within us which opposes the physical body and is consequently not subject to its laws. First of all, it cannot be subject to the laws of growth and decay. For this something contains truth within it. Now truth cannot have a yesterday and a to-day, it cannot be one thing one day and another the next, like objects of sense. Therefore truth must be something eternal. And when the philosopher turns away from the perishable things of sense and towards truth, he is turning towards an eternal element that lives within him. If we immerse ourselves wholly in spirit, we shall live wholly [71]in truth. The things of sense around us are no longer present merely in their physical form. "And he accomplishes this most perfectly," says Socrates, "who approaches everything as much as possible with the spirit only, without either looking round when he is thinking, or letting any other sense interrupt his reflecting; but who, making use of pure thought only, strives to grasp everything as it is in itself, separating it as much as possible from eyes and ears, in short from the whole body, which only disturbs the soul and does not allow it to attain truth and insight when associated with the soul.... Now is not death the release and separation of the soul from the body? And it is only true philosophers who are always striving to release the soul as far as they can. This, therefore, is the philosopher's vocation, to deliver and separate the soul from the body.... Therefore it would be foolish if a man, who all his life has taken measures to be as near death as possible, should, when it comes, rebel against it.... In truth the real seekers after wisdom aspire to die, and of all men they are those who least fear [72]death." Moreover Socrates bases all higher morality on liberation from the body. He who only follows what his body ordains is not moral. Who is valiant? asks Socrates. He is valiant who does not obey his body but the demands of his spirit when these demands imperil the body. And who is temperate? Is not this he who "does not let himself be carried away by desires, but who maintains an indifferent and moral demeanour with regard to them. Therefore are not those alone temperate who set least value on the body and live in the love of wisdom?" And so it is, in the opinion of Socrates, with all virtues.

Thence Socrates goes on to characterise intellectual cognition. What is it after all, to cognise? Undoubtedly we arrive at it by forming judgments. I form a judgment about some object; for instance, I say to myself, what is in front of me is a tree. How do I arrive at saying that? I can only do it if I already know what a tree is. I must remember my conception of a tree. A tree is a physical object. If I remember a tree, I therefore remember a physical object. I say [73]of something that it is a tree, if it resembles other things which I have previously observed and which I know to be trees. Memory is the medium for this knowledge. It makes it possible for me to compare the various objects of sense.

But this does not exhaust my knowledge. If I see two similar things, I form a judgment and say, these things are alike. Now, in reality, two things are never exactly alike. I can only find a likeness in certain respects. The idea of a perfect similarity therefore arises within me without having its correspondence in reality. And this idea helps me to form a judgment, as memory helps me to a judgment and to knowledge. Just as one tree reminds me of others, so am I reminded of the idea of similarity by looking at two things from a certain point of view. Thoughts and memories therefore arise within me which are not due to physical reality.

All kinds of knowledge not borrowed from sense-reality are grounded on such thoughts. The whole of mathematics consists of them. He would be a bad geometrician who could [74]only bring into mathematical relations what he can see with his eyes and touch with his hands. Thus we have thoughts which do not originate in perishable nature, but arise out of the spirit. And it is these that bear in them the mark of eternal truth. What mathematics teach will be eternally true, even if tomorrow the whole cosmic system should fall into ruins and an entirely new one arise. Conditions might prevail in another cosmic system, to which our present mathematical truths would not be applicable, but these would be none the less true in themselves.

It is only when the soul is alone with itself that it can bring forth these eternal truths. It is at these times related to the true and eternal, and not to the ephemeral and apparent. Hence Socrates says: "When the soul returning into itself reflects, it goes straight to what is pure and everlasting and immortal and like unto itself; and being related to this, cleaves unto it when the soul is alone, and is not hindered. And then the soul rests from its mistakes, and is like unto itself, even as the eternal is, with whom the soul is now [75]in touch. This state of soul is called wisdom.... Look now whether it does not follow from all that has been said, that the soul is most like the divine, immortal, reasonable, unique, indissoluble, what is always the same and like unto itself; and that on the other hand the body most resembles what is human and mortal, unreasonable, multiform, soluble, never the same nor remaining equal to itself.... If, therefore, this be so, the soul goes to what is like itself, to the immaterial, to the divine, immortal, reasonable. There it attains to bliss, freed from error and ignorance, from fear and undisciplined love and all other human evils. There it lives, as the initiates say, for the remaining time truly with God."

It is not within the scope of this book to indicate all the ways in which Socrates leads his friends to the eternal. They all breathe the same spirit. They all tend to show that man finds one thing when he goes the way of transitory sense-perception, and another when his spirit is alone with itself. It is to this original nature of spirit that Socrates [76]points his hearers. If they find it, they see with their own spiritual eyes that it is eternal. The dying Socrates does not prove the immortality of the soul, he simply lays bare the nature of the soul. And then it comes to light that growth and decay, birth and death, have nothing to do with the soul. The essence of the soul lies in the true, and this can neither come into being nor perish. The soul has no more to do with the becoming than the straight has with the crooked. But death belongs to the becoming. Therefore the soul has nothing to do with death. Must we not say of what is immortal, that it admits of mortality as little as does the straight of the crooked? Starting from this point, "must we not ask," adds Socrates, "that if the immortal is imperishable, is it not impossible for the soul to come to an end when death arrives? For from what has been already shown, it does not admit of death, nor can it die any more than three can be an even number."

Let us review the whole development of this dialogue, in which Socrates brings his [77]hearers to behold the eternal in human personality. The hearers accept his thoughts, and they look into themselves to see if they can find in their inner experiences something which assents to his ideas. They make the objections which strike them. What has happened to the hearers when the dialogue is finished? They have found something within them which they did not possess before. They have not merely accepted an abstract truth, but they have gone through a development. Something has come to life in them which was not living in them before. Is not this to be compared with an initiation? And does not this throw light on the reason for Plato's setting forth his philosophy in the form of conversation? These dialogues are nothing else than the literary form of the events which took place in the sanctuaries of the Mysteries. We are convinced of this from what Plato himself says in many passages. Plato wished to be, as a philosophical teacher, what the initiator into the Mysteries was, as far as this was compatible with the philosophical manner of communication. It is evident how Plato feels himself in harmony [78]with the Mysteries! He only thinks he is on the right path when it is taking him where the Mystic is to be led. He thus expresses himself on the subject in the Timæus. "All those who are of right mind invoke the gods for their small or great enterprises; but we who are engaged in teaching about the universe,—how far it is created and uncreated,—have the special duty, if we have not quite lost our way, to call upon and implore the gods and goddesses that we may teach everything first in conformity with their spirit, and next in harmony with ourselves." And Plato promises those who follow this path, that divinity, as a deliverer, will grant them illuminating teaching as the conclusion of their devious and wandering researches.

It is especially the Timæus that reveals to us how the Platonic cosmogony is connected with the Mysteries. At the very beginning of this dialogue there is mention of an initiation. Solon is initiated by an Egyptian priest into the formation of the worlds, and the way in which eternal truths are [79]symbolically expressed in traditional myths. "There have already been many and various destructions of part of the human race," says the Egyptian priest to Solon, "and there will be more in the future; the most extensive by fire and water, other lesser ones through countless other causes. It is also related in your country that Phaëthon, the son of Helios, once mounted his father's chariot, and as he did not know how to drive it, everything on the earth was burnt up, and he himself slain by lightning. This sounds like a fable, but it contains the truth of the change in the movements of the celestial bodies revolving round the earth and of the annihilation of everything on the earth by much fire. This annihilation happens periodically, after the lapse of certain long periods of time." This passage in the Timæus contains a plain indication of the attitude of the initiate towards folk-myths. He recognises the truths hidden in their images.

The drama of the formation of the world is brought before us in the Timæus. Any one who will follow up the traces which lead to this formation of the cosmos arrives at a [80]dim apprehension of the primordial force from which all things proceeded. "Now it is difficult to find the Creator and Father of the universe, and when we have found Him, it is impossible to speak about Him so that all may understand." The Mystic knew what this "impossibility" means. It points to the divine drama. God is not present in what belongs merely to the senses and understanding. In those He is only present as nature. He is under a spell in nature. Only one who awakens the divine within himself is able to approach Him. Thus He cannot at once be made comprehensible to all. But even to one who approaches Him, He does not appear Himself. The Timæus says that also. The Father made the universe out of the body and soul of the world. He mixed together, in harmony and perfect proportions, the elements which came into being when He, pouring Himself out, gave up His separate existence. Thereby the body of the world came into being, and stretched upon it, in the form of a cross, is the soul of the world. It is what is divine in the world. It found the death of the cross so that the world might [81]come into existence. Plato may therefore call nature the tomb of the divine, a grave, however, in which nothing dead lies but the eternal, to which death only gives the opportunity of bringing into expression the omnipotence of life. And man sees nature in the right light when he approaches it in order to release the crucified soul of the world. It must rise again from its death, from its spell. Where can it come to life again? Only in the soul of initiated man. Then wisdom finds its right relation to the cosmos. The resurrection, the liberation of God, that is wisdom. In the Timæus the development of the world is traced from the imperfect to the perfect. An ascending process is represented imaginatively. Beings are developed. God reveals Himself in their development. Evolution is the resurrection of God from the tomb. Within evolution, man appears. Plato shows that in man there is something special. It is true the whole world is divine, and man is not more divine than other beings. But in other beings God is present in a hidden way, in man he is manifest. At the end of the Timæus we [82]read: "And now we might assert that our study of the universe has attained its end, for after the world was provided and filled with mortal and immortal living beings, it, this one and only begotten world, has itself become a visible being embracing everything visible, and an image of the Creator. It has become the God perceptible to the senses, and the greatest and best world, the fairest and most perfect which there could be." But this one and only begotten world would not be perfect if the image of its Creator were not to be found amongst the images it contains. This image can only be engendered in the human soul. Not the Father Himself, but the Son, God's offspring, living in the soul, and being like unto the Father, him man can bring forth.

Philo, of whom it was said that he was the resurrected Plato, characterised as the "Son of God" the wisdom born out of man, which lives in the soul and contains the reason existing in the world. This cosmic reason, or Logos, appears as the book in which "everything in the world is recorded and delineated." It also appears as the Son of [83]God, "following in the paths of the Father, and creating forms, looking at their archetypes." The platonising Philo addresses this Logos as Christ, "As God is the first and only king of the universe, the way to Him is rightly called the 'Royal Road.' Consider this road to be philosophy ... the road which the company of the ancient ascetics took, who turned away from the entangling fascination of pleasure and devoted themselves to the noble and earnest cultivation of the beautiful. The law names this Royal Road, which we call true philosophy, God's word and spirit."

It is like an initiation to Philo when he enters upon this path, in order to meet the Logos who, to him, is the Son of God. "I do not shrink from relating what has happened to me innumerable times. Often when I wished to put my philosophical thoughts in writing, in my accustomed way, and saw quite clearly what was to be set down, I nevertheless found my mind barren and rigid, so that I was obliged to desist without having accomplished anything, and seemed to be hampered with idle fancies. At the same [84]time I could not but marvel at the power of the reality of thought, with which it rests to open and to close the womb of the human soul. Another time, however, I would begin empty and arrive, without any trouble, at fulness. Thoughts came flying like snowflakes or grains of corn invisibly from above, and it was as though divine power took hold of me and inspired me, so that I did not know where I was, who was with me, who I was, or what I was saying or writing; for just then the flow of ideas was given me, a delightful clearness, keen insight, and lucid mastery of material, as if the inner eye were able to see everything with the greatest distinctness."

This is a description of a path to knowledge so expressed that we see that any one taking this path is conscious of flowing in one current with the divine, when the Logos becomes alive within him. This is also expressed clearly in the words: "When the spirit, moved by love, takes its flight into the most holy, soaring joyously on divine wings, it forgets everything else and itself. It only clings to and is filled with that of [85]which it is the satellite and servant, and to this it offers the incense of the most sacred and chaste virtue."

There are only two ways for Philo. Either man follows the world of sense, that is, what observation and intellect offer, in which case he limits himself to his personality and withdraws from the cosmos; or he becomes conscious of the universal cosmic force, and experiences the eternal within his personality. "He who wishes to escape from God falls into his own hands. For there are two things to be considered, the universal Spirit which is God, and one's own spirit. The latter flees to and takes refuge in the universal Spirit, for one who goes beyond his own spirit says that it is nothing and connects everything with God; but one who avoids God, abolishes the First Cause, and makes himself the cause of everything which happens."

The Platonic view of the universe sets out to be knowledge which by its very nature is also religion. It brings knowledge into relation with the highest to which man can attain through his feelings. Plato will only [86]allow knowledge to hold good when feeling may be completely satisfied in it. It is then more than science, it is the substance of life. It is a higher man within man, that man of which the personality is only an image. Within man is born a being who surpasses him, a primordial, archetypal man, and this is another secret of the Mysteries brought to expression in the Platonic philosophy. Hippolytus, one of the Early Fathers, alludes to this secret. "This is the great secret of the Samothracians (who were guardians of a certain Mystery-cult), which cannot be expressed and which only the initiates know. But these latter speak in detail of Adam, as the primordial, archetypal man."

The Platonic Dialogue on Love, or the Symposium, also represents an initiation. Here love appears as the herald of wisdom. If wisdom, the eternal word, the Logos, is the Son of the Eternal Creator of the cosmos, love is related to the Logos as a mother. Before even a spark of the light of wisdom can flash up in the human soul, a dim impulse or desire for the divine must be present in it. Unconsciously the divine must draw [87]man to what afterwards, when raised into his consciousness, constitutes his supreme happiness. What Heraclitus calls the "daimon" in man (see p. 49) is connected with the idea of love. In the Symposium, people of the most various ranks and views of life speak about love,—the ordinary man, the politician, the scientific man, the satiric poet Aristophanes, and the tragic poet Agathon. They each have their own view of love, in keeping with their different experiences of life. The way in which they express themselves shows the stage at which their "daimon" has arrived (cf. p. 49). By love one being is attracted to another. The multiplicity, the diversity of the things into which divine unity was poured, aspires towards unity and harmony through love. Thus love has something divine in it, and owing to this, each individual can only understand it as far as he participates in the divine.

After these men and others at different degrees of maturity have given utterance to their ideas about love, Socrates takes up the word. He considers love from the point of view of a man in search of knowledge. For [88]him, it is not a divinity, but it is something which leads man to God. Eros, or love, is for him not divine, for a god is perfect, and therefore possesses the beautiful and good; but Eros is only the desire for the beautiful and good. He thus stands between man and God. He is a "daimon," a mediator between the earthly and the divine.

It is significant that Socrates does not claim to be giving his own thoughts when speaking of love. He says he is only relating what a woman once imparted to him as a revelation. It was through mantic art that he came to his conception of love. Diotima, the priestess, awakened in Socrates the daimonic force which was to lead him to the divine. She initiated him.

This passage in the Symposium is highly suggestive. Who is the "wise woman" who awakened the daimon in Socrates? She is more than a merely poetic mode of expression. For no wise woman on the physical plane could awaken the daimon in the soul, unless the daimonic force were latent in the soul itself. It is surely in Socrates' own soul that we must also look for this "wise woman." [89]But there must be a reason why that which brings the daimon to life within the soul should appear as an outward being on the physical plane. The force cannot work in the same way as the forces which may be observed in the soul, as belonging to and native to it. We see that it is the soul-force which precedes the coming of wisdom which Socrates represents as a "wise woman." It is the mother-principle which gives birth to the Son of God, Wisdom, the Logos. The unconscious soul-force which brings the divine into the consciousness is here represented as the feminine element. The soul which as yet is without wisdom is the mother of what leads to the divine. This brings us to an important conception of mysticism. The soul is recognised as the mother of the divine. Unconsciously it leads man to the divine, with the inevitableness of a natural force.

This conception throws light on the view of Greek mythology taken in the Mysteries. The world of the gods is born in the soul. Man looks upon what he creates in images as his gods (cf. p. 33). But he must force his way through to another conception. He must [90]transmute into divine images the divine force which is active within him before the creation of those images. Behind the divine appears the mother of the divine, which is nothing else than the original force of the human soul. Thus side by side with the gods, man represents goddesses.

Let us look at the myth of Dionysos in this light. Dionysos is the son of Zeus and a mortal mother, Semele. Zeus wrests the still immature child from its mother when she is slain by lightning, and shelters it in his own side till it is ready to be born. Hera, the mother of the gods, incites the Titans against Dionysos, and they tear him in pieces. But Pallas Athene rescues his heart, which is still beating, and brings it to Zeus. Out of it he engenders his son for the second time.

In this myth we can accurately trace a process which is enacted in the depths of the human soul. Interpreting it in the manner of the Egyptian priest who instructed Solon about the nature of myths (cf. p. 78 et seq.), we might say, it is related that Dionysos was the son of a god and of a mortal mother, that he was torn in pieces and afterwards [91]born again. This sounds like a fable, but it contains the truth of the birth of the divine and its destiny in the human soul. The divine unites itself with the earthly, temporal human soul. As soon as the divine, Dionysiac element stirs within the soul, it feels a violent desire for its own true spiritual form. Ordinary consciousness, which once again appears in the form of a female goddess, Hera, becomes jealous at the birth of the divine out of the higher consciousness. It arouses the lower nature of man (the Titans). The still immature divine child is torn in pieces. Thus the divine child is present in man as intellectual science broken up. But if there be enough of the higher wisdom (Zeus) in man to be active, it nurses and cherishes the immature child, which is then born again as a second son of God (Dionysos). Thus from science, which is the fragmentary divine force in man, is born undivided wisdom, which is the Logos, the son of God and of a mortal mother, of the perishable human soul, which unconsciously aspires after the divine. As long as we see in all this merely a process in the soul and look upon it as a picture of this [92]process, we are a long way from the spiritual reality which is enacted in it. In this spiritual reality the soul is not merely experiencing something in itself, but it has been released from itself and is taking part in a cosmic event, which is not enacted within the soul, in reality, but outside it.

Platonic wisdom and Greek myths are closely linked together, so too are the myths and the wisdom of the Mysteries. The created gods were the object of popular religion, the history of their origin was the secret of the Mysteries. No wonder that it was held to be dangerous to "betray" the Mysteries, for thereby the origin of the gods of the people was "betrayed." And a right understanding of that origin is salutary, a misunderstanding is injurious.

THE WISDOM OF THE MYSTERIES AND THE MYTH

The Mystic sought forces and beings within himself which are unknown to man as long as he remains in the ordinary attitude towards life. The Mystic puts the great question about his own spiritual forces and the laws which transcend the lower nature. A man of ordinary views of life, bounded by the senses and logic, creates gods for himself, or when he gets to the point of seeing that he has made them, he disclaims them. The Mystic knows that he creates gods, he knows why he creates them, he sees, so to say, behind the natural law which makes man create them. It is as though a plant suddenly became conscious, and learned the laws of its growth and development. As it is, it develops in lovely [94]unconsciousness. If it knew about the laws of its own being, its relation to itself would be completely changed. What the lyric poet feels when he sings about a plant, what the botanist thinks when he investigates its laws, this would hover before a conscious plant as an ideal of itself.

It is thus with the Mystic with regard to the laws, the forces working within him. As one who knew, he was forced to create something divine beyond himself. And the initiates took up the same attitude to that which the people had created beyond nature; that is to the world of popular gods and myths. They wanted to penetrate the laws of this world of gods and myths. Where the people saw the form of a god, or a myth, they looked for a higher truth.

Let us take an example. The Athenians had been forced by the Cretan king Minos to deliver up to him every eight years seven boys and seven girls. These were thrown as food to a terrible monster, the Minotaur. When the mournful tribute was to be paid for the third time, the king's son Theseus accompanied it to Crete. On his arrival there, [95]Ariadne, the daughter of Minos interested herself in him. The Minotaur dwelt in the labyrinth, a maze from which no one could extricate himself who had once got in. Theseus desired to deliver his native city from the shameful tribute. For this purpose he had to enter the labyrinth into which the monster's booty was usually thrown, and to kill the Minotaur. He undertook the task, overcame the formidable foe, and succeeded in regaining the open air with the aid of a ball of thread which Ariadne had given him.

The Mystic had to discover how the creative human mind comes to weave such a story. As the botanist watches the growth of plants in order to discover its laws, so did the Mystic watch the creative spirit. He sought for a truth, a nucleus of wisdom where the people had invented a myth.

Sallust discloses to us the attitude of a mystical sage towards a myth of this kind. "We might call the whole world a myth," says he, "which contains bodies and things visibly, and souls and spirits in a hidden manner. If the truth about the gods were taught to all, the unintelligent would disdain [96]it from not understanding it, and the more capable would make light of it. But if the truth is given in a mystical veil, it is assured against contempt and serves as a stimulus to philosophic thinking.'

When the truth contained in a myth was sought by an initiate, he was conscious of adding something which did not exist in the consciousness of the people. He was aware of being above that consciousness, as a botanist is above a growing plant. Something was expressed which was different from what was present in the mythical consciousness, but it was looked upon as a deeper truth, symbolically expressed in the myth. Man is confronted with his own sense-nature in the form of a hostile monster. He sacrifices to it the fruits of his personality, and the monster devours them, and continues to do so till the conqueror (Theseus) awakes in man. His intuition spins the thread by means of which he finds his way again when he repairs to the maze of the senses in order to slay his enemy. The mystery of human knowledge itself is expressed in this conquering of the senses. The [97]initiate knows that mystery. It points to a force in human personality unknown to ordinary consciousness, but nevertheless active within it. It is the force which creates the myth, which has the same structure as mystical truth. This truth finds its symbol in the myth.

What then is to be found in the myths? In them is a creation of the spirit, of the unconsciously creative soul. The soul has well-defined laws. In order to create beyond itself, it must work in a certain direction. At the mythological stage it does this in images, but these are built up according to the laws of the soul. We might also say that when the soul advances beyond the stage of mythological consciousness to deeper truths, these bear the same stamp as did the myths, for one and the same force was at work in their formation.

Plotinus, the philosopher of the Neo-Platonic school (A.D. 204-269), speaks of this relation of mythical representation to higher knowledge in reference to the priest-sages of Egypt. "Whether as the result of rigorous investigations, or whether instinctively when [98]imparting their wisdom, the Egyptian sages do not use, for expressing their teaching and precepts, written signs which are imitations of voice and speech; but they draw pictures, and in the outlines of these they record, in their temples, the thought contained in each thing, so that every picture contains knowledge and wisdom, and is a definite truth and a complete whole, although there is no explanation nor discussion. Afterwards the contents of the picture are drawn out of it and expressed in words, and the cause is found why it is as it is, and not otherwise."

If we wish to find out the connection of mysticism with mythical narratives, we must see what relationship to them there is in the views of the great thinkers, those who knew their wisdom to be in harmony with the methods of the Mysteries. We find such harmony in Plato in the fullest degree. His explanations of myths and his application of them in his teaching may be taken as a model (cf. p. 78 et seq.). In the Phædrus, a dialogue on the soul, the myth of Boreas is introduced. This divine being, who was seen in the rushing wind, one day saw the fair Orithyia, [99]daughter of the Attic king Erectheus, gathering flowers with her companions. Seized with love for her, he carried her off to his grotto. Plato, by the mouth of Socrates, rejects a rationalist interpretation of this myth. According to this explanation, an outward, natural fact is poetically symbolised by the narrative. A hurricane seized the king's daughter and hurled her over the rocks. "Interpretations of this sort," says Socrates, "are learned sophistries, however popular and usual they may be.... For one who has pulled to pieces one of these mythological forms must, to be consistent, elucidate sceptically and explain naturally all the rest in the same way.... But even if such a labour could be accomplished, it would in any case be no proof of superior talents in the one carrying it out, but only of superficial wit, boorish wisdom, and ridiculous haste.... Therefore I leave on one side all such enquiries, and believe what is generally thought about the myths. I do not examine them, as I have just said, but I examine myself to see whether I too may perhaps be a monster, more complicated [100]and therefore more disordered than the chimæra, more savage than Typhon, or whether I represent a more docile and simple being, to whom some particle of a virtuous and divine nature has been given."

We see from this that Plato does not approve of a rationalistic and merely intellectual interpretation of myths. This attitude must be compared with the way in which he himself uses myths in order to express himself through them. When he speaks of the life of the soul, when he leaves the paths of the transitory and seeks the eternal in the soul, when, therefore, images borrowed from sense-perception and reasoning thought can no longer be used, then Plato has recourse to the myth. Phædrus treats of the eternal in the soul, which is portrayed as a car drawn by two horses winged all over, and driven by a charioteer. One horse is patient and docile, the other wild and headstrong. If an obstacle comes in the way of the car the troublesome horse takes the opportunity of impeding the docile one and defying the driver. When the car arrives where it has to follow the gods up the [101]celestial steep, the intractable horse throws the team into confusion. If it is less strong than the good horse, it is overcome, and the car is able to go on into the supersensible realm. It thus happens that the soul can never ascend without difficulties into the kingdom of the divine. Some souls rise more to the vision of eternity, some less. The soul which has seen the world beyond remains safe until the next journey. One who, on account of the intractable horse, has not seen beyond, must try again on the next journey. These journeys signify the various incarnations of the soul. One journey signifies the life of the soul in one personality. The wild horse represents the lower nature, the docile one the higher nature; the driver, the soul longing for union with the divine.

Plato resorts to the myth in order to describe the course of the eternal spirit through its various transformations. In the same way he has recourse, in other writings, to symbolical narrative, in order to portray the inner nature of man, which is not perceptible to the senses.

Plato is here in complete harmony with the [102]mythical and allegorical manner of expression used by others. For instance there is in ancient Hindu literature a parable attributed to Buddha.

A man very much attached to life, who seeks sensuous pleasures and will die at no price is pursued by four serpents. He hears a voice commanding him to feed and bathe the serpents from time to time. The man runs away, fearing the serpents. Again he hears a voice, warning him that he is pursued by five murderers. Once more he escapes. A voice calls his attention to a sixth murderer, who is about to behead him with a sword. Again he flees. He comes to a deserted village. There he hears a voice telling him that robbers are shortly going to plunder the village. Having again escaped, he comes to a great flood. He feels unsafe where he is, and out of straw, wood, and leaves he makes a basket in which he arrives at the other shore. Now he is safe, he is a Brahmin.

The meaning of this allegory is that man has to pass through the most various states before attaining to the divine. The four [103]serpents represent the four elements, fire, water, earth, and air. The five murderers are the five senses. The deserted village is the soul which has escaped from sense-impressions, but is not yet safe if it is alone with itself, for if its lower nature lays hold of it, it must perish. Man must construct for himself the boat which is to carry him over the flood of the transitory from the one shore, the sense-nature, to the other, the eternal, divine world.

Let us look at the Egyptian mystery of Osiris in this light. Osiris had gradually become one of the most important Egyptian divinities; he supplanted other gods in certain parts of the country; and an important cycle of myths was formed round him and his consort Isis.

Osiris was the son of the Sun-god, his brother was Typhon-Set, and his sister was Isis. Osiris married his sister, and together they reigned over Egypt. The wicked brother, Typhon, meditated killing Osiris. He had a chest made which was exactly the length of Osiris' body. At a banquet this chest was offered to the person whom it [104]exactly fitted. This was Osiris and none other! He entered the chest. Typhon and his confederates rushed upon him, closed the chest, and threw it into the river. When Isis heard the terrible news she wandered far and wide in despair, seeking her husband's body. When she had found it, Typhon again took possession of it, and tore it in fourteen pieces which were dispersed in many different places. Various tombs of Osiris were shown in Egypt. In many places, up and down the country, portions of the god were said to be buried. Osiris himself, however, came forth from the nether-world and vanquished Typhon. A beam shone from him upon Isis, who in consequence bore a son, Harpocrates or Horus.

And now let us compare this myth with the view which the Greek philosopher, Empedocles (B.C. 490-430) takes of the universe. He assumes that the one original primeval being was once broken up into the four elements, fire, water, earth, and air, or into the multiplicity of being. He represents two opposing forces, which within this world of existence bring about growth and decay, [105]love and strife. Empedocles says of the elements:

They remain ever the same, but yet by combining their forces
Become transformed into men and the numberless beings besides.
These are now joined into one, love binding the many together.
Now once again they are scattered, dispersing through hatred and strife.
What then are the things in the world from Empedocles' point of view? They are the elements in different combinations. They could only come into being because the Primeval Unity was broken up into the four essences. Therefore this primordial unity was poured into the elements. Anything confronting us is part of the divinity which was poured out. But the divinity is hidden in the thing; it first had to die that things might come into being. And what are these things? Mixtures of divine constituents effectuated by love and hatred. Empedocles says this distinctly:

See, for a clear demonstration, how the limbs of a man are constructed,
[106]
All that the body possesses, in beauty and pride of existence,
All put together by love, are the elements there forming one.
Afterwards hatred and strife come, and fatally tear them asunder,
Once more they wander alone, on the desolate confines of life.
So it is with the bushes and trees, and the water-inhabiting fishes,
Wild animals roaming the mountains, and ships swiftly borne by their sails.
Empedocles therefore must come to the conclusion that the sage finds again the Divine Primordial

Unity, hidden in the world by a spell, and entangled in the meshes of love and hatred. But if man finds the divine, he must himself be divine, for Empedocles takes the point of view that a being is only cognised by its equal. This conviction of his is expressed in Goethe's lines: "If the eye were not of the nature of the sun, how could we behold light? If divine force were not at [107]work in us, how could divine things delight us?"

These thoughts about the world and man, which transcend sense-experience, were found by the Mystic in the myth of Osiris. Divine creative force has been poured out into the universe; it appears as the four elements; God (Osiris) is killed. Man is to raise him from the dead with his cognition, which is of divine nature. He is to find him again as Horus (the Son of God, the Logos, Wisdom), in the opposition between Strife (Typhon) and Love (Isis). Empedocles expresses his fundamental conviction in Greek form by means of images which border on myth. Love is Aphrodite, and strife is Neikos. They bind and unbind the elements.

The portrayal of the content of a myth in the manner followed here must not be confused with a merely symbolical or even allegorical interpretation of myths. This is not intended. The images forming the contents of a myth are not invented symbols of abstract truths, but actual soul-experiences of the initiate. He experiences the images with his spiritual organs of perception, just [108]as the normal man experiences the images of physical things with his eyes and ears. But as an image is nothing in itself if it is not aroused in the perception by an outer object, so the mythical image is nothing unless it is excited by real facts of the spiritual world. Only in regard to the physical world, man is at first outside the exciting causes, whereas he can only experience the images of myths when he is within the corresponding spiritual occurrences. In order, however, to be within them, he must have gone through initiation. Then the spiritual occurrences within which he is perceiving are, as it were, illustrated by the myth-images. Any one who cannot take the mythical element as such illustration of real spiritual occurrences, has not yet attained to the understanding of it. For the spiritual events themselves are supersensible, and images which are reminiscent of the physical world are not themselves of a spiritual nature, but only an illustration of spiritual things. One who lives merely in the images lives in a dream. Only one who has got to the point of feeling the spiritual element in the image as he feels in the [109]sense-world a rose through the image of a rose, really lives in spiritual perceptions. This is the reason why the images of myths cannot have only one meaning. On account of their illustrative character, the same myths may express several spiritual facts. It is not therefore a contradiction when interpreters of myths sometimes connect a myth with one spiritual fact and sometimes with another.

From this standpoint, we are able to find a thread to conduct us through the labyrinth of Greek myths. Let us consider the legend of Heracles. The twelve labours imposed upon Heracles appear in a higher light when we remember that before the last and most difficult one, he is initiated into the Eleusinian mysteries. He is commissioned by King Eurystheus of Mycenæ to bring the hell-hound Cerberus from the infernal regions and take it back there again. In order to undertake the descent into hell, Heracles had to be initiated. The Mysteries conducted man through the death of perishable things, therefore into the nether-world, and by initiation they rescued his eternal part from perishing. As a Mystic, he could [110]vanquish death. Heracles having become a Mystic overcomes the dangers of the nether-world. This justifies us in interpreting his other ordeals as stages in the inner development of the soul. He overcomes the Nemæan lion and brings him to Mycenæ. This means that he becomes master of purely physical force in man; he tames it. Afterwards he slays the nine-headed Hydra. He overcomes it with firebrands and dips his arrows in its gall, so that they become deadly. This means that he overcomes lower knowledge, that which comes through the senses. He does this through the fire of the spirit, and from what he has gained through the lower knowledge, he draws the power to look at lower things in the light which belongs to spiritual sight. Heracles captures the hind of Artemis, goddess of hunting: everything which free nature offers to the human soul, Heracles conquers and subdues. The other labours may be interpreted in the same way. We cannot here trace out every detail, and only wish to describe how the general sense of the myth points to inner development.

A similar interpretation is possible of the [111]expedition of the Argonauts. Phrixus and his sister Helle, children of a Bœotian king, suffered many things from their step-mother. The gods sent them a ram with a golden fleece, which flew away with them. When they came to the straits between Europe and Asia, Helle was drowned. Hence the strait is called the Hellespont. Phrixus came to the King of Colchis, on the east shore of the Black Sea. He sacrificed the ram to the gods, and gave its fleece to King Æetes. The king had it hung up in a grove and guarded by a terrible dragon. The Greek hero Jason undertook to fetch the fleece from Colchis, in company with other heroes, Heracles, Theseus, and Orpheus. Heavy tasks were laid upon Jason by Æetes for the obtaining of the treasure, but Medea, the king's daughter, who was versed in magic, aided him. He subdued two fire-breathing bulls. He ploughed a field and sowed in it dragon's teeth from which armed men grew up out of the earth. By Medea's advice he threw a stone into their midst, whereupon they killed each other. Jason lulls the dragon to sleep with a charm of Medea's and is then able [112]to win the fleece. He returns with it to Greece, Medea accompanying him as his wife. The king pursues the fugitives. In order to detain him, Medea slays her little brother Absyrtus, and scatters his limbs in the sea. Æetes stays to collect them, and the pair are able to reach Jason's home with the fleece.

Each of these facts requires a deep elucidation. The fleece is something belonging to man, and infinitely precious to him. It is something from which he was separated in times of yore, and for the recovery of which he has to overcome terrible forces. It is thus with the eternal in the human soul. It belongs to man, but man is separated from it by his lower nature. Only by overcoming the latter, and lulling it to sleep, can he recover the eternal. This becomes possible when his own consciousness (Medea) comes to his aid with its magic power. Medea is to Jason what Diotima was to Socrates, a teacher of love (cf. p. 88). Man's own wisdom has the magic power necessary for attaining the divine after having overcome the transitory. From the lower nature there can [113]only arise a lower human principle, the armed men who are overcome by spiritual force, the counsel of Medea. Even when man has found the eternal, the fleece, he is not yet safe. He has to sacrifice part of his consciousness (Absyrtus). This is exacted by the physical world, which we can only apprehend as a multiple (dismembered) world. We might go still deeper into the description of the spiritual events lying behind the images, but it is only intended here to indicate the principle of the formation of myths.

Of special interest, when interpreted in this way, is the legend of Prometheus. He and his brother Epimetheus are sons of the Titan Iapetus. The Titans are the offspring of the oldest generation of gods, Uranus (Heaven) and Gæa (Earth). Kronos, the youngest of the Titans, dethroned his father and seized upon the government of the world. In return, he was overpowered, with the other Titans, by his son Zeus, who became the chief of the gods. In the struggle with the Titans, Prometheus was on the side of Zeus. By his advice, Zeus banished the Titans to the nether-world. But in [114]Prometheus there still lived the Titan spirit, he was only half a friend to Zeus. When the latter wished to exterminate men on account of their arrogance, Prometheus espoused their cause, taught them numbers, writing, and everything else which leads to culture, especially the use of fire. This aroused the wrath of Zeus against Prometheus. Hephaistos, the son of Zeus, was commissioned to make a female form of great beauty, whom the gods adorned with every possible gift. She was called Pandora, the all-gifted one. Hermes, messenger of the gods, brought her to Epimetheus, the brother of Prometheus. She brought him a casket, as a present from the gods. Epimetheus accepted the present, although Prometheus had warned him against receiving any gift from the gods. When the casket was opened, every possible human evil flew out of it. Hope alone remained, and this because Pandora quickly closed the box. Hope has therefore been left to man, as a doubtful gift of the gods. By order of Zeus, Prometheus was chained to a rock on the Caucasus, on account of his relation to man. An eagle perpetually gnaws his liver, [115]which is as often renewed. He has to pass his life in agonising loneliness till one of the gods voluntarily sacrifices himself, i.e., devotes himself to death. The tormented Prometheus bears his sufferings steadfastly. It had been told him that Zeus would be dethroned by the son of a mortal unless Zeus consented to wed this mortal woman. It was important for Zeus to know this secret. He sent the messenger Hermes to Prometheus, in order to learn something about it. Prometheus refused to say anything. The legend of Heracles is connected with that of Prometheus. In the course of his wanderings Heracles comes to the Caucasus. He slays the eagle which was devouring the liver of Prometheus. The centaur Chiron, who cannot die, although suffering from an incurable wound, sacrifices himself for Prometheus, who is thereupon reconciled with the gods.

The Titans are the force of will, proceeding as nature (Kronos) from the original universal spirit (Uranus). Here we have to think not merely of will-forces in an abstract form, but of actual will-beings. Prometheus is one of them, and this describes his nature. [116]But he is not altogether a Titan. In a certain sense he is on the side of Zeus, the Spirit, who enters upon the rulership of the world after the unbridled force of nature (Kronos) has been subdued. Prometheus is thus the representative of those worlds which have given man the progressive element, half nature-force, half spiritual force, man's will. The will points on the one side towards good, on the other, towards evil. Its fate is decided according as it leans to the spiritual or the perishable. This fate is that of man himself. He is chained to the perishable, the eagle gnaws him, he has to suffer. He can only reach the highest by seeking his destiny in solitude. He has a secret which is that the divine (Zeus) must marry a mortal (human consciousness bound up with the physical body), in order to beget a son, human wisdom (the Logos) which will deliver the deity. By this means consciousness becomes immortal. He must not betray this secret till a Mystic (Heracles) comes to him, and annihilates the power which was perpetually threatening him with death. A being half animal, half human, a centaur, is [117]obliged to sacrifice itself to redeem man. The centaur is man himself, half animal, half spiritual. He must die in order that the purely spiritual man may be delivered. That which is disdained by Prometheus, human will, is accepted by Epimetheus, reason or prudence. But the gifts offered to Epimetheus are only troubles and sorrows, for reason clings to the transitory and perishable. And only one thing is left—the hope that even out of the perishable the eternal may some day be born.

The thread running through the legends of the Argonauts, Heracles and Prometheus, is continued in Homer's Odyssey. Here we find ourselves compelled to use our own method of interpretation. But on closer consideration of everything which has to be taken into account, even the sturdiest doubter must lose all scruples about such an interpretation. In the first place, it is a startling fact that it is also related of Odysseus that he descended into the nether-world. Whatever we may think about the author of the Odyssey in other respects, it is impossible to imagine his representing a mortal descending to the [118]infernal regions, without his bringing him into connection with what the journey into the nether-world meant to the Greeks. It meant the conquest of the perishable and the awakening of the eternal in the soul. It must therefore be conceded that Odysseus accomplished this, and thereby his experiences and those of Heracles acquire a deeper significance. They become a delineation of the non-sensuous, of the soul's progress of development. Hence the narrative in the Odyssey is different from what is demanded by a history of outer events. The hero makes voyages in enchanted ships. Actual geographical distances are dealt with in most arbitrary fashion. It is not in the least a question of what is physically real. This becomes comprehensible, if the physically real events are only related for the sake of illustrating the development of a soul. Moreover the poet himself at the opening of the book says that it deals with a search for the soul:

"O Muse, sing to me of the man full of resource, who wandered very much after he had destroyed the sacred city of Troy, and [119]saw the cities of many men, and learned their manners. Many griefs also in his mind did he suffer on the sea, although seeking to preserve his own soul, and the return of his companions."

We have before us a man seeking for the soul, for the divine, and his wanderings during this search are narrated. He comes to the land of the Cyclopes. These are uncouth giants, with only one eye and that in the centre of the forehead. The most terrible, Polyphemus, devours several of Odysseus' companions. Odysseus himself escapes by blinding the Cyclopes. Here we have to do with the first stage of life's pilgrimage. Physical force or the lower nature has to be overcome. It devours any one who does not take away its power, who does not blind it. Odysseus next comes to the island of the enchantress Circe. She changes some of his companions into grunting pigs. She also is subdued by Odysseus. Circe is the lower mind-force, which cleaves to the transitory. If misused, it may thrust men down even deeper into bestiality. Odysseus has to overcome it. Then he is able to descend into the [120]nether-world. He becomes a Mystic. Now he is exposed to the dangers which beset the Mystic on his progress from the lower to the higher degrees of initiation. He comes to the Sirens, who lure the passer-by to death by sweet magic sounds. These are the forms of the lower imagination, which are at first pursued by one who has freed himself from the power of the senses. He has got so far that his spirit acts freely, but is not initiated. He pursues illusions, from the power of which he must break loose. Odysseus has to accomplish the awful passage between Scylla and Charybdis. The Mystic, at the beginning of the path wavers between spirit and sensuousness. He cannot yet grasp the full value of spirit, yet sensuousness has already lost its former attraction. All Odysseus' companions perish in a shipwreck; he alone escapes and comes to the nymph Calypso, who receives him kindly and takes care of him for seven years. At length, by order of Zeus, she dismisses him to his home. The Mystic has arrived at a stage at which all his fellow-aspirants fail; he alone, Odysseus, is worthy. He enjoys for a time, which is [121]defined by the mystically symbolic number seven, the rest of gradual initiation. Before Odysseus arrives at his home, he comes to the isle of the Phæaces, where he meets with a hospitable reception. The king's daughter gives him sympathy, and the king, Alcinous, entertains and honours him. Once more does Odysseus approach the world and its joys, and the spirit which is attached to the world, Nausicaa, awakes within him. But he finds the way home, to the divine. At first nothing good awaits him at home. His wife, Penelope, is surrounded by numerous suitors. Each one she promises to marry, when she has finished weaving a certain piece of work. She avoids keeping her promise by undoing every night what she has woven by day. Odysseus is obliged to vanquish the suitors before he can be reunited to his wife in peace. The goddess Athene changes him into a beggar so that he may not be recognised at his entrance; and thus he overcomes the suitors. Odysseus is seeking his own deeper consciousness, the divine powers of the soul. He wishes to be united with them. Before the Mystic can find them, he must [122]overcome everything which sues for the favour of that consciousness. The band of suitors spring from the world of lower reality, from perishable nature. The logic directed against them is a spinning which is always undone again after it has been spun. Wisdom (the goddess Athene) is the sure guide to the deepest powers of the soul. It changes man into a beggar, i.e., it divests him of everything of a transitory nature.

The Eleusinian festivals, which were celebrated in Greece in honour of Demeter and Dionysos, were steeped in the wisdom of the Mysteries. A sacred road led from Athens to Eleusis. It was bordered with mysterious signs, intended to bring the soul into an exalted mood. In Eleusis were mysterious temples, served by families of priests. The dignity and the wisdom which was bound up with it were inherited in these families from generation to generation. (Instructive information about the organisation of these sanctuaries will be found in Karl Bötticher's Ergänzungen zu den letzten Untersuchungen auf der Akropolis in Athen, Philologus, Supplement, [123]vol. iii, part 3.) The wisdom, which qualified for the priesthood, was the wisdom of the Greek Mysteries. The festivals, which were celebrated twice a year, represented the great world-drama of the destiny of the divine in the world, and of that of the human soul. The lesser Mysteries took place in February, the greater in September. Initiations were connected with the festivals. The symbolical presentation of the cosmic and human drama formed the final act of the initiations of the Mystics, which took place here.

The Eleusinian temples had been erected in honour of the goddess Demeter. She was a daughter of Kronos. She had given to Zeus a daughter, Persephone, before his marriage with Hera. Persephone, while playing, was carried away by Hades (Pluto), the god of the infernal regions. Demeter wandered far and wide over the earth, seeking her with lamentations. Sitting on a stone in Eleusis, she was found by the daughters of Keleus, ruler of the place; in the form of an old woman she entered the service of his family, as nurse to the queen's son. She [124]wished to endow this boy with immortality, and for this purpose hid him in fire every night. When his mother discovered this, she wept and lamented. After that the bestowal of immortality was impossible. Demeter left the house. Keleus then built a temple. The grief of Demeter for Persephone was limitless. She spread sterility over the earth. The gods had to appease her, to prevent a great catastrophe. Then Zeus induced Hades (Pluto) to release Persephone into the upper world, but before letting her go, he gave her a pomegranate to eat. This obliged her to return periodically to the nether-world for evermore. Henceforward she spent a third of the year there, and two-thirds in the world above. Demeter was appeased and returned to Olympus; but at Eleusis, the place of her suffering, she founded the cult which should keep her fate in remembrance.

It is not difficult to discover the meaning of the myth of Demeter and Persephone. It is the soul which lives alternately above and below. The immortality of the soul and its perpetually recurring transformation by birth [125]and death are thus symbolised. The soul originates from the immortal—Demeter. But it is led astray by the transitory, and even prevailed upon to share its destiny. It has partaken of the fruits in the nether-world, the human soul is satisfied with the transitory, therefore it cannot permanently live in the heights of the divine. It has always to return to the realm of the perishable. Demeter is the representative of the essence from which human consciousness arose; but we must think of it as the consciousness which was able to come into being through the spiritual forces of the earth. Thus Demeter is the primordial essence of the earth, and the endowment of the earth with the seed-forces of the produce of the fields through her, points to a still deeper side of her being. This being wishes to give man immortality. She hides her nursling in fire by night. But man cannot bear the pure force of fire (the spirit). Demeter is obliged to abandon the idea. She is only able to found a temple service, through which man is able to participate in the divine as far as this is possible.

The Eleusinian festivals were an eloquent [126]confession of the belief in the immortality of the human soul. This confession found symbolic expression in the Persephone myth. Together with Demeter and Persephone Dionysos was commemorated in Eleusis. As Demeter was honoured as the divine creatress of the eternal in man, so in Dionysos was honoured the ever-changing divine in the world. The divine poured into the world and torn to pieces in order to be spiritually reborn (cf. p. 90) had to be honoured together with Demeter. (A brilliant description of the spirit of the Eleusinian Mysteries is found in Edouard Schuré's book, Sanctuaires d'Orient. Paris, 1898.)

THE MYSTERY WISDOM OF EGYPT

When leaving thy body behind thee, thou soarest into the ether,
    Then thou becomest a god, immortal, not subject to death.

In this utterance of Empedocles (cf. p. 55) is epitomised what the ancient Egyptians thought about the eternal element in man and its connection with the divine. The proof of this may be found in the so-called Book of the Dead, which has been deciphered by the diligence of nineteenth-century investigators (cf. Lepsius, Das Totenbuch der alten Ägypter, Berlin, 1842). It is "the greatest continuous literary work which has come down to us from ancient Egypt." All kinds of instructions and prayers are contained in it, which were put into the tomb [128]of each deceased person to serve as a guide when he was released from his mortal tenement. The most intimate ideas of the Egyptians about the Eternal and the origin of the world are contained in this work. These ideas point to a conception of the gods similar to that of Greek mysticism.

Osiris gradually became the favourite and most universally recognised of the various deities worshipped in different parts of Egypt. In him were comprised the ideas about the other divinities. Whatever the majority of the Egyptian people may have thought about Osiris, the Book of the Dead indicates that the priestly wisdom saw in him a being that might be found in the human soul itself. Everything said about death and the dead shows this plainly. While the body is given to earth, and kept by it, the eternal part of man enters upon the path to the primordial eternal. It comes before the tribunal of Osiris, and the forty-two judges of the dead. The fate of the eternal part of man depends on the verdict of these judges. If the soul has confessed its sins and been deemed reconciled to eternal justice, [129]invisible powers approach it and say: "The Osiris N. has been purified in the pool which is south of the field of Hotep and north of the field of Locusts, where the gods of verdure purify themselves at the fourth hour of the night and the eighth hour of the day with the image of the heart of the gods, passing from night to day." Thus, within the eternal cosmic order, the eternal part of man is addressed as an Osiris. After the name Osiris comes the deceased person's own name. And the one who is being united with the eternal cosmic order also calls himself "Osiris." "I am the Osiris N. Growing under the blossoms of the fig-tree is the name of the Osiris N." Man therefore becomes an Osiris. Being Osiris is only a perfect stage in human development. It seems obvious that even the Osiris who is a judge within the eternal cosmic order is nothing else but a perfect man. Between being human and divine, there is a difference in degree and number. The mystic view of the mystery of "number" underlies this. Osiris as a cosmic being is One, yet on this account he exists undivided in each human soul. Each person [130]is an Osiris, yet the One Osiris must be represented as a separate being. Man is in course of development; at the end of his evolutionary career, he becomes divine.

In taking this view, we must speak of divinity, or becoming divine, rather than of a separate divine being, complete in himself.

It cannot be doubted but that according to this view only he can really enter upon the Osiris existence, who has reached the portals of the eternal cosmic order as an Osiris. Thus, the highest life which man can lead must consist in his changing himself into Osiris. Even during mortal life, a true man will live as a perfect Osiris as far as he can. He becomes perfect when he lives as an Osiris, when he passes through the experiences of Osiris. In this way, we see the deeper significance of the Osiris myth. It becomes the ideal of the man who wishes to awaken the eternal within him.

Osiris is torn to pieces and killed by Typhon. The fragments of his body are preserved and cared for by his consort, Isis. After his death he let a ray of his own light fall upon her, and she bore him Horus. This [131]Horus takes up the earthly tasks of Osiris. He is the second Osiris, still imperfect, but progressing towards the true Osiris.

The true Osiris is in the human soul, which at first is of a transitory nature; but as such, it is destined to give birth to the eternal. Man may, therefore, regard himself as the tomb of Osiris. The lower nature (Typhon) has killed the higher nature in him. Love in his soul (Isis) must take care of the dead fragments of his body, and then the higher nature, the eternal soul (Horus) will be born, which can progress to Osiris life. The man who is aspiring to the highest kind of existence must repeat in himself, as a microcosm, the macrocosmic universal Osiris process. This is the meaning of Egyptian initiation. What Plato (cf. p. 80) describes as a cosmic process, i.e., that the Creator has stretched the soul of the world on the body of the world in the form of a cross, and that the cosmic process is the release of this crucified soul,—this process had to be enacted in man on a smaller scale if he was to be qualified for Osiris life. The candidate for initiation had to develop himself in such a way that his [132]soul-experience, his becoming an Osiris, became blended into one with the cosmic Osiris process.

If we could look into the temples of initiation in which people underwent the transformation into Osiris, we should see that what took place represented microcosmically the building of the cosmos. Man who proceeded from the "Father" was to give birth to the Son in himself. What he actually bears within him, divinity hidden under a spell, was to become manifest in him. This divinity is kept down in him by the power of the earthly nature; this lower nature must first be buried in order that the higher nature may arise.

From this we are able to interpret what we are told about the incidents of initiation. The candidate was subjected to mysterious processes, by means of which his earthly nature was killed, and his higher part awakened. It is not necessary to study these processes in detail, if we understand their meaning. This meaning is contained in the confession possible to every one who went through initiation. He could say: "Before [133]me was the endless perspective at the end of which is the perfection of the divine. I felt that the power of the divine is within me. I buried what in me keeps down that power. I died to earthly things. I was dead. I had died as a lower man, I was in the nether-world. I had intercourse with the dead, i.e., with those who have already become part of the chain of the eternal cosmic order. After my sojourn in the nether-world, I arose from the dead. I overcame death, but now I have become different. I have nothing more to do with perishable nature. It has in me become saturated with the Logos. I now belong to those who live eternally, and who will sit at the right hand of Osiris. I myself shall be a true Osiris, part of the eternal cosmic order, and judgment of life and death will be placed in my hands." The candidate for initiation had to submit to the experience which made such a confession possible to him. Thus this was an experience of the highest kind.

Let us now imagine that a non-initiate hears of such experiences. He cannot know what has really taken place in the initiate's [134]soul. In his eyes, the initiate died physically, lay in the grave, and rose again. What is a spiritual reality at a higher stage of existence appears when expressed in the form of sense-reality as an event which breaks through the order of nature. It is a "miracle." So far initiation was a miracle. One who really wished to understand it must have awakened within him powers to enable him to stand on a higher plane of existence. He must have approached these higher experiences through a course of life specially adapted for the purpose. In whatever way these prepared experiences were enacted in individual cases, they are always found to be of quite a definite type. And so an initiate's life is a typical one. It may be described independently of the single personality. Or rather, an individual could only be described as being on the way to the divine if he had passed through these definite typical experiences.

Such a personality was Buddha, living in the midst of his disciples. As such an one did Jesus appear to his community. Nowadays we know of the parallelism that exists [135]between the biographies of Buddha and of Jesus. Rudolf Seydel has convincingly proved this parallelism in his book, Buddha und Christus. (Compare also the excellent essay by Dr. Hübbe-Schleiden, "Jesus ein Buddhist.") We have only to follow out the two lives in detail in order to see that all objections to the parallelism are futile.

The birth of Buddha is announced by a white elephant, which descends from heaven and declares to the queen, Maya, that she will bring forth a divine man, who "will attune all beings to love and friendship, and will unite them in a close alliance." We read in St. Luke's Gospel: "To a virgin espoused to a man whose name was Joseph, of the house of David; and the virgin's name was Mary. And the angel came in unto her, and said, 'Hail, thou that art highly favoured.... Behold, thou shalt conceive in thy womb, and bring forth a son, and shalt call his name Jesus. He shall be great, and shall be called the Son of the Highest.'"

The Brahmins, or Indian priests, who know what the birth of a Buddha means, interpret Maya's dream. They have a [136]definite, typical idea of a Buddha, to which the life of the personality about to be born will have to correspond. Similarly we read in Matthew ii. et seq., that when Herod "had gathered all the chief priests and scribes of the people together, he demanded of them where Christ should be born." The Brahmin Asita says of Buddha: "This is the child which will become Buddha, the redeemer, the leader to immortality, freedom, and light." Compare with this Luke ii. 25: "And, behold, there was a man in Jerusalem, whose name was Simeon; and the same man was just and devout, waiting for the consolation of Israel: and the Holy Ghost was upon him.... And when the parents brought in the child Jesus, to do for him after the custom of the law, then took he him up in his arms, and blessed God, and said, Lord, now lettest thou thy servant depart in peace, according to thy word: for mine eyes have seen thy salvation, which thou hast prepared before the face of all people; a light to lighten the Gentiles, and the glory of thy people Israel."

It is related of Buddha that at the age of twelve he was lost, and found again under a [137]tree, surrounded by poets and sages of the olden time, whom he was teaching. With this incident the following passage in St. Luke corresponds: "Now his parents went to Jerusalem every year at the feast of the passover. And when he was twelve years old, they went up to Jerusalem after the custom of the feast. And when they had fulfilled the days, as they returned, the child Jesus tarried behind in Jerusalem; and Joseph and his mother knew not of it. But they, supposing him to have been in the company, went a day's journey; and they sought him among their kinsfolk and acquaintance. And when they found him not, they turned back again to Jerusalem, seeking him. And it came to pass that after three days they found him in the temple, sitting in the midst of the doctors, both hearing them, and asking them questions. And all that heard him were astonished at his understanding and answers" (Luke ii. 41-47).

After Buddha had lived in solitude, and returned, he was received by the benediction of a virgin, "Blessed is thy mother, blessed is thy father, blessed is the wife to whom [138]thou belongest." But he replied, "Only they are blessed who are in Nirvana," i.e., who have entered the eternal cosmic order. In St. Luke's Gospel (xi. 27), we read: "And it came to pass, as he spake these things, a certain woman of the company lifted up her voice and said unto him. 'Blessed is the womb that bare thee, and the paps which thou hast sucked.' But he said, 'Yea rather, blessed are they that hear the word of God, and keep it.'"

In the course of Buddha's life, the tempter comes to him and promises him all the kingdoms of the earth. Buddha refuses everything in the words: 'I know well that I am destined to have a kingdom, but I do not desire an earthly one. I shall become Buddha and make all the world exult with joy." The tempter has to own that his reign is over. Jesus answers the same temptation in the words: "Get thee hence, Satan, for it is written, Thou shalt worship the Lord thy God, and him only shalt thou serve. Then the devil leaveth him" (Matthew iv. 10, 11). This description of the parallelism might be extended to many other points with the same result.

[139]The life of Buddha ended sublimely. On a journey, he felt ill; he came to the river Hiranja, near Kuschinagara. There he lay down on a carpet which his favourite disciple, Ananda, spread for him. His body began to be luminous from within. He died transfigured, his body irradiating light, saying, "Nothing endures."

The death of Buddha corresponds with the transfiguration of Jesus. "And it came to pass about eight days after these sayings, he took Peter and John and James, and went up into a mountain to pray. And as he prayed, the fashion of his countenance was altered, and his raiment was white and glistering."

Buddha's earthly life ends at this point, but it is here that the most important part of the life of Jesus begins,—His suffering, death, and resurrection. Other accounts of Buddha's death need not here be considered, even though they reveal profound aspects.

The agreement in these two redemptive lives leads to the same conclusion. The narratives themselves indicate the nature of this conclusion. When the priest-sages hear what [140]kind of birth is to take place, they know what is involved. They know that they have to do with a Divine man; they know beforehand what kind of personality it is who is appearing. And therefore his course of life can only correspond with what they know about the life of a Divine man. In the wisdom of their Mysteries such a life is traced out for all eternity. It can only be as it must be; it comes into manifestation like an eternal law of nature. Just as a chemical substance can only behave in a certain definite way, so a Buddha or a Christ can only live in a certain definite way. His life is not described merely by writing a casual biography; it is much better described by giving the typical features which are contained for all time in the wisdom of the Mysteries. The Buddha legend is no more a biography in the ordinary sense than the Gospels are meant to be a biography in the ordinary sense of the Christ Jesus. In neither is the merely accidental given; both relate the course of life marked out for a world-redeemer. The source of the two accounts is to be found in the mystery traditions and [141]not in outer physical history. Jesus and Buddha are, to those who have recognised their Divine nature, initiates in the most eminent sense. Hence their lives are lifted out of things transitory, and what is known about initiates applies to them.[4] The casual incidents in their lives are not narrated. Of such it might be announced "In the beginning was the Word, and the Word was with God, and the Word was a God and the Word was made flesh and dwelt among us."

But the life of Jesus contains more than that of Buddha. Buddha's ends with the Transfiguration; the most momentous part of the life of Jesus begins after the Transfiguration. In the language of initiates this means that Buddha reached the point at [142]which divine light begins to shine in men. He faces mortal death. He becomes the light of the world. Jesus goes farther. He does not physically die at the moment when the light of the world shines through him. At that moment he is a Buddha. But at that very moment he enters upon a stage which finds expression in a higher degree of initiation. He suffers and dies. What is earthly disappears. But the spiritual element, the light of the world, does not. His resurrection follows. He is revealed to his followers as Christ. Buddha, at the moment of his Transfiguration, flows into the blissful life of the Universal Spirit. Christ Jesus awakens the Universal Spirit once more, but in a human form, in present existence. Such an event had formerly taken place at the higher stages of initiation. Those initiated in the spirit of the Osiris myth attained to such a resurrection. In the life of Jesus, this "great" initiation was added to the Buddha initiation. Buddha demonstrated by his life that man is the Logos, and that he returns to the Logos, to the light, when his earthly part dies. In Jesus, the Logos himself became [143]a person. In him, the Word was made flesh.

Therefore, what was enacted in the innermost recesses of the temples by the guardians of the ancient Mysteries has been apprehended, through Christianity, as a historical fact. The followers of Christ Jesus confessed their belief in Him, the initiate, of unique and supreme greatness. He proved to them that the world is divine. In the Christian community, the wisdom of the Mysteries was indissolubly bound up with the personality of Christ Jesus. That which man previously had sought to attain through the Mysteries was now replaced by the belief that Christ had lived on earth, and that the faithful belonged to him.

Henceforward, part of what was formerly only to be gained through mystical methods, could be replaced, in the Christian community, by the conviction that the divine had been manifested in the Word present amongst them. Not that for which each individual soul underwent a long preparation was now decisive, but what those had heard and seen who were with Jesus, and what [144]was handed down by them. "That which was from the beginning, which we have heard, which ... our hands have handled, of the Word of life ... that which we have seen and heard declare we unto you, that ye also may have fellowship with us." Thus do we read in the first Epistle of St. John. And this immediate reality is to embrace all future generations in a living bond of union, and as a church is mystically to extend from race to race. It is in this sense that the words of St. Augustine are to be understood, "I should not believe the Gospels unless the authority of the Catholic Church induced me to do so." Thus the Gospels do not contain within themselves testimony to their truth, but they are to be believed because they are founded on the personality of Jesus, and because the Church from that personality mysteriously draws the power to make the truth of the Gospels manifest.

The Mysteries handed down traditionally the means of arriving at truth; the Christian community itself propagates the truth. To the confidence in the mystical forces which spring up in the inmost being of man, during [145]initiation, was added the confidence in the One, primordial Initiator.

The Mystics sought to become divine, they wished to experience divinity. Jesus was divine, we must hold fast to Him, and then we shall become partakers of His divinity, in the community founded by Him; this became Christian conviction. What became divine in Jesus was made so for all His followers. "Lo, I am with you alway, even unto the end of the world." The one who was born in Bethlehem has an eternal character independent of time. The Christmas anthem thus speaks of the birth of Jesus, as if it took place each Christmas, "Christ is born to-day, the Saviour has come into the world to-day, to-day the angels are singing on earth."

In the Christ-experience is to be seen a definite stage of initiation. When the Mystic of pre-Christian times passed through this Christ-experience, he was, through his initiation, in a state which enabled him to perceive something spiritually,—in higher worlds,—to which no fact in the world of sense corresponded. He experienced that [146]which surrounds the Mystery of Golgotha in the higher world. If the Christian Mystic goes through this experience by initiation, he at the same time beholds the historical event which took place on Golgotha, and knows that in that event, enacted within the physical world, there is the same content as was formerly only in the supersensible facts of the Mysteries. Thus there was poured out on the Christian community, through the "Mysteries of Golgotha," that which formerly had been poured out on the Mystics within the temples. And initiation gives Christian Mystics the possibility of becoming conscious of what is contained in the "Mystery of Golgotha," whereas faith makes man an unconscious partaker of the mystical stream which flowed from the events depicted in the New Testament, and which has ever since been pervading the spiritual life of humanity.

FOOTNOTES:

[4]The great initiates raised themselves through initiation up into the sphere of the Logos and carried this Logos influence with them in their human life. The fundamental difference between them and Jesus was the fact that the Logos in the course of its evolution individualised itself into One Divine Individuality who descended into Jesus of Nazareth at the Baptism, and so that the Logos manifested its whole Divine individuality through the personality of Jesus as far as it was possible to express Divinity by human means. Such was the unique character of the Christ Jesus.

THE GOSPELS

The accounts of the life of Jesus which can be submitted to historical examination are contained in the Gospels. All that does not come from this source might, in the opinion of one of those who are considered the greatest historical authorities on the subject (Harnack), be "easily written on a quarto page."

But what kind of documents are these Gospels? The fourth, that of St. John, differs so much from the others, that those who think themselves obliged to follow the path of historical research in order to study the subject, come to the conclusion: "If John possesses the genuine tradition about the life of Jesus, that of the first three Evangelists (the Synoptists) is untenable. If the Synoptists are right, the Fourth Gospel must be [148]rejected as a historical source" (Otto Schmiedel, Die Hauptprobleme der Leben Jesu Forschung, p. 15). This is a statement made from the standpoint of the historical investigator.

In the present work, in which we are dealing with the mystical contents of the Gospels, such a point of view is neither to be accepted nor rejected. But attention must certainly be drawn to such an opinion as the following: "Measured by the standard of consistency, inspiration, and completeness, these writings leave very much to be desired, and even measured by the ordinary human standard, they suffer from not a few imperfections." This is the opinion of a Christian theologian (Harnack, Wesen des Christentums).

One who takes his stand on a mystical origin of the Gospels easily finds an explanation of what is apparently contradictory, and also discovers harmony between the fourth Gospel and the three others. For none of these writings are meant to be mere historical tradition in the ordinary sense of the word. They do not profess to give a historical [149]biography (cf. p. 140 et seq.). What they intended to give was already shadowed forth in the traditions of the Mysteries, as the typical life of a Son of God. It was these traditions which were drawn upon, not history. Now it was only natural that these traditions should not be in complete verbal agreement in every Mystery centre. Still, the agreement was so close that the Buddhists narrated the life of their divine man almost in the same way in which the Evangelists narrated the life of Christ. But naturally there were differences. We have only to assume that the four Evangelists drew from four different mystery traditions. It testifies to the extraordinary personality of Jesus that in four writers, belonging to different traditions, he awakened the belief that he was one who so perfectly corresponded with their type of an initiate, that they were able to describe him as one who lived the typical life marked out in their Mysteries. They each described his life according to their own mystic traditions. And if the narratives of the first three Evangelists resemble each other, it proves nothing more than that they [150]drew from similar mystery traditions. The fourth Evangelist saturated his Gospel with ideas which are, in many respects, reminiscent of the religious philosopher, Philo (cf. p. 82). This only proves that he was rooted in the same mystic tradition as Philo.

There are various elements in the Gospels. Firstly, facts are related, which seem to lay claim to being historical. Secondly, there are parables, in which the narrative form is only used to symbolise a deeper truth. And, thirdly, there are teachings characteristic of the Christian conception of life. In St. John's Gospel there is no real parable. The source from which he drew was a mystical school which considered parables unnecessary.

The part played by ostensibly historical facts and parables in the first three Gospels is clearly shown in the narrative of the cursing of the fig tree. In St. Mark xi. 11-14, we read: "And Jesus entered into Jerusalem, and into the temple: and when he had looked round about upon all things, and now the eventide was come, he went out unto Bethany with the twelve. And on the morrow, when they were come from Bethany, [151]he was hungry: and seeing a fig tree afar off having leaves, he came, if haply he might find any thing thereon: and when he came to it, he found nothing but leaves; for the time of figs was not yet. And Jesus answered and said unto it, No man eat fruit of thee hereafter for ever." In the corresponding passage in St. Luke's Gospel, he relates a parable (xiii. 6, 7): "He spake also this parable; A certain man had a fig tree planted in his vineyard; and he came and sought fruit thereon, and found none. Then said he unto the dresser of his vineyard, Behold these three years I come seeking fruit on this fig tree, and find none: cut it down; why cumbereth it the ground?" This is a parable symbolising the uselessness of the old teaching, represented by the barren fig tree. That which is meant metaphorically, St. Mark relates as a fact appearing to be historical. We may therefore assume that, in general, facts related in the Gospels are not to be taken as only historical, or as if they were only to hold good in the physical world, but as mystical facts; as experiences, for the recognition of which spiritual vision is [152]necessary, and which arise from various mystical traditions. If we admit this, the difference between the Gospel of St. John and the Synoptists ceases to exist. For mystical interpretation, historical research has not to be taken into account. Even if one or another Gospel were written a few decades earlier or later than the others, they are all of like historical value to the mystic, St. John's Gospel as well as the others.

And the "miracles" do not present the least difficulty when interpreted mystically. They are supposed to break through the laws of nature. They only do this when they are considered as events which have so come about on the physical plane, in the perishable world, that ordinary sense-perception could see through them offhand. But if they are experiences which can only be fathomed on a higher stage of existence, namely the spiritual, it is obvious that they cannot be understood by means of the laws of physical nature.

It is thus first of all necessary to read the Gospels correctly; then we shall know in what way they are speaking of the Founder [153]of Christianity. Their intention is to relate his life in the manner in which communications were made through the Mysteries. They relate it in the way in which a Mystic would speak of an initiate. Only, they give the initiation as the unique characteristic of one unique being. And they make salvation depend on man's holding fast to the initiate of this unique order. What had come to the initiates was the "kingdom of God." This unique being has brought the kingdom to all who will cleave to him. What was formerly the personal concern of each individual has become the common concern of all those who are willing to acknowledge Jesus as their Lord.

We can understand how this came about if we admit that the wisdom of the Mysteries was imbedded in the popular religion of the Jews. Christianity arose out of Judaism. We need not therefore be surprised at finding engrafted on Judaism, together with Christianity those mystical ideas which we have seen to be the common property of Greek and Egyptian spiritual life. If we examine national religions, we find various [154]conceptions of the spiritual; but if, in each case, we go back to the deeper wisdom of the priests, which proves to be the spiritual nucleus of them all, we find agreement everywhere. Plato knows himself to be in agreement with the priest-sages of Egypt when he is trying to set forth the main content of Greek wisdom in his philosophical view of the universe. It is related of Pythagoras that he travelled to Egypt and India, and was instructed by the sages in those countries. Thinkers who lived in the earlier days of Christianity found so much agreement between the philosophical teachings of Plato and the deeper meaning of the Mosaic writings, that they called Plato a Moses with Attic tongue.

Thus Mystery wisdom existed everywhere. In Judaism it acquired a form which it had to assume if it was to become a world-religion.

Judaism expected the Messiah. It is not to be wondered at that when the personality of an unique initiate appeared, the Jews could only conceive of him as being the Messiah. Indeed this circumstance throws light on the fact that what had been an [155]individual matter in the Mysteries became an affair of the whole nation. The Jewish religion had from the beginning been a national religion. The Jewish people looked upon itself as one organism. Its Jao was the God of the whole nation. If the son of this God were to be born, he must be the redeemer of the whole nation. The individual Mystic was not to be saved apart from others, the whole nation was to share in the redemption. That one is to die for all is founded on the fundamental ideas of the Jewish religion.

It is also certain that there were mysteries in Judaism, which could be brought out of the dimness of a secret cult into the popular religion. A fully-developed mysticism existed side by side with the priestly wisdom which was attached to the outer formalism of the Pharisees. This mystery wisdom is spoken of among the Jews just as it is elsewhere. When one day an initiate was speaking of it, and his hearers sensed the secret meaning of his words, they said: "Old man, what hast thou done? Oh, that thou hadst kept silence! Thou thinkest to navigate the boundless ocean without sail or mast. This is what [156]thou art attempting. Wilt thou fly upwards? Thou canst not. Wilt thou descend into the depths? An immeasurable abyss is yawning before thee." And the Kabbalists, from whom the above is taken, also speak of four Rabbis; and these four Rabbis sought the secret path to the divine. The first died; the second lost his reason; the third caused monstrous evils, and only the fourth, Rabbi Akiba, went in and out of the spiritual world in peace.

We thus see that within Judaism also there was a soil in which an initiate of an unique kind could develop. He had only to say to himself: "I will not let salvation be limited to a few chosen people. I will let all people participate in it." He was to carry out into the world at large what the elect had experienced in the temples of the Mysteries. He had to be willing to take upon himself to be, in spirit, to his community, through his personality, that which the cult of the Mysteries had heretofore been to those who took part in them. It is true he could not at once give to the whole community the experiences of the Mysteries, nor would he have wished [157]to do so. But he wished to give to all the certainty of the truth contemplated in the Mysteries. He wished to cause the life, which flowed within the Mysteries, to flow through the further historical evolution of humanity, and thus to raise mankind to a higher stage of existence. "Blessed are they that have not seen, and yet have believed." He wished to plant unshakably in human hearts, in the form of confidence, the certainty that the divine really exists. One who stands outside initiation and has this confidence will certainly go further than one who is without it. It must have weighed like a mountain on the mind of Jesus to think that there might be many standing outside who do not find the way. He wished to lessen the gulf between those to be initiated and the "people." Christianity was to be a means by which every one might find the way. Should one or another not yet be ripe, at any rate he is not cut off from the possibility of sharing, more or less unconsciously, in the benefit of the spiritual current flowing through the Mysteries. "The Son of Man is come to seek and to save that which was [158]lost." Henceforward even those who cannot yet share in initiation may enjoy some of the fruits of the Mysteries. Henceforth the Kingdom of God was not to be dependent on outward ceremonies: "Neither shall they say, Lo here! or, Lo there! for, behold, the Kingdom of God is within you." With Jesus the point in question was not so much how far this or that person advanced in the kingdom of the spirit, as that all should be convinced that that kingdom exists. "In this rejoice not, that the spirits are subject unto you; but rather rejoice, because your names are written in heaven." That is, have confidence in the divine. The time will come when you will find it.

THE LAZARUS MIRACLE

Amongst the "miracles" attributed to Jesus, very special importance must be attached to the raising of Lazarus at Bethany. Everything combines to assign a prominent position in the New Testament to that which is here related by the Evangelist. We must bear in mind that St. John alone relates it, the Evangelist who by the weighty words with which he opens his Gospel claims for it a very definite interpretation.

St. John begins with these sentences: "In the beginning was the Word, and the Word was with God, and the word was a God.... And the Word was made flesh, and dwelt among us, and we beheld his glory, a glory as of the only begotten of the Father, full of grace and truth."

One who places such words at the [160]beginning of his narrative is plainly indicating that he wishes it to be interpreted in a very deep sense. The man who approaches it with merely intellectual explanations, or otherwise in a superficial way, is like one who thinks that Othello on the stage really murders Desdemona. What then is it that St. John means to say in his introductory words? He plainly says that he is speaking of something eternal, which existed at the beginning of things. He relates facts, but they are not to be taken as facts observed by the eye and ear, and upon which logical reason exercises its skill. He hides behind facts the "Word" which is in the Cosmic Spirit. For him, the facts are the medium in which a higher meaning is expressed. And we may therefore assume that in the fact of a man being raised from the dead, a fact which offers the greatest difficulties to the eye, ear, and logical reason, the very deepest meaning lies concealed.

Another thing has to be taken into consideration. Renan, in his Life of Jesus, has pointed out that the raising of Lazarus undoubtedly had a decisive influence on the end [161]of the life of Jesus. Such a thought appears impossible from the point of view which Renan takes. For why should the fact that the belief was being circulated amongst the populace that Jesus had raised a man from the dead appear to his opponents so dangerous that they asked the question, "Can Jesus and Judaism exist side by side?" It does not do to assert with Renan: "The other miracles of Jesus were passing events, repeated in good faith and exaggerated by popular report, and they were thought no more of after they had happened. But this one was a real event, publicly known, and by means of which it was sought to silence the Pharisees. All the enemies of Jesus were exasperated by the sensation it caused. It is related that they sought to kill Lazarus." It is incomprehensible why this should be if Renan were right in his opinion that all that happened at Bethany was the getting up of a mock scene, intended to strengthen belief in Jesus. "Perhaps Lazarus, still pale from his illness, had himself wrapped in a shroud and laid in the family grave. These tombs were large rooms hewn out of the rock, and [162]entered by a square opening which was closed by an immense slab. Martha and

Mary hastened to meet Jesus, and brought him to the grave before he had entered Bethany. The painful emotion felt by Jesus at the grave of the friend whom he believed to be dead (John xi. 33, 38) might be taken by those present for the agitation and tremors which were wont to accompany miracles. According to popular belief, divine power in a man was like an epileptic and convulsive element. Continuing the above hypothesis, Jesus wished to see once more the man he had loved, and the stone having been rolled away, Lazarus came forth in his grave-clothes, his head bound with a napkin. This apparition naturally was looked upon by every one as a resurrection. Faith knows no other law than the interest of what it holds to be true." Does not such an explanation appear absolutely naïve, when Renan adds the following opinion: "Everything seems to suggest that the miracle of Bethany materially contributed to hasten the death of Jesus"? Yet there is undoubtedly an accurate perception underlying this [163]last assertion of Renan. But with the means at his disposal he is not able to interpret or justify his opinion.

Something of quite special importance must have been accomplished by Jesus at Bethany, in order that such words as the following may be accounted for: "Then gathered the chief priests and the Pharisees a council, and said, 'What do we? for this man doeth many miracles'" (John xi. 47). Renan, too, conjectures something special: "It must be acknowledged," he says, "that John's narrative is of an essentially different kind from the accounts of miracles of which the Synoptists are full, and which are the outcome of the popular imagination. Let us add that John is the only Evangelist with accurate knowledge of the relations of Jesus with the family at Bethany, and that it would be incomprehensible how a creation of the popular mind could have been inserted in the frame of such personal reminiscences. It is, therefore, probable that the miracle in question was not amongst the wholly legendary ones, for which no one is responsible. In other words, I think that something took [164]place at Bethany which was looked upon as a resurrection." Does not this really mean that Renan surmises that something happened at Bethany which he cannot explain? He entrenches himself behind the words: "At this distance of time, and with only one text bearing obvious traces of subsequent additions, it is impossible to decide whether, in the present case, all is fiction, or whether a real fact which happened at Bethany served as the basis of the report that was spread abroad." Might it not be that we have to do here with something of which we might arrive at a true understanding merely by reading the text in the right way? In that case, we should perhaps no longer speak of "fiction."

It must be admitted that the whole narrative of this event in St. John's Gospel is wrapped in a mysterious veil. To show this, we need only mention one point. If the narrative is to be taken in the literal, physical sense, what meaning have these words of Jesus: "This sickness is not unto death, but for the glory of God, that the Son of God might be glorified thereby." This is the [165]usual translation of the words, but the actual state of the case is better arrived at, if they are translated, "for the vision (or manifestation) of God, that the Son of God might be manifested thereby." This translation is also correct according to the Greek original. And what do these other words mean, "Jesus said unto her, I am the resurrection, and the life: he that believeth in me, though he were dead, yet shall he live"? (John xi. 4, 25). It would be a triviality to think that Jesus meant to say that Lazarus had only become ill in order that Jesus might manifest His skill through him. And it would again be a triviality to think that Jesus meant to assert that faith in Him brings to life again one who in the ordinary sense is dead. What would there be remarkable about a person who has risen from the dead, if after his resurrection he were the same as he was before dying? Indeed what would be the meaning of describing the life of such a person in the words, "I am the resurrection and the life"? Life and meaning at once come into the words of Jesus if we understand them to be the expression of a spiritual [166]occurrence and then, in a certain sense, literally as they stand in the text. Jesus actually says that He is the resurrection that has happened to Lazarus, and that He is the life that Lazarus is living. Let us take literally what Jesus is in St. John's Gospel.

He is "the Word that was made flesh." He is the Eternal that existed in the beginning. If he is really the resurrection, then the Eternal, Primordial has risen again in Lazarus. We have, therefore, to do with a resurrection of the eternal "Word," and this "Word" is the life to which Lazarus has been raised. It is a case of illness, not one leading to death, but to the glory, i.e., the manifestation of God. If the eternal Word has reawakened in Lazarus, the whole event conduces to manifest God in Lazarus. For by means of the event Lazarus has become a different man. Before it, the Word, or spirit did not live in him, now it does. The spirit has been born within him. It is true that every birth is accompanied by illness, that of the mother, but the illness leads to new life, not to death. In Lazarus that part of him [167]becomes ill from which the "new man," permeated by the "Word," is born.

Where is the grave from which the "Word" is born? To answer this question we have only to remember Plato, who calls man's body the tomb of the soul. And we have only to recall Plato's speaking of a kind of resurrection when he alludes to the coming to life of the spiritual world in the body. What Plato calls the spiritual soul, St. John denominates the "Word." And for him, Christ is the "Word." Plato might have said, "One who becomes spiritual has caused something divine to rise out of the grave of his body." For St. John, that which took place through the life of Jesus was that resurrection. It is not surprising, therefore, if he makes Jesus say, "I am the resurrection."

There can be no doubt that the occurrence at Bethany was an awakening in the spiritual sense. Lazarus became something different from what he was before. He was raised to a life of which the Eternal Word could say, "I am that life." What then took place in [168]Lazarus? The spirit came to life within him. He became a partaker of the life which is eternal. We have only to express his experience in the words of those who were initiated into the Mysteries, and the meaning at once becomes clear. What does Plutarch (vide supra p. 26 et seq.) say about the object of the Mysteries? They were to serve to withdraw the soul from bodily life and to unite it with the gods. Schelling thus describes the feelings of an initiate:

"The initiate through his initiation became a link in the magic chain, he himself became a Kabir. He was admitted into an indestructible association and, as ancient inscriptions express it, joined to the army of the higher gods" (Schelling, Philosophie der Offenbarung). And the revolution that took place in the life of one who received initiation cannot be more significantly described than in the words spoken by Ädesius to his disciple, the Emperor Constantine: "If one day thou shouldst take part in the Mysteries, thou wilt feel ashamed of having been born merely as a man."

If we fill our souls with such feelings as [169]these, we shall gain the right attitude towards the event that took place at Bethany, and have a peculiarly characteristic experience through St. John's narrative. A certainty will dawn upon us which cannot be obtained by any logical interpretation or by any attempt at rationalistic explanation. A mystery in the true sense of the word is before us. The

"Eternal Word" entered into Lazarus. In the language of the Mysteries, he became an initiate (vide p. 132 et seq.), and the event narrated to us must be the process of initiation.

Let us look upon the whole occurrence as though it were an initiation. Lazarus is loved by Jesus (John xi. 36). No ordinary affection can be meant by this, for it would be contrary to the spirit of St. John's Gospel, in which Jesus is "The Word." Jesus loved Lazarus because he found him ripe for the awakening of "the Word" within him. Jesus had relations with the family at Bethany. This only means that Jesus had made everything ready in that family for the final act of the drama, the raising of Lazarus. The latter was a disciple of Jesus, such an [170]one that Jesus could be quite sure that in him the awakening would be consummated. The final act in a drama of awakening consisted in a symbolical action. The person involved in it had not only to understand the words, "Die and become!" He had to fulfil them himself by a real, spiritual action. His earthly part, of which his higher being in the Spirit of the Mysteries must be ashamed, had to be put away. The earthly must die a symbolic-real death. The putting of his body into a somnambulic sleep for three days can only be denoted an outer event in comparison with the greatness of the transformation which was taking place in him. An incomparably more momentous spiritual event corresponded to it. But this very process was the experience which divides the life of the Mystic into two parts. One who does not know from experience the inner significance of such acts cannot understand them. They can only be suggested by means of a comparison.

The substance of Shakespeare's Hamlet may be compressed into a few words. Any one who learns these words may say that in [171]a certain sense he knows the contents of Hamlet; and logically he does. But one who has let all the wealth of the Shakespearian drama stream in upon him knows Hamlet in a different way. A life-current has passed through his soul which cannot be replaced by any mere description. The idea of Hamlet has become an artistic, personal experience within him.

On a higher plane of consciousness, a similar process takes place in man when he experiences the magically significant event which is bound up with initiation What he attains spiritually, he lives through symbolically. The word "symbolically" is used here in the sense that an outer event is really enacted on the physical plane, but that as such, it is nevertheless a symbol. It is not a case of an unreal, but of a real symbol. The earthly body has really been dead for three days.[5] [172]New life comes forth from death. This life has outlived death. Man has gained confidence in the new life.

It happened thus with Lazarus. Jesus had prepared him for resurrection. His illness was at once symbolic and real, an illness which was an initiation (cf. p. 132 et seq.), and which leads, after three days, to a really new life.

Lazarus was ripe for undergoing this experience. He wrapped himself in the garment of the Mystic, and fell into a condition of lifelessness which was symbolic death. And when Jesus came, the three days had elapsed. "Then they took away the stone from the place where the dead was laid. And Jesus lifted up his eyes and said, 'Father, I thank thee that thou hast heard me'" (John xi. 41). The Father had heard Jesus, for Lazarus had come to the final act in the great drama of knowledge. He had learned how resurrection is attained. An initiation into the Mysteries had been consummated. It was a case of such an initiation as had been understood as such during the whole of antiquity. It had taken place through [173]Jesus, as the initiator. Union with the divine had always been conceived of in this way.

In Lazarus Jesus accomplished the great miracle of the transmutation of life in the sense of immemorial tradition. Through this event, Christianity is connected with the Mysteries. Lazarus had become an initiate through Christ Jesus Himself, and had thereby become able to enter the higher worlds. He was at once the first Christian initiate and the first to be initiated by Christ Jesus Himself. Through his initiation he had become capable of recognising that the "Word" which had been awakened within him had become a person in Christ Jesus, and that consequently there stood before him in the personality of his awakener, the same force which had been spiritually manifested within him. From this point of view, these words of Jesus are significant, "And I knew that thou hearest me always: but because of the people which stand by I said it, that they may believe that thou hast sent me." This means that the point is to make evident this fact: in Jesus lives the "Son of [174]the Father" in such a way that when he awakens his own nature in man, man becomes a Mystic. In this way Jesus made it plain that the meaning of life was hidden in the Mysteries and that they were the path to this understanding. He is the living Word; in Him was personified what had been immemorial tradition. And therefore the Evangelist is justified in expressing this in the sentence, "in Him the Word was made flesh." He rightly sees in Jesus himself an incarnated Mystery. On this account, St. John's Gospel is a Mystery. In order to read it rightly, we must bear in mind that the facts are spiritual facts. If a priest of the old order had written it, he would have described traditional rites. These for St. John took the form of a person, and became the life of Jesus.

An eminent modern investigator of the Mysteries, Burkhardt in Die Zeit Konstantins, says that they "will never be cleared up." This is because he has not found out how to explain them. If we take the Gospel of St. John and see in it the working out in symbolic-corporeal reality the drama of [175]knowledge presented by the ancients, we are really gazing upon the Mystery itself.

In the words, "Lazarus, come forth," we can recognise the call with which the Egyptian priestly initiators summoned back to every-day life those who, temporarily removed from the world by the processes of initiation, had undergone them in order to die to earthly things and to gain a conviction of the reality of the eternal. Jesus in this way revealed the secret of the Mysteries. It is easy to understand that the Jews could not let such an act go unpunished, any more than the Greeks could have refrained from punishing Æschylus, if he had betrayed the secrets of the Mysteries.

The main point for Jesus was to represent in the initiation of Lazarus before all "the people which stood by," an event which in the old days of priestly wisdom could only be enacted in the recesses of the mystery-temples. The initiation of Lazarus was to prepare the way to the understanding of the "Mystery of Golgotha." Previously only those who "saw," that is to say, who were initiated, were able to know something of [176]what was achieved by initiation, but now a conviction of the Mysteries of higher worlds could also be gained by those who "had not seen, and yet had believed."

FOOTNOTES:

[5]This and other circumstances connected with the so-called raising of Lazarus from the dead are to be understood in the light of the fact, that Lazarus' death-sleep was at the same time symbolic

and real—it was in other words a symbolic reality, a reality symbolising other realities, and but for the action of Christ, Lazarus would have remained dead.

THE APOCALYPSE OF ST. JOHN

At the end of the New Testament stands a remarkable document, the Apocalypse, the secret Revelation of St. John. We have only to read the opening words to feel the deep mystic character of this book. "The Revelation of Jesus Christ, which God gave unto him, to shew unto his servants how the necessary things are shortly going to happen; and this is sent in signs by the angel of God unto his servant John." What is here revealed is "sent in signs." Therefore we must not take the literal meaning of the words as they stand, but seek for a deeper meaning of which the words are only signs. But there are other things also which point to a hidden meaning. St. John addresses himself to the seven churches in Asia. Not actual, material churches are meant; the number seven is [178]the sacred number, chosen on account of its symbolic meaning. The actual number of the Asiatic churches was different. And the manner in which St. John arrived at the revelation also points to something mysterious. "I was in the Spirit on the Lord's day, and heard behind me a great voice, as of a trumpet, saying, 'What thou seest, write in a book, and send it unto the seven churches.'" Thus, we have to do with a revelation received by St. John in the spirit. And it is the revelation of Jesus Christ. Wrapped in a hidden meaning there appears what Christ Jesus manifested to the world. Therefore we must also look for this hidden meaning in the teachings of Christ. This revelation bears the same relation to ordinary Christianity as was borne by the revelation of the Mysteries, in pre-Christian times, to the people's religion. On this account the attempt to treat the Apocalypse as a mystery appears to be justified.

The Apocalypse is addressed to seven churches. For the reason of this we have only to single out one of the seven messages sent. In the first of these it is said, "Unto [179]the angel of the church of Ephesus write; these things saith he that holdeth the seven stars in his right hand, who walketh in the midst of the seven golden candlesticks; I know thy works, and thy labour, and thy patience, and how thou canst not bear them which are evil: and thou hast tried them which say they are apostles, and are not, and hast found them liars: and hast borne, and hast patience, and for my name's sake hast laboured, and hast not fainted. Nevertheless I have somewhat against thee, because thou hast left thy highest love. Remember therefore from whence thou art fallen, and repent, and do the best works; or else I will come unto thee quickly, and will remove thy candlestick out of his place, except thou repent. But this thou hast, that thou hatest the deeds of the Nicolaitanes, which I also hate. He that hath an ear, let him hear what the Spirit saith unto the churches; to him that overcometh will I give to eat of the tree of life, which is in the midst of the paradise of God." This is the message addressed to the angel of the first community. The angel, who represents the spirit of this [180]community, has entered upon the path pointed out by Christianity. He is able to distinguish between the false adherents of Christianity and the true. He wishes to be Christian, and has founded his work on the name of Christ. But it is required of him that he should not bar his own way to the highest love by any kind of mistakes. He is shown the possibility of taking a wrong course through such errors. Through Christ Jesus the way for attaining to the divine has been pointed out. Perseverance is needed for advancing further in the spirit in which the first impulse was given. It is possible to believe too soon that one has the right spirit. This happens when the disciple lets himself be led a short way by Christ and then leaves his leadership, giving way to false ideas about it. The disciple thereby falls back again into the lower self. He has left his "highest love." The knowledge which is attached to the senses and intellect may be raised into a higher sphere, becoming wisdom, by being spiritualised and made divine. If it does not reach this height, it remains amongst perishable things. Christ Jesus has pointed out [181]the path to the Eternal, and knowledge must with unwearied perseverance follow the path which leads to its becoming divine. Lovingly must it trace out the methods which transmute it into wisdom. The Nicolaitanes were a sect who took Christianity too lightly. They saw one thing only, that Christ is the Divine Word, the Eternal Wisdom which is born in man. Therefore they concluded that human wisdom was the Divine Word, and that it was enough to pursue human knowledge in order to realise the divine in the world. But the meaning of Christian wisdom cannot be construed thus. The knowledge which in the first instance is human wisdom is as perishable as anything else, unless it is first transmuted into divine wisdom. "Thou art not thus," says the "Spirit" to the angel of Ephesus; "thou hast 'not relied' merely upon human wisdom. Thou hast patiently trodden the Christian path. But thou must not think that the 'highest' love is not needed to attain to the goal. Such a love is necessary which far surpasses all love to other things. Only such can be the 'highest' love. The path to the divine is an infinite one, and it is to be [182]understood that when the first step has been gained, it can only be the preparation for ascending higher and higher." Such is the first of these messages, as they are to be interpreted. The meaning of the others may be found in a similar way.

St. John turned, and saw "seven golden candlesticks," and "in the midst of the seven candlesticks one like unto the Son of Man, clothed with a garment down to the foot, and girt about the paps with a golden girdle. His head and his hairs were white like wool, as white as snow; and his eyes were as a flame of fire." We are told (i. 20) that "the seven candlesticks are the seven churches." This means that the candlesticks are seven different ways of attaining to the divine. They are all more or less imperfect. And the Son of Man "had in his right hand seven stars" (v. 16). The seven stars are the angels of the seven churches (v. 20). The guiding spirits, or daimons (cf. p. 87), of the wisdom of the Mysteries have here become the guiding angels of the churches. The churches are represented as bodies for spiritual beings, [183]and the angels are the souls of those bodies, just as human souls are the guiding powers of human bodies. The churches are the imperfect ways to the divine, and the souls of the churches were to become guides along those paths. For this purpose they must themselves have for their leader the being who has in his right hand seven stars. "And out of his mouth went a sharp two-edged sword: and his countenance was as the sun shineth in his strength." This sword is also found in the Mysteries. The candidate for initiation was terrified by a flashing sword (cf. p. 18). This indicates the situation of one who wishes to know the divine by experience, so that the face of wisdom may shine upon him like the sun. St. John also goes through this experience. It is to be a test of his strength (cf. p. 18). "And when I saw him, I fell at his feet as dead. And he laid his right hand upon me, saying unto me, Fear not" (v. 17). The candidate for initiation must pass through the experiences which otherwise man only undergoes at the gate of death. His guide must lead him beyond the region in which birth and death have a [184]meaning. The initiate enters upon a new life. "And I was dead; and, behold, I am alive for evermore, Amen; and have the keys of hell and of death."

Thus prepared, St. John is led on to learn the secrets of existence. "After this I looked, and, behold, a door was opened in heaven: and the first voice which I heard was as it were of a trumpet talking with me; which said, Come up hither, and I will shew thee things which must be hereafter." The messages to the seven spirits of the churches make known to St. John what is to take place in the physical world in order to prepare the way for Christianity. What he now sees "in the Spirit" takes him to the spiritual fountain-head of things, hidden behind physical evolution, but which will be realised, in a spiritualised age, in the near future, by means of physical evolution. The initiate experiences now in the spirit what is to happen in the future,—"And immediately I was in the spirit: and, behold, a throne was set in heaven, and one sat on the throne. And he that sat was to look upon like a jasper and a sardine stone: and there was [185]a rainbow round about the throne, in sight like unto an emerald." In this way is described the source of things in the world of sense, in the pictures in which it appears to the seer. "And round about the throne were four and twenty seats: and upon the seats I saw four and twenty elders sitting, clothed in white raiment; and they had on their heads crowns of gold" (iv. 2-4). The beings far advanced on the path of wisdom thus surround the fountain-head of existence, to gaze on its infinite essence and bear testimony to it. "And in the midst of the throne, and round about the throne, were four beasts full of eyes before and behind. And the first beast was like a lion, and the second beast like a calf, and the third beast had a face as a man, and the fourth beast was like a flying eagle. And the four beasts had each of them six wings about him; and they were full of eyes within: and they rest not day and night, saying, Holy, holy, holy, Lord God Almighty, which was, and is, and is to come." It is not difficult to see that the four beasts represent the supersensible life underlying physical forms of life. Afterwards, when the trumpets [186]sound, they lift up their voices, i.e., when the life expressed in sense-forms has been transmuted into spiritual life.

In the right hand of him who sits on the throne is the book in which the path to the highest wisdom is traced out (v. 1). There is only one worthy to open the book. "Behold, the Lion of the tribe of Juda, the Root of David, hath prevailed to open the book and to loose the seven seals thereof." The seven seals of the book denote that human wisdom is sevenfold. That this is so is again connected with the sacred character of the number seven. The mystic wisdom of Philo designates as seals the eternal cosmic thoughts which come to expression in things. Human wisdom seeks for those creative thoughts; but only in the book, which is sealed with them, is divine truth to be found. The fundamental thoughts of creation must first be unveiled, the seals must be opened, before what is in the book can be revealed. Jesus, the Lion, has power to open the seals. He has given a direction to the great creative thoughts which, through them, leads to wisdom. The Lamb that was slain and that [187]has bought its divinity with its blood, Jesus, who drew down the Christ into Himself and who thus, in the supreme sense, passed through the Life-Death-Mystery, opens the book (v. 9, 10). And as each seal is opened (vi), the four beasts declare what they know.

At the opening of the first seal, St. John sees a white horse, on which sits a rider with a bow. The first universal power, an embodiment of Creative Thought, becomes visible. It is put into the right direction by the new rider, Christianity. Strife is allayed by the new faith. At the opening of the second seal a red horse appears, ridden by one who takes away from the earth Peace,—the second universal power, so that humanity may not neglect, through sloth, to cultivate divine things. The opening of the third seal shows the universal power of Justice, guided by Christianity. The fourth brings the power of Religion which, through Christianity, has received new dignity.

The meaning of the four beasts thus becomes plain. They are the four chief universal powers, to which Christianity gives a new direction: War (the lion); Peaceful Work [188](the bull); Justice (the being with the human face); and Religious Enthusiasm (the eagle). The meaning of the third being becomes clear when it is said, at the opening of the third seal, "A measure of wheat for a penny, and three measures of barley for a penny," and that the rider holds "a pair of balances." And at the opening of the fourth seal a rider becomes visible whose name "was Death, and Hell followed with him." This rider is Religious Justice (vi. 6, 8). When the fifth seal is opened there appear the souls of those who have already acted in the spirit of Christianity. Creative thought itself, embodied in Christianity, shows itself here; but by this Christianity is at first meant only the first Christian community, which was transitory like other forms of creation. The sixth seal is opened (vi.); it is made evident that the spiritual world of Christianity is an eternal world. The people at large seem to be permeated by that spiritual world out of which Christianity itself proceeded. What it has itself created becomes sanctified. "And I heard the number of them which were sealed: and there were sealed an hundred and [189]forty and four thousand of all the tribes of the children of Israel" (vii. 4). They are those who prepared for the Eternal before the coming of Christianity, and who were transformed by the Christ-impulse.

The opening of the seventh seal follows. It becomes evident what true Christianity is to be in the evolution of the world. The seven angels, "which stood before God," appear (Rev. viii. 2). Again these angels are spirits from the ancient Mysteries transferred to Christianity. They are the spirits who lead to the vision of God in a really Christian way. Therefore what is next accomplished is a leading to God: it is an "initiation" which is bestowed upon St. John. The proclamations of the angels are accompanied by the necessary signs during initiations. "The first angel sounded and there followed hail and fire mingled with blood, and they were cast upon the earth: and the third part of trees was burnt up, and all green grass was burnt up." And similar things take place when the other angels sound their trumpets.

At this point we see that this was not [190]merely an initiation in the old sense, but that a new one was taking the place of the old. Christianity was not to be confined, like the ancient Mysteries, to a few elect ones. It was to belong to the whole of humanity. It was to be a religion of the people; the truth was to be ready for each one who "has ears to hear." The old Mystics were singled out from a great number; the trumpets of Christianity sound for every one who is willing to hear them. Whether he draws near or not depends on himself. This is the reason why the terrors accompanying this initiation of humanity are so enormously enhanced. What is to become of the earth and its inhabitants in a far distant future is revealed to St. John at his initiation. Underlying this is the thought that initiates are able to foresee in higher worlds what is realised in the lower world only in the future. The seven messages present the meaning of Christianity to that age, the seven seals represent what was then being prepared through Christianity for future accomplishment. The future is veiled and sealed to the uninitiated; it is unsealed in initiation. [191]When the earthly period is over during which the seven messages hold good, a more spiritual time will begin. Then life will no more flow on as it appears in physical forms, but even outwardly it will be a copy of its supersensible forms. These latter are represented by the four animals and the other seal-pictures. In a still later future appears that form of the earth which the initiate experiences through the trumpets.

Thus the initiate prophetically goes through what is to happen. And the Christian initiate learns how the Christ-impulse interposes and works on in earthly evolution. After it has been shown how all that is too much attached to perishable things perishes to attain true Christianity, there appears the mighty angel with a little book open in his hand, which he gives to St. John. "And he said unto me, Take it, and eat it up; and it shall make thy belly bitter, but it shall be in thy mouth sweet as honey" (x. 9). St. John was not only to read the little book, he was to absorb it and let its contents permeate him. What avails any knowledge unless man is vitally and thoroughly imbued [192]with it? Wisdom has to become life, man must not merely recognise the divine, but become divine himself. Such wisdom as is written in the book no doubt causes pain to the perishable part of man, "it shall make thy belly bitter," but so much the more does it make happy the eternal part, "but it shall be in thy mouth sweet as honey."

Only by such an initiation can Christianity become actual on the earth. It kills everything belonging to the lower nature. "And their dead bodies shall lie in the street of the great city, which spiritually is called Sodom and Egypt, where also our Lord was crucified." By this is meant the followers of Christ, who are ill-treated by the temporal powers. But what is ill-treated is only the mortal part of human nature, which they will afterwards have conquered. Thereby their fate is a copy of the prefiguring fate of Christ Jesus. "Spiritually Sodom and Egypt" is the symbol of a life which cleaves to the outer and is not changed by the Christ-impulse. Christ is everywhere crucified in the lower nature. When the lower nature conquers, all remains dead. The dead bodies [193]of men lie about in the public places of cities. Those who overcome the lower nature and awaken the crucified Christ hear the trumpet of the seventh angel, "the kingdoms of this world are become the kingdoms of our Lord, and of his Christ, and he shall reign for ever and ever" (xi. 15). "And the temple of God was opened in heaven, and there was seen in his temple the ark of his testament" (xi. 19).

In the vision of these events, the initiate sees renewed the old struggle between the lower and the higher natures. For everything which the candidate for initiation formerly had to go through must be repeated in one who follows the Christian path. Just as Osiris was threatened by the evil Typhon so now "the great dragon, that old serpent" (xii. 9) must be overcome. The woman, the human soul, gives birth to lower knowledge, which is an adverse power if it is not raised to wisdom. Man must pass through that lower knowledge. In the Apocalypse it appears as the "old serpent." From the remotest times the serpent had been the symbol of knowledge in all mystic wisdom. [194]Man may be led astray by this serpent,—knowledge,—if he does not bring to life in him the Son of God, who crushes the serpent's head. "And the great dragon was cast out, that old serpent, called the Devil, and Satan, which deceiveth the whole world: he was cast out into the earth, and his angels were cast out with him" (xii. 9). In these words we can see what it was that Christianity wished to be:—a new kind of initiation. What had been attained in the Mysteries was to be attained in a new form. For in them too the serpent had to be overcome, but this was no longer to take place in the old way. The one, primeval mystery, the Christian mystery, was to replace the many mysteries of antiquity. Jesus, in whom the Logos had been made flesh, was to become the initiator of the whole of humanity, and humanity was to be his own community of Mystics.

What was to take place was not a separation of the elect, but a linking together of all. As each grows up to it so does he become a Mystic. The good tidings are announced to all, he who has an ear to hear hastens to [195]learn the secrets. The voice of the heart is to decide in each individual case. It is not that one person at a time is introduced into the Mystery-temples, but that the word is to be spoken to all, to one it will then appeal more strongly than to another. It will be left to the daimon, the angel within each individual, to decide how far the latter may be initiated. The whole world is a Mystery-temple. Not only is salvation to come to those who see the wonderful processes in the special temples for initiation,—processes which give them a guarantee of eternal life, but "Blessed are they that have not seen, and yet have believed." Even if at first they grope in the dark, the light may nevertheless come to them later. Nothing is to be withheld from any one; the way is to be open to all.

The latter part of the Apocalypse describes clearly the dangers threatening Christianity through anti-Christian powers, and the final triumph of Christianity. All other gods are merged in the one Christian divinity: "And the city had no need of the sun, neither of the moon to shine in it: for the glory of God did lighten it, and the Lamb [196]is the light thereof" (xxi. 23). The secret of the Revelation of St. John is that the Mysteries are no longer to be kept under lock and key. "And he saith unto me, Seal not the sayings of the prophecy of this book, for the time is at hand."

The author of the Apocalypse has set forth what he believes to be the relation of his church to the churches of antiquity. He wished to express in a spiritual mystery what he thought about the Mysteries themselves. He wrote his mystery on the isle of Patmos, and he is said to have received the "Revelation" in a grotto. These details indicate that the revelation was of a mystery character.

Thus Christianity arose out of the Mysteries. Its wisdom is born as a mystery in the Apocalypse, but a mystery which transcends the limits of the old mystery world. The separate Mysteries were to become one universal one.

It may appear to be a contradiction to say that the secrets of the Mysteries became manifest through Christianity, and that nevertheless a Christian mystery is to be seen again in the spiritual visions of the [197]writer of the Apocalypse. The contradiction disappears directly we reflect that the secrets of the ancient Mysteries were revealed by the events in Palestine. Through these there became manifest what had previously been veiled in the Mysteries. There is now a new secret, namely what has been introduced into the evolution of the world by the appearance of the Christ. The initiate of ancient times, when in the spiritual world, saw how evolution points the way to the as yet hidden Christ. The Christian initiate experiences the unseen effects of the manifested Christ.

JESUS AND HIS HISTORICAL BACKGROUND

In the wisdom of the Mysteries is to be sought the soil out of which grew the spirit of Christianity. All that was needed was the gaining ground of the fundamental conviction that this spirit must be introduced into life in greater measure than had been the case with the Mysteries. But such a conviction was widely spread, as may be seen from the manner of life of the Essenes and Therapeutæ, who existed long before Christianity arose.

The Essenes were a secluded sect, living in Palestine, whose numbers at the time of Christ were estimated at four thousand. They formed a community which required that its members should lead a life which developed a higher life within the soul, and brought about a new birth. The aspirant [199] for admission was subjected to a severe test, in order to ascertain whether he were ripe for preparing himself for a higher life. If he was admitted, he had to undergo a period of probation, and to take a solemn oath that he would not betray to strangers the secrets of the Essenian discipline. The object of this life was the conquest of the lower nature in man, so that the spirit latent within him might be awakened ever more and more. One who had experienced up to a certain point the spirit within him was raised to a higher grade, and enjoyed a corresponding degree of authority, not forced from without, but conditioned by the nature of things.

Akin to the Essenes were the Therapeutæ, who dwelt in Egypt. We get all desirable details of their mode of life in a treatise by the philosopher Philo, On the Contemplative Life. (The dispute as to the authenticity of this work must now be regarded as settled, and it may be rightly assumed that Philo really described the life of a community existing long before Christianity, and well known to him. Cf. on the subject, G.R. Mead's Fragments of a Faith Forgotten.) A [200] few passages from Philo's treatise will give an idea of the main tenets of the Therapeutæ. "The dwellings of the members of the community are extremely simple, only affording necessary shelter from extreme heat and cold. The dwellings are not built close together, as in towns, for contiguity has no attraction for one who wishes for solitude; nor are they at a great distance one from another, in order that the social relations, so dear to them, may not be made difficult, and that they may easily be able to assist each other in case of an attack by brigands. In each house is a consecrated room called a temple or monasterion, a small room or cell in which the mysteries of the higher life are cultivated.... They also possess works by ancient authors who once directed their school, and left behind many explanations about the customary method used in allegorical writings.... Their interpretation of sacred writings is directed to the deeper meaning of allegorical narratives."

We thus see that what had been striven after in the narrower circle of the Mysteries was being made general. But such a [201] generalisation naturally weakened their severe character. The Essene and Therapeutic communities form a natural transition from the Mysteries to Christianity. But Christianity wished to extend to humanity in general what with the Essenes and Therapeutæ was an affair of a sect. This of course prepared the way for a still further weakening of the old severe forms.

The existence of such sects makes it possible to understand how far the time was ripe for the comprehension of the mystery of Christ. In the Mysteries, a man was artificially prepared for the dawning upon his consciousness, at the appropriate time, of the spiritual world. Within the Essene or Therapeutic community the soul sought, by a certain mode of life, to become ripe for the awakening of the higher man. A further step forward is that man struggles through to a feeling that a human individuality may have evolved to higher and higher stages of perfection in repeated earth lives. One who had arrived at a glimpse of this truth would also be able to feel that in Jesus a being of lofty spirituality had appeared. The loftier the [202]spirituality, the greater the possibility of accomplishing something of importance. Thus the individuality of Jesus could become capable of accomplishing the deed which the Evangelists so mysteriously indicate in the Baptism by John, and which, by the way in which they speak of it, they so clearly point out as of the utmost importance. The personality of Jesus became able to receive into its own soul Christ, the Logos, who was made flesh in that soul. Thenceforward the Ego of Jesus of Nazareth was the Christ, and the outer personality was the vehicle of the Logos. The event of the Ego of Jesus becoming the Christ is enacted in the Baptism by St. John. During the period of the Mysteries, "union with the Spirit" was only for those who were initiated. Amongst the Essenes, a whole community cultivated a life by means of which all its members were able to arrive at the mystical union. In the coming of Christ, something, i.e., the deeds of Christ, was placed before the whole of humanity, so that all might share in the mystical union.

THE NATURE OF CHRISTIANITY

The deepest effect must have been produced upon believers in Christianity by the fact that the Divine, the Word, the eternal Logos, no longer came to them in the dim twilight of the Mysteries, as Spirit only, but that when they spoke of the Logos, they were made to think of the historical, human personality of Jesus. Formerly the Logos had only been seen in different degrees of human perfection. The delicate, subtle differences in the spiritual life of personalities could be observed, and the manner and degree in which the Logos became living within those seeking initiation. A higher degree of maturity was to be interpreted as a higher stage of evolution of spiritual life. The preparatory steps had to be sought in a [204]spiritual life already passed through, and the present life was to be regarded as the preparatory stage for future degrees of spiritual evolution. The conservation of the spiritual power of the soul and the eternity of that force might be stated in the words of the Jewish occult teaching in the book of Sohar, "Nothing in the world is lost, nothing falls into the void, not even the words and voice of man: everything has its place and purport." Personality was but a metamorphosis of the soul, which develops from one personality to another. The single life of the personality was only considered as a link in the chain of development stretching backwards and forwards.

This Logos metamorphosing itself in the many separate human personalities has through Christianity been directed away from these to the one unique personality of Jesus. What had previously been distributed throughout the world was now united in a single personality. Jesus became the unique God-Man. In Jesus something was present once which must appear to man as the greatest of ideals, and with which, in [205]the course of man's repeated earthly lives, he ought to be more and more united. Jesus took upon Himself the divinisation of the whole of humanity. In Him was sought what formerly could only be sought in a man's own particular soul. One did not any more behold the divine and eternal within the personality of a man; all that was now beheld in Jesus. It is not the eternal part of the soul that conquers death and is raised through its own power as divine, but it is that which was in Jesus, the one God that will appear and raise the souls.

It follows from this that an entirely new meaning was given to personality. The eternal, immortal part had been taken from it. Only the personality, as such, was left. If immortality be not denied, it has to be admitted as pertaining to the personality itself. Out of the belief in the soul's eternal metamorphosis came the belief in personal immortality. The personality acquired infinite importance, because it was the only thing which was left to man.

Henceforth there is nothing between the personality and the infinite God. A direct [206]relation with Him must be established. Man was no longer capable of himself becoming divine, in a greater or less degree. He was simply man, standing in a direct but outward relation to God. This brought quite a new note into the conception of the world for those who knew the point of view held in the ancient Mysteries. There were many people in this position during the first centuries of Christianity. They knew the nature of the Mysteries. If they wished to become Christians, they were obliged to come to an understanding with the older conceptions. This brought them most difficult conflicts within their souls. They sought in most various ways to effect a settlement between the two tendencies in the conception of the world. This conflict is reflected in the writings of early Christian times: in those of heathens attracted by the sublimity of Christianity, as well as in the writings of those Christians who found it hard to give up the conceptions of the Mysteries. Slowly did Christianity grow out of these Mysteries. On the one hand Christian convictions were presented in the form of the Mystery truths, [207]and on the other, the Mystery wisdom was clothed in Christian words.

Clement of Alexandria (ob. 217 A.D.), a Christian writer whose education had been pagan, is an instance of this, "God has not forbidden us to rest from good deeds when keeping the sabbath. He permits those who can grasp them to share in the divine mysteries and in the sacred light. He has not revealed to the crowd what is not suitable for them. He judged it fitting to reveal it only to a few, who are able to grasp it and to work out in themselves the unspeakable mystery which God confided to the Logos, not to the written word. And God hath set some in the Church as apostles; and some prophets; and some evangelists; and some pastors and teachers; for the perfecting of the saints, for the work of the ministry, for the edifying of the body of Christ." Individual souls in those days sought by very different paths to find the way from the ancient views to the Christian ones. And the one who thought he was on the right path called others heretics. In the meanwhile, the Church grew stronger and stronger [208]as an outward institution. The more power it gained, the more did the path, recognised as the right one by the decisions of councils, take the place of personal investigation. It was for the Church to decide who deviated too far from the divine truth which she guarded. The idea of a "heretic" took firmer and firmer shape. During the first centuries of Christianity, the search for the divine path was a much more personal matter than it afterwards became. A long distance had been travelled before Augustine's conviction became possible: "I should not believe in the truth of the Gospels unless the authority of the Catholic Church forced me to do so" (cf. p. 143).

The conflict between the method of the Mysteries and that of the Christian religion acquired a special stamp through the various Gnostic sects and writers. We may class as Gnostics all the writers of the first Christian centuries who sought for a deep, spiritual meaning in Christian teachings. (A brilliant account of the development of the Gnosis is given in G.R.S. Mead's book mentioned above, Fragments of a Faith Forgotten.) We [209]understand the Gnostics when we look upon them as saturated with the ancient wisdom of the Mysteries, and striving to understand Christianity from that point of view. For them, Christ was the Logos, and as such of a spiritual nature. In His primal essence, He cannot approach man from without. He must be awakened in the soul. But the historical Jesus must bear some relation to the spiritual Logos. This was the crucial point for the Gnostics. Some settled it in one way, some in another. The essential point common to them all was that to arrive at a true understanding of the Christ-idea, mere historical tradition was not enough, but that it must be sought either in the wisdom of the Mysteries, or in the Neo-Platonic philosophy which was derived from the same source. The Gnostics had confidence in human wisdom, and believed it capable of bringing forth a Christ by whom the historical Christ could be measured: in fact, through whom alone the latter could be understood and beheld in the right light.

Of special interest from this point of view is the doctrine given in the books of [210]Dionysius the Areopagite. It is true that there is no mention of these writings till the sixth century; it matters little when and where they were written, the point is that they give an account of Christianity which is clothed in the language of the Neo-Platonic philosophy and presented in the form of a spiritual contemplation of the higher world. At all events this is a form of delineation which belongs to the first Christian centuries. In older times the truth was handed on in the form of oral tradition; the most important things were not entrusted to writing. The Christianity described in the writings of Dionysius is set forth in the mirror of the Neo-Platonic conception of the world. Sense-perception troubles man's spiritual vision. He must reach out beyond the senses. But all human ideas are primarily derived from observation by the senses. What man perceives with his senses, he calls existence; what he does not so perceive, he calls non-existence. Therefore if he wishes to open up an actual view of the Divine, he must rise above existence and non-existence, for these also, as he conceives them, have their origin [211]in the sphere of the senses. In this sense God is neither existent nor non-existent; he is super-existent. Consequently he cannot be attained by means of ordinary cognition, which has to do with existing things. We have to be raised above ourselves, above our sense-observation, above our reasoning logic, if we are to find the way to spiritual vision. Thence we are able to get a glimpse into the perspectives of the Divine.

But this super-existent Divinity has brought forth the Logos, the basis of the universe, filled with wisdom. To him man's lower powers are able to attain. He is present in the cosmos as the spiritual Son of God, he is the Mediator between God and man. He may be present in man in various degrees. He may for instance be realised in an external institution, in which those diversely imbued with his spirit are grouped into a hierarchy. A "church" of this kind is the outer reality of the Logos, and the power which lives in it lived in a personal way in the Christ become flesh, in Jesus. Thus the Church is through Jesus united to God: Jesus is its meaning and crowning-point.

[212]One thing was clear to all Gnosis, that one must come to an understanding about the personality of Jesus. Christ and Jesus must be brought into connection with one another. Divinity was taken away from human personality and must, in one way or another, be recovered. It must be possible to find it again in Jesus. The Mystic had to do with a degree of divinity within himself, and with his earthly personality. The Christian had to do with the latter, and also with a perfect God, far above all that is attainable by humanity. If we hold firmly to this point of view, a fundamental mystic attitude of the soul is only possible when the soul's spiritual eyes are opened; when, through finding higher spiritual possibilities within itself, the soul throws itself open to the light which issues from Christ in Jesus. The union of the soul with its highest powers is at the same time union with the historical Christ. For mysticism is an immediate consciousness and feeling of the divine within the soul. But a God far transcending everything human can never dwell in the soul in the real sense of the word. The Gnosis and all subsequent [213]Christian mysticism represent the effort, in some way or other, to lay hold of that God, and to apprehend Him directly in the soul.

A conflict in this case was inevitable. It was really only possible for a man to find his own divine part, but this is both human and divine,—the divine at a certain stage of development. Yet the Christian God is a definite one, perfect in himself. It was possible for a person to find in himself the power to strive upwards to this God, but he could not say that what he experienced in his own soul, at any stage of development, was one with God. A great gulf was fixed between what it was possible to find in the soul, and what Christianity called divine. It is the gulf between science and faith, between knowledge and religious feeling.

This gulf does not exist for the Mystic in the old sense of the word. For he knows for a certainty that he can only comprehend the divine by degrees, and he also knows why this is so. It is clear to him that this gradual attainment is a real attainment of real divine life, and he finds it difficult to speak of a perfect, isolated divine principle. [214]A Mystic of this kind does not seek a perfect God, but he wishes to experience the divine life. He seeks to be made divine, not to gain an external relation to the Godhead.

It is of the essence of Christianity that its mysticism in this sense starts with an assumption. The Christian Mystic seeks to behold divinity within him, but at the same time he looks up to the historical Christ as his physical eyes do to the sun. Just as the sun is the means by which physical eyes behold physical objects, so does the Christian Mystic intensify his inner nature that it may behold the divine, and the light which makes such vision possible for him is the fact of the appearance of Christ. It is He who enables man to attain his highest possibilities. It is in this way that the Christian Mystics of the Middle Ages differ from the Mystics of the ancient Mysteries (cf. my book, Mystics of the Renaissance).

CHRISTIANITY AND HEATHEN WISDOM

At the time of the first beginnings of Christianity, there appear in heathen civilisation conceptions of the universe which seem to be a continuation of the Platonic philosophy, and which may also be taken as a deepening and spiritualisation of the wisdom of the Mysteries. The beginning of such conceptions is to be dated from Philo of Alexandria (B.C. 25-A.D. 50). From his point of view the processes which lead to the divine take place in the innermost part of the human soul. We might say that the temple in which Philo seeks initiation is wholly within him, and his higher experiences are the Mysteries. In his case processes of a purely spiritual nature replace the initiatory ceremonies of the sanctuary.

[216]According to Philo, sense-observation and knowledge gained through the logical intellect do not lead to the divine. They have merely to do with what is perishable. But there is a way by which the soul may rise above these methods. It must come out of what it calls its ordinary self: from this it must withdraw. Then it enters a state of spiritual exaltation and illumination, in which it no longer knows, thinks, and judges in the ordinary sense of the words; for it has become merged, identified with the divine, which is experienced in its essence, and cannot be imparted in thought-concepts or abstract ideas. It is experienced, and one who goes through this experience knows that no one can impart it, for the only way of reaching it is to live it. The visible world is an image of this mystic reality which is experienced in the inmost recesses of the soul. The world has come forth from the invisible, inconceivable God. The harmony of the cosmos, which is steeped in wisdom, and to which sense-phenomena are subject, is a direct reflection of the Godhead, its spiritual image. It is divine spirit poured out into the [217]world,—cosmic reason, the Logos, the offspring or Son of God. The Logos is the mediator between the world of sense and the unimaginable God. When man steeps himself in knowledge, he becomes united with the Logos, which is embodied in him. The person who has developed spirituality is the vehicle of the Logos. Above the Logos is God; beneath is the perishable world. It is man's vocation to form the link between the two. What he experiences in his inmost being, as spirit, is the universal Spirit. Such ideas are directly reminiscent of the Pythagorean manner of thinking (cf. p. 57 et seq.).

The centre of existence is sought in the inner life, but this life is conscious of its cosmic value. St. Augustine was thinking in virtually the same way as Philo, when he said: "We see all created things because they are; but they are, because God sees them." And he adds, concerning what and how we see: "And because they are, we see them outwardly; because they are perfect, we see them inwardly."

Plato has the same fundamental idea (cf. [218]p. 63 et seq.). Like Plato, Philo sees in the destiny of the human soul the closing act of the great cosmic drama, the awakening of the divinity that is under a spell. He thus describes the inner actions of the soul: the wisdom in man's inner being walks along, "tracing the paths of the Father, and shapes the forms while beholding the archetypes." It is no personal matter for man to create forms in his inner being; they are the eternal wisdom, they are the cosmic life.

This is in harmony with the interpretation of the myths of the people in the light of the Mysteries. The Mystic searches for the deeper truth in the myths (cf. p. 94 et seq.). And as the Mystic treats the myths of paganism, Philo handles Moses' story of the creation. The Old Testament accounts are for him images of inner soul-processes. The Bible relates the creation of the world. One who merely takes it as a description of outer events only half knows it. It is certainly written, "In the beginning God created the heaven and the earth. And the earth was without form and void, and darkness was on the face of the deep. And [219]the spirit of God moved on the face of the waters." But the real inner meaning of the words must be lived in the depths of the soul. God must be found within, then He appears as the "Primal Splendour, who sends out innumerable rays, not perceptible by the senses, but collectively thinkable." This is Philo's expression. In the Timæus of Plato, the words are almost identical with the Bible ones, "Now when the Father, who had created the universe, saw how it had become living and animated, and an image of the eternal gods, he felt pleasure therein." In the Bible we read, "And God saw that it was good."

The recognition of the divine is for Philo, as well as for Plato and in the wisdom of the Mysteries, to live through the process of creation in one's own soul. The history of creation and the history of the soul which is becoming divine, in this way flow into one. Philo is convinced that Moses' account of the creation may be used for writing the history of the soul which is seeking God. Everything in the Bible thereby acquires a profoundly symbolical meaning, of which Philo becomes [220]the interpreter. He reads the Bible as a history of the soul.

We may say that Philo's manner of reading the Bible corresponds to a feature of his age which originated in the wisdom of the Mysteries. He indeed relates that the Therapeutæ interpreted ancient writings in the same way. "They also possess works by ancient authors who once directed their school and left behind many explanations about the customary method pursued in allegorical writings.... The interpretation of such writings is directed to the deeper meaning of the allegorical narratives" (cf. p. 200). Thus Philo's aim was to discover the deeper meaning of the "allegorical" narratives in the Old Testament.

Let us try to realise whither such an interpretation could lead. We read the account of creation and find in it not only a narrative of outward events, but an indication of the way which the soul has to take in order to attain to the divine. Thus the soul must reproduce in itself, as a microcosm, the ways of God, and in this alone can its efforts after wisdom consist. The drama of the universe [221]must be enacted in each individual soul. The inner life of the mystical sage is the realisation of the image given in the account of creation. Moses wrote not only to relate historical facts, but to represent pictorially the paths which the soul must travel if it would find God.

All this, in Philo's conception of the universe, is enacted within the human soul. Man experiences within himself what God has experienced in the universe. The word of God, the Logos, becomes an event in the soul. God brought the Jews from Egypt into Palestine; he let them go through distress and privation before giving them that Land of Promise. That is the outward event. Man must experience it inwardly. He goes from the land of Egypt, the perishable world, through the privations which lead to the suppression of the sense-nature, into the Promised Land of the soul, he attains the eternal. With Philo it is all an inward process. The God who poured Himself forth into the world consummates His resurrection in the soul when that soul understands His creative word and echoes it. Then man has [222]spiritually given birth within himself to divinity, to the divine spirit which became man, to the Logos, Christ. In this sense knowledge was, for Philo and those who thought like him, the birth of Christ within the world of spirit. The Neo-Platonic philosophy, which developed contemporaneously with Christianity, was an elaboration of Philo's thought. Let us see how Plotinus (A.D. 204-269) describes his spiritual experiences:

"Often when I come to myself on awaking from bodily sleep and, turning from the outer world, enter into myself, I behold wondrous beauty. Then I am sure that I have been conscious of the better part of myself. I live my true life, I am one with the divine and, rooted in the divine, gain the power to transport myself beyond even the super-world. After thus resting in God, when I descend from spiritual vision and again form thoughts, I ask myself how it has happened that I now descend and that my soul ever entered the body at all, since, in its essence, it is what it has just revealed itself to me. What can the reason be for souls forgetting God the Father since they come [223]from the beyond and belong to Him, and, when they forget Him, know nothing of Him or of themselves? The first false step they take is indulging in presumption, the desire to become, and in forgetfulness of their true self and in the pleasure of only belonging to themselves. They coveted self-glorification, they rushed about in pursuit of their desires and thus went astray and fell completely away. Thereupon they lost all knowledge of their origin in the beyond, just as children, early separated from their parents and brought up elsewhere, do not know who they themselves and their parents are." Plotinus delineates the kind of life which the soul should strive to develop. "The life of the body and its longings should be stilled, the soul should see calm in all that surrounds it: in earth, sea, air, and heaven itself no movement. It should learn to see how the soul pours itself from without into the serene cosmos, streaming into it from all sides; as the sun's rays illuminate a dark cloud and make it golden, so does the soul, on entering the body of the world encircled by the sky, give it life and immortality."

[224]It is evident that this vision of the world is very similar to that of Christianity. Believers of the community of Jesus said: "That which was from the beginning, which we have heard, which we have seen with our eyes, which we have looked upon, and our hands have handled, of the Word of life ... declare we unto you." In the same way it might be said in the spirit of Neo-Platonism, "That which was from the beginning, which cannot be heard and seen, must be spiritually experienced as the Word of life."

And so the old conception of the universe is developed and splits into two leading ideas. It leads in Neo-Platonism and similar systems to an idea of Christ which is purely spiritual; on the other hand, it leads to a fusion of the idea of Christ with a historical manifestation, the personality of Jesus. The writer of the Gospel of St. John may be said to unite these two conceptions. "In the beginning was the Word." He shares this conviction with the Neo-Platonists. The Word becomes spirit within the soul, thus do the Neo-Platonists conclude. The Word was made flesh in Jesus, thus does St. John [225]conclude, and with him the whole Christian community. The inner meaning of the manner in which the Word was made flesh was given in all the ancient cosmogonies. Plato says of the macrocosm: "God has extended the body of the world on the soul of the world in the form of a cross." The soul of the world is the Logos. If the Logos is to be made flesh, he must recapitulate the cosmic process in fleshly existence. He must be nailed to the cross, and rise again. In spiritual form this most momentous thought of Christianity had long before been prefigured in the old cosmogonies. The Mystic went through it as a personal experience in initiation. The Logos become man had to go through it in a way that made this fact one that is true for or valid to the whole of humanity. Something which was present under the old dispensation as an incident in the Mysteries becomes a historical fact through Christianity. Hence Christianity was the fulfilment not only of what the Jewish prophets had predicted, but also of the truth which had been prefigured in the Mysteries.

[226] The Cross of Golgotha gathers together in one fact the whole cult of the Mysteries of antiquity. We find the cross first in the ancient cosmogonies. At the starting-point of Christianity it confronts us in an unique event which has supreme value for the whole of mankind. It is from this point of view that it is possible for the reason to apprehend the mystical element in Christianity. Christianity as a mystical fact is a milestone in the process of human evolution; and the incidents in the Mysteries, with their attendant results, are the preparation for that mystical fact.

ST. AUGUSTINE AND THE CHURCH

The full force of the conflict which was enacted in the souls of Christian believers during the transition from paganism to the new religion is exhibited in the person of St. Augustine (A.D. 354-430). The spiritual struggles of Origen, Clement of Alexandria, Gregory Nazianzen, Jerome, and others are full of mysterious interest when we see them calmed and laid to rest in the mind of Augustine.

In Augustine's personality deep spiritual needs developed out of a passionate nature. He passed through pagan and semi-Christian ideas. He suffered deeply from the most appalling doubts of the land which attack one who has felt the impotence of many varieties of thought in the face of spiritual problems, and who has tasted the depressing [228]effect of the question: "Can man know anything whatever?"

At the beginning of his struggles, Augustine's thoughts clung to the perishable things of sense. He could only picture the spiritual to himself in material images. It is a deliverance for him when he rises above this stage. He thus describes it in his Confessions: "When I wished to think of God, I could only imagine immense masses of bodies and believed that was the only kind of thing that could exist. This was the chief and almost the only cause of the errors which I could not avoid." He thus indicates the point at which a person must arrive who is seeking the true life of the spirit. There are thinkers, not a few, who maintain that it is impossible to arrive at pure thought, free from any material admixture. These thinkers confuse what they feel bound to say about their own inner life, with what is humanly possible. The truth rather is that it is only possible to arrive at higher knowledge when thought has been liberated from all material things, when an inner life has been developed in which images of reality do not cease when [229]their demonstration in sense-impressions comes to an end. Augustine relates how he attained to spiritual vision. Everywhere he asked where the divine was to be found. "I asked the earth and she said 'I am not it' and all that was upon the earth said the same. I asked the ocean and the abysses and all that lives in them, which said, 'We are not thy God, seek beyond us.' I asked the winds, and the whole atmosphere and its inhabitants said, 'The philosophers who sought for the essence of things in us were under an illusion, we are not God.' I asked the sun, moon, and stars, which said, 'We are not God whom thou seekest.'" And it came home to St. Augustine that there is only one thing which can answer his question about the divine—his own soul. The soul said, "No eyes nor ears can impart to thee what is in me. For I alone can tell thee, and I tell thee in an unquestionable way." "Men may be doubtful whether vital force is situate in air or in fire, but who can doubt that he himself lives, remembers, understands, wills, thinks, knows, and judges? If he doubts, it is a proof that he is alive, he remembers why he doubts, he [230]understands that he doubts, he will assure himself of things, he thinks, he knows that he knows nothing, he judges that he must not accept anything hastily." Outer things do not defend themselves when their essence and existence are denied, but the soul does defend itself. It could not be doubtful of itself unless it existed. By its doubt it confirms its own existence. "We are and we recognise our being, and we love our own being and knowledge. On these three points no illusion in the garb of truth can trouble us, for we do not apprehend them with our bodily senses like external things." Man learns about the divine by leading his soul to know itself as spiritual, so that it may find its way, as a spirit, into the spiritual world. Augustine had battled his way through to this knowledge. It was out of such an attitude of mind that there grew up in pagan nations the desire to knock at the gate of the Mysteries. In the age of Augustine, such convictions might lead to becoming a Christian. Jesus, the Logos become man had shown the path which must be followed by the soul if it would attain the goal which it sees when in [231]communion with itself. In A.D. 385, at Milan, Augustine was instructed by St. Ambrose. All his doubts about the Old and New Testaments vanished when his teacher interpreted the most important passages, not merely in a literal sense, but "by lifting the mystic veil by force of the spirit."

What had been guarded in the Mysteries was embodied for Augustine in the historical tradition of the Evangelists and in the community where that tradition was preserved. He comes by degrees to the conviction that "the law of this tradition, which consists in believing what it has not proved, is moderate and without guile." He arrives at the idea, "Who could be so blind as to say that the Church of the Apostles deserves to have no faith placed in it, when it is so loyal and is supported by the conformity of so many brethren; when these have handed down their writings to posterity so conscientiously, and when the Church has so strictly maintained the succession of teachers, down to our present bishops?"

Augustine's mode of thought told him, that with the coming of Christ other conditions [232]had set in for souls seeking after the spirit than those which had previously existed. For him it was firmly established that in Christ Jesus had been revealed in outer historical fact that which the Mystic had sought in the Mysteries through preparation. One of his most significant utterances is the following, "What is now called the Christian religion already existed amongst the ancients and was not lacking at the very beginnings of the human race. When Christ appeared in the flesh, the true religion already in existence received the name of Christian." There were two ways possible for such a method of thought. One way is that if the human soul develops within it the forces which lead it to the knowledge of its true self, it will, if it only goes far enough, come also to the knowledge of the Christ and of everything connected with him. This would have been a mystery-wisdom enriched through the Christ event. The other way is taken by Augustine and is that by which he became the great model for his successors. It consists in cutting off the development of the forces of the soul at a certain point, and in borrowing [233]the ideas connected with the coming of Christ from written accounts and oral traditions. Augustine rejected the first way as springing from pride of the soul; he thought the second was the way of true humility. Thus he says to those who wished to follow the first way: "You may find peace in the truth, but for that humility is needed, which does not suit your proud neck." On the other hand, he was filled with boundless inward happiness by the fact that since the coming of Christ in the flesh, it was possible to say that every soul can come to spiritual experience which goes as far as it can in seeking within itself, and then, in order to attain to the highest, has confidence in what the written and oral traditions of the Christian Church tell us about the Christ and his revelation. He says on this point: "What bliss, what abiding enjoyment of supreme and true good is offered us, what serenity, what a breath of eternity! How shall I describe it? It has been expressed, as far as it could be, by those great incomparable souls who we admit have beheld and still behold.... We reach a point at which we [234]acknowledge how true is what we have been commanded to believe and how well and beneficently we have been brought up by our mother, the Church, and of what benefit was the milk given by the Apostle Paul to the little ones...." (It is beyond the scope of this book to give an account of the alternative method which is evolved from the Mystery Wisdom, enriched through the Christ event. The description of this method will be found in An Outline of Occult Science, see advt., front page.) Whereas in pre-Christian times one who wished to seek the spiritual basis of existence was necessarily directed to the way of the Mysteries, Augustine was able to say, even to those souls who could find no such path within themselves, "Go as far as you can on the path of knowledge with your human powers, thence trust (faith) will carry you up into the higher spiritual regions." It was only going one step further to say, it is natural to the human soul only to be able to arrive at a certain stage of knowledge through its own powers: thence it can only advance further through trust, through faith in written and [235]oral tradition. This step was taken by the spiritual movement which assigned to knowledge a certain sphere above which the soul could not rise by its own efforts, but everything which lay beyond this domain was made an object of faith which has to be supported by written and oral tradition and by confidence in its representatives. Thomas Aquinas, the greatest teacher within the Church (1224-1274), has set forth this doctrine in his writings in a variety of ways. His main point is that human knowledge can only attain to that which led Augustine to self-knowledge, to the certainty of the divine. The nature of the divine and its relation to the world is given by revealed theology, which is not accessible to man's own researches and is, as the substance of faith, superior to all knowledge.

The origin of this point of view may be studied in the theology of John Scotus Erigena, who lived in the ninth century at the court of Charles the Bald, and who represents a natural transition from the earliest ideas of Christianity to the ideas of Thomas Aquinas. His conception of the universe is [236]couched in the spirit of Neo-Platonism. In his treatise De Divisione Naturæ, Erigena has elaborated the teaching of Dionysius the Areopagite. This teaching started from a God far above the perishable things of sense, and it derived the world from Him (Cf. p. 208 et seq.). Man is involved in the transmutation of all beings into this God, Who finally becomes what He was from the beginning. Everything falls back again into the Godhead which has passed through the universal process and has finally become perfected. But in order to reach this goal man must find the way to the Logos who was made flesh. In Erigena this thought leads to another: that what is contained in the writings which give an account of the Logos leads, when received in faith, to salvation. Reason and the authority of the Scriptures, faith and knowledge stand on the same level. The one does not contradict the other, but faith must bring that to which knowledge never can attain by itself.

The knowledge of the eternal which the [237]ancient Mysteries withheld from the multitude became, when presented in this way by Christian thought and feeling, the content of faith, which by its very nature had to do with something unattainable by mere knowledge. The conviction of the pre-Christian Mystic was that to him was given knowledge of the divine, while the people were obliged to have faith in its expression in images. Christianity came to the conviction that God has given his wisdom to mankind through revelation, and man attains through his knowledge an image of this divine revelation. The wisdom of the Mysteries is a hothouse plant, which is revealed to a few individuals ripe for it. Christian wisdom is a Mystery revealed as knowledge to none, but as a content of faith revealed to all. The standpoint of the Mysteries lived on in Christianity, but in a different form. All, not only the special individual, were to share in the truth, but the process was that at a certain point man owned his inability to penetrate farther by means of knowledge, and thence ascended to faith. Christianity brought the content of the Mysteries out of the obscurity of the [238]temple into the clear light of day. The one Christian movement mentioned led to the idea that this content must necessarily be retained in the form of faith.

The Mystical Life of Jesus

While the Gospels offer a glimpse into the final years of Christ's public life, they are strikingly silent about his formative years, travels, and inner teachings. This silence has led many to ask: What was hidden? What has been lost—or deliberately omitted?

In The Mystical Life of Jesus, H. Spencer Lewis, founder of the Rosicrucian Order (AMORC), dares to fill in the blanks.

Drawing from Eastern archives, ancient mystery traditions, and esoteric Christian records, Lewis reconstructs a version of Jesus's life that spans continents, initiations, and sacred teachings. This is not the passive lamb of conventional Sunday school lessons—it is the portrait of a world-traveling adept, trained in the mystical schools of Egypt, India, and beyond, whose mission was far greater than martyrdom.

Lewis claims that Jesus did not simply die for humanity—he came to teach it how to live in conscious union with the Divine.

Here you'll find references to hidden brotherhoods, secret manuscripts, and teachings passed down through oral and initiatory traditions—claims that will challenge orthodox minds and inspire seekers of hidden truth.

Placed second in this compilation, The Mystical Life of Jesus expands upon the metaphysical foundation laid by Steiner, offering a historical and mystical narrative of Christ's life beyond the veil of scripture. Whether taken as spiritual allegory or hidden history, it invites the reader to see Jesus as both man and initiate—teacher and embodiment of divine light.

EXPLANATION

EXPLANATION OF THE TERMS "ARYAN" AND "GREAT WHITE BROTHERHOOD"

These special terms are defined by Rosicrucians as follows: In the Rosicrucian teachings the word Aryan is used to denote the prehistoric culture and root-language behind Sanskrit and most extant Indo- European languages today. Dictionaries state that the word Aryan comes from the Sanskrit arya, an adjective meaning noble. The Oxford English Dictionary defines Aryan as "A member of the Aryan family; one belonging to, or descended from, the ancient people who spoke the parent Aryan language." This family of languages includes Sanskrit, Zend, Persian, Greek, Latin, Celtic, Teutonic, and Slavonic—in other words, the present-day Indo-European languages. Rosicrucians also define Aryan as referring to the prehistoric Atlantean wise beings—the "Light Bearing" or "Enlightened Ones." As far as race is concerned, the original wise beings who taught the Aryan language and culture were called Atlanteans, and as a distinctive racial type, disappeared in prehistoric times. However, it was their sacred Atlantean culture—the traditions, institutions, and hieroglyphic alphabet known as Sensar— which was cultivated as Sanskrit, the ancient Aryan language of the Hindus of India.

In Rosicrucian terminology the Great White Brotherhood (G.W.B.) consists of all the enlightened soul personalities who, independent of religions and traditions, are commissioned to work in one of the twelve paths of the ancient mystical tradition. It is that invisible body of mystics composed of the most exalted and advanced spiritual leaders in various lands throughout the world. The word White in this phrase alludes to Light, the illumination of understanding, wisdom, and spirituality as expressed by enlightened soul personalities, and has nothing to do with race. Rosicrucians realize that these cosmic masters work in the service of humanity. The Rosicrucian Order, AMORC, is only one of the channels that has been used and is still being used by the G.W.B. for the development and progress of humanity's own spiritual and esoteric unfoldment and for the improvement of civilization.

INTRODUCTION

IT IS A fact that very often truth is far more interesting than fiction. It is particularly so in regard to the life of Jesus. Perhaps it is due to the cosmic cycle through which humanity is passing, or perhaps it is due solely to our intellectual development, but people have become more interested in the life of the Great Redeemer than they have been in any other period since the dawn of Christianity.

In my contact with seekers for spiritual truths, covering twenty- five years, I have found that inevitably the student of mysticism, metaphysics, psychology and occultism is drawn to a more minute and analytical study of the life and teachings of the Christ, Jesus. His whole career, his doctrines, parables, miracles, and illuminating inferences, gradually fascinate and attune the spiritual side of mystical students, and they become restless until they can fathom the mysteries of Jesus's life.

Why there are any mysteries in the life of Jesus is revealed in chapters in this book. After many years of careful study and research, even to the extent of visiting the holy and mystical places of Europe, Palestine, and Egypt, I am still unprepared to say whether the church authorities who authorized the incomplete, partly erroneous, and greatly veiled life of Jesus as it appears in the Christian Bible were justified in their actions or not. Certain it is, not all are prepared even today to comprehend, nor apprehend, the mystical significance of most of the mysteries associated with pristine Christianity. That there are thousands, perhaps several millions, now ready for the truth is undeniable; but even so, they are but a small fraction of those who have accepted and found peace and salvation through the offerings of the Christian church.

To those who in orthodox sincerity will reject much that is presented in this book, I can say only: "Hold fast to that which is good!" If your faith, your knowledge, and your conviction in regard to Christian matters serves you well, and there is no inner urge to look beyond the veil, then do not do so. Permit nothing to weaken or lessen your adoration and worship of him who is your Savior and your Lord.

To those who believe that a more intimate knowledge of Jesus, the Son of God, the Master, the Avatar, and the Mystic, will endear him to their hearts, and to those who feel that the inner self needs more light on the mysteries of his mission, I present the chapters of The Mystical Life of Jesus as a comprehensive survey of things long held in seclusion by a few, but now deserving of wider circulation.

The story of the life and mission of Jesus as presented in this book makes no sectarian appeal. I know, as a fact, that the Jesus revealed herein is acceptable to as many Jews as Gentiles, to as many Roman Catholics as Protestants; and in these days of religious controversy and profound concern regarding the growth of the numberless thousands who do not attend any church and who seem to be losing their interest in religious matters, I am happy to say that I know that thousands will find in this book a key to their problem and an incentive to reread the Christian Bible and reconsider their rejection of the church.

I said I know these things. Through my official capacity I am in daily contact with many thousands of such persons in North America and thousands in other lands. In my public lectures throughout the United States for twelve years, in personal interviews with the spiritually restless among the populace, and in journeys to foreign lands, I have seen the effect of these truths. Parts of the chapters in this book have been used in public discourses, some of the interesting facts have been used in private lessons, and others have been presented in personal conversations. The result has always been an awakening of interest in the life and teachings of Jesus, and generally a happy realization that Jesus and his doctrines were wholly acceptable in the newer revelations.

In the past few years, certain pamphlets have appeared claiming to contain hidden facts regarding the life of Jesus. In most cases these stories contained such improbabilities or inconsistencies as to condemn them as fabrications. Several of the most popular of these have claimed that they were the result of a discovery of some rare manuscript or record hitherto hidden in a secluded monastery. The real origin of all that was dependable in such pamphlets was the uncovering of certain holy books of the ancients which did contain casual references to incidents in the life of Jesus rejected by the church authorities when the first versions of the Bible were authentically compiled.

The facts contained in this book are not drawn from any newly discovered manuscripts, writings, or records. In fact, it cannot be said that the facts contained herein are new to either the founders of the early Christian church, to the most profound and analytical writers of spiritual subjects, or to the most advanced of mystics in many lands.

The Rosicrucian archives in foreign lands, embracing the records of the Essenes, the Nazarenes, and the Nazarites, as well as the complete records of the Great White Brotherhood in Tibet, India, and Egypt, have always been sources of knowledge for the worthy inquirer into the history of all avatars and especially into the history of Jesus. It is from this dependable source that all the facts contained in this book have been drawn—not at one time and not without years of labor and indefatigable study and service.

Wherever possible, verification or substantiation has been secured from the writings and records of the early church leaders, historians, or archivists. Extracts have also been taken from the writings of Jews, and even from the so-called heathens, whenever possible. Such citations are plainly indicated.

I wish to take this opportunity to thank all those who in past years have carefully examined portions of my writings on this subject and have called my attention to additional points which should be covered. I wish also to thank those members in my tour to the Near East during the months of January, February, and March of this year, who acted as my companions in my special researches, and aided my secretary and myself in securing the information needed to give personal verification to the important statements contained in this book. It was a glorious work and I hope that these many companions will find some rewards for their efforts in the book which I have dedicated to them.

—H. Spencer Lewis

Egyptian Temple, Rosicrucian Park San Jose, California April 15, 1929

*Biblical quotations in this edition are from the New Revised Standard Version (NRSV) translation of the Bible.

18

Chapter 1

THE MYSTERY OF THE ESSENES
BEFORE ONE CAN properly understand and appreciate the history and real story of the birth and life work of the Master Jesus, one must have an understanding of the ancient organizations and schools which contributed to the preparation for his coming.

Within the last 100 years, a great many notations in sacred literature have been discovered relating to the Essenian community and the activities of this organization in Palestine just prior to and during the lifetime of the Master Jesus. Many of these notations have verified the references to the Essenes by such eminent historians as Philo and Josephus, and have explained many of the mysterious references found in the sacred writings of the Hebrews as translated in the Christian Bible.

The possible relationship of the Essenes to the early Christian activities has not only aroused the interest of hundreds of eminent theologians and biblical authorities, but it has caused one question to be asked by thousands of students of mystical literature: "Why has the history or story of the Essenes been withheld from general knowledge?"

The answer is: Those who knew the story desired to keep the Essenian community shrouded in mystery to protect its work and teachings from being publicly discussed and eventually scoffed at by those students or professors of orthodox Christianity who have labored so diligently to make even a greater mystery of Christ and Christianity.

The Rosicrucian records have always had extensive details of the activities of the Essenian organization, and no initiate of the Rosicrucian Order, or no profound student of the ancient mysteries who became worthy of contact with the ancient records, was ever left in ignorance regarding the Essenes. Today the veil can be drawn aside and some of the facts regarding the Essenes be revealed to the world because of the advancement that has been made in the study of occult literature and the broad-minded view that is taken by the average educated student of spiritual and mystical subjects. For this reason I feel justified in giving the following facts in regard to the Essenes.

In the first place, it probably will be sufficient in this brief outline of their organization to say that the Essenes were a branch of the illuminated Great White Lodge, which had its birth in the country of Egypt during the years preceding Akhnaton, Egyptian pharaoh and founder of the first monotheistic religion, who supported and encouraged the existence of a \ to teach the mystic truths of life.

The several mystic schools of Egypt, which were united under one head constituting the G.W.B., assumed different names in different parts of the world, in accordance with the language of each country and the peculiarities of the general religious or spiritual thought of the people. We find that at Alexandria, the members of the organization there assumed the name of Essenes. Scientists have speculated considerably in regard to the origin of this word and its real meaning. So many unsatisfactory speculations upon its root have been offered in the past that there is still considerable doubt, in the minds of most authorities, regarding it.

The word truly comes from the Egyptian word kashai, which means "secret." And there is a Jewish word of similar sound, chsahi, meaning "secret" or "silent"; and this word would naturally be translated into essaios or "Essene," denoting "secret" or "mystic." Even Josephus found that the Egyptian symbols of light and truth are represented by the word choshen, which transliterates into the Greek as essen. Historical references have been found also wherein the priests of the ancient temples of Ephesus bore the name of Essene. A branch of the organization established by the Greeks translated the word Essene as being derived from the Syrian word asaya, meaning "physician," into the Greek word therapeutes, having the same meaning.

The Rosicrucian records clearly state that the original word was meant to imply a secret organization, and while most of the members became physicians and healers, the organization was devoted to many other humanitarian practices besides the art of healing, and not all of its members were physicians in any sense.

The spread of the organization into the many lands near Egypt was slow and natural, in accordance with the awakening consciousness of the people; and we find that the Essenes became a very definite branch of the G.W.B. representing the outer activities of that organization, which was primarily a school of learning and instruction. Thus, for several centuries before the dawn of the Christian era, the Essenes, as an active band of workers, maintained two principal centers. One was in Egypt on the banks of Lake Moeris, where the great Master Moria- El the Illustrious was born in his first known incarnation, educated, prepared for his great mission, and established the principle and law of baptism as a spiritual step in the process of initiation. The other principal Essenian center was first established in Palestine, at Engaddi, near the Dead Sea.

Going through the Rosicrucian records pertaining to the Essenes, I find thousands of notations regarding these two branches, and from them I have selected the following statements as being the most interesting and most definite in their connection with the mystical life of Jesus.

The branch in Palestine had to contend with the despotism of the rulers of that country and the jealousy of the priesthood. These conditions forced the Essenes in Palestine to hold themselves in greater silence and solitude than they had been accustomed to in Egypt. Before they moved from their small buildings and sacred enclosure at Engaddi, to the ancient buildings on Mount Carmel, their principal activity seemed to be the translation of ancient manuscripts and the preservation of such traditions and records as constituted the foundation of their teachings.

It is recorded that when the time came for them to move from Engaddi to Mount Carmel, their greatest problem was the secret movement of these manuscripts and records. Fortunately for us, they succeeded in preserving the rarest of the manuscripts that came out of Egypt, and in other ways preserved the ancient, traditional stories and teachings. It is from these that we derive most of our knowledge regarding both the Essenes and the G.W.B. A picture of how they lived, and what they believed and taught, undoubtedly constitutes a story of intense interest to all modern students of mysticism and sacred literature.

Every member of the Essenes in Egypt or Palestine, or of the Therapeutae, as they were called in other lands, had to be a pure- blooded descendant of the Aryan race. This point is very important in connection with the facts that will be revealed regarding the birth and life of the Master Jesus. Likewise, they were students of the Avestan writings and adhered to the principles taught therein, which laid great stress upon a healthy body and a powerful mind. Before any qualified Aryan could become an adept in the organization, he or she had to be prepared in childhood under certain teachers and instructors, raised with a healthy body, and needed to exercise certain mental powers under test.

Every adult applicant who was allowed to partake of the daily meal in the communal building was assigned at the time of initiation to a definite mission in life, and this mission had to be adhered to regardless of all obstacles and all temptations, even to the sacrifice of one's life. Some chose to be physicians or healers, others artisans, teachers, missionaries, translators, scribes, and so forth. Whatever worldly things they possessed at the time of their initiation had to be donated to the common fund, from which all drew only as was needed. The simple life they led, free from any indulgence in the pleasures common to the public, made it unnecessary for them to draw upon these funds except in rare instances.

Immediately upon initiation, each member adopted a robe of white composed of one piece of material, and wore sandals only in such weather or at such times as was absolutely necessary. Their attire was so distinct or unique that among the populace they were known as the Brothers and Sisters in White Clothing. The term Essene was not popularly known, and only the learned knew of it. This accounts for the lack of references to the Essenes in most of the popular histories or writings of the time.

They lived in well-kept buildings, usually within a sacred or well- protected enclosure, in community fashion. All of their affairs were regulated by a committee or council of judges or councilors, 100 in number, who met once a week to regulate the activities of the organization and to hear the reports of the workers in the field. All disagreements, all complaints, all tests and trials were heard by this council, and one of the regulations indicates that they were always cautious in expressing opinions of one another or of those outside of the organization, and they were not critical of the lives or affairs of the people they were trying to reform or assist. They also adhered strictly to one of their laws: "Judge not— lest ye be judged also."

It is possible to set forth here their definite articles of faith as recorded in ancient, secret writings. While these articles of faith appear in slightly different words in the various branches of the Essenian organization, they are undoubtedly based upon the articles of faith adopted by the G.W.B. at the time of the establishment of the Essenian organization.

1.   God is principle; Gods attributes manifest only through matter to the outer being. God is not a person, nor does God appear to the outer person in any form of cloud or glory. (Note the similarity of this article to the statement of John 4:24: "God is spirit and those who worship [God] must worship in spirit and in truth")

2.   The power and glory of God's dominion neither increases nor diminishes by human belief or disbelief; and God does not set aside [God's] laws to please human beings.

3.   The human ego is of God, and at one with God, and is consequently immortal and everlasting.

4.   The forms of man and woman are manifestations of the truth of God, but God is not manifest in the form of man or woman as a being.

5. The human body is the temple in which the soul resides, and from the windows of which we view God's creations and evolutions.

6. At the transition or separation of the soul and body, the soul enters that secret state where none of the conditions of the earth have any charms, but the soft breezes and great power of the Holy Ghost bring comfort and solace to the weary or the anxious who are awaiting future action. Those who fail, however, to exercise the blessings and gifts of God, and who follow the dictates of the tempter and of the false prophets and the ensnaring doctrines of the wicked, remain in the bosom of the earth until they are freed from the binding powers of materialism, purified, and assigned to the secret kingdom. (This explains the ancient, mystical term of earth bound, referring to those who are still enslaved to material temptations for a time after transition.)

7. To keep holy the one sacred day of the week that the soul may commune in spirit and ascend to contact with God, resting from all labors, and discriminating in all actions.

8. To keep silent in disputes, to close the eyes before evil, and to stop the ears before blasphemers. (This is the original of the ancient law, "to speak no evil, to see no evil, and to hear no evil.")

9. To preserve the sacred doctrines from the profane, never speak of them to those who are not ready or qualified to understand, and be prepared always to reveal to the world that knowledge which will enable humans to rise to greater heights.

10. To remain steadfast in all friendships and all communal relations, even unto death; in all positions of trust never to abuse the power or privilege granted; and in all human relationships to be kind and forgiving, even to the enemies of the faith.

Every department of the organization was supervised by stewards, who were in charge of the material things turned into the general fund by every member. This general fund was called the poor fund and was used to relieve the sufferings of the poor in every land. This point reminds us of the statement in Matthew 19:21: "Sell your possessions, and give the money to the poor . . . then come, follow me."

Hospices were established by the Essenes in various communities for the care of the sick and the poor, especially during epidemics of famine or disease. These places were called Bethsaida. We find in this feature of their work the origin of the hospices and hospitals which became well known some centuries later. A special staff of workers who were connected with these places came to be called Hospitalers. Herein we find the origin of another branch of the community that later became a more or less separate organization. The Essenes also established rescue homes in various communities and at the entrance to most cities had a place called a gate, where strangers or those in need of something to eat or guidance would be cared for temporarily. Recent discoveries in Jerusalem have revealed the existence of a gate known as the Essene Gate.

The Essenes disliked life in cities, and established themselves in communities of small villages outside of the walls or limits of practically every city where they existed. In such communities members had their own little houses and gardens, and those who did not marry lived in a community house. Marriage was not forbidden among the Essenes, as is commonly believed, but their ideals regarding marriage were very high, and only those who were well mated and whose mating was approved by the higher officials were permitted to marry.

Women were permitted to become associate members of the organization, and in only a few cases were they allowed to enter even the early grades of study of the work. This was not because there was any belief among the Essenes that women were inferior to men in either spiritual or mental capacity, but because the Essenian branch of the G.W.B. was strictly an organization of men, to carry on the work throughout each community. But sisters, mothers, and daughters of the men in each Essenian community were permitted to be a part of the community and become associate members. Those of the women who were not married, and who did not care to marry, often adopted orphan children as their own, and in this way carried on a form of humanitarian work for the organization.

In considering their more private affairs, we find that there were not servants, for servitude was considered unlawful, and each household had to be cared for by the members of the household. Some of the rules and regulations recorded in the Rosicrucian records would indicate that their ideas regarding servants and servitude were quite fanatical according to our modern point of view. We must remember that in the days when these rules were adopted, most servants in every wealthy household, or the servants of a king or potenrate of any kind, were like slaves, and, of course, among the Essenes every man and woman was a free being, and slavery or serfdom of any kind was absolutely prohibited. In each community everyone took part in any work that pertained to the entire community, and all had a certain amount of menial work to do. The new initiates had to work in the fields and at certain times serve at the community tables or in the kitchen and at the tables of the rescue houses.

As with many other branches of the G.W.B., the Essenes never entered into contracts or agreements which required oaths or any form of writing. It became well known about them that their word was equal to any agreement or contract in writing. They had a definite set of rules and regulations for their lives, which were well known by all those with whom they had any dealing, and the highest potentates of the land knew that the Essenes could not be bound by any oaths, but were highly responsible when they gave their word in any promise.

Even Josephus, in writing about the Essenes of 146 B.C., stated that the Essenes were exempted from the necessity of taking the oath of allegiance to Herod. Most certainly they would make no promise in the name of God, nor swear to anything in the name of God, for to them, as with the Jews who inherited the idea from them, the name of God was to be mentioned only in a sacred manner in their temples, and at all other times the name of God was unpronounceable. In disagreements with strangers, the Essenes would pay any price demanded of them or make sacrifices as requested rather than to enter into arguments or have any strained relationships. It was for this reason that the Essenes were thought well of by the Pharisees and other sects in Palestine, although these other sects severely criticized the religious practices of the Essenes.

Speaking of oaths, however, I am permitted to give herewith the official oath which was taken by male initiates and which was the only oath they ever admitted. It was given upon their own honor, at the time of entering the final degree of initiation, or what we would call the fourth degree of their advancement into the organization. The oath is as follows:

I promise herewith, in the presence of my elders, and the Brothers of the Order, ever to exercise true humbleness before God and manifest justice toward all men; to do no harm, either of my own volition or at the command of others, to any living creature; always to abhor wickedness, and assist in righteousness and justice; to show fidelity to all men, particularly to those who may be my superiors in counsel; and when placed in authority, I shall never abuse the privileges or power temporarily given unto me, nor attempt to belittle others by a worldly display of my mental or physical prowess; truth shall ever have my adoration and I shall shun those who find pleasure in falsehood; I will keep my hands clean from theft, and keep my soul free from the contamination of worldly gain; my passions I will restrain, and never indulge in anger nor any outward display of unkind emotions; I shall never reveal the secret doctrines of our brotherhood, even at the hazard of life, except to those who are worthy of them; I shall never communicate the doctrines in any form, but the one form in which received; I shall not add to nor subtract from the teachings, but shall ever attempt to preserve them in their pristine purity, and will defend the integrity of the books and records of our order, the names of the masters, legislators, and my elders.

After the initiate had reached what we might call the fourth degree and had taken the foregoing obligation, he was admitted to the common table to partake of the one great symbolical meal of the day, at which time meditation and contemplation, as well as discussion of the problems of the work, formed part of the period.

It is interesting to note that all the food used by the Essenes was prepared according to the rules and regulations stated in the old documents, in a scientific but simple manner, and while vegetables and especially many forms of raw foods were used, it is not true that all flesh foods were forbidden. There was never any form of over-eating or banqueting, and certainly the rules of moderation in all things pertained to eating and drinking as well; hence there was no gluttony nor intoxication.

The Essenes seldom took part in public discussions and never participated in discussions of religion or politics. They were most often silent when others spoke, and silence seemed to be their motto. They were well trained in the use of the voice and in making incantations, and knew the value of vowel sounds to such a degree that by training they became very soft spoken, even in ordinary con-versation. Because of this they were often known as the soft-spoken ones.

It is but natural that the Essenes would have developed not only magnetic personalities, accompa-nied by clean bodies, clean raiment, and clean habits, but they developed such beautiful auras that on many occasions these auras became visible to the profane. This especially mystified the Jews who were unfamiliar with the development of a mystical nature, even though their own religion and tra-ditions contained many wonderful mystical laws which they failed to put into practical application. It was customary for all Essenes to wash their hands and feet upon entering their own homes or the homes of anyone else, and to cleanse their hands and feet before any ceremony, and before each daily prayer. In their individual homes the Essenes spent much time before the altar in their sanctums, or in the study of the rare manuscripts and books which were circulated among them according to their degree of advancement. They were particularly well versed in astrology, elementary astronomy, natural history, geometry, elementary chemistry and alchemy, comparative religions, mysticism, and natural law.

Those who were the physicians in the organization were evidently a curiosity to the peoples of Pales-tine who were accustomed to the healing methods of that land, which included the exercising of charms, incantations in high-pitched voices, the reciting of weird formulas, the striking of crude mu-sical instruments, and the use of strong drugs. The Essenes spoke softly to their patients and used certain vowel sounds without any evidence of a formula. They often performed the greatest cures by the simple laying on of hands or by instructing the patient to retire to the silence of his home and sleep while the cure was conducted in a psychic manner.

All Essenes promised to educate their children in the teachings and principles which constituted the foundation of the Essenian belief. They raised each child within the scope of the organization until the child's twelfth year, when it was accepted on probation, which lasted until the twenty-first year, at which time the males were admitted to the first degree, and generally reached the fourth degree about the thirtieth year. The females were admitted on their twenty-first birthday to associate membership, and remained in that the rest of their lives if they proved worthy by the manner of their living.

Only an occasional Essene was permitted to preach to the public or perform public miracles, and then never as a matter of demonstration, but solely as a matter of service. Those in the organization who had lived the greatest number of incarnations, and were therefore the most highly evolved, were selected as their leaders, and, from among these, one was selected during each cycle to go out into the world and organize the work in a new land.

The Essenes looked forward to the coming of a great Savior who would be born within the fold of their organization and who would be a reincarnation of the greatest of their past leaders. Through their highly evolved knowledge and intimate psychic contact with the Cosmic, they were well informed of coming events, and the Essenian literature and the literature of many countries contain references to the prophets among the Essenes. Manahem was one of their prophets who became famous through the prophecy that Herod would reign.

There seemed to be a regulation or an unwritten law among the Essenes that none of their members should be engaged in a daily task that was destructive, but always constructive. Therefore we find that the list of prominent Essenes included weavers, carpenters, vine planters, gardeners, merchants, and those contributing to the good and welfare of the public There never were any in the organization who were armorers, slaughterers of cattle, nor engaged in any practice or business that destroyed the least living thing.

It must be very apparent to my readers that the Essenes would appear to have been one of the sects of Palestine and would have been, therefore, classified as such by the Jews and by the governmental authorities. For this reason we often read in newly discovered records a reference to the Essenes as one of the sects in Palestine. It would be natural for the Jews to consider the Essenes as a religious organization, instead of a communal or mystical one, and certainly an organization opposed to the Jewish doctrines and practices. Under these conditions it would be natural for the Essenes to establish their homes in certain communities where others of the same organization lived and where they could have that form of neighborly companionship which strengthened their interests.

These Essenes were not Jews by birth, by blood, or by religion, and were often referred to as Gentiles, and we find them classified as Gentiles in many of the sacred writings, even in the Christian Bible.

Editor's Note: Archaeological discoveries made in 1946— some 17 years after this chapter was written—go far to enlarge our knowledge of the Essenes and to confirm the statements made here concerning them. Read the article by Edmund Wilson in the May 14, 1955, issue of the magazine The New Yorker, as well as his book Scrolls from the Dead Sea, published by Oxford University Press, New York and Toronto (1955).

Editor's Note: Corroborative evidence of the cultural activities of the Essenes is shown in a report appearing in the New York Times of April 2, 1953. This concerns the discovery of a series of important manuscripts on the shore of the Dead Sea, 25 miles east of Jerusalem. We quote: "The archaeologist (G. Lankester Harding, Director of Antiquities, in Jordan) said the scrolls had been found several months ago in a cave near the ruins of a settlement now known as Khirbet Qumran. He added that it was fairly certain that the settlement was the home of the Essenes about 1,900 years ago and that the scrolls were from their library, and probably were hidden in caves for safe keeping." This new find included hitherto unknown Apocrypha and "descriptions of the conduct and organization of the Essenes, who lived in Palestine from the second century B.C. to the second century A.D. The Essenes were distinguished by their strict asceticism and such characteristics as the community of property, the practice of charity, and the pursuit of virtue."

19

Chapter 2

THE NEIGHBORS OF JESUS
TO FURTHER UNDERSTAND the greatness of the advent of the Master Jesus, one should know something of the people and the conditions of the country in which he was born, and with which he had to contend at the beginning of his mission.

In the first place, Palestine was not one nation of one language, with interests that held one people in common bonds, but a land of many nations, of many languages, and many diverse interests. It was a country of mixed and hostile peoples, whose interests were not only diverse, but so divided and so opposed that peace and harmony among them was impossible. Those of the Jewish faith were not all Hebrews, and those who were Hebrews were such through the beginning of a new race that had its origin at the time of the Exodus out of Egypt. Among these Hebrews were many in whose veins was Aryan blood by intermarriage; therefore, there were various castes. Hence among the Hebrews, as among those of the Jewish faith, there were those who would not recognize others in the same faith, and who believed that God had ordained the distinctions which they established.

In the midst of these people there were the heathens, whose temples were rapidly rising, and whose rites and customs were becoming prevalent. To the northeast there were the nomads, wild people living without restraint or regulation, but the vast majority of the people throughout the northeast were Syrians, Greeks, and heathens. To the east and to the west of Palestine, the Egyptian, Phoenician, and the Grecian rites contended for mastery, and in the very heart of Palestine itself the Greek language was dominant and the Grecian rites prevailed.

The educated classes throughout Palestine spoke Greek. The language of the tribes of Israel had undergone a great change, and the ancient Hebrew language, as it was called, had given place to the Aramaean dialect, except in the academies and theological schools.

In the northern section, known as Upper Galilee, lived people who were known as Gentiles. Tiberius itself was wholly non-Jewish. Gaza had its own deity. Joppa was influenced by a heathen religion, according to the Jews. Caesarea was essentially a heathen city and, to the Jews, was the symbol of Rome—the Rome of Edom—and was therefore to be destroyed; for Caesarea and Jerusalem, from the viewpoint of the Jews, could never exist at the same time.

The rabbis of the Jewish religion considered that the only real and true land of Israel was that portion immediately south of Antioch. Yet strange to say, it was here that the first Gentile church was organized and that we find the first Christian disciples.

Palestine, and especially Jerusalem, was most certainly a heathen district just before the coming of the Master Jesus. While it is true that the Jewish religion was well established, it most certainly did not include the multitudes, and it did not include all of the highest rank and power. Judaism itself was quite a problem at this time. The Pharisees and Sadducees were the two other largest sects, if we may be permitted to consider the Essenes as a sect from the Jewish point of view; but the former two held opposite principles and hated each other, while the Essenes, of course, could not be a part of either of them.

There was one common emotion which bound all these people of Palestine in one universal feeling. The high and the low, the learned and the unlearned, the rich and the poor, the heathen, the Jew, the common person or the ruling ones, united in their intense dislike for the Gentiles.

In the financial world the Hebrews represented the wealth and influence of the nations; for all money transactions and great trade dealings were in their hands. Merchandise from the Far East came through Palestine by means of Arab caravans and through the Phoenician ports, where fleets of ships owned by the Jews and operated by Gentile sailors were ever ready to convey the wares to other parts of the world. The Jews as traders and bankers were keenly alive to the value of this situation, and through their financial influence wielded a considerable power in the political world also. They were able to obtain secrets of state and to secure such positions in the civil and military service of the other Gentile nations as permitted them to manipulate the intricacies of diplomacy so as to further the interests of the Hebrews.

It must be remembered that the orthodox Jews or Hebrews were intensely Hebraic. To their own they were very hospitable, a trait which they considered a great virtue, and to strangers, especially to the Gentiles, they manifested the very opposite in all actions.

The people living in Jerusalem, which was the most advanced habitation in Palestine, had special agents in, and corresponded with, the important parts of the world; and letters were carried from Jerusalem to many other cities by messengers and by peddlers. The wealthy Jews gave great fortunes for the support and defense of the Jewish faith, and such donations were always looked upon as investments that would bring great returns. The Hebrews had their own rulers in most cities and were allowed to have the same status as the Romans, or the rights of Asiatic citizens, and the special privileges which they demanded because of having been instructed by their God to enjoy such privileges as God's chosen people. Having the status of Romans entitled them to a civil government of their own, independent of the rule of the tribunals in the cities in which they lived. They enjoyed such unlimited religious liberties and exacted such religious privileges as they denied to natives in their own lands who were not of their faith.

The ruling class of the Hebrews made themselves obnoxious to the other citizens in each section of the land by closing their stores on the sabbath and going about idly in gorgeous attire, with marked display of contempt and abhorrence of everything around them. It was their secret desire to convert to Judaism the relatives of all those who wielded power, influence, and wealth, because through such converts they would promote the interests of Israel, and it was freely predicted that the ultimate aim of the proselyting was to wipe the Gentiles out of Palestine.

In the synagogues, which represented the meeting places of the ruling class of the Hebrews, the separation of the classes was strictly observed, and the women were considered as unprepared for a position in the church. We see the attitude toward women in many passages of the Jewish liturgy used in the synagogues, where thanksgiving is expressed in the following words: "Blessed art thou, Lord and God, that thou hast not made me a woman." Women were considered as having no souls and no degree of spirituality that could be developed, and they were therefore incapable of ever becoming angelic. It is always interesting to those of the Western world today in traveling through the Oriental countries to find that all the statues of angels are of the masculine sex. This idea of a soulless woman is retained in all Latin languages; for we find that word angel is always of the masculine sex. No rabbi would permit himself to be closeted with a woman in religious discussion, nor to deal with a woman in regard to spiritual matters.

Secretly, or silently, the Jews or the orthodox of Israel resented the fact that the scepter of power had been taken away from Judea and the chosen people of God subjected to the government of Rome. This was a humiliation which the Jews hoped to see undone. Israel hoped that the day would come when its people would rise in power and when their "King of Glory" would appear and reestablish the power and kingdom of Israel again.

And thus Israel waited. In silence and with suppressed emotion, the faithful anticipated the coming of the great day.

In my recent journey through Egypt, I felt the same suppressed emotion on the part of the Egyptians. As they moved about in silence with cold, emotionless expressions on their faces, and refrained from speaking of the days that were, and the days that would come, one could sense that inwardly there was a great fire burning which wanted only the signal to burst into a conflagration that would sweep throughout the whole country. The Egyptians, too, are waiting now for the day to come when the great power and illumination that resides within their traditions and their secret archives will make them the potent rulers of their land. Just as one could easily sense the possibility of a great conflagration in that land, so one may understand and appreciate the condition that existed in Palestine at the time of the birth of the Master Jesus. Uneasiness had seized the people; for they had felt the yoke upon their necks and they realized that they were being held in bondage and could stand it but a short time longer.

In a social way, vice and degrading practices had become popular with the masses, and the moral standard was akin to licentiousness. Intrigue and crime were found even in the courts of law. The governing power was divided between the two classes, the nobility and the priesthood. The nobility sought only gratification of the baser senses, trying to keep within the law only as far as it permitted them to gain their selfish ends. Most of them professed to be of the sect of Sadducees. On the other hand, the priestly element, or the Pharisees, known as the "pure, separate ones," were constantly warring in their determined effort to secure power and force strict adherence to the letter of their laws. The Sadducees were their enemies, especially when the latter were favored in any way with rank or position.

The masses were downtrodden and held in ignorance of the true conditions, but they believed that there was a possibility of rising above their environment through the coming of a great leader. It is no wonder that these persons, mostly unlearned and inexperienced in the things of life, united with any movement which promised them freedom from their bondage or an opportunity to rise to heights which they sensed in their dream world. Thus, in many ways these uncultured and uneducated ones followed leaders and principles which left them in serious situations and sorely disappointed. It was the great hope that the coming of the expected Messiah would change all of the sorrowful conditions and bring about a solidification and unification of the people of Israel. How this was to come about, no one knew; and only the pretenders who headed the false movements attempted to explain.

The House of David, out of which the true leader of the people of Israel should come, had long since passed into the hands of strangers. The high priesthood, out of which a great Messiah might come, was Jewish only by profession, being politically Roman and Greek in culture, and by birth anything but of the great House of David. Therefore, the great Deliverer who would lead them out of bondage as Moses had done, could not come through the lineage of those who were presently at the head of the nation, nor could this person come through those who were of the priesthood.

One phrase remained in the consciousness of the people: "From among my [brothers and sisters] I shall raise one who shall guide my people!"

20

Chapter 3

THE PARENTS OF JESUS

NO PROPER CONSIDERATION can be given to the birth and childhood of Jesus without first becoming acquainted with the parents of Jesus and their relationship to the mystical facts involved. Therefore, let me state the first important facts, as proved by our records, and then submit the evidence pertaining thereto.

Jesus was born of Gentile parents through whose veins flowed Aryan blood, and in whose hearts and minds had been implanted the teachings of the Essenes, as well as the more secret teachings of the G.W.B. This is the simple, definite statement found throughout the Rosicrucian records.

In the Christian Bible, in the Talmud, and in many reliable works, we find verification of these statements. The parents of Jesus lived in Galilee. There is no possible dispute on this point, and they were therefore Galileans in the full meaning of the term. So our first consideration should be of Galilee and the Galileans.

In Matthew 4:15, we read: "Galilee of the Gentiles." Strange as it may seem, the average Bible student gives little thought to this expression and loses sight of its very important significance. Jesus himself was called the Galilean. For this reason, we must look upon Jesus as having been classified by his own people, or by the people of Palestine at least, as one who was different from them. This warrants us in investigating the real situation and discovering why the Galileans were Gentiles, and why Gentiles lived in Galilee.

In I Maccabees 5:15, we read that messengers from Galilee, with torn clothing and in great anguish, came to Judas Maccabaeus and reported that "the people of Ptolemais and Tyre and Sidon, and all Galilee of the Gentiles, had gathered together against them to 'annihilate us.'" And Judas told Simon, his brother, to choose certain men to go to Galilee and rescue the Jews who were in Galilee, that they might not be persecuted by the Gentiles. Simon took 3,000 men into Galilee, where he fought many battles with the "heathens," and the Jews living in Galilee with their wives and children were brought safely into Judea.

Here we see at once an intimation of the conditions that existed in part of Palestine, and how the orthodox Jews looked upon the Galileans as being not only Gentiles, and of a different religion and race, but as enemies to their best interests.

The transfer of the Jews living in Galilee referred to above was made in 164 B.C. At about the same time, Judas Maccabaeus rescued his brothers who lived among the "heathens" in the north of the country (and east of the Jordan) and brought them all to Jerusalem. According to this account and many others, there were Jews in Galilee long after 164 B.C. Therefore, Galilee continued as a nation of Gentiles or "heathens" until the year 103 B.C., when Aristobulus, grandson of Simon, and first king of the Jews (Maccabees), forced all those living in Galilee to adopt circumcision and the Mosaic law.

We will see by this that the Gentiles living in Galilee, which included the parents of Jesus, were Aryans by blood, Gentiles by natural religious classification, mystics by philosophical thought, and Jews by forced adoption. In other words, the Gentiles of Galilee after 103

B.C. were forced to adopt circumcision and respect the Mosaic law, and in accordance with this law all children at a certain age had to accept the Jewish faith in a formal way by appearing at the synagogue for probationary admission to the church. If this combination of circumstances and conditions will be kept in mind by my readers, it will enable them to understand the many strange statements that appear in sacred literature.

In the cuneiform inscriptions of Tiglath-Pileser, there is reference to the conquest of Galilee, but it is generally misunderstood, as are many of the other statements regarding Galilee, because few know that Galilee is also referred to as the land of Hamath. The same name, Hamath, is used in the Old Testament, but it seems that modern students of the ancient writings did not recognize in this particular word the name of the ancient capital of Galilee. However, let it be known now that Hamath is the famous hot springs, half an hour south of Tiberius, on the western shore of the Sea of Galilee.

Often in the Old Testament one may read of the "entrance to Hamath" and it always refers to parts of the northern boundary of Palestine. It is the Wady Alhammans, near Magdala, three miles northwest of Tiberius, where Mary Magdalene was born. In other parts of the Bible we read that the king of Hamath, who sent his son to salute David, was a Galilean; Solomons storehouse or granaries which he built in Hamath were situated near the Sea of Galilee.

The true spelling of the name is Hammoth, or Hammath, the Assyrian form being Hammati, which means "hot springs." Many other quotations could be used to show that Hamath was in Galilee. And we will find by other references that a great many Assyrians were sent to Hamath as colonists, and further reference reveals that the Assyrians were all Aryans. Even Sargon II tells how he deported the Median chief with kinsmen to Hamath.

It was because of this settlement of Aryans in the vicinity of Galilee, and the resulting race of Aryans in that community, that the Aryans of Egypt who were members of the G.W.B. and of the Essenian organization directed their people to go to northern Palestine, and live on the shores of Galilee and associate with people of their own race. There are also many historical notations in Egyptian records, and especially in the ancient records of the G.W.B., to show that there was close communion and intercourse between the Aryans of Galilee and the Aryans of Egypt.

Our records also show that at the time of the birth of Jesus, the Galileans spoke a language which was not Hebrew. The fact has been known among students of sacred literature for several centuries that the Master Jesus spoke another language besides Hebrew, and there are indications that he spoke several tongues. These indications have greatly puzzled the students of sacred literature, and much speculation has existed among authorities in regard to this matter.

The common agreement among these authorities is that Jesus presented most of his parables and teachings to the populace in the Aramaic language, and they also believe that he used some other language that was not Hebrew. Our records clearly show that he used Greek and Aramaic in his general discourses and conversations, and used Hebrew only when he was speaking to those who did not understand the other languages. Most of his beautifully poetic parables and discourses were in either the Aramaic or the Greek language. We will discuss, later, the manner in which Jesus became educated in the Greek language. We will find the use of these foreign phrases in the words of Jesus, in such verses of the Bible as Mark 5:41, Mark 7:34, Mark 14:36, and in many other places.

The Galilean dialect was a constant source of jest for the Jews. Peter was also of Galilee and of the Gentile race, and we find in Matthew 26:73 that some said to Peter: "Certainly you are also one of them, for your accent betrays you." There are many historical notes that show that the Jews recognized the Galileans by the fact that these Gentiles could not distinguish the various Semitic gutturals.

The foregoing are but a few of the hundreds of facts which might be submitted to show that the parents of Jesus were Gentiles and of a different tongue than the Jews. This makes us question at once the genealogy which is so exhaustively presented in the Bible in an attempt to show that Jesus was a descendant of the House of David. This genealogy in the Bible is presented in two places by two different authors, and the generations in each table do not agree. But aside from this discrepancy, the genealogy is only an attempt on the part of later admirers and followers of Jesus to make it appear that he was of the House of David, as hoped and prayed for by the Jews.

It must be borne in mind that at no time during his lifetime did Jesus himself refer to his ancestors or forebears, or intimate to the Jews that he was the Messiah of the House of David whom they had anticipated. And we find nothing in any historical records of a contemporary nature, or among the authentic Jewish records, to show that during the lifetime of Jesus, or even during the first 100 or more years after his time, that the Jews or anyone else believed that he was of the House of David. Just when the genealogy attempting to show such a connection was prepared and introduced in the sacred writings is not known, but it is most certainly a very late addition to the writings.

Now we must deal with another phase of the history of the parents, and of Jesus himself. In much of the Christian literature Jesus is referred to as the Nazarene, and it is commonly believed that this means to indicate that Jesus was born, or spent most of his lifetime, in Nazareth. It is strange how students of biblical literature, and especially those who have written so exhaustively on the life of Jesus, and who have presented in their teachings and preachments the picturesque details of his life, have never given proper thought to the tide Nazarene, or investigated its real meaning. It is assumed by all of these authorities, writers, and teachers, that if Jesus was a Nazarene, he must have been of the city called Nazareth, and since he and his parents lived in Galilee, the city of Nazareth must have been in that locality. On the basis of such reasoning, it is generally proclaimed that Nazareth was the home town of the parents of Jesus, and that Nazareth in Galilee was the place where Jesus spent his childhood.

I have been just recently in Nazareth and made exhaustive inquiries for the purpose of verifying the statements contained in the Rosicrucian records. Probably most of my readers will be surprised to learn that at the time Jesus was born there was no city or town in the whole of Galilee known as

Nazareth, and that the city in Galilee which now bears that name is not only a city of more recent years, but was named and came into existence because of the demand on the part of investigators to find some place that would answer to the name of Nazareth in Galilee.

First of all, we must make plain that the title Nazarene did not imply that the person who bore that title was of a city called Nazareth. Rather, the title was given by the Jews to those strange people outside of their own religion who seemed to belong to some secret sect or cult that had existed in northern Palestine for many centuries. We find in the Christian Bible that even John the Baptist was called the Nazarene. We also find many other references to persons who were known as Nazarenes. In Acts 24:5, we find some man being condemned as a mover of sedition among the Jews throughout the world and being called a "ringleader of the sect of the Nazarenes." Whenever the Jews came in contact with one in their country who had a different religion, and especially a mystical understanding of the things of life, and who was living in accordance with some code of philosophical or moral ethics that was different from those of the Jews, he or she was called a Nazarene for the want of a better name.

There was a definite sect called the Nazarenes, and we find them referred to in the Jewish records as a sect of primitive Christians, or in other words, those who were essentially prepared for and ready to accept the Christian doctrines. In fact, the Jewish encyclopedias and authorities seem to agree that the term Nazarene embraced all those Christians who had originally been both Jews, and who neither would nor could give up their original mode of life, but who attempted to adjust the new doctrines with the old. The Jewish encyclopedias also state that it is quite evident that the Nazarenes and the Essenes had many characteristics in common and were therefore of a mystical tendency. In fact, the Essenes and the Nazarenes were considered heretics by the learned Jews, but there is this difference or distinction in the use of the two terms: the Essenes were not as well known to the populace of Palestine as were the Nazarenes, and seldom was someone called an Essene unless the person was well informed and knew the difference between the Essenes and the Nazarenes; whereas many Essenes and even those of other sects who lived an atypical life or who did not accept the Jewish religion were called Nazarenes.

Jerome, the famous biblical authority, refers to the fact that in his day there still existed among the Jews, in all the synagogues of the East, a heresy condemned by the Pharisees, and the followers of it were called Nazarenes. He said that they believed that Christ, the Son of God, was born of the Virgin Mary, and they held Christ to be the one who suffered under Pontius Pilate and ascended to heaven. "But," said Jerome, "while they pretended to be both Jewish and Christian, they were neither."

Turning to the highest Roman Catholic authorities, we find that the title Nazarene, as applied to Christ, occurs only once in the Douai version of the Bible, and this authority states that the term Jesus Nazarenus is uniformly translated "Jesus of Nazareth," but this is a mistake in translation, for it should read "Jesus the Nazarene." Nowhere in the Old Testament do we find the word Nazareth as referring to a city existing anywhere in Palestine, but we do find in the New Testament references to Jesus returning to a city called Nazareth. These references are a result of translating the phrase, "Jesus returning to the Nazarenes" to read, "Jesus returning to Nazareth." The interesting point here is emphasized by the Roman Catholic authorities, for they show that whereas Jesus was commonly referred to as the Nazarene, he was not of that sect at all.

Taking the Jewish and Roman Catholic records together, and comparing them with the information contained in our own records, we find that the Nazarenes constituted a sect of Jews who, while attempting to adhere to the ancient Jewish teachings, did believe in the coming of a Messiah who would be born in an unusual manner and who would become the Savior of their race. After the ministry of Jesus began, these Nazarenes accepted Jesus as the Messiah and even accepted the doctrines he taught while still trying to adhere to many of the fundamentals of their Jewish religion. The Jewish records state that the Nazarenes rejected Paul, the Apostle of the Gentiles, and that some of the Nazarenes exalted Jesus only as a just person.

There was another term for such heretics among the Jews, and this was Nazarite. According to the Jewish authorities, the term was applied to those who lived apart or separate from the Jewish race, because of some distinctive religious, moral, or ethical belief. The Jewish records state that such persons were often those who would not take wine or drink anything made from grapes, or those who would not cut a hair of their heads, or who would not touch the dead during any funeral ceremony. These same records state that the history or origin of Nazariteship in ancient Israel is obscure. They state that Samson was a Nazarite, as was his mother, and that Samuel's mother promised to dedicate him to the sect of Nazarites. The Jewish records state also that it was common for parents to dedicate their minor children to the Nazarite sect, and they distinctly say that there are references to the fact that Jesus was said to have been dedicated to the Nazarites while still in the womb. The Jewish records say that Luke 1:15 refers to this dedication. Helena, the Queen, and Miryam of Palmyra are mentioned as Nazarites in the Jewish records, and many other persons famous in sacred literature were known to be Nazarites.

That the terms Nazarite and Nazarene had naught to do with a city or town called Nazareth is plainly indicated by many historical records. We have said that the present town of Nazareth in Galilee received its name because a place had to be found that would fit the common understanding in regard to the village in which the parents of Jesus lived and where he spent his boyhood. During the first few centuries after Christ, when the Christian doctrines were in the making and the founders of the Roman Catholic Church and religious students in general were searching for every historical site connected with the life of Jesus, each spot, place, and incident in the career of this great person was eagerly tabulated and glorified. My recent visit through Palestine made plain to me that this desire to find historical, sacred sites and glorify them has not ended and will probably continue for hundreds of years. The absurdity of most of this becomes apparent when even the casual tourist discovers that three, four, and five different places are pointed out as being the spot where some particular incident in the life of Jesus occurred.

In searching for a place that would answer to the name of Nazareth in Galilee, great difficulty was experienced, since no such city was mentioned in the Old Testament, and none of the ancient maps of the time of Christ revealed such a site. A very small settlement, however, called En Nasira was found far from the Sea of Galilee, and this was immediately renamed Nazareth and associated with the early life of the child Jesus. This discovery of the town of En Nasira was made in the third century after Christ, and since then has been known as the town of Nazareth, but even today it is lacking in any of the evidences which would warrant the use of that name.

In Mark 6:1,2, the statements are made that Jesus went back to his own country and his disciples followed him, and when the sabbath day was come, he began to teach in the synagogue. In the fourth verse of that chapter, Jesus referred to the fact that he was a prophet in his own country, among his own kin, and in his own house. These statements have been taken to refer to Nazareth, the town in which many biblical students believe Jesus was born and in which he spent his childhood.

Now, if Jesus did return to his home town and did preach in a synagogue to great multitudes, it could not have been at En Nasira, or the so-called town of Nazareth; for even in the second and third centuries after the birth of Jesus, En Nasira or Nazareth had no synagogue and was not large enough to have any building in which multitudes could have listened to Jesus, nor were there multitudes in that vicinity to hear him. So the references in Mark to his hometown could not refer to En Nasira. En Nasira was only a settlement around a spring which was at that time called the "Spring of the Guard House," but I find that now in recent years it has been changed and is called "St. Mary's Well." This change of name and the giving of a religious significance to some unimportant site in Palestine is typical of the changes that are being rapidly made in that country for the benefit of tourists.

Turning to the old Jewish records, we find these state that only in the books of the New Testament, written long after the lifetime of Jesus, is the town of Nazareth mentioned as a village in Galilee, and that such a place is not mentioned in the Old Testament, in the historical writings of Josephus, nor in the Talmud. During the lifetime of Jesus, the town of Joppa was the important city in the locality of Galilee. It was the one which attracted all tourists and is referred to most often in historical writings.

In the Roman Catholic records and in their encyclopedias, we find that the town of En Nasira was known as a strictly Jewish village up to the time of Constantine and is referred to as one being inhabited wholly by Jews. Therefore, this little village surrounding a well could not have been the center of the Gentile population of Galilee. At the present time, there is a small church or chapel in Nazareth which I visited, and it is supposed to stand above the grotto where Mary and Joseph lived at the time that the archangel announced to Mary the forthcoming birth of the incarnation of the Logos.

All of the foregoing facts point out very clearly that Mary and Joseph and the child born to them were considered, along with many others in their locality, as Nazarenes, Nazarites, or people of a non-Jewish sect. And the many other references to this sect clearly show that it was one which held such religious and mystical views as permitted the acceptance of the fundamentals of the Christian doctrine. Taking this into consideration, we have at once an interesting picture of the conditions existing in and around Palestine just prior to the Christian era.

We have, first of all, a large number of men and women, even children, who were either Jewish by birth, Gentile by birth, or of various races and bloods, but who had refused to adopt wholly or completely the Mosaic law and were Jewish only because the laws of the land forced them to adopt circumcision, to appear in the synagogue when twelve years of age, and to be enrolled as Jews. Yet these persons were mystically inclined in their beliefs and followed the Jewish teachings only so far as they revealed God and God's laws and served them in their study of divine principles. They were prepared by some school or some system which made them ready to accept the higher mystical teachings as they were revealed from time to time by the progressive minds or by the teachings of avatars. On the other hand, there was the one definite organization of mystics known as the Essenes, which conducted many forms of humanitarian activities, including hospices, rescue homes, and places for the care of the poor and needy. The Essenes had their northern center in Galilee, among the Aryans, because they had been directed to this locality by the center of their organization in Egypt, known as the G.W.B. The Essenes were not popularly known, were quiet and unostentatious in their activities, and were distinguished by the populace only by their white raiment. The Nazarites, the Nazarenes, and the Essenes mingled freely and undoubtedly sought to carry on their independent activities without interference one with the other, although they unquestionably had many ideals and purposes in common. But the Nazarites and Nazarenes were popularly recognized and known to the populace, and for this reason all who did not accept the Jewish faith, or who were heretical in their Jewish beliefs, were classified as Nazarenes and Nazarites, not as Essenes.

In and around the shores of the Sea of Galilee lived these people— mostly Gentiles of Aryan blood of the several sects, Nazarenes, Nazarites, and Essenes. They, too, were looking for the coming of the great Master, the great Avatar, the great Messiah, who would not only redeem Palestine but the whole world, and who would bring contentment to Israel and all peoples. These mystics contemplated, with true understanding, the reincarnation of one of their own great masters. We must bear in mind that the belief in reincarnation was not only an established belief among these mystics, who were classified as heretics and as Gentiles, but also among the most orthodox of the Jewish people at that time. This accounts for the many references in sacred literature, and even in the Christian Bible, to a great leader, a great teacher, as having been someone else at some other time; for they believed that the greatest among them were great because of previous preparation, previous existence, and previous attainments. Naturally they looked for the new great master, the new redeemer of the world, to come out of the past in a new body and as a well prepared individual of high attainments. The Rosicrucian records show that not only did each of the homes of these Essenes and Nazarenes and Nazarites have a sanctum, in which daily prayers and solemn meditations were held, but many hours of each day and evening were given to mystical practices and the development of a spiritual power within their beings. This made possible the many miracles they performed and the great work which they did among the poor and needy.

They were well advanced in the understanding of most of the mystical laws which the Rosicrucians and other mystics of the world today study and practice, and they knew the potentialities of certain spiritual laws when applied specifically for any definite purpose. To them, such miracles as incarnations of a highly divine nature, and the coming of a great leader into their midst, through uncontaminated material laws, were not impossible, nor improbable, and they lived a life typical of that which the mystics of today believe is lived by the masters in Tibet and in parts of India and Egypt.

Joseph was not only a devout Essene, and a carpenter by trade, in keeping with the rules of the organization, but Mary, his wife, was an associate member of the organization. Yet both of them had been forced to accept the Jewish religion and had identified themselves in a purely formal way with the faith in accordance with the law of the land.

With these facts in mind, let us now approach the interesting subject of the birth of Jesus.

21

Chapter 4

THE VIRGIN BIRTH OF AVATARS

THIS INCIDENT IN the life of avatars is one that is very difficult to approach and more difficult to present to those who have not attained that high degree of mystical understanding and awakening which naturally would bring to the student a spiritual understanding of the conception and birth of avatars.

I realize fully that the standard Christian story of the virgin birth of Jesus is one that is not accepted by those who reject any of the Christian doctrines. In fact, the authorized Christian version of the virgin birth is a very difficult one for the uninitiated and undeveloped mystic to comprehend, and it certainly appears to be an impossible story to those who are of an analytical mind and who do not comprehend any of the mystical laws and principles as taught by the ancient masters.

Perhaps I will do better than others who have attempted, in the past, to reduce the mystical phase of the birth of Jesus to a semi-mystical presentation, and perhaps I may fail altogether. I am not limited by any creeds or dogmas which require that I shall adhere to a standardized version; and if I fail to make my reader comprehend, or perhaps apprehend, the real mystery of the virgin birth, it will be because I have been limited solely by an inadequate vocabulary to express in general terms that which every mystic understands inwardly, and because of the inability of some of my readers to read between the lines of my statements and realize what I cannot reduce to such crude things as printed words.

First of all, it should be understood by those who approach this great mystery with an open and unbiased mind, that Jesus was not the first great Master, Avatar, or Son of God to be "born of a virgin." The authorized Christian version of the virgin birth of Jesus presents the story as though it were unique and exclusively a Christian manifestation. If nowhere else in the history of God's messengers on earth, or the working out of God's plans for the redemption of humans in all ages and cycles, there had ever been a similar incident or a similar manifestation of the great mystic powers of the universe, operating as an unusual manifestation of God's omnipotent ways, then the mystery of the conception and birth of this great person would be more difficult to explain and to comprehend.

To the mystics of the Orient in all lands and of all ages, the great mystery of the virgin and spiritual birth of a Son of God is accepted not only as a possibility but as a fact natural to the life of every great avatar. Christians or students of Christian literature in America who are accustomed to hear the mystery of the virgin birth referred to as one of the problems of faith, and one of the doctrinal points upon which the faith of thousands of Christians is broken, are surprised when they tour through foreign lands to find that even those who are not Christians and who are of the Moslem,

Hindu, Buddhist, or other faiths, find no difficulty in accepting the story of a divine, spiritual conception and birth, and believe that this one feature of the life of the Master Jesus is the only one which is consistent with the claim that Jesus was the great Redeemer and Savior of the world.

In fact, during my recent trip through lands which brought me in contact with persons of Oriental faiths, I found most of them who were not Christians expressing themselves on this subject in this wise: "If you Christians believe that Jesus was a Son of God, or the divinely appointed messenger to redeem any part of the world through the message he had to give, then you must believe that he was divinely conceived and born, for there can be no question of such distinctive birth if he was a divine messenger." When I explained to some of them that there were so-called Christians or students of the Christian doctrine who could not accept the idea of divine conception and birth, but who still believed that Jesus was a great master, a divinely appointed messenger, a true Son of God, and an avatar of unusual authority from on high, these people merely smiled and said that such a viewpoint was an absurdity, for—according to their viewpoint—no one humanly conceived and born could attain any degree of divine authority which would make that person the Christ.

Thus we see that the great problem resolves itself into a problem not of the fact of the virgin birth or the divinity of Jesus, but a problem of human comprehension on the part of the consciousness in the Occidental world as compared with the consciousness we find in the Oriental world. In other words, we are face to face with the fact that not the validity of the claim of the virgin birth of Jesus should be given serious thought by students of spiritual mysticism in the Western world, but the lack of understanding and comprehension on the part of those millions who have not yet attained the proper degree of spiritual understanding regarding the spiritual laws operating in such important events.

The Oriental of any of the various faiths points out to us of the Occidental world the fact that we are attempting to struggle with a principle in the spiritual world with which we are least acquainted, and for a comprehension of which we are least prepared. The mystics of all lands agree that until human beings are prepared, through spiritual development and comprehension of the higher laws, to understand easily the actuality of spiritual conception and divine birth in its sublime fullness, we are not ready in any sense to understand the teachings and the true message brought to this world by any of the great avatars, especially that of the last and greatest of them all, Jesus the Christ.

This does not mean that it is impossible for the sincere student of Christian doctrines to comprehend at least the mystical laws involved in the possibility of a divine birth, but it does mean that such a student must try to see and comprehend the mysticism that is fundamental in all of the Christian doctrines. The Rosicrucians hold the same viewpoint that the Orientals hold in this regard; namely, that the orthodox Christianity in the Western world today too greatly slights the mysticism and mystical principles which are fundamental to Christianity and which constituted the pristine Christianity of ancient times. In other words, too much thought is given to the literal meaning of words and the material interpretation of all of the principles involved in Christianity, which leaves almost a total neglect of the pure mysticism that makes possible a real understanding or spiritual comprehension of Christianity in its original form.

Added to this is the reluctance on the part of the Occidental world to accept as facts and actual possibilities the so-called miracles of the Bible. I do not agree with such authorities as the late William

Jennings Bryan and others who have claimed that the scientific trend of our thinking and our highly scientific education in the Occidental world has tended to blind us to the spiritual truths in the Bible or in all sacred literature. I do not believe that materialistic science is in any way responsible for the Occidental's inability to understand the higher spiritual statements found in the sacred writings of the Bible or the other books of other creeds. I believe that this inability on the part of the minds of the Western world is due to the unawakened status of the spiritual side of our natures and the absence, except in the various occult and metaphysical schools of the Western world, of such general teachings along spiritual lines as would properly prepare us for an understanding of that which is accepted readily and understood thoroughly by the Oriental mind.

I have said that we should bear in mind that Jesus was not the first of the great teachers, who came as messengers of God, to be born of a virgin or to have been conceived by Divine Principle. A few references to similar incidents in the past may help my readers to understand what is meant by this statement.

It is a fact that divine births and divine conceptions were so currently accepted among the ancients that whenever they heard of one who was greatly distinguished in human affairs, they immediately classified such a person as having been born of supernatural lineage. Even in the polytheistic religions, various gods were declared to have descended from Heaven and been made incarnate in humans. The learned Thomas Maurice, in his unusual book called Indian Antiquities, goes so far as to state that "in every age and in almost every religion of the Asiatic world, there seems uniformly to have flourished an immemorial tradition that one god had, from all eternity, begotten another god." I may add that our own records of ancient traditions and sacred writings contain many references to religious movements in antiquity, in which the great leader was claimed to be "God's Begotten Son."

India had a number of avatars or divine messengers who were incarnated through divine conception, and two of them bore the name of Krishna, or Krishna the Savior. Now Krishna was born of a chaste virgin called Devaki, who, on account of her purity, was selected to become the mother of God. In this instance, we find a very ancient story of a virgin giving birth to a divinely conceived messenger of God.

Buddha was considered and believed by all his followers to have been begotten of God and born of a virgin whose name was Maya or Mary. In the ancient stories of the birth of Buddha, as understood by all the Orientals and found in their sacred writings long before the Christian era, we read how the divine power, called the Holy Ghost, descended upon the virgin Maya. In the ancient Chinese version of the story, the Holy Ghost is called Shing-Shin.

The Siamese, likewise, had a god and savior who was virgin born and whom they called Codom. In this ancient story, the beautiful young virgin had been informed in advance that she was to become the mother of a great messenger of God, and one day while in her usual period of meditation and prayer, she was impregnated by divine sunbeams. When the boy was born, he grew up in a remarkable manner, became a protege of wisdom, and performed miracles.

When the first Europeans visited Cape Comorin, the most southerly extremity of the Indian subcontinent, they were surprised to find the natives worshiping a Lord and Savior who had been divinely conceived and born of a virgin.

The serpent was used as a mystical symbol in the early sacred writings of various schools of religion. It was very often used as an emblem of the Word or Logos, and in this sense it became the symbol of the tempter in the fall of humans. The serpent was also the emblem of the Holy Ghost or the power that impregnated the life in the virgin. In this sense it was the incarnation of the "Logos." The emblem shown above represents the serpent as found engraved or carved on many ancient monuments to represent the "Logos." The Ophites also venerated this same symbol as an emblem of Jesus the Christ.

When the first Jesuit missionaries visited China, they wrote in their reports that they were appalled at finding in the polytheistic religion of that country a story of a redeeming master who had been born of a virgin and divinely conceived. This god was said to have been born in 3468 B.C. Lao-Tze, the famous Chinese teacher, was claimed to have been born of a virgin, black in complexion, and described as marvelous and as beautiful as jasper.

In Egypt, long before the dawn of Christianity, and long before any of the writers of the present Christian Bible were born, or any of its doctrines conceived of as Christian, the Egyptian people had several messengers of God who were born of virgins through divine conception. Horus was known to all the ancient Egyptians as having been born of the virgin Isis, and his conception and birth was considered one of the three great mysteries or mystical doctrines of the Egyptian religion. To them, every incident in connection with the conception and birth of Horus was pictured, sculpted, adored, and worshiped as are the incidents of the conception and birth of Jesus among the Christians today. Another Egyptian god called Ra was born of a virgin. I have seen on one of the ancient walls of a temple along the Nile, a beautifully carved picture representing the god Thoth— the messenger of God— telling the maiden, Queen Mautmes, that she is to give birth to a divine Son of God, who will be the king and redeemer of her people.

Turning to Persia, we find that Zoroaster was the first of the world redeemers acclaimed to have been born in innocence through the conception of a virgin. Ancient carvings and pictures of this great messenger show him surrounded by an aura of light that filled the humble place of his birth. Cyrus, king of Persia, was also believed to have been of divine origin. In the records of his time, he was referred to as the Christ or the anointed Son of God and was considered as God's messenger.

Even Plato, who was born in Athens, 429 B.C., was believed by the populace to have been a divine Son of God by a pure virgin called Perictione. It is recorded in the ancient records that the father of Plato, who was known as Aris, had been admonished in a spiritual dream to hold pure and sacred the person of his wife until after the divine conception and birth of the child that was to come, and that this child's conception would be by divine means.

Apollonius, who was still living and performing great miracles and teaching in various lands during the early part of the life of Jesus, was also born of a virgin mother according to the stories that were recorded of him during and shortly after his time. According to these stories, the mother of Apollonius in 41 B.C. was informed by a god in a dream that she would give birth to a great messenger of God who would be known as Apollonius.

Speaking of famous miracle workers and teachers who left behind them unquestioned records of great work in behalf of humanity, we find that Pythagoras, who was born about 570 B.C., had divine honors paid to him through and after his lifetime. According to the sacred writings about him, his mother conceived him through a spectre, or the Holy Ghost, which appeared to her. His father, or foster father, was also informed through a vision that his wife was to bring forth a son through divine conception and that the son would become a benefactor to humanity.

The story of Aesculapius is very interesting. He became a great performer of miracles, a messenger with a divine message for all humanity, and was considered a true Son of God. When the Messenians sought to learn of the birth of Aesculapius, they consulted the oracle of Delphi and were informed that an invisible God or Holy Ghost of the Divine Kingdom was his father, that Coronis was his earthly mother, and that he was born at Epidaurus.

According to the story, when Coronis experienced the sacred event of divine conception, she sought to conceal her pregnancy from her father because she did not believe that she could make worldly people understand the strange occurrence. So she went into hiding at Epidaurus, where the child was delivered months later in a lowly and humble goat stable on a mountainside. A herder of goats, named Aristhenes, going in search of a goat and a dog missing from his fold, discovered the young child in the stable and would have carried him home had he not seen, when approaching the child, that its head was encircled with fiery rays which told him that the child was a divine being. His report of the finding of the child spread throughout the land, and people from all quarters flocked to the stable to pay homage to the Son of God and brought valuable presents which they laid at the feet of the infant. The child was honored as a god not only in Phoenicia and Egypt, but the worship of him passed into Greece and Rome.

Even on this side of the great ocean, the natives of North and South America had gods that were supposed to have been divinely born. Long before the landing of Columbus, the inhabitants of ancient Mexico worshiped a savior and world redeemer whom they called Quetzalcoatl, who was born of a pure virgin according to the traditions which the church leaders, who came with Columbus, discovered in the ancient writings carved on the walls of the temples. According to the story, then long established, a messenger from Heaven had announced to his mother that she would bear a son by divine conception, and that he would be the savior of the world. There was an established Mexican hieroglyphic which conveyed the story of the divine conception and birth of this Mexican god. The Mayas of Yucatan also had a virgin-born god, corresponding to Quetzalcoatl, whose name was Zama; and he was termed "the only begotten son of the Supreme God." In Central America and Peru, there were other divinely conceived and uniquely born gods.

I think I have shown, in just these few out of the many hundreds of well-recorded instances, that among the Orientals, and especially among those peoples whose religions had a well developed mystical basis, the idea of virgin or divine birth was not an improbability, but a well-accepted possibility. It has been said by many of the critics of the story of the virgin birth of Jesus, that if Jesus had been conceived and born as stated in the Christian records, it is strange that none of the contemporary writers, none of his disciples, not even Jesus himself, ever referred to this fact during his lifetime, and that only many years after his passing did the story of his divine conception and birth become established. This sort of argument would be sound and reasonable only if the virgin birth was unique with Jesus or, in other words, if he had been the first and only great messenger of God to have been considered of divine origin and birth. But if we consider that it was common belief among the peoples of the Oriental lands, and of Egypt and Palestine, that every great messenger, every avatar, every

Son of God ordained by divine decree to raise the status of the peoples of that time was born of divine conception, then we can understand why in the case of Jesus, neither his disciples nor the historians considered the event of such outstanding importance as to write about it, be enthusiastic over it, or make of it the unusual miracle that the Christian church makes of it today.

In tracing back the very complete records of the ancient pre-Christian avatars and Sons of God that greatly influenced the development of civilization, we find in the Rosicrucian records and in some other writings that are fragmentary, that the disciples and followers of each of these avatars or messengers devoted more time and thought to the recording of the sayings, teachings, and demonstrations of the avatars than to the recording of the events connected with their births and transitions. Even in the score or more cases where the divine conceptions and divine births of these pre-Christian avatars in various lands are recorded, the statements are brief, concise, and very often merely incidental to the story being told. The facts of the virgin birth are disposed of hurriedly as though they were of secondary importance and to be taken for granted by the reader of the life of each of these avatars.

In no case do we find that the disciples and followers of the avatars considered the divine conception and birth as a feature for adoration and worship, as we find in the case of the Christian teachings today. Very often the statements in regard to these miraculous births were made as briefly as we, at the present time, refer to the fact that some great person was born on such and such a date, with the assumption that every person is born and must be born at some place in a manner in keeping with his or her race and the conditions of the country in which the event occurred.

I am sure that when these facts are taken into consideration, those who have heretofore been puzzled because so few historical references can be found in ancient writings regarding the divine conception and birth of Jesus will realize that they have been seeking for something that, from the Oriental point of view, was not the outstanding or important event of his life. It is a fact that among the Orientals the lives and teachings and practical demonstrations of the teachings on the part of these avatars were considered all that was important about them, and the incidents of birth and location of birth, and of their ultimate passing, were points to be considered only by those intimately associated with the avatars and were recorded merely for the purpose of completing the record.

The next important point to have in mind is the fact that the reason for the general acceptance by mystics of the fact of divine conception lies in the common belief among the mystics and Oriental philosophers that the power of thought or the power of a mental or audible word is capable of impregnating matter and bringing lifeless matter into consciousness. If we try to assume that the impregnation of matter in a mystical manner like this is an unusual miracle of doubtful nature, never having been proved, and not acceptable except on the basis of unfounded faith, then we must also assume that all the fundamental teachings of the mystics of the Orient, and all of the claims made in occult and mystical literature by competent teachers and by those whose fame and integrity have been well established, are false, unfounded, unreliable, and unworthy of our consideration. And if we assume this, then there is little hope for us in the teachings that come from the Orient, and little reason for us to believe in the superior power and hidden, secret principles of divine energy.

The mystics of all ages have claimed, and through the so-called miracles have proved to themselves, that certain latent, potent principles can be invoked by humans and are applied by God in the creative processes of the universe. The very creation of the world itself is considered by all the mystics of the Orient as the first great demonstration of the potency of the Logos, or the power of the Word breathed into space where no life existed, resulting in immediate impregnation and the manifestation of living matter. The mystics of the Orient rightfully contend that in the beginning all nonliving matter was impregnated with life by a divine process, without the application of material laws. No other conception is possible to their understanding or acceptable to them. And if the first great impregnation of life in this manner is accepted, why should there be any question of lesser demonstrations in the case of an individual being, or the impregnation of a single cell of life?

Mystics of all times have demonstrated that even the spoken word, composed of a properly intoned vowel, has the power to disturb the status of matter and to set it into vibration or to change its elementary nature or its chemical composition. In demonstration of this, mystics of the Orient—and some highly evolved ones of the Occident— have learned how to utter a sound, or to produce a sound upon a violin string or other musical instrument, which would cause a manifestation in matter.

It is common with the Rosicrucians and with mystics of other schools who have learned how, and who have developed to the proper degree of perfection in these things, to utter vowel sounds or, by mental concentration, to direct invisible, potent energies to such focal points as would cause a manifestation in nonliving and living matter. It is the aim and ambition of millions of students of mystical law to attain that degree of perfection where they can perform seeming miracles of this kind. To these mystics and to the rational mind comprehending the laws involved, it would seem that if humans are capable of applying these mystical principles in such a manner as this, it certainly would not be improbable, let alone impossible, for the Mind of God to have directed certain powers to impregnate matter and bring about not only the virgin birth with which we are dealing in this chapter of the book, but many similar manifestations of an unusual nature.

Therefore, the Rosicrucian of evolved understanding, or the mystic of spiritual attainment, readily and understandingly accepts the virgin birth of Jesus and sees in it no violation of natural or spiritual law, nor any exception to truly scientific principles. Those who cannot accept the virgin birth or divine birth of the Master Jesus are probably laboring under the limiting comprehension of materialistic consideration and have not attained a spiritual development in their evolution which makes possible the comprehension and apprehension of the higher laws.

There is but one point upon which the Rosicrucians and the mystics of the Orient disagree with the fundamentalist or strictly orthodox of the Christian church, and this is in the uniqueness of the conception and birth of the Master Jesus. The Christian doctrines teach that Jesus was the only begotten Son of God, and the only instance where the Word was made flesh and where God sent upon the earth a Divine Son to redeem the world. The Rosicrucians understand that Jesus was not the first and only, but the last and greatest of all the messengers of God conceived in this manner and born on earth.

This brings us to another point of consideration before presenting the ancient, mystical story of the birth of Jesus. In a previous chapter, I stated that the Essenes, the Nazarenes, and the mystics of Palestine anticipated the coming of a great master who would be the incarnation of one of the former great leaders. I also stated that it was the common belief among the Jews that the Messiah which they expected would likewise be the incarnation of one of their former deliverers. In these statements you will note the belief on the part of the people of the Orient in the fact of reincarnation, which was an established belief throughout the entire Oriental world and which is today a positive principle in the religious and philosophical thought of more than three quarters of the earth's population, questioned only by part of the people in the Western world.

The Orientals also knew, through previous experiences, that the great avatars and messengers of God, who came to them from time to time as the evolution of the races required, were the reincarnation of the previous great souls on earth and had attained in each incarnation a higher and still higher degree of spiritual expression and mastership. Just when each one of these messengers would appear in a final incarnation it was impossible for them to tell, but since all incarnations were progressive, and since each messenger was greater and more advanced than the preceding one, the Essenes, the Nazarenes, and even the Jews of Palestine anticipated that the messenger who would come to them would be greater than any of the preceding avatars and would probably be the reincarnation of one of the greatest of those who had served them in the past.

It was natural for the Jews to feel that such a messenger or Messiah would be the reincarnation of one of their previous deliverers, perhaps Moses, and most certainly of the House of David. On the other hand, the Essenes and those of the Aryan race believed (and based their belief upon a better understanding of the mystical laws than the Jews possessed) that the new great master and redeemer for the world would be of the Aryan race, in the form of a reincarnation of one of the great masters who had served the world in other lands and who would not be limited to the tribes of Israel.

For this reason, the Essenes in Palestine and in Egypt and other locations fully anticipated that from their own race and from among the members of their own organization would come the next great master, because the Essenes represented at this time the group of most highly evolved and spiritually trained beings on earth.

22

Chapter 5

THE MYSTICAL BIRTH OF JESUS
BEFORE GIVING THE account of the birth of Jesus as it is recorded in the ancient Rosicrucian records, I wish to call to the attention of my readers the following important points.

At the time of the birth of Jesus, the Essenian community as a part of the G.W.B. was not only well established in various parts of Egypt and Palestine with its largest center of members in Egypt, located at Alexandria, and its very large community district in Galilee, but the organization maintained a great secret temple at Heliopolis in Egypt where the supreme officers met and where the highest ceremonies of the organization were held. This temple was often referred to in ancient records as the Temple of Helios, or the "temple of the sun." In Palestine, a smaller temple for the sacred ceremonies of the Essenes in and around Jerusalem was located close to one of the Jerusalem gates. It was in this temple in Jerusalem that officers of the Essenian organization in Palestine assembled for their high ceremonies.

Perhaps it is necessary to explain at this point, also, that in all the ancient temples of the G.W.B., Including those of the Essenes, the young daughters of the highest members of the organization served as virgins or as vestals for certain periods of their lives and were under the guardianship of the organization. In all the Rosicrucian branches throughout the world today, including those in North America, there are several vestals associated with each temple or lodge representing the spiritual consciousness of the Cosmic. These girls are always daughters of parents who have been in the organization for some time. They are highly respected and aided in every way to high attainments in all the ethical, cultural, and educational principles of the land.

With these points in mind, I now present what is probably the oldest and most complete story of the virgin birth or divine birth of the Master Jesus, as it has been recorded and preserved in the archives of the Rosicrucian organization in Egypt, India, and Tibet. I have had to condense the story slightly for presentation in this book, in order that the entire volume might not become too large, but I have not eliminated any essential detail nor altered any of the important mystical phrases.

The following story is the one that is generally accepted with perfect understanding by the mystics of the G.W.B., and I trust that the mystics of the Western world will find in it a perfect explanation of this greatest of all mystical mysteries.

In the days of the mystic sects and sacred cults of the G.W.B. of the Orient, there was one Joachim who was high priest in the holy Temple of Helios at the outer gate of Jerusalem. He was a devout follower of the sacred rituals and had pledged to give all that was his to the great work. And when the time came that his wife, Anna, was to have a child, they agreed that if it should be a girl, and she should show in her infancy that she was divinely ordained, she should become a Dove in the holy temple and remain a virgin of the sacred sanctum. And in the ninth month Anna bore a child, and it was a girl as the astrologers (magi) of the temple had predicted. When the days were accomplished, Anna purified herself, and gave the child the breast, and called its name Mary because the sun at birth was in the sign of Libra.

When the child was six months old it was taken by the parents to the temple that the child might be examined and that which it carried from its last life revealed in the presence of the priests and the magi. The child was placed in the sanctum upon its own feet, with its face toward the East, while the mother sat upon a white cloth at the foot of the vestal fire. The baby was urged to walk and it did walk. The priests and magi noticed that the child took seven steps and then knelt upon its knees before its mother in the sanctum. And as the magi chanted, the mother lifted up her child and cried aloud to the heavens: "As the Lord my God liveth, thou shalt not walk upon this earth until I give thee to the temple of the Lord." And the priests glorified in the fulfillment of the prophecy that Joachim, their high priest, should give to the temple a virgin.

The mother was true to her promise. She made a sanctuary in her home and placed a cloth from the Temple of Helios upon the floor on which the child Mary should walk so that she set foot not upon the earth until the day of her deliverance to the temple. The mother suffered nothing common or unclean to pass by her child and called the undefiled virgins of the priests of the temples to lead her about the improvised sanctuary and to carry her into the rose gardens when the sun was mellow.

The child's first birthday came and there was a sacred feast at the home of Joachim and Anna, and all the priests and scribes and magi of the temples of the community were present. Joachim brought the child Mary from the sanctuary to the priests, and she was sprinkled with undefiled water and the petals of the rose, and the magi officially proclaimed her name to be Mary, the Dove of Helios. The priests blessed her and prayed to God, saying: "O God of our Hearts, bless this child and make her name, as the magi have just proclaimed it to be, a name to be eternally named in all generations of the children of God." And all present said, "So be it, So be it, Amen!"

Her mother then took the Dove to the sanctuary to give it breast, and she sang a song to God saying: "I sing thee a song, O holy child, a song unto God, for [God] hath given me the fruit of righteousness. Harken, ye scribes of the twelve kingdoms of our land, for the Holy Dove is with me and God abideth with us." And when the feast was ended they went away rejoicing, each of the twelve scribes to bring the great tidings to their twelve temples of the twelve kingdoms.

The months passed and the child became two years old and there was another birthday feast. And Joachim said, "Let us carry Mary to the temple, that we may render the vow which we promised, lest perchance God refuse us the privilege and our gift become unacceptable." But Anna, her mother, said: "Seest not that Mary is wise and strong for her years and blessed with an understanding not of this life but that which she carried with her to the mouth of my womb when she was born? In another year she will be stronger and of wisdom sufficient to permit her to journey to the temple alone without her father and mother as in the past." And Joachim agreed.

And when the child became three years of age and was exceedingly bright with inner understanding, Joachim called the priests and scribes of the twelve kingdoms and invited the undefiled virgins of the priests to escort Mary to the temple. The virgins came with the sacred lamps burning with joy at the gift of God to the temple. But Mary refused escort and was carried only by her mother to the temple gate, that her feet might not touch the earth. The virgins were within the temple chanting and incensing the sanctum when Mary was received at the outer portal by the priests of Helios. The child was then taken into the temple and placed on the third step leading to the altar while the sacred fire burned and the priest prayed to God, saying: "God hath magnified [God's] purposes and [God's] name in all generations, and through this child God will manifest [God's] redemption to the children of this land." And he blessed the child, and she danced with joy and walked from the altar into the sanctum and knelt before the shekinah.

As the parents made their way toward the door of the temple they turned and saw that the child asked not to go. And as the virgins and priests and the scribes and magi walked to the West of the temple they cast rose leaves upon the kneeling child. The parents marveled at the child's desire to remain alone in the great temple. When they had departed and the child was alone, Mary saw her own child body floating as a dove in the air, and from out of the space above the shekinah there appeared a hand as though of an angel giving Mary as she floated a morsel of food. And a voice, as if from the angel, said: "Behold, this is to be thy food henceforth, for no longer shalt thou find milk at the mother's breast, for thou hast sucked that which God hath provided and now thou shalt eat only that which thy kin shall serve thee."

At the time Mary became twelve years of age she was made womanly with functions which gave sign and symbol that her day had come to fulfill the vow of her parents. A council was held of the priests and the magi, who said: "Behold, Mary the Dove is become twelve years old and she giveth sign that her day either to dwell within the temple or be given in marriage has come. Shall we take her now or wait the allotted time of twelve years and eleven months?" And the magi replied: "Go before the altar and ask God to show that which is right and whatever God shall manifest to thee, that also will we do."

And Joachim, as high priest, entered the sanctum and placed upon his official garment the triangular breastplate, and prayed for illumination. And a form appeared to him, saying, "Joachim, Joachim, go forth and summon the widowers of the [community] who hath homes and let them take a sacred staff apiece, and Mary shall be given to be cared for to him to whom God shall show a sign." And Joachim reported that which was given to him, and the scribes were informed to bring forth the widowers of their kingdoms.

Now there was one, by name Joseph, who was of the Essenian community at Galilee, and who was a devout brother of the temple of his kingdom; and when he heard that all the widowers were summoned to Helios, he laid down his axe and tools with which he was building a house, and hastened to meet the others. When all the widowers were assembled before the Temple of Helios, the high priest selected 144 sacred staffs and purified them before the altar and gave each of the widowers a staff. But there was no sign given by which Joachim could tell the answer to the selection the voice promised.

Joseph was the last to receive a staff and as he lifted it in sacred salutation to the high priest, behold a white dove went out of the rod and hovered over the head of Joseph. And the high priest said to Joseph: "Thou hast been allotted to receive the virgin which hath been given to Helios, to keep with thyself in thy home." But Joseph refused, saying he knew not what was intended by the gathering and that he had two sons and he was old, and the virgin appeared to be a young girl not yet thirteen as was the law.

The high priest admonished Joseph, reminding him what God did to Dathan and Abiram and Korah, how the earth opened and they were swallowed up because of their gainsaying. And Joseph feared and offered to take the virgin and to keep with himself the Dove of Helios. And he said to Mary: "Behold, I have received thee from the temple of God, and I will leave thee in my house and go to finish my building and will come to thee." And thus came Mary to live with Joseph, the widower and builder, as the virgin of the community.

And there came a time when the council of the priests of Helios was called to make plans for the making of a new curtain for the temple. And the priests said, "Let us call the undefiled virgins of our community and also our Dove of the temple." And when the call was answered, there were seven virgins. And Mary was sent for as the Dove of the temple. When they were within the temple, the high priest ordered that lots should be cast to see who should spin the gold for the curtain and who should spin the green, the scarlet, the purple, the blue, and the fine linen and silk. And the true purple and scarlet fell to the lot of Mary, their Dove. And she took the materials and went away to her home.

As she worked upon her spinning there appeared to her a figure of a great master who said: "Fear not! I come to bring thee a message of great joy, Mary, Holy Virgin and Sacred Dove of Helios, for thy day hath come to fulfill the prophecy of the magi! Thou hast found favor with God and thy [brothers and sisters], and now thou shalt conceive from the word of God." And when Mary heard this she disputed, saying: "Shall I conceive from the word of God? And yet shall I bear as every woman beareth?"

And the voice of the figure said: "Not in the manner of thy understanding shalt thou conceive, but in the manner of thy understanding shalt thou bear. For though the lips of man may kiss thee as the hands of the high priest hath blessed thee, so shalt the seed of man be thy heritage; but the word of God shall be breathed upon thee and its power shall make thee holy and bless the seed that it may be of God. Wherefore, also, that holy life which shall be born of thee shall be called the Son of God, and he shall attain the name Jesus because he shall be the God in [humanity] and will become the God with [humanity.]" And Mary answered: "It shall be according to the word of God!"

Mary wrought the purple and the scarlet and took it to the high priest. He spoke to Mary and told her he had been informed that her day had come to conceive and he blessed her and rejoiced with her, and told her that her name would be holy in all the generations of the earth. Mary went away, in time of preparation, to her cousin Elizabeth and stayed there until her condition was so manifest that she again sought the privacy of her home sanctuary.

Her sixth month came and Joseph returned from his housebuilding and found Mary was with child and he was surprised and sorrowful. He smote his face and threw himself upon the sackcloth of the sanctuary and wept bitterly, saying: "With what face shall I look to my God? for I receive a virgin, and the Dove of our temple, and have not guarded over her and she has been defiled by man? Who hath done this thing in my home? Is not the history of Adam repeated in me?"

And Joseph arose from his sackcloth and called Mary and said to her: "Why hast thou who walked the seven steps and was raised to the third step of the Holy of Holies in our temple, permitted man to defile thee? Didst thou not receive food from the hands of an angel as a token that thou wast not to accept from the profane that which would feed the earthly desires?" And she wept bitterly that Joseph did not know and that he should mistrust her, and she cried: "I am pure and know no man!" And Joseph was filled with awe and challenged her words, saying: "Whence then is it that thou art thus?" And she said with sweetness of voice: "As our God liveth I know not how this came but through the word! As I slept [God] came unto me with pureness of spirit, freed from the mortal body, and whereas [God] breathed not the breath of lust but spake with the breath of the word of God, I conceived in fact as God first conceived in thought; and as the thought preceded the creation of the world, so with me the most holy of all words preceded the quickening that came upon me." And Joseph was afraid lest those who knew not of the laws of a God would misunderstand and mis-judge, and he was in a quandary. But in the night there came to him the voice of the master, saying: "Be not afraid, for that which she hath conceived is of the Holy Spirit, and she shall bear a son and the Heavenly Hosts shall call his name Jesus because the Holy Spirit, through the word of God, shall be in him."

And there came later a scribe to the home of Joseph to inquire about his absence from a meeting of the community. And the scribe saw that

Mary was with child and he went forthwith to the high priest and was ready to attest that Mary had been defiled. And the high priest sent for Joseph and Mary and gave them hearing and listened knowingly to Mary's declaration of innocence and purity and then reasoned with the scribe. The magi consulted, and it was decided that the test should be given whereby their auras would manifest the color of sin, if sin there be upon them. And each was given a drink from the vessel containing the radiant water and they were placed in the dark and naught but pureness of light came from them and no sin was made manifest. And the high priest said: "If the God of our temple manifests not thy sin through [Gods] laws, then I cannot judge you." And he dismissed them as pure in heart and clean in body.

The day came when Joseph found it necessary to journey with Mary to avoid censure because of his predicament and Mary's strange experience. And they came to a cave where they rested at Mary's request, for she believed her hour at hand. Joseph sought aid and met a woman who came to the cave and met Mary and heard the strange story and believed it not. And in all directions Joseph saw that the heavens and the earth and the distant people upon it were silent and motionless and he knew that the presence of God was upon the face of the earth and that some miracle was about to be wrought.

While he and the woman waited in the cave, a great light came into the darkness and repelled them and it hovered over Mary. And the light became smaller in size and more dense in whiteness until it enveloped Mary and then slowly reduced to naught. And as Joseph and the woman watched in the silence the light was gone and there came the cry of a baby's voice and an angel appeared and said unto them: "At this hour, in humility of spirit, and with pureness of mind, to a virgin in the temple there is now born the Son of God, conceived by the Holy Spirit through the word of God. And his name will become Jesus, for that is the name of God into which the fire of spirit and the power of the word is given. But I warn thee not to tell to the profane that which has happened, for they will believe thee not but will say that unto a virgin some mortal man hath given child; and they will curse thee as a defiler of thy trust."

Joseph and Mary made ready to depart from the cave where they had been some time and were met by the magi who came, saying: "Where is the great King whose star in the heavens declares his birth? This hour should see him and his parents upon the highway, for his hour of birth is passed." And Joseph said: "I come unto Judea with the Son of God, not the King, for his Kingdom is not of the land but of the hearts of [men and women]."

And when Herod heard that a great king was born who fulfilled the strange predictions of the prophets, he made inquiries and was troubled. And when the magi of the G.W.B. heard what Herod threatened, they warned Joseph, while blessing Mary and giving to her of their script, gold, frankincense, and myrrh. And Joseph and Mary proceeded on their way by another road.

23

Chapter 6

THE BIRTHPLACE AND THE MAGI

IT MAY NOT be generally realized that there is a very interesting story in connection with the birthplace of the Holy Child, as for many centuries the exact location of the place has been an important point of discussion and is even disputed at the present time among the highest authorities.

We note in the Christian Gospel of Matthew the inference that Jesus was born in a house in Bethlehem. The words of Matthew are:

"In the time of King Herod, after Jesus was born in Bethlehem of Judea, [magi] from the East came to Jerusalem, asking, 'Where is the child who has been born king of the Jews? For we observed his star in the East, and have come to pay him homage.' . . . On entering the house, they saw the child with Mary his mother; and they knelt down and paid him homage."

No comments are made in the usual Christian Bible in regard to the statement in Matthew that Mary and the child were in a house, and this difference of location usually passed unnoticed. We must bear in mind that the writer of the Book of Luke distinctly implies that the child was born in a stable, in the following words:

"And she gave birth to her firstborn son and wrapped him in bands of cloth, and laid him in a manger, because there was no place for them in the inn."

Just why the almost universal impression exists that Jesus was born in a manger when there are two different statements in that regard will be explained in a moment. The fact of the matter is that in the early Christian days there was a third version of the place of birth that was exceedingly popular and based upon information not generally revealed in the present day Christian stories.

We find, for instance, that Eusebius, the first ecclesiastical historian, who played an important part in the Council of Nicaea, in A.D. 325, when most of the important traditions of the Christian church were discussed and decided, brought the matter of the birthplace of Jesus before the council for a positive decision. In his discussions he said little about a house or a manger being the reputed birthplace of the Holy Child, but said that the infant Jesus had been born in a cave instead. And he referred to the fact that at the time of Constantine a magnificent temple had been erected on the site of the cave, so that Christians might worship the place where the Savior was born.

In the apocryphal gospel called Protevangelion written by James, a brother of Jesus, we find reference to the cave again in the following words: "But on a sudden the cloud became a great light in the cave, so their eyes could not bear it."

Of the prominent leaders of the Christian church in the early days, we find that Tertullian (A.D.

200), Jerome (A.D. 375), and others, said that Jesus was born in a cave, and all the heathens of Palestine point to the cave in their land to this very day as the birthplace of the Christ Child.

We find also that Canon Farrar said: "That the actual place of Christ's birth was a cave, is a very ancient tradition, and this cave used to be shown as the scene of the event, even so early as the time of Justin Martyr in A.D. 150."

Now the facts of the matter are that Matthew was nearly correct when he said that Jesus was born in a house, for the cave in which the child was born was more than an empty excavation under a rock, or a hollow place in the mountainside. The Rosicrucian records and the Essenian records have always contained the statement that the child of Mary and Joseph was born in an Essenian grotto on the highway near Bethlehem.

I have previously referred to the fact that the Essenes possessed certain rescue houses and hospices in various parts of Palestine, and three of these were grottos. Usually such grottos were partly natural and partly artificial, and we know that grottos of this kind were quite common throughout Palestine and adjoining lands, for in early Christian days it was found safer and better to build grottos than large structures above ground when the purpose of such places was protection, isolation, and safety. The number of grottos still existing in Palestine always surprises the investigating tourists, and many of them are large enough to contain from ten to twenty rooms of a fair size, free from moisture, dampness, heat, or cold.

The Essenes made their three grottos very large, very convenient in location, and well protected from casual observation and attack by Bedouins or other tribes. Such grottos were located from twenty to sixty feet below the earths surface, with rooms that were approached by well-cut stone stairways descending at a wide angle and well lighted by apertures in the side of the rock or rocks that protected the entrance way. Some of the rooms were carefully hewn out of solid rock while others were partly natural in their formation. In most cases, the surface of the rock walls of the rooms was covered with a mud cement over which decorations or paint of some kind were applied in an artistic manner.

Oil lamps, hung from the ceilings or set in niches in the walls, furnished ample illumination; and small apertures between the rooms, or rising upward into traversed channels, provided a proper circulation of air. Seats, or the foundations for lounges, were cut in the sides of some of the walls or were formed of rocks in the center or end of the rooms. There was always a well close to each of these places, and provision was made in each room for a large jar of fresh water. The floor of these rooms was usually finished with partly smoothed stones, much like flagging, and only in one or two of the smaller rooms used for storage or some other purpose was the floor left with its ground finish. These grottos were usually furnished with convenient places for sleeping, eating, rest, recreation, and the care of the sick. In every way the appointments and equipment within these grottos were equal to those found in the mud, stone, or clay structures that were built above ground. Thus, a grotto home, or hospice, was not considered less costly or less elegant than one that was built above the surface.

It was into the Essenian grotto near Bethlehem that Joseph and Mary went for the birth of the child. A few references in the ancient Essenian and Rosicrucian records regarding the event would indicate that it had been quite common for the women of the Essenian organization to go to one of the Essenian hospices for the delivery of their children. A number of these places were prepared to take care of the sick, the injured, and the needy, as hospitals do, and it was traditional among the Essenes, as it is today among the Jewish people, to give considerable thought and to provide special facilities for women at the time of delivery. We might almost say that some of these early hospices were the originals of the present-day [birthing suites] so well established in various parts of the world.

I recently visited this Essenian grotto near Bethlehem and carefully investigated the size, shape, and arrangement of the rooms, and I cannot see how any one of the millions of persons who have seen the birthplace of the Holy Child can believe that there ever was any justification in calling it a manger. The large reception room in the center of the grotto, surrounded by many private rooms, immediately indicated that it was either a very large home, much larger than any home commonly found in Palestine, or a public place of some kind.

The stone stairway descending to the rooms would certainly suggest that the place could not have been used as a stable. When one sees the careful carving of the stones, the decorations still visible in many places, the care with which the floors were finished, and the arrangement of the rooms leading off from the central room, one is impressed at once with the fact that this was undoubtedly a very well planned and cared for hospice of some kind. Even today, the rooms are dry enough, warm enough, and comfortable enough for pleasant living, and when one sees the crude structures above ground that are usually provided for cattle (when any structures are provided at all), it is quite evident that no one would have gone to such trouble and expense for the sake of providing a stable for cattle.

At one of the famous Christian councils held by the early church leaders, when so many of the doctrines, teachings, and disputed points of tradition were being discussed and definitely settled, it was finally voted that the best way to end all of the argument about the birthplace of Jesus was to arbitrarily determine that a manger was the nature of the enclosure in which he was born. This arbitrary decision settled the matter for all time, so far as the church was concerned, and regardless of the many authentic records that still exist, it is probable that the story of the birth occurring in a lowly manger will remain a part of the Christian traditions.

One other important point in connection with the place of birth and the event of the birth of the Holy Child is likewise interesting. This pertains to the visit of the magi and the homage they paid to the Holy Child. According to the authorized Christian versions the three magi were led by a great star which caused them to journey "from the East" to the very locality in which the child was born. And they carried with them treasures and gifts of gold, frankincense, and myrrh.

The story of the star appearing in the heavens at this particular time has always been a fascinating one, and it is also one that skeptics or doubters of the Christian traditions have looked upon as a fantastic element, introduced in the account merely to make it picturesque. But long ago scientific astronomers, who investigated this matter with their charts of the periodicity of famous comets and moving star-like bodies, discovered that at or about the time of the birth of the Holy Infant, there was a great star or heavenly body that was making its rapid movement across the heavens above these lands.

Not only did this discovery, which has been substantiated by many scientists for many years, tend to verify the story of a symbol that could have led the magi in their journey, but the many ancient traditions regarding similar stories reveal the fact that it was a common belief among the magi, the astrologers, the Chaldeans, and the mystics of the Oriental countries, that whenever a great comet appeared in the sky and moved across the heavens, a leader or great avatar was about to be born who would prove to be a Savior or Redeemer. So well established was this belief, and so many interesting mystical points are involved in it, that I believe it worthwhile to take a little time at this point to speak of these matters.

It is true that in the story told in the Book of Luke, the writer says nothing about magi from the "East." However, he says that shepherds came and worshiped the young child, and that these shepherds had been keeping their flocks by night, and that the angel of the Lord appeared before them saying, "I am bringing you good news of great joy for all the people: to you is born this day in the city of David a Savior, who is the Messiah [the Christ], the Lord."

That statement in the Book of Luke was evidently written for the purpose of trying to explain the ancient belief that when a great star appeared, moving across the heavens, it was a message from God that a Savior was born, and the writer of Luke reduces the idea to a definite statement made by the Lord to the shepherds in the field.

In investigating the origin of this belief, we find from the old Essenian and Rosicrucian records that when the divine child called Krishna was born, a great star in the heavens proclaimed the fact, and Krishna was immediately adored and honored by the magi, who brought gifts to him. The old records state that the gifts consisted of sandalwood and perfumes. Likewise, at the time of the birth of Buddha, a great moving star in the heavens proclaimed his divinity, and the magi again visited the place of birth and paid homage and presented gifts.

The birth of Confucius in 351 B.C. was heralded by a great star moving across the heavens. This was observed by the magi, who found the location of the great child through the movement of the star, and went to the place of birth and paid homage: We find the same story in regard to Mithras, the Persian savior, Socrates, Aesculapius, Bacchus, Romulus, and a host of others.

We must remember that astrology was the one highly developed science among the magi and mystics of the Oriental lands, and that out of this science grew the present-day science of astronomy. It may be inappropriate, but I cannot fail to take this opportunity of stating that the ancient practice or art of astrology was more highly developed than it is today, and it did not deal with the petty things of luck and misfortune with which our present-day astrology deals, and which so shamefully blasphemes an ancient and honorable mystical science.

The magi referred to in the Bible were not just astrologers, or mediocre philosophers, who might have also been shepherds in the field, or ordinary persons of everyday affairs, but were the learned instructors and high representatives of the great academies and mystery schools of the Orient. The title of magus was granted only to one who had attained the very high degree of initiation in the mystery schools by proving to be a master of the arts and sciences, and by being a highly evolved mystic in every sense. The magi were consulted by the kings, potentates, and learned people of all lands, not only in regard to matters of astrology or astronomy, but in regard to history, medicine, natural law, spiritual law, and hundreds of other subjects which required profound thinking and unusual learning to explain or comprehend. They were the great oracles for the learned. They even occupied the position of the highest advisers in courts and councils of last appeal involving disputes of many kinds.

That a few of these magi should have observed the symbolic star and noted its significance was but natural in their time. But we must not presume that their observance of the star occurred only a few hours before the birth of the Holy Child, and that they hurriedly left their sanctums or their places of occupations and journeyed rapidly across lands to the birthplace. According to the ancient records at our disposal, we find that, as in all other cases, where the symbolic star had been noticed, the movement of this particular star had been observed for many months prior to the birth of the Holy Infant. For several weeks prior to the birth, close and careful tabulations had been made regarding the movement of the star and the probable time of its ultimate significance. And those who had been selected by the mystery schools to journey to the place of birth and represent the Essenes and the G.W.B. had started on their way to Palestine several weeks prior to the time of the birth.

We find from the records, also, that these magi knew the story of the selection of Mary as the pre-ordained mother of the Holy Child, the location of the home of Mary and Joseph in Palestine, and the arrangements that Mary should go to a particular grotto hospice near Bethlehem for the delivery of her child. The record states that Mary was at the hospice three days before the child was born, awaiting the important hour. The magi were in the vicinity of Bethlehem, also awaiting the hour.

When the star appeared in the heavens at its highest point and then began its sudden and rapid descent toward the horizon, the magi knew that the day and hour had come—and they had but to journey a short distance to the grotto to see the child that had been expected. They brought not only the things that are itemized in the Christian account, but greetings from the highest officials of the G.W.B., jewels of a symbolic nature for the mother and father, and a rosary containing a rare emblem for the infant to wear about its neck, that it might ever after be identified as the anticipated Son of God.

The magi, after having officially visited the child and formally presented their gifts and greetings, journeyed on to Mount Carmel and there made a report of the birth, and left official instructions for the keepers of the monastery and school at Carmel in regard to the education and care of the child throughout its infancy and childhood. Then these magi went on to Egypt and made their report to the high priests and the supreme officers of the G.W.B.

Chapter 7

THE BIRTHDATE OF THE HOLY CHILD

THERE HAS ALWAYS been considerable discussion regarding the year in which Jesus was born, but it is not my purpose to participate in this dispute at this time. The fact of the matter is that the actual year, according to the various calendars then existing and now existing, is of little consequence, for a definite year in one calendar would be a different year in another calendar. It would be very difficult for most people to work out a calendar which would enable them to figure correctly the true year of birth.

That the writers of the books of the Bible were confused in regard to the actual year is very apparent after even a casual examination of their statements. For instance, in the Book of Matthew, we are informed that Jesus was born in the days of Herod, the king, and the writer of the Book of Luke states that Jesus was born when Cyrenius was governor of Syria or later. These two statements have caused a great deal of discussion, for the days of Herod ended 4 B.C., and biblical authorities state that Cyrenius was governor of Syria from 4 B.C. to 1 B.C., and again in A.D. 6. Even the matter of the taxing referred to in the stories indicates that a different year is referred to than is commonly accepted as the year of the birth of Jesus.

The very interesting point in regard to the time of birth, however, pertains to the day of the month and the month itself.

For many centuries after the life of Jesus, the Christian church founders and eminent ecclesiastical authorities were unable to decide as to the birth date of Jesus. Among the early Christians, the anniversary of the Nativity was celebrated with a great festival in May, sometimes in April, and on other occasions in January. Some of the earliest traditions in the Christian church definitely stated that May 20 was the correct date, while some of the church leaders insisted that April 19 or 20 was the true and correct date. Even up until the fifth century after the life of Jesus, the matter was still in dispute, but in that century, the community at Rome held one of its famous councils and made a definite decision by selecting December 25, or midnight of December 24, as the true time. And in this decision we find a very beautiful and important mystical story.

It must be understood by my readers that the many facts revealed in this book which are different from the authorized Christian versions of the life of Jesus are not facts which were concealed during the early Christian days, but were known to all of the leaders of the Christian church and to the high ecclesiastical authorities who gathered in councils from time to time and established the doctrines, traditions, and forms of ceremony to be officially a part of the Christian theology. What motives these early authorities had for disregarding facts known to them, and for withholding from the masses certain facts of intense interest to us at the present time, and in changing other facts to symbolical falsehoods, must be left to the intuition of my readers. The popular statement that "the end justifies the means" was unquestionably one of the thoughts in their minds.

We find in the writings of these early authorities a statement made many times that certain changes and inventions which they established in connection with the traditions of the life of Jesus were "theological necessities." In other words, in order to utilize many of the ancient, mystical ceremonies which church authorities derived from the temples of Egypt and from the doctrines and practices of the Essenes and the G.W.B., they had to invent certain points and principles in connection with the life and work of Jesus so as to make these ceremonies adaptable and consistent. In order to establish a new theology and many new doctrines, they had to ignore and set aside many facts which would have been inconsistent with their decisions.

When, however, it came to some important points that had to be definitely decided, they were forced to rely upon the ancient principles and doctrines that had been established and were known to the true spiritual laws so that they would have some foundation upon which to base their decisions. The decision that midnight of December 24 was the actual birth time of Jesus was one such case, and the reason for this is intensely interesting from a mystical point of view. This decision, however, conflicted with one of the points in the traditional story of his birth, namely, the story that at the time of the birth shepherds were in the field caring for their flocks. It has always been said by those who knew the conditions in Palestine at that time that the latter part of December is not a season when shepherds are in the fields caring for their flocks at night or at any other hour of the day, and that this incident was introduced in the story when the belief was common that Jesus was born in the month of April or May.

However, the great fact which the church leaders had to take into consideration in reaching their decision was that throughout all the preceding centuries, all the other great avatars who had been born of virgins, who were Sons of God, and who were known as Redeemers or Saviors, had been born on or about December 25. The other fact that they could not fail to consider was that there was a spiritual law or a cosmic law for the birth of these great avatars on December 25, and that no Redeemer of the world could have been born at any other time.

We must bear in mind that the birth of a great avatar or a Son of God is not a simple incident in the scheme of things, nor a casual accident of conditions. The birth of an avatar is the result of certain laws preordained and established in the cosmic scheme and coincident with a series of events leading up to and culminating in the Divine Birth. The cosmic birth of Jesus, as of every other avatar, is an interesting story in itself and has no place in this chapter. But in order that my reader may be familiar with the manifestations of this great cosmic law, I will present the following facts from the historical records of the G.W.B.

In the first place, there is a correspondence between the spiritual law, cosmic law, and mundane law pertaining to a universal condition manifesting about December 23, 24, or 25 of each year. It is at this time that a cosmic change occurs called the Birth of the God Sol, and this event was always celebrated by the ancients as the Accouchement of the Queen of Heaven or the Celestial Virgin of the Sphere.

In India this period was one of great rejoicing everywhere. Many centuries before the Christian era, this period in December was celebrated as a religious festival, at which time the people decorated their homes with garlands and they were prolific in their gifts and presents to friends and relatives. So far back in antiquity can this religious festival in December be traced that its origin is lost in obscurity.

In China, also, long before the Christian period, the people recognized this period of the winter solstice as a holy time, and on December 24 or 25 they closed all their shops, their courts, and their places of business activities. Among the ancient Persians, their most splendid ceremonials were in honor of Mithras, whose birthday was recorded as having occurred on December 25.

Among the ancient Egyptians for many centuries, December 25 was celebrated as the birthday of several of their gods. We find this referred to in all of the histories of the religions of ancient peoples, as, for instance, in the book entitled Religion of the Ancient Greeks, by De Septehenes, who says: "The ancient Egyptians fixed the pregnancy of Isis (the Queen of Heaven and the virgin mother of the Savior Horus) on the last days of March and towards the end of December they placed the commemoration of her delivery."

In some cases the celebration of the birth dates of some of these ancient gods was changed by high proclamation, just as the birth date of Jesus was changed from May to December. The birth date celebration of Krishna is now held in July or August.

In Bonwicks Egyptian Belief we find a verification of what is contained in the Rosicrucian records. He says in regard to Horus: "He is the great god— loved of Heaven. His birth was one of the greatest mysteries of the Egyptian religion. Pictures representing it appeared on the walls of temples. One passed through the holy adytum to the still more sacred quarters of the temple known as the birthplace of Horus. He was presumably the child of deity. At Christmas time, or that answering to our festival, his image was brought out of that sanctuary with peculiar ceremonies, as the image of the infant Bambino is still brought out and exhibited in Rome."

The Christian figure of the Bambino, or the Christ child. It is this form carved in marble or stone that is exposed in the churches on Christmas morning and kept on view from Christmas to Epiphany. It is claimed that Saint Francis of Assisi was the originator of this statue in the 13th century, but research has revealed that a similar statue of a Holy Child was exhibited on Christmas Day in many lands before the Christian era.

It is interesting to note here that the word Bambino is now a sacred word among the foreign Christians, and it is a term used for representations of the infant Christ Jesus in swaddling clothes. It is customary in Rome to bring out to public view, early on Christmas morning, an image of the Bambino carried with great ceremony for the public to salute and greet, in honor of the original birthday. This little incident of Roman Christian ceremony is just a continuation of the ancient customs established in the mystic lands by the G.W.B.

Osiris, son of the holy virgin, or Neith, was born on December 25; and the Greeks celebrated this day as the birthday of Hercules. Bacchus and Adonis were also born on December 25. Tertullian, Jerome, and other founders of the early Christian church, who labored so diligently in the formation of Christian doctrines, ceremonies, and creeds, inform us in their early writings that the ceremony of the celebration of the birthday of Adonis on December 25 took place in a cave and that the cave in which they celebrated this mystery was in Bethlehem, and was, in fact, the same cave in which the child Jesus was born. This is but another verification of the fact that the Essenian grotto in which the Holy Child of Mary and Joseph was born had been used for the celebration of previous avatars, such as Adonis. This is why the magi knew where to find the new avatar on his birthday.

The fact that December 25 was celebrated generally as a day associated with the birth of Sol, or the cosmic birthday of certain laws and principles manifested by the Sun, is shown in many ancient records of the early Christian celebrations in Rome. We can turn to the writings of the Reverend Mr. Gross, who has written very thoroughly and authentically in regard to these matters, and read as follows: "In Rome, before the time of Christ, a festival was observed on the 25th of December, under the name of Natalis Solis Invicti (birthday of Sol, the Invincible). It was a day of universal rejoicing illustrated by illuminations and public games. All public business was suspended, declarations of war and criminal executions were postponed, friends made presents to one another, and the slaves were indulged with great liberties."

It is interesting to note, also, that among the ancient Germans centuries before the birth of Christ, these people celebrated annually, at the time of the winter solstice, a sacred period which they called their Yule-feast. On this occasion all agreements were renewed, the gods were consulted as to the future, sacrifices were made to the various gods, and the people indulged in jovial hospitality. Of this ancient ceremony the word Yule still survives as the old name for Christmas, and the ancient custom of burning the Yule log on Christmas Eve is still the usual practice.

It is interesting to note also that the word Yule in French is called Noel, which is the equivalent of the Hebrew or Chaldee word Nule. Among the ancient Scandinavians there was a yearly celebration at the winter solstice that was observed as the mother-night, and the feast was called Jul. It was in honor of Freyr, the Holy Son of the supreme god and goddess. The celebration included all sorts of demonstrations of joy and happiness, and the bestowing of gifts.

In Great Britain and Ireland the Druids celebrated December 25 as a holy day and burned great fires and lights on the tops of hills. Even in ancient Mexico, the last week of December was celebrated as a sacred feast, in honor of the birth of a god.

The use of evergreens and mistletoe at Christmas time is derived from ancient practices. Tertullian, the early church leader to whom I referred previously, writing from a distant land to his colleagues at home, described this custom of December 25 and the use of evergreens and mistletoe. Saying that it was "rank idolatry," he described how the natives of this region decked their doors "with garlands of flowers and evergreens."

From the foregoing we see that when the G.W.B. in Egypt set down in its records the statement that the day and hour of the winter solstice was the cosmic period for the birth of avatars, as observed in all the ancient notations, it was not ordaining a time or arbitrarily establishing by decree a period for the celebration of the birthdays, but was merely proclaiming what it had observed and proceeded to state how the cosmic law had made itself manifest. Just why avatars should be born in the winter solstice, and why so many of humanity's great leaders were actually born at such a time, is a matter that deals with the principles of reincarnation, cosmic cycles of existence, and cosmic laws relative to the periodicity of the stages of advancing civilization. Such points as these have no place in the present volume.

Of course, those who are interested in the profound mystical principles and spiritual laws of the universe, and who are anxious to know just how these affect every man and woman in his or her personal development and attunement with the Cosmic Consciousness, will make contact with some school or system which deals with these subjects thoroughly, conscientiously, and without bias or prejudice.

Naturally such information is never sold and never put into book form for public sale at any price. For this reason the seekers will vainly search among bookstores or in the offerings of private publishers or commercial movements for the information desired. Only such organizations as the Rosicrucians, for instance, or branches of the

G.W.B. operating in foreign lands, will give the seeker this information in a private, personal way, and with no other motive than the benefit that each individual will derive from the instruction, if he or she is found worthy to have such knowledge.

25

Chapter 8

THE CHILDHOOD OF JESUS

WE FIND TWO periods in the authorized Christian version of the life of Jesus which are passed over without comment and without detail. These are the years constituting his childhood and up to and including his appearance before the learned authorities in the synagogue, and the period from that time until the beginning of his mission in the Holy Land as an adult.

The silence in Christian literature regarding these two periods has unquestionably been responsible for a great many discussions that have led to severe criticism of the entire story of his life. Aside from the orthodox version of his birth, which so many reject because they do not understand it, the two gaps in the story of his life referred to above have constituted excellent reasons for the rejection of the story of the remainder of his life. Those who cannot accept the immaculate conception and divine birth of Jesus do not hesitate to point out the two gaps in the early part of his life as proof that the real story of the life of Jesus has never been told.

The highest critics of the authorized version of the life of Jesus point out with some justification that if the biblical accounts did not go into such detail and put such great stress upon the events of his conception and birth, the absence of details regarding his childhood and youth would be immaterial and would cast no reflection upon the entire story of the latter part of his life. But when every important and casual event leading up to his birth, and the events of the birth itself, are recorded by so many witnesses and glorified in such detail, there appears to be some significance in the silence regarding his youth.

Surely those who felt it their duty to gather, record, and preserve the essential and nonessential points regarding the birth, and all that led up to it, must have had access to the facts pertaining to his childhood, and these facts must have been more definitely recorded and better known to a larger number of persons than the events pertaining to the conception and birth of Jesus. Why, then, the silence and the complete absence of those details which would have been highly interesting and extremely illuminating to those who would adore Jesus and seek to worship every phase of his life?

Be it known, therefore, that the facts regarding the childhood and youth of Jesus are not lacking and are not absent in those records which were kept and are still preserved by those groups of persons and organizations which have not been influenced by the rulings of religious councils or the dictates of synods and who do not find in those facts any event or any incident belittling to the greatness and supreme mastership of Jesus the Christ.

I am aware that some of the facts pertaining to the childhood and youth of Jesus have become public in various lands at various times and that some of these facts have found their way into the mystical writings of the Occidental world. But the complete story and the most important details have been withheld by those organizations who know them well in the belief that until the Western world was ready to understand them in their richness and illuminating significance, it would be better to withhold them. There is no reason why these facts should not be revealed at this time, and I am glad to say that the authorities who have the records in their archives, and with whom I have recently held consultations in this regard, agree that the present recklessness throughout the Western world in regard to religious matters, and especially the desire on the part of so many millions of persons for a more complete outline of the life of Jesus, warrants the publication of the facts now given for the first time in Western sacred literature.

That Jesus must have had some unusual preparation and very thorough education is quite apparent to any student of Christian doctrines and to every analyst of the life of this great teacher. The mere fact that at an early age he could astound the learned of his country by his ability to answer and ask profound questions proves that during the first ten or more years of his life, he was carefully educated and carefully trained. We may assume with perfect reason and logic that as a Son of God or a messenger of God, he was inspired continuously and could find in his immediate contact with the Consciousness of God the illuminating thoughts which he expressed. But with the same reasonable logic, we must believe that he had to receive that education and training in the mundane schools of this world, which would make it possible for him to express those ideas and those thoughts in the words and tongue, in the images and pictures, understood by the multitude.

The greatest of the masters in an have undoubtedly painted their masterpieces under inspiration. Nevertheless, each of these masters had to be trained in the technique of expressing that inspiration in a medium that would convey the thought, the idea, the picture, from one mind to another. The greatest of the composers have unquestionably written under inspiration, and by their own admission they have found that the most beautiful passages in their music came to them as from Heaven; nevertheless, these artists had to be trained in the technique of expressing that which was inspired within their souls.

No matter how completely and perfectly Jesus may have been in spiritual contact with the Cosmic Mind and with the Consciousness of God, he had to have that training, that education, and that practice in the use of words and in the expression of thought which enabled him to say the most beautiful things in the most beautiful language ever spoken. We cannot conceive of an uneducated, untrained, unprepared instrument speaking such thoughts and doing such things as he did, even under the most perfect inspirational contact, without preparation and training.

The argument that any such training and preparation in mundane schools and at the hands of earthly advisers, instructors, and guardians would weaken the claim of divine preparation and unique Sonship, is absolutely absurd. Have we any reason to believe that the mother of Jesus did not teach the little child to walk or to eat? Or shall we assume that these things were divinely inspired in him, and that from the moment of birth such things were known to him? After all, is not the matter of walking upright, instead of crawling about, a matter of earthly wisdom and regulation, and not a rule of the Cosmic or an establishment of God, which God would inspire in the minds or consciousness of all beings? Is not the use of certain words, of certain languages, and the grouping of these words into grammatical phrases, a result of human regulations and rules rather than cosmic laws and principles? If these things are earthly products, then they must be acquired at the hands of humans and must be taught by humans.

Most certainly Jesus was taught to speak the Hebrew, the Aramaic, and the Greek languages, for we cannot conceive of God's having inspired the knowledge of these languages in the consciousness of Jesus without earthly education. For why should these three languages have been selected by God as the modes of expression on the part of one who was to be a Redeemer of all peoples in all lands, with many tongues? If Jesus was taught how to speak and teach several languages, with the ability to interpret the inspiration of his soul into sounds and words that would convey meaning to others, there is no reason to believe that he was not taught other things necessary to carry out his great mission in life. All this is for the purpose of presenting the logic and reasonableness of his education, and not for the purpose of attempting to prove that he must have had such education. There are ample records to show how and where he was educated, and we will deal with these at this time.

In the first place, I have already shown that Jesus was born in the family of two devout Essenes and in a community of Essenes. This in itself was sufficient to guarantee the young child the very highest education obtainable in any land at that time. Not only were the preparatory schools conducted by the Essenes sufficient to give every child an excellent education at the hands of teachers and masters who had been trained in many lands and raised to the highest degree of ethical and literary attainments, but the associations and connections which the Essenes maintained with their other branches in foreign lands guaranteed a very liberal education to this special Son of God and this special charge of the Essenian community.

We are told in the accounts of his birth how the magi, who were the learned individuals of the mystery temples and the chief instructors of the highest principles of education, came to the birthplace of Jesus to pay homage to him as the preordained avatar of the new cycle. This acknowledgment on the part of the great magi indicates that the little child was anticipated and expected by the Essenes and by the Great White Lodge in all lands, and that he would be guided and protected throughout his life. To assume that these magi paid such homage and adoration to one whom they knew to be the great and expected leader of humanity, and then did not show any further interest in his education, development, and training, and played no part in the development of his life, is to assume something that would be more of a mystery than any other phase of the life of Jesus as it appears in the authorized Christian version.

I have said that at the time of the birth of Jesus, the Essenes constituted a large community in Galilee, and that they had hospices and refuge houses in various parts of Palestine for the care of the poor and needy. They also maintained the Supreme Temple in distant Egypt and minor temples in Palestine and other places. I must point out now one other fact that has been held in secrecy for many centuries, and that will probably explain many strange references in the sacred literature of the Christians and other sects.

The Nazarenes, the Nazarites, and the Essenes had united their interests in regard to one essential work—a work that is referred to by many authorities in religious and sacred histories and encyclopedias as being one of the common interests which bound the Nazarenes, the Nazarites, and the Essenes. This work was the maintenance of a great school, college, and monastery on Mount Carmel. The introduction of this historical place into the life of Jesus may seem surprising to a great many of my readers. For this reason a brief resume of the history of Mount Carmel may be not only appropriate, but of value to those who wish to make further research in this regard.

Just when Mount Carmel became the secret, sacred place for the maintenance of an isolated, protected school of mystics and of the

G.W.B. is not definitely known. The earliest historical incidents of a religious nature connected with Mount Carmel are those associated with the lives of Elijah and his son. The ancient Jewish documents, as well as many of the writings preserved by the Roman Catholic Church, which in later years became greatly interested in the Mount of Carmel, show that from the earliest known period of the history of this Mount, a tabernacle, monastery, or temple of some kind was located there, and that when Elijah went to this mountain to carry out the many marvelous things recorded of him, he found a temple and an altar there. We also know, from references in various records, that many of the great masters of the G.W.B. spent part of their lives on this mountain in the temple or monastery. Even Pythagoras spent part of his life there, and in the history of his life this retreat of Mount Carmel is referred to as "sacred above all mountains and forbidden of access to the vulgar." We find even in the Roman Catholic records, which have traced the history of Mount Carmel very carefully, references to the fact that "in ancient times the sacredness of Carmel seems to have been known to other nations besides Israel; thus in the list of places conquered by the Egyptian King, Thothmes the Third, there is a probable reference at Number 48 to the 'Holy Headland' of Carmel." Those who are students of Rosicrucian history know that Thothmes III was one of the great founders of the early mystery schools of Egypt and a leader in the movement that became the G.W.B. The Rosicrucian records also point out that Thothmes III conquered Carmel in the year 1449 B.C. and released it to those who sought to maintain in this out-of-the-way place a school and monastery for the mystery teachings.

Now it is well known that Elijah was a Nazarite and an Essene, and that both the Jewish and Roman Catholic records refer to him as such. This one fact alone would be sufficient to indicate the nature of the demonstrations which Elijah performed on Mount Carmel and the nature of the monastery and temple maintained on the summit of the mountain.

In many of the old stichometrical lists and writings and papers of the ancient ecclesiastical writers, mention appeared of an apocryphal Apocalypse of Elias, from which some citations are said to be found in I Corinthians 2:9, and elsewhere in the Bible. This old book or Apocalypse of Elias was known to the mystics of the G.W.B. and is known to all of the Oriental Rosicrucians as a very sacred record of

the early history and teachings of the Essenes and the Nazarenes. In the early Christian centuries and during the lifetime of the Master Jesus, the Apocalypse of Elias was well known and used in the sacred classes of the most advanced members of the organization. But like many other very valuable and illuminating records of early periods dealing with the more secret teachings, it was withdrawn from public use and became "lost."

However, in 1893, Maspero, the famous historical writer, connected with the Rosicrucian Order of Egypt, found a Coptic translation of it in one of the Order's monasteries in Upper Egypt. Since then several other translations in other languages have been discovered in the archives of the G.W.B., and parts of these have been used in the recently issued higher teachings of the Rosicrucians. From this Apocalypse of Elias and from the other Rosicrucian records, we learn much about the establishment of the monasteries and schools at Carmel, which were known as "the school of the prophets" or "the school of the Essenes."

As years passed by, the attendance at the school and monastery at Carmel became so large that a community was established there, composed of those who were students. They adopted a distinct form of dress and remained within the monastery grounds throughout their entire lives except for the periods when they went forth to other lands as missionaries. It was here that many of the most ancient manuscripts were translated and illuminated on parchment and sent to the various archives of the G.W.B. throughout the world. A wonderful library was also maintained at Carmel for many centuries. Members of this community were present at Saint Peters first sermon on Pentecost, and they built a chapel in honor of this occasion. Many other historical structures existed there, such as El-Khadr, the school of the prophets; El-Muhraka, the traditional spot of Elias's sacrifice; Elias's Grotto; and the monastery itself.

About 400 years after the Christian period, the monastery and school at Mount Carmel were abandoned as the principal place of education for the G.W.B. The wonderful library and the thousands of manuscripts and records were transferred to the secret monastery of Tibet, where these things are now preserved, and where the greatest school of mysticism and sacred literature in the world is maintained. Some centuries after this abandonment, an order of a monkish nature was established in Carmel, and the members of this organization claimed to be descendants of those of the original organization, but likewise claimed to be Roman Catholic in faith. This contention caused much dispute for several centuries, and it was finally settled when Pope Innocent XII in 1698 decided that the claim of direct succession was not correct and that the new organization had no connection with the early Carmelite organization. Out of this decision grew the present organization known as the Carmelites, or White Friars, as they are called in England, which is a Roman Catholic organization popularly known as the Carmelite Order. Today in the midst of the ruins of the ancient Essenian structure can be seen the Roman Catholic convent of the Carmelite organization.

According to the Rosicrucian records, we find that in the sixth year of his life, the youthful Jesus was placed in the school at Carmel and began his preparation and training as a Son of God and an avatar. There is no question about the authenticity of this statement. It is recorded in too many places and in too many different ways, and it is verified by so many later incidents in his life, that any question of this fact cannot be reasonably raised. The records further intimate that while he was an apt and perhaps unusually bright student, he was given every special advantage that the entire organization, not only in Palestine, but in Egypt as well, could give to one that was known to be their special charge and the greatest among them. It is also recorded that young Jesus was not entered in the school under the name of Jesus, but under the name of Joseph, and this presents another interesting fact for those who desire the most intimate details of his life.

It is commonly believed by biblical students that the name of Jesus was given to the child at the time of his circumcision, in accordance with the custom of the land. This is based upon the fact that he was called Jesus later in his life, and that before his birth it was said that his name would be or should be Jesus. The Gospel of St. Luke tells us the familiar story of how an angel appeared to Mary and told her that the unborn child would be called Jesus. But this statement and that in Matthew are really prophecies. They say simply that Mary shall bring forth a child who shall be known as Jesus. In the historical record presented in Chapter 5 of this book, we find that Mary was told that the "holy life which shall be born to thee, shall be called the Son of God, and he shall attain the name of Jesus."

Nowhere in the Christian Bible do we find the statement that he should be christened Jesus at the time of the circumcision, but we do find reference to such naming at his circumcision in the Gospel of the Infancy of Jesus. But these statements were added to these gospels on the presumption that the name he bore later in life was the name that was given to him at circumcision. The Gospels were written long after the lifetime of Jesus, and they contained similar assumptions and inferences without foundation. From the time that the disciples knew Jesus or came in contact with him, until the close of his life, he was known as Jesus and bore that name. Since they never knew him or contacted him before he bore that name, they had no reason to believe that he ever had any other name. The fact that such a name was predicted for him, and that he eventually attained such a name, causes us to investigate the meaning of the name Jesus.

We know that the word Christ comes from the Greek word Christos which means "Messiah." We find that the word Christos was introduced to other nations when the Septuagint was prepared about 100 B.C., and that it was used to translate the word Mashiach, which means "the anointed one," or, in its more complete form, Meschiach, meaning "Yahvehs Anointed." Cyrus is called "the anointed," and in Psalm 105:15, the plural form "anointed ones" is used to apply to the patriarchs. In the Old Testament, the word "anointed" is limited to mean a Jewish king, except in the case of Cyrus and the patriarchs, which exceptions prove that it could mean a person great in more ways than one. The word or title Christos had been used in the mystery schools and in the Orient for the name and title of many of the former avatars.

Going back to the Septuagint, we find that the Greek word Christos originally came from the name of one of the Egyptian deities. There was old Hermes, whose name has been corrupted or translated into "Hiram of Tyre," who built the temple without the noise of axe or hammer. The Latin form of this name is Mercury, while the Greek form is Hermes, and the Egyptian form was Tachut. Now in Hebrew, the word Tachath, which is called Thoth occasionally in Greek, means "under" and "beneath." Thoth was the Lord or God of Maa, or the Egyptian Maa or Maat, meaning "truth." And Maa kHeru, meaning "true words" is the basis from which came the Greek form Merkury or Mercury.

The Egyptian letter or diphthong kH is a highly aspirated H and by the Greeks is usually transcribed as X and, vice versa, the value of the Greek X is usually transcribed as ch. The kHeru of the Egyptians would be therefore cheru or Ch-R. These latter letters form the famous XR or the cryptogram of the early Christians, which I personally saw and traced on several stones of the tombs in the catacombs of Rome. It is generally accepted in all Christian historical records that this XP referred to Christ, and in the Greek Gospel of John, Jesus is called the Logos, which is a word having a similar meaning. Therefore, we see that the term Christ was a tide to be specifically applied to and attained by one who had been especially born and deified as a messenger of God.

Now the word Jesus presents the same understanding. The old Hebrew form of the word as found in the Old Testament is Joshua, or Jeshua, and was often rendered as Jesu. The Greek form of the name is responsible for the final s. Originally, the Hebrew form of Joshua meant "helped of Yahveh," while the later Hebrew form means "to deliver" or "to save." Therefore, Jesus came to be known as meaning "savior."

In the Synoptic Gospels we do not find the disciples at first calling their master by the name of Jesus, but they did call him Rabbi meaning "teacher" and Adonai meaning "master," and other titles of respect and love.

The record of his entrance into the school at Carmel shows that he was entered as Joseph, the son of Mary and Joseph, and the reincarnation of Zoroaster, the "Son of God." When and how he attained the name of Jesus is explained in another part of this work.

26

Chapter 9

JESUS ENTERS THE PRIESTHOOD

THE ONE DEFINITE comment made on the early life of Jesus in the popular stories of his life, especially those of churchly origin, tells about the wonderful impression which

the child made upon the learned doctors and masters at the time of his visit to Jerusalem in his thirteenth year. Even among the most advanced of Christian theologians and in nearly all of the extensive histories of his life, the real facts pertaining to this visit to Jerusalem are misunderstood or misrepresented through a lack of knowledge of what actually occurred.

I have already said that Jesus and his parents lived as Gentiles in the Gentile section of Palestine but had to obey the Jewish customs and regulations of the land. One of these regulations was that in accordance with strict Jewish law, it devolved upon each boy in his thirteenth year to attend one of the feasts at Jerusalem. He had to appear officially under certain conditions and at a certain place for a definite ceremony, and he then became what was called a Son of the Commandment, or of the Torah. The usual time for such a visit was on the first paschal feast after the boy had passed his twelfth birthday.

According to the story, the parents of Jesus took him with their other children in the company of other Nazarenes to Jerusalem. The text of the Christian version seems to indicate that it was "their wont to go" up to the temple. This is evidently a mistake on the part of the writers or translators, because as Gentiles, the parents of Jesus were not accustomed to attending all of the feasts and ceremonies of the Jewish church, for the law did not require that of any but those who were strictly orthodox and wholeheartedly affiliated with the Jewish religion. Since Jesus was the first born of the children in the family and, therefore, the oldest, he was the only one of the children of Mary and Joseph who had attained the age when such visits were compulsory, and so this must have been their first obedience to this law of the land. I find that even some of the highest critics of Christian literature agree that the phrase "it was their wont" to go, should be read in that sense which puts the participle in the present tense and not in the past. Hence we understand how glad Mary and Joseph were to avail themselves of this opportunity to visit the Holy Sanctuary in Jerusalem and to bring their wonderful child before those officials who would conduct a formal examination.

This paschal feast in Jerusalem was held in the spring. Caponius was acting as procurator and Annas ruled in the temple as high priest. Out of Galilee walked this holy family, accompanied by a host of other Gentiles, Nazarenes, Nazarites, Essenes, and some Jews, chanting as they went and making of the event a gala occasion. The ranks of these travelers were swelled by other festive bands who united in chanting the Psalms of Ascent to the accompaniment of the flute. Unquestionably they also discussed the spiritual principles involved in the ceremonies to be held.

It was a long journey as we would view it in these days. Recently I made the trip in a very fast automobile from Nazareth to Jerusalem, and I found that it required the better part of a day to do it. All through the beautiful section of Palestine which these pilgrims had to traverse, composed of hills and valleys, magnificently tinted with the beautiful green of that country and spotted with flowers, one could still see the ancient trail of footpaths that led up over the hills and down into the valleys in almost a straight line from the present site called Nazareth to Jerusalem and over which the pilgrims walked in their journeys to and fro. Even today the natives of that country walk these same paths or ride on their donkeys garbed as in the times of Christ, presenting a picture that carries one back hundreds of years.

When the tired pilgrims finally reached the gates of Jerusalem, the problem of being housed and cared for must have been a serious matter, for the feast brought nearly the entire population of Palestine into the environs of Jerusalem for three or four days. The Essenes, Nazarites, and Nazarenes were fortunate inasmuch as at the city gate, and in places nearby, there were special houses and structures owned by the Essenes and Nazarenes for the care of their own people and for pilgrims and strangers who needed their care.

The scene must have been a glorious one for the youthful child, making perhaps the first long trip in his life. The school at Carmel is but a short distance from the villages of Galilee, as compared with the long distance that stretches between them and Jerusalem, and we may easily realize how impressed the child must have been with the sight of so many pilgrims, the chanting, the music of the flute, the wayside prayers, the excitement, and finally the greetings and preparations at the city gate.

So little has been told about the Temple and Sanctuary where Jesus attended the feast that perhaps a few words about this place will be of interest to my readers. As the pilgrims reached the place of the Temple, they found it necessary to ascend a mount crested by beautiful buildings symmetrically proportioned and gigantic enough to hold within their walls not fewer than 200,000 persons. The mount on which the structures stood rose abruptly from out of the valley, much like an island that rises out of the sea. And around it, in the greenness of the valley, was a mass of walls, palaces, houses, and streets reflecting the bright sunlight from the snowy marble and glittering gold. About 1,000 square feet of the mount was occupied by the Sanctuary and Temple. At the northwestern angle and connected with the main structure was the Castle of Antonia held by the Roman garrison. The lofty walls were pierced by massive gates. One unused gate known as the Tedi was on the north; on the east was the Susa Gate which opened on the arched roadway to the Mount of Olives. There were also the two Huldah Gates, which led by tunnels from the priest-suburb Ophel into the outer court. On the west were four other gates.

Within the gates the court was surrounded by double colonnades with benches here and there for those who resorted to prayer, or for conferences. The southern double colonnades, with a wide space between, were the most magnificent. The eastern colonnade was the most venerable, and was known as the ancient Solomons Porch. Entering the court from the bridge under the Tower of John, the pilgrim would pass along the southern colonnade to the eastern extremity over which rose a tower known as the Pinnacle, that is referred to in the history of the Temptation. From this lofty pinnacle, the priests each morning watched and announced the sunrise, and 450 feet beneath this tower yawned the Kedron Valley. Within these colonnaded areas were the meeting places of the first and lowest of the three sanhedrins, known as the Temple; the second or intermediate court of appeal usually held in what was called the Court of the Priests; and the highest of the courts known as the Great Sanhedrin, which was often referred to as the Hall of Hewn Square Stones.

Passing out of the colonnades and porches, one would enter the court of the Gentiles, or what the Jews called the Mount of the House, which was the widest on the west side. This was called the chol, or profane place, to which the Gentiles retired during the feast, and it was here also that the marketplace was located for the sale of various needful articles, along with the money changers. Beyond this Gentile section was a wall which marked a space beyond which no Gentile or person not strictly orthodox might proceed. Thus, the Gentiles— which included the Essenes, Nazarites, Nazarenes, and those who had not adopted the Jewish faith completely— had to assemble in a special place set aside for them.

The Sanctuary itself was on a higher terrace than the Court of the Priests. Twelve steps led up to its porch, and here in separate chambers was kept all that was necessary for the sacrificial services. A two-leaved gate opened into the Sanctuary which was divided into two parts. The holy place had the golden candlestick in the south, and the table of the Shewbread in the north, with the golden altar of incense between them. The mystical Veil referred to so often in the ceremonies of the mystery temples of Egypt, from which the Veil in the Jewish sanctuary was derived, concealed the entrance to the most Holy Place, which was an empty place in the Temple containing nothing but the piece of rock, the Eben Shethiyah, or foundation stone, which, according to tradition, covered the mouth of the pit, and on which the world was founded.

These few details cannot give an adequate idea of the vastness of the temple buildings, for all around the Sanctuary and colonnaded courts were various chambers and outbuildings which served different purposes connected with the services.

It was in the Gentile section of the entire enclosure that Joseph and his parents along with the others of their class assembled. It was necessary for the Gentiles to be present only for the first two days of the feast. On the third day, therefore, were held the special ceremonies for the strictly orthodox. Thus, for the rest of those in attendance, the third and following days were so-called half-holy days when it was lawful for all in attendance to return home if need be. It was at this time that Joseph was brought before the learned doctors immediately after the ceremony for examination and questioning. Undoubtedly there were many other children of his age present on this occasion, and undoubtedly the questioning was the same for all of them. Yet we are told that the answers which Joseph gave provoked intense interest in him, and that after the usual questions had been asked of all the children, and the parents and children had proceeded on their way, young Joseph was retained for further questioning and a special examination.

We are told in old records that on the last days of the feast, and when the actual feast itself had been celebrated and the usual ceremonies completed, it was customary for the doctors of the Temple-Sanhedrin to come out upon the terrace of the Temple and there preach or discuss certain doctrines and conduct a forum, or ask questions of those in whom they were especially interested. It was in such an audience as this, out on the terrace and informally conducted, that Joseph was found after his parents had started on their way home with their other children and missed him, according to the Christian version of the story.

As I have intimated, there was nothing extraordinary about the fact that one or more children had been retained by the doctors for special examination. Many writers of the life of Jesus, and many Christian authorities who have analyzed this incident in his life, have attempted to speculate upon the nature of the questions and answers which brought Jesus to the attention of these doctors. Some of them seem to have come to the conclusion that Jesus was taking part in one of the usual scientific classes designated as Kallah, at which time not only the doctors but the most analytical of the Jewish scholars discussed the doctrines, practices, customs, and habits of the Jewish religion. Such sessions required considerable preparation on the part of the lecturing rabbis or doctors and considerable Talmudic knowledge on the part of the attendants.

Many of these discussions dealt with the establishment of new rules and regulations, as well as the authoritative interpretation of Jewish rules. For instance, the great Hillel took part in a discussion in this court regarding the propriety of offering the Passover on the sabbath. By his great logic he proved that it was appropriate to do so and was honored for his services in this regard. It is hardly to be believed that the youthful Joseph could or would participate in such discussions as were common to the Kallah, even if the learned doctors had considered him old enough or wise enough to be present. Furthermore, the fact that Joseph was a Gentile, and not of the strictly orthodox faith, would have prevented him from participating in this class. And there is another consideration: these classes were held in the last month of summer (Elul) before the feast of the new year, and in the last winter month (Adar) immediately before the feast of the Passover, but it was in the spring that Joseph attended the paschal feast.

Another speculation on the part of some theological writers is to the effect that perhaps the parents of Joseph, realizing that the boy was about to enter into a new cycle of his life, informed him regarding his divine birth and Sonship and that he in turn presented these facts to the learned doctors at the temple and discussed the important principles involved. This explanation is more unsound than any other, for the simple reason that the young man was on his way to the Temple in obedience to a law which definitely outlined the procedure and the purpose of the occasion. Thus, it would have availed him nothing to have argued in behalf of his special appointment from on high. It is very doubtful, indeed, if the doctors assembled at the court would have permitted him to make any plea or explanation in behalf of his own divine place in life, and certainly they would not have set aside other tasks to listen to any such unique presentation.

We can thoroughly understand just what did happen when we examine the facts in the case and reenact the entire scene. The youths of Palestine were called upon to come to the Temple in their thirteenth year in order to partake of the paschal feast, and thereby acknowledge obedience to the Jewish religious law. It was a purely formal registration intended to supply the church with a complete list of those who had attained that age where they could be counted as of the faith or out of it. It was natural, therefore, that before being permitted to partake of the feast, every youngster was questioned in a categorical manner, being asked a list of questions, which would reveal the religious faith and ideas of each applicant. These questions had been asked for many years and were considered a standard catechism. The catechism for Gentiles was different from that used for those who were strictly orthodox and born in the faith. In other words, the questions asked of those who were assembled in the Gentile section of the court were quite different from those asked of the youths assembled in the orthodox section.

Our records indicate that Joseph had been somewhat prepared by his education at Carmel and by his contact with the orthodox Jews to answer the questions that would be asked of a Gentile registrant at the feast. It was the belief that only such questions would be asked of him as were asked of other youths, and that he would answer them in proper manner, that made his parents leave their child alone in the class for youths while they went into an adjoining building where adult Gentiles were given a different examination preparatory to participating formally in the paschal feast. It was probably the plan that after young Joseph had finished his examination and had entered the Sanctuary along with the other youths in the Gentile class, he would meet his parents out in the general court and proceed with them on their return.

According to the story, the parents proceeded homeward with their other children and with a large band of others who were returning to Galilee, and it was not until they were halfway home that they discovered that young Joseph was not in the large party of pilgrims. The fact that his absence was not noticed during the first pan of the trip plainly indicates that young Joseph was relied upon to take care of himself and to look after his own interests, and that the parents were more concerned with the care of the younger members of the family.

That young Joseph was well educated, unusually alert of mind, and in every sense well prepared to take care of himself is not only indicated by this incident but by what actually happened in Jerusalem. It is recorded that during the formal examination, while young Joseph was answering the categorical questions put to all of the youths, he gave explanations concerning some doctrinal points that involved a new angle, a broader insight, and a higher idealism regarding the mystical side of the theological points. This so surprised the learned doctors that they asked young Joseph to remain after the class had completed its work and after they had all partaken of the paschal feast. He was then called before a group of learned doctors of the Great Sanhedrin and further questioned, and he was then requested to remain within the temple grounds until the following day, when he would be interviewed by a court composed of the highest officials, high priests, and learned teachers. It was here that young Joseph was found on the third day. According to the records, I find that young Joseph did not put any particular emphasis upon his divine appointment as a Messenger of God, nor refer in any particular manner to the preordained mission of his life. He did reveal the fact that he was a special student of the Essenes at Mount Carmel, and that it was his intention to carry out the plans of the organization and visit the higher schools of instruction in foreign lands, including the academy and mystery school at Heliopolis. What this may have indicated to the minds of the learned Jewish doctors is not definitely stated. One question put to young Joseph does indicate that they immediately suspected him of being a selected leader for the future work of his community. However, this in itself would not have aroused any curiosity or particular interest on the part of these doctors, and evidently it did not antagonize them, inasmuch as they did not express any idea regarding young Joseph's apparent refusal to do otherwise than accept merely the formal commandment making him an adopted Jew of the country.

Their surprise and keen interest centered around the unusual insight that young Joseph had regarding religious, theological, and mystical principles, and his very clear exposition of spiritual laws. For this reason they were amazed at his "combinative insight," or unusual spiritual intelligence, and "discerning answers." If young Joseph had revealed to these doctors some of the principles taught by the Essenes and was the apt student which the organization records in its reports, then he must have astounded these doctors who were learned only in the traditional teachings of their own faith and unaccustomed to the newer and higher ideas taught in the Essenian schools.

Young Joseph did reveal, however, in very positive terms, that in a few months he would finish the preliminary courses of instruction at the school at Carmel, and that in accordance with the rules and regulations of the organization, he would leave Galilee early in the fall to go to the schools in foreign lands, and that he would not return to Palestine for many years. Thus he explained his reasons for not doing more than formally obeying the command to appear for registration and not promising to attend the synagogues regularly or becoming a true disciple of the Jewish faith. The fact that he had been circumcised made him potentially a Jew so far as fundamental preparation for admission into the Jewish faith as a Gentile was concerned, but there was no way by which the Jewish clerics could force this young man, or any other of the Gentile youths, to become an orthodox follower of the Jewish religion.

Young Joseph was not the first ambitious youth of the country who had gone to Egypt and other lands to acquire a higher education or to make more successful contacts with the larger things in life, and the fact of his determination to travel for the betterment of his education did not cause any surprise in the minds of these doctors. However, his entire attitude and the free and easy manner in which he spoke of his plans did surprise these authorities who were accustomed to having the youths of the land show them greater consideration and less independence.

So when the parents of young Joseph found him sitting in the midst of a group of learned doctors and succeeded in calling him aside and reminded him of their concern and sorrow when they missed him, he may have made the reply which Christian literature has made very famous, and which our records do not reveal at all. But if he did say that he had been very busy attending to his Fathers business, we can understand that he was referring to the entire scheme of his life. Certainly he must have felt that he was about his Father's business when he was making plain to his inquisitors the nature of his beliefs and convictions, the reason for his contemplated journeys to other lands, and his inability to become a devout attendant at the synagogues in Palestine.

After young Joseph and his parents returned to their home village, he was sent again to the school on Mount Carmel, there to live and finish his term of preliminary instruction.

27

Chapter 10

JESUS ENTERS THE SECRET PRIESTHOOD
LITTLE IS INTIMATED in the Christian Gospels about the life of Jesus between the time of his appearance before the learned doctors in Jerusalem and the beginning of his mission in Palestine. In fact, the first revelation regarding the preparation of Jesus for his work as a Son of God is in connection with his baptism in the River Jordan. We are told that at this time Jesus came out of Galilee and permitted himself to be known to the public.

Certainly the baptism of Jesus could not have been the beginning of his preparation for the ministry; and most certainly more preparation than this was required to carry on the work which he efficiently conducted for so many years. I have intimated in previous parts of this book why it is unreasonable to believe that Jesus required no preparation for his ministry, and I have tried to show that his whole life demonstrated deep study, careful preparation, and unusual guidance during his youth.

We now approach a period in his life that is not only interesting because it is generally unknown to the students of Christian doctrines, but is highly significant in the light of the work which he accomplished during his lifetime.

According to the Essenian records, young Joseph completed his official schooling early in the fall, when he was still in his thirteenth year. With all of his precociousness and brilliant mind, he was not permitted to shorten the usual period of study and preparation in the School of the Prophets at Carmel. Therefore, we must presume that he was given careful attention and tutored by those who added such special subjects to his instructions as would have kept him engaged in his attainment of knowledge until the prescribed time had come for his transfer to other teachers and other schools.

The records also outline very clearly and definitely the incidents of his life from the time of the transfer from Carmel until he was ready for his great mission. The details of these incidents in his life are too exhaustive and unimportant to present in toto in a book of this size and character, but the essential points and the interesting incidents may be outlined as follows:

According to the instructions sent to the school at Carmel from the Supreme Temple at Heliopolis, the young avatar was to complete his education by a thorough study of the ancient religions and teachings of the various sects and creeds most influential in the development of civilization. In other words, he was to become familiar with the tenets of the so-called heathen religions before taking up the study of the development of the pagan beliefs and rites into the higher principles and creeds taught in the mystery schools of Egypt.

In modern times, students preparing for the ministry must become familiar with comparative religions, but they are able to do this in great universities, where the sacred books and writings of the ancient religions are expounded, analyzed, and carefully digested before the modern forms of theology are undertaken. Students do not have to leave their own lands and journey into distant places in order to contact and become acquainted with the ancient religions or schools of ethics.

In the time of which I am writing, however, it was considered absolutely necessary for students of religion or philosophy to journey to the very seat of each of the ancient religions, where they might have access to copies of the authentic versions of each religion and an opportunity to live among the people, thus becoming intimately acquainted with the rituals, rites, and practices of the tenets. Many of the great avatars in the past had journeyed to distant places for this purpose, and it was in this way that knowledge of the various ancient teachings had become universally disseminated.

So young Joseph was placed in the charge of two magi, who came to Carmel for the purpose of conducting the youth to his first distant school and place of experience. The records show that Joseph was permitted to spend about a week with his parents in Galilee, while the magi made their preparations and held various consultations with the officials at the Carmel school. They also instructed the parents of Joseph as to what they should expect and what they should do in his absence. The records further state that when Joseph and the magi started from Galilee, a special ceremony of the Essenes was held in one of their small assembly places. Then, without attracting unnecessary attention, the magi and the boy proceeded with a number of others who were going a short distance of the way, in a caravan, by the shortest route to Jagannath. This city was located on the east coast of India, and its present-day name is Puri. It had been the center of pure Buddhism for many centuries; and on a mountain near the outlying districts of the town there was a monastery or school containing many of the ancient Buddhist writings and the most learned instructors of Buddhas doctrines. It required nearly a year for the magi, young Joseph, and others, who joined the caravan en route, to reach this point in India, while the magi continued to instruct Joseph. During their many trials and tribulations they pointed out to him the sufferings of humanity, the weaknesses and strengths of the peoples ideals, and the popular fallacies of the day.

According to the records, young Joseph remained a little over a year in this monastery school and became thoroughly familiar with the ancient teachings and the evolved rituals of the Buddhist faith. The principal teacher of young Joseph at this time was one known as Lamaas, to whom young Joseph took such a great liking that later in his life he sent for Lamaas to come and unite with the Essenes in Palestine.

When it came time for young Joseph to leave the monastery at Jagannath, visits were made to the valley of the Ganges with a several months's stop at Benares. We must bear in mind that the great monastery and world headquarters of the G.W.B. had not yet been established at a spot in Tibet; for if it had been, Joseph and his magi would have undoubtedly proceeded to this place and remained there for a considerable time. In Benares, young Joseph had an opportunity to pursue the study of ethics, natural law, languages, and similar subjects constituting the offerings of several of the great schools there which were renowned for their culture and learning. It was in Benares that young Joseph became greatly interested in the Hindu method of healing, and he took a short course in the Hindu principles under Udraka, who was reputed to be the greatest of the Hindu healers.

After a visit to other parts of India, merely for the purpose of contacting the art, law, and culture of the peoples, Joseph returned to the monastery at Jagannath, where he remained for two more years. His advancement in the subjects being taught was such that he was appointed a teacher in a small town called Katak, and this gave him his first opportunity to become familiar with the art of teaching or instructing by the use of parables or stories.

As a result of his contact with eminent teachers and the learned of Benares, young Joseph was visited by a high priest from Lahore. It appears from the records that he had already introduced new ideas and truly mystical principles in his discourses and instructions to children, and these appealed to the most learned of his hearers, but aroused the antagonism of the unlearned and strictly orthodox Hindus. Therefore, early in his life he learned what it meant to have enemies as well as followers. The high priest from Lahore tried to persuade young Joseph to change his teachings slightly and at the same time cease his journeys among the lower castes and common people. Here was Joseph's first temptation to hold himself aloof from the common touch and to change his attitude so as to appeal to the aristocracy and the influential. However, young Joseph refused to listen to the petitions of the high priests, and he even refused to accept gifts that were offered.

It was while he was thus drinking the bitter draughts of life, that Joseph received the sad news that his father in Galilee had passed on, and that his mother was grieving, and none was able to comfort her. Messengers informed him that no word had come from him and that his mother was unable to learn of his whereabouts. Even though she had been informed by the Essenes that silence on the part of young Joseph had been predicted, and that he was safe, she could not be consoled. It was at this time that young Joseph expressed himself for the first time in definite words, which were recorded and are still preserved. According to the several translations of the message which he sent by the Essenian messengers to his mother, it read as follows:

Beloved mother: Be not grieved, for all is well for father as with you. He has completed his present work here on earth and has done so nobly. None in any walk of life can charge him with deceit, dishonesty, nor wrong intention. In his period of life here he has completed many great tasks and is gone from our midst truly prepared to solve the problems that await him in the future. Our God, the Father of all of us, is with him now as [God] was with him heretofore; but even now the Heavenly Hosts guard his footsteps and protect him on his way. Therefore, why should you weep and suffer? Tears will not conquer your grief, and your sorrow cannot be vanquished by any emotion of your heart or mind.

Let your soul be busy in meditation and contact with him who is gone, and if thou art not idle, there will be no time for grief. When grief throbs through the heart, and anguish causes you pain, permit yourself to rise to higher planes and indulge in the ministry of love. Your ministry has always been that of love, and in the brotherhood thou canst find many opportunities to answer the call of the world for more love. Therefore, let the past remain the past. Rise above the cares of earthly things and give your life to those who still live with us here on earth. When your life is done, you will find it again in the morning sun, or even in the evening dew, as in the song of birds, the perfume of the flowers, and the mystic lights of the stars at night. For it will not be long before your problems and toils here on earth will be solved also, and when all is counted and arranged you will be ready for greater fields of effort and prepared to solve the greater problems of the soul. Try then, to be content until I come to you soon and bring to you richer gifts than any that you have ever seen and greater than those made of gold or precious stones. I am sure that my brothers will care for you and supply your needs, and I am always with you in mind and spirit.

Your son, Joseph

This letter and other writings, written during the years which followed and which have been carefully preserved and recorded, plainly indicate the rapid development of his mind and the marvelous comprehension he had of cosmic laws and principles.

It is stated in some ancient records that after Joseph had completed the studies of the Buddhistic teachings and the Hindu doctrines in India, he journeyed to Lhasa in Tibet. While still in India, a messenger came to Joseph with some manuscripts from a Buddhist temple in Lhasa, sent by Mengtse, who was considered the greatest of all the Buddhist sages. For a considerable period messengers from Lhasa brought manuscripts to young Joseph, and it was this intercourse and the effects it had upon his life that may have caused him to journey to Lhasa personally. However, when Joseph was ready to leave Jagannath, his journey took him westward toward Persia, where, in the city of Persepolis, arrangements had been made for his further studies. This was one of the ancient cities of the kings and the center of the learned magi of that country who were known as Hor, Lun, and Mer. One of these magi, a very old man, was one of the three who had visited the infant at the time of his birth in the Essenian grotto and had brought to him gifts from the monastery of Persia.

Great homage was paid to Joseph by these magi and by the priests of the temple. Other learned individuals from various sections of Persia came to Persepolis and remained there as instructors and students during the time of Joseph's education. It is even recorded that at the close of each day when the instructors had finished the day's lesson, they asked Joseph to become their teacher and inform them of the higher principles which he seemed to comprehend through inspiration.

It was here that Joseph finally made plain to the elders that the greatest instruction he had to give was that which he had obtained in the silence after meditating upon some important law given to him in the course of his reading and studying. Thus, Joseph established a system of entering the silence which became an important feature in later mystical methods. It was in this city, also, that Joseph demonstrated considerable healing power. After months of analysis of the power within his being and a careful study of the principles involved, he revealed to his elders his belief that the faith or mental attitude and attunement on the part of the patients had a considerable effect upon the results. This laid the foundation for the later teachings of the secret conclaves of the disciples of Jesus—inner or psychic attunement and mental preparations are necessary in all forms of spiritual healing.

After a year spent in Persia, Joseph and his guides proceeded to the Euphrates. Here he contacted the greatest sages of Assyria as well as magi from other lands who came to see him and hear him speak; for he had already attracted great attention as an interpreter of the spiritual laws in a more understandable, mystical manner. Joseph spent considerable time in the cities and towns of Chaldea and in the lands between the Tigris and the Euphrates. His healing powers and methods were becoming so rapidly perfected that it is recorded that multitudes in these lands were benefited by his methods. It was also about this time that the magi who were his guides informed him that the development of the ability to heal would be one of the tests in his final examination of preparedness for his ultimate mission.

From this country Joseph and the guides journeyed through the ruined Babylon, and spent some time in examining the fallen temples, ruined gates, and the empty palaces. It was here that he became familiar with the trials and tribulations of the early tribes of Israel when they were held in captivity in Babylon, and he saw where Daniel and the Hebrew children had experienced their great tests. He was unquestionably impressed with the sins of pagans and the error of ancient beliefs.

Then Joseph and his guides journeyed to Greece, where he came in contact with some of the Athenian philosophers. He was under the personal direction and care of Apollonius, who opened up the ancient records of Grecian lore for him. In this country Joseph attracted unusual attention among the wise and the magi, and they implored him to remain a long time; but his itinerary had been definitely decided upon, and in a few months he sailed from Grecian shores for Alexandria.

He stayed but a short time at Alexandria, just long enough to visit some of the ancient shrines and to be entertained by the special messengers who went there to greet him. He was taken immediately thereafter to the city of Heliopolis and settled in a private home specially arranged for him. He had several servants, a beautiful garden, and a personal attendant whose records as a scribe would place him today in the category of a personal secretary.

Very shortly after his arrival in Heliopolis, Jesus was approached by representatives of the pagan priesthood of Egypt, who had heard of his teachings and his demonstrations of mystical power and disapproved of them. Once again he learned to drink of the bitters of life through many trials and tribulations which would have tempted the average person to accede to the advice of the priesthood and resort to hypocrisy and deceit in regard to his purposes and intentions.

It was at this point in his life that Joseph began his preparatory initiations for the entrance into the higher grades of the G.W.B. I will treat these in my next chapter, for the details are worthy of complete presentation.

28

Chapter 11

JESUS ATTAINS MASTERSHIP
IN ORDER TO understand the advancement of Jesus through the various grades of the priest-hood leading to mastership, it is necessary to explain the operation of the G.W.B. in which he became an initiate.

The G.W.B. referred to so often in the preceding chapters was a nonsectarian organization formed in a primitive way by the ancestors of Amenhotep IV, pharaoh of Egypt, who became better known in philosophical literature as Akhnaton. We do not definitely know which of these ancestors was the first to proclaim the foundation of the organization, but we do know that Thothmes III established many of the important rules and regulations for the conduct of the organization, and that these regulations were in effect for many centuries.

In one of the Rosicrucian records, we find that at the close of his reign as pharaoh of Egypt in 1447 B.C., there were thirty nine men and women constituting the high council of the secret organization. The council meetings were held in one of the halls of the temple at Karnak in Luxor where Thothmes III had erected two obelisks on which were carved the famous cartouche which became the seal of the G.W.B. and which is used in Egypt and America today as the seal of the organization known as the Rosicrucian Order. In establishing this cartouche as the seal of the organization, we find the following words written in the record in regard to its use: "In testimony of the great work of our teacher (Master) to be forever a mark of honor and loyalty."

The son and grandson of Thothmes III sponsored the continuation of the secret group and permitted it to increase in size and activity. In 1378 B.C., was born Akhnaton, the great-grandson of Thothmes III. He became the great reorganizer and founder of the present rules and regulations of the worldwide organization known as the G.W.B., which developed out of the secret organization established in ancient times.

The original plan of the secret organization was to bring the wisest men and women in Egypt together, and especially the most advanced of the magi, for the purpose of discussing, analyzing, recording, and preserving the great knowledge that constituted the light of the world. Egypt had become the center of the world's culture and scientific knowledge, as is attested by the remarkable attainments made by her people under the leadership of the learned individuals in the sciences generally. To Egypt came students from all parts of the world, to obtain the highest education and to contact the mystery schools, as they were called, under the direction of this secret society.

Akhnaton was the reincarnation of one of the previous great avatars and became what historians call the world's first great individual. He, too, had a great message for the world, and during his short lifetime he accomplished more for the advancement of philosophy, religion, and ethics than any individual preceding him. It was he who began a very strenuous attack upon the heathen priesthoods of Egypt which held the masses in slavery, and it was he who established the world's first monotheistic religion, for Akhnaton declared that there were not many gods, but only One, "the ever living, sole God." In his doctrines, which he introduced into the G.W.B., he laid the foundation for the present- day monotheism and for most of the doctrines and creeds used in the Christian and Hebrew religions.

It was while Akhnaton was pharaoh that the children of Israel dwelt in Egypt and the leaders of those tribes became initiates of the G.W.B. It was also at this time that Moses, as one of the initiates, became acquainted with the fundamentals of the religion which he afterward modified to present to those who followed him out of Egypt into Palestine. It was also to Akhnaton that Moses made his appeal for aid in taking the tribes of Israel out of Egypt, and it was through the aid thus given by Akhnaton and by the G.W.B. in secrecy that the tribes of Israel evaded the heathen priesthood and had a safe journey.

As stated in an earlier part of this book, branches of the G.W.B. were established under various names in many parts of the world during the first ten centuries before Christ. The original body of members in Egypt became the international council or supreme body maintaining the name of the G.W.B. and eventually adopting the rose cross emblem as their esoteric symbol. But the branches established in various parts of the world were permitted to adopt such names as were significant in the various languages or symbolical to the peoples with whom they had to deal. Thus it was that a large branch formed at Heliopolis adopted the name of Essenes, which name was later used by the followers in the northern part of Palestine; whereas in Greece the name of Therapeutae was used, and other names in other places. All these branches, however, used the same seals and symbols, adhered to the same general rules and regulations, and paid allegiance to the supreme body known as the G.W.B. in Egypt.

Out of the organizations monasteries, schools, and temples, and its branches, came most of the famous philosophers, teachers, priests, and avatars of the future. Today we find that in the branches of the organization known as the Rosicrucian Order, which name has become practically the exclusive worldly name for the organization, there are students in preparation for the ministry, for positions as teachers and professors in colleges, those who are to become eminent physicians in various schools of therapeutics, including medicine and surgery, and those who are also preparing for research work in the various fields of science. We also find in the membership, hundreds of thousands of men and women who are students of the teachings of the Rosicrucian Order, because of the personal benefit they derive and the assistance the organization gives them through private teachings and instruction for the betterment of their living, the attainment of personal evolution, and the awakening of those latent or dormant faculties which enable them to achieve the highest degree of success and happiness in their individual careers.

Therefore, it was natural that the new avatar should be one of this organization, as had been most of the avatars in preceding centuries. It was also perfectly logical and reasonable for this young Son of God to have his footsteps directed toward the organizations great schools and teachers in Egypt, where he might complete his preparations and receive his final instructions before entering upon his divine mission.

Before initiates of the G.W.B. could go out into the world and proclaim the doctrines and teachings which would enlighten civilization and bring about the gradual evolution of humanity, they had to be tested and tried in such ways as would not only prove to the entire organization their worthiness, but would also make them familiar with the tests and trials they would inevitably face during their mission.

Thus we find Joseph now at the threshold of his final preparation and ready for the symbolical tests and initiations leading to the degree and attainment of mastership which would qualify him to go out into the world and fulfill the mission for which he had been cosmically and divinely ordained.

When Jesus was ready for his entrance into the organization's supreme college and monastery at Heliopolis, he found that the first requirement called for three months of meditation, prayer, and study in the quiet of his own home, during which time many of the organizations eminent masters would contact him in the cosmic or psychic sense, through mental processes.

The records show that he was surrounded, as we have stated, with every comfort and convenience, and for his study he was given many of the rarest manuscripts containing the texts of ancient doctrines and creeds. Then came the first of the tests. It is stated that one night at the midnight hour, a door in his chamber was opened, and a priest in Oriental garb came to Joseph and pleaded with him that he abandon his intention of staying in Egypt and receiving the authority of the G.W.B., because his mission and plans were antagonistic to the priesthood of Egypt, and the priesthood was plotting to take his life or to imprison him.

The priest offered various methods whereby Joseph might secretly and easily leave Egypt and return safely to Palestine. Young Joseph had seen many evidences of the enmity which his presence in Egypt had aroused, and as I have said before, he was drinking of the bitter cup. For this reason the pleading and offering of the priest were certainly tempting. But young Joseph absolutely refused to abandon his plans or to change his decision. Joseph summed up his argument with this statement: "I shall not bargain with deceit, nor sell my soul for the safety of my body. I shall deceive no one, and I will be no partner of hypocrisy. Return to your people and tell them that I shall remain true to God and to myself."

His decision was reported to the organizations high authorities, and Joseph was commanded to appear before them. Then the hierophant placed his hand on Joseph's head and gave him a scroll on which was written just one word, Sincerity. Joseph knew that this had been a test of his sincerity and that he had yielded not to temptation.

Some weeks later another messenger called upon Joseph in his home and presented a very interesting story. This messenger claimed that he had at one time been in the same position as Joseph, and he had suffered all the trials and enmity of the priesthood of Egypt while remaining steadfast in his determination to become a master. He claimed that he had attained high degrees in the organization and had finally been admitted to their great ceremonies and to their secret conclaves. But then he had found that all of the work was corruption and that their rites were sacrificial, in which innocent children, women, men, and animals were burned as offerings to false gods. He had finally escaped and now urged Joseph to think well of the future and to stop before it was too late.

When Joseph questioned him as to how he had gained access to his chamber, the man replied that as a trusted priest of the organization he knew of passageways and doors that permitted him to enter any of the organizations structures. Joseph then accused the man of being a traitor and said that he would refuse to listen to one whose hands were not clean and who could not show a higher purpose than he had shown. The man disappeared, and again Joseph was brought before the hierophant who once more placed his hand upon Josephs head and handed a scroll to him which contained but one word, Justice. And Joseph learned that this was another test and that he had passed it successfully.

About a month later, another priest approached him one afternoon, when he was in the midst of meditation in the quietness of his sanctum. This priest began to comment on the grandeur and richness of the rooms in which Joseph dwelt, and he called the attention of Joseph to the fact that the great teachers in Egypt had undoubtedly provided these luxurious surroundings for Joseph because to them Joseph was the greatest of them all, and that the healing Joseph had accomplished in foreign lands, the wonderful interpretation he had given in answer to questions asked in India and Persia had proved that he was the greatest philosopher, the greatest mystic, and the greatest teacher in all the world.

Therefore, he urged that Joseph should not submit to the dictates of the G.W.B., but go out into the world at once and organize a priesthood of his own which would overthrow all others and bring triumphant victory to him personally. It is recorded that this man made eloquent pleas to young Joseph and pointed out to him the rosy path to fame and popular acclaim, bringing to him wealth, honor, and unlimited power. The man left the presence of Joseph at the psychological moment of his beautiful presentation, and for many days Joseph wrestled with the idea that had been implanted in his mind. But always there came from within the voice of the Divine Self pointing out clearly the duty for which he had been cosmically ordained.

Finally Joseph sent a message to the man and stated that he was thankful for the contest that had raged within him and for the victory which had come to the better self, and that he wanted not glory, fame, nor wealth, but only an opportunity to serve and to keep the faith while life was in his body. Once again he was called before the hierophant, and this time a scroll was handed to him upon which was written the one word, Faith. And Joseph learned that this was another test of his faith and that he had passed it successfully.

Thus Joseph completed the first of the three preliminary degrees of initiation, which were really degrees of test and trial, before being admitted into the organizations important fourth degree. Having passed these tests, and further examinations which were held before the conclave of high priests, he was finally honored with the title of Master and admitted into the highest circle as a duly prepared and qualified Master of the G.W.B.

This title of Master was always used by the Essenes in speaking of Jesus throughout his entire ministry, when the conversations dealt with his public affairs or reference was made in general conversation aside from any of his special activities as a divine Son of God. The title of Master was also used by many of the Jews who greatly admired Jesus for his work among them and especially for the valuable instructions which he gave. It was always reverently used by those who understood its real meaning, just as it is reverently used by the Rosicrucians today when they speak of the Great Master Jesus.

29

Chapter 12

JESUS ATTAINS CHRISTHOOD
HAVING ATTAINED THE degree of Mastership in the
G.W.B. placed Joseph among the most learned of the high priests and second only to the hierophant of the organization.

This entitled him to attend the highest conclaves, to have access to the most sacred and sublime ceremonies, to indulge in the transcendental experiences at certain cosmic periods of the year, and to attune himself by the highest spiritual laws with the Consciousness of God.

It may be argued that since Jesus was divinely ordained, divinely conceived, and divinely born, and predetermined to be the Son of God and the Savior of the world, that no earthly power and certainly no earthly council could either grant or fail to grant him the privilege of such attunement with the Consciousness of God. This is unquestionably true. Nowhere in the records with which I am dealing and nowhere in the present-day teachings of the Rosicrucians is it intimated that if Jesus had not passed through the preparation and experiences outlined by the G.W.B., he would have been unable to attune himself just as completely with the Divine Consciousness or become conscious of the Godhood or Christhood within him.

From the very hour of his birth all of the magi, high priests, and most learned advisers of the organization were his inferiors in divine attunement and soul preparation for the great mission. It was no presumption on the part of these great leaders to perform their time-honored duty of accepting Joseph as a neophyte and giving him every one of the tests and trials and offering him every opportunity for development as had been offered to the greatest among them. Nor did Joseph himself consider the attitude assumed by the organization in treating him as a neophyte, and as one who had to be prepared, a failure of recognition, on their part, of his superior position among them. We shall see later on that even after Joseph had completed all the preparation that the organization prescribed for him, and they had acknowledged him ready for his mission in life, he voluntarily offered himself for a final act of preparation in the knowledge that all these things were necessary for the work he desired to accomplish and which had been cosmically planned for him.

Naturally, I wish it were possible for me to outline here the further initiations, ceremonies, and steps of preparation through which Joseph passed during the years in which he remained in Egypt. These things are never revealed to those who are not high initiates; and Jesus himself, during his entire mission, revealed them to no one but his apostles, whom he carefully selected and whom he constituted as his sacred council and initiated as he had been initiated. I hardly think that any of my readers expect these things to be published in any book of this kind or in any book for the general public; and

I am sure that the most learned and reasonable of my readers would doubt the authenticity of any printed record which claimed to contain such details.

It is possible, however, to speak of the last and final stage of his preparation for the ministry, which was held in the chambers of the Great Pyramid now known as the Pyramid of Cheops.

Much has been said in various books and magazine articles in recent years about the chambers and secret rooms of the Great Pyramid, and space in this volume does not permit even a brief explanation of the intricate arrangement of the passageways and ancient chambers that are built within and beneath this great structure. The average tourist to Egypt sees the several pyramids that are grouped almost as a unit just outside of Cairo and close to the famous Sphinx. These tourists are generally told that the Great Pyramid was built as a tomb, and that it is a solid structure built over a burial chamber. Even the most ingenious of the guides who escort the tourists to the pyramids refuse to admit that there are secret chambers and ceremonial rooms within this unique building. However, during my recent visit to the Pyramid, and while in the company of several high officers of the Rosicrucian Order of Egypt and a number of officers of the Order in America, we were permitted to enter these secret rooms and to verify the facts contained in our records.

It may be surprising to my readers to know that in the ancient times, or in the times with which we are dealing, the entrance way to the principal ceremonial rooms of the Pyramid was not through any doorways in the Pyramid itself, but through a secret passageway built between the two huge paws of the Sphinx. These paws rest upon a high foundation wall, forming two sides of a court in front of the Sphinx, in the center of which stood an altar. Back of this altar, still partly in ruins, and just beneath the breast of the Sphinx, was the well-guarded, secret doorway, opening only by application of certain secret contrivances which only a few knew. It led under the sands and the foundation walls of the Pyramid to long subterranean passageways under the Sphinx and to the great reception hall far below the surface surrounding the Pyramid.

It was to the outer court in front of the Sphinx that the neophytes who were well prepared and deemed worthy of the secret of the entrance way to the Pyramids were brought and given their first induction into the mysteries of the higher degrees. Such ceremonies usually occurred at midnight, when the neophytes and the few who conducted the outer-court ceremony wended their way separately to this sacred spot, guarded and protected by trusted sisters and brothers who remained at distant points from the Sphinx and the Pyramid as watchers and sentinels. Only those who once actually passed through the ceremony within the Pyramid knew of the secret entrance way and the existence of the rooms and passageways.

Joseph was brought before this outer court of the Sphinx and clothed in purple robes during the preliminary ceremony held at midnight. At the completion of the ceremony, he was escorted through the subterranean passageway to the reception room beneath the Pyramid. After further ceremony here in this room, the sublime ceremony of being raised to the highest pinnacle of initiation began. This was performed by escorting Joseph up various inclines to the several different levels within the Pyramid, on each of which was a small chamber.

After having reached the highest of these chambers, practically in the center of the Pyramid, the final ceremony took place. During this the royal diadem was placed upon the head of Joseph, indicating that he was no longer a neophyte, nor even a peer among the Masters of the G.W.B., but the greatest of them all. For over an hour a pontifical ceremony was conducted, culminating in a period of silence and meditation while Joseph knelt before the altar. Then a great light filled the chamber, which was otherwise lighted only by candles and three torches. A white dove descended in the light and rested on the head of Joseph while the hierophant rose, and various bells in the chambers beneath began pealing the great announcement to the world. A slight figure rising behind the hierophant like an angelic being commanded Joseph to rise while the voice of this being proclaimed: "This is Jesus the Christ; arise!" And all within the chamber united in saying "Amen." The symbol to the left is called in Christian mysticism the Monogram of Christ. It is also often used as a symbol of Christianity. The author of this book traced this monogram on the face of a number of tombs in the catacombs at Rome and in some of the ancient carvings of Egypt. Early Christian missionaries were misled by the discovery of this symbol in foreign lands, and believed it indicated the presence of earlier Christian missionaries. The symbol was in use long before Christianity adopted it. It was the original monogram of Osiris. The sacred banner of Constantine called the Labarum, on which was placed the sign by which he was to conquer, was inscribed with the sacred monogram. It was also the mystical sign of Jupiter Ammon. The monogram had a mystical origin in the mystery teachings of the Egyptian Mystery

Schools, and it has been found engraved on a medal of Ptolemy, king of Cyrene. An identical monogram was also found on the coins of Herod the Great, issued before the Christian era. The Roman Catholic Encyclopedia claims that the X and the P are the first two letters of a Greek work meaning "Christ." (The letter R in Greek looks like P; X is the English Ch.) This authority also admits that the monogram was used in pre-Christian periods as a mystical emblem. The monogram composed of X.RN., shown on the right, is another symbol of the title "Our Lord Jesus Christ."

The foregoing is but a very brief, greatly condensed outline of the final ceremony. The complete details present one of the most picturesque and elaborate settings ever recorded in the organization's secret writings, and it is known that no such ceremony has ever occurred since then.

As the ceremony ended, the officers and members of the high council surrounded Joseph, who had now attained the name Jesus and had been acknowledged the Christ, and paid homage to him and proclaimed him the incarnation of the Word, or the Living Logos. Then followed the ceremonial march to the chambers below, where the first of the Lords suppers was held as a symbolical feast.

Messengers were sent the next day, in all directions from Egypt to every land in which the organizations branches were located, to proclaim the coming of the Savior and the announcement of his mission of redemption. Among these was one John from the Essenian community in Palestine, who had been a student at the schools in Egypt, preparing for his mission in life. He was known to be the reincarnation of Elijah, and he was sent to Palestine, the land in which, as Elijah, he had once before served as an avatar and had attended the monastery at Carmel. It was his mission, like that of the other messengers sent to other lands, to proclaim the coming of the Christ. And so all the peoples who were ready for the coming of the Lord

were duly notified, and the great work of Jesus the Christ began.

30

Chapter 13

THE MYSTIC BEGINNING OF CHRIST'S MISSION

THEN JOHN REACHED Palestine he appeared in public in the most humble clothing and with great humility. His work was to announce among the lowly and the humble in spirit the coming of the great Redeemer. He presented an entirely new idea inasmuch as he preached the doctrine of baptism for redemption or regeneration.

It may not be out of place here to state that baptism, or the immersion in water and the use of water for purification in a symbolical or cosmic sense, was introduced into the rites and ceremonies of the G.W.B. in Egypt by one who was known as El-Moria. He was one of the great avatars in the organizations early days, and he had learned through meditation and Cosmic Illumination that water would cleanse in a cosmic sense as well as a physical sense. It was through his learned discussions before the organizations high council in this regard that pools of purified water were introduced in front of every altar in the mystery temples of Egypt and other lands.

It was this same great avatar who first introduced public baptism for spiritual regeneration by holding such ceremonies at Lake Moeris, in the Fayum district of Egypt, around which centered one of the earliest of the advanced civilizations of Egypt.

Recently I made a trip to this place in company with others of our Order. There I saw the beautiful lake which is still a mystery to those who have tried to discover the source of its beautiful water, far from the Nile and in the very heart of desert lands. Here many of us reenacted in the utmost sublimity the early form of baptism and symbolically celebrated the ancient rite. According to the records of the Rosicrucian Order, this is the first time that scores of men and women united in one reverential party to participate in this ceremonial rite since the days before Christ, and of course it was the first time in the history of the world that such a group of persons from America ever received baptism at the shore of Lake Moeris. For hundreds of years this beautiful lake has never been visited by European or American tourists, and for a thousand years its history and its connection with the Christian rite of baptism has remained unknown except to those in the Rosicrucian Order and those in the high branches of the G.W.B. in Tibet, India, and Egypt.

John was looked upon by the Jewish people as one of the sturdy race of Judah. Since he came from the wilderness into their midst in pious clothing, they looked upon him as an ascetic. His camel's hair cloak was a symbol of penitence, and his words were those of an ancient prophet. John picked out the banks of the Jordan as his special territory for the work he wished to do. Appealing, as he intended, to the lowly and the humble, he attracted the attention of multitudes, who seemed to drink in his words and find hope in his proclamations.

In selecting the valley of the Jordan, he had chosen a place that seemed to be separated from the rest of the world and filled with terrifying contrasts to the rest of Palestine. Around about was the rough land of volcanic formation and volcanic destruction. In fact, the part of the shores selected by John was known as the Sea of Solitude, but it was here that the Essenes had originally held such wonderful ceremonies and had established one of their first communities. It was truly holy ground to John. John's message was that which most of the Jews had hoped to hear in their lifetimes—the coming of the Messiah. But he warned them that they must prepare for this coming and prepare for it in a true spirit of repentance. His earnestness, and the power with which he proclaimed that only the repentant, the purified, and those who were purged of all sin would see the Messiah, shocked the holy ones and antagonized the strictly orthodox.

From all parts of Palestine came those who wanted to hear the message of John and witness his strange ceremonies in the waters of the river. About this time word came from other lands that other prophets were foretelling the coming of the Messiah. Over and over was repeated the ancient prophecy that out of the land of Egypt would come the Son of God.

Camps were built around the lake where earnest souls remained for weeks, many of them hoping that the Messiah would appear in the midst of the thousands who gathered there on feast days. A number asked permission to form a group to take up the work of John and to serve under him in the beginning of a holy war. Rumors of this plan reached the rulers of Palestine, and the priests at Jerusalem began to feel uneasy at the excitement of the populace. Other conditions in Palestine seemed to indicate that a great crisis was at hand. Tiberius, now seventy-four years of age, was indulging in such debauchery at Capri as was rapidly hastening his transition. Pontius Pilate was continuing his persecution of the Jews and becoming more furious. It was in the midst of these conditions that Jesus the Christ quietly and without recognition returned to Galilee and greeted his mother, brothers, and sisters in their little home. He awaited patiently the hour when the first message was to be given. To Jesus came the reports of the work being done by John, and how John was insisting that all who were worthy of regeneration and redemption must be baptized by water. Finally Jesus decided that he should set the great example among the Gentiles of Galilee by proceeding to the Jordan and submitting to John's baptism.

And so it was that Jesus entered the throngs of those standing by the shores of the Jordan listening to the preachments of John. Here he heard the voice of John thundering, "Repent ye, prepare ye the way of the Lord, make his path straight." As he baptized each applicant, he made his famous prophecy of the coming of the Messiah, saying: "I baptize you with water only, but he will baptize you with fire."

Jesus stepped forward, and he and John faced each other for the first time since they had met in one of the conclaves in Egypt. Instantly John knew that he was in the presence of the Christ, and he folded his arms across his chest with the right hand over his heart, and the left hand over his right breast, making the salutation common among the Essenes. Jesus replied by making a similar sign. Words passed between John and Jesus which have been variously recorded, but which constituted the formal recognition on the part of John that was due the great Master before him. Then Jesus stepped into the water and submitted voluntarily to the baptism. As stated in the preceding chapter, this act clearly shows that Jesus recognized the necessity of formal preparation and ceremonial procedure, even though he knew of the divine, cosmic appointment of his Messiahship.

It is one of the important doctrines of the G.W.B. that spiritual illumination and Cosmic Consciousness enter our being only when we are ready. There is an ancient belief based upon the mystic teachings of the Orient that when each individual is ready for the coming of the Master, who is to guide and instruct her or him in the higher things of life, the Master will appear. But the emphasis here should be placed upon readiness, which includes worthiness and sincerity of purpose. Unless one is truly ready and properly prepared by instruction, guidance, and the help that lies in the process based upon spiritual laws, no Master will appear, no bursting of inner Cosmic Consciousness will become manifest, and no great illumination of transcendental light will come. Worthiness must be attained, preparedness made manifest, and readiness earned by voluntary effort.

Just as John was sent ahead to prepare the way, just as the great avatars of the past found it necessary to preach and teach in order to prepare the many for spiritual regeneration, and just as Jesus taught his disciples and hosts of others that they might mentally comprehend and spiritually apprehend the laws and principles leading to spiritual awakening, so have the teachers and Masters in the mystery schools in all lands maintained the systems of instruction and methods of preparation that have proved to be adequate and efficient. The seeker for divine effulgence and Cosmic Consciousness who attempts to await the coming of the Master and the brightness of illumination without study and preparation, and without association with those who are likewise qualified to aid and assist, delays the coming of the great day and often closes the door to the coming of the Master. It is in this fact that we find warrant for the establishment of the churches and for the maintenance of the secret orders and societies devoted to the spiritual preparation of humanity.

Another monogram for Christ is that formed of three letters, supposed to be the first two and last letters of the Greek word for "Jesus," but the last letter was finally changed to the Latin letter S so that the I.H.S. stood for Jesus Hominum Salvator— "Jesus, the Savior of Humanity." The letters were also used to mean In Hoc Salus and In Hoc Signo, meaning "In this Cross is Salvation," or "By This Sign, Conquer." The / and J in the early Latin language were identical in form, and in the early monograms composed of the letters I.H.S., the mark of abbreviation was put above the letters. These abbreviation marks were later misunderstood or so crudely carved that they were considered to be a cross over the H, and in this wise a new monogram was evolved appearing as shown above, with the cross resting on the letter H. This monogram is now the official emblem as adopted by the Jesuits.

So Jesus entered the water and immersed his body in it, while John stood by ready to give him humble benediction. As Jesus rose erectly in the water, and before John could speak, a great light came down from the heavens and surrounded Jesus and remained with him as a magnificent, blinding aura of iridescent illumination. John stepped back, more in fear of the brilliancy of the light than through astonishment, and the multitudes stood aghast, speechless and spellbound by the sight before their eyes.

Then from out of the heavens there descended a great, white, luminous dove, as bright as molten silver and as magnificent as the spiritual light which surrounded the body of Christ. The dove lighted upon the shoulder of Jesus, and while all stood silent and motionless, a voice came from the center of their attention, melodious but resounding like a trumpet call, proclaiming: "This is my beloved

Son!" John knew, as did the other Essenes who were assembled there, that the Holy Ghost had descended upon Mary, and had created in Jesus a new being— the divine being of Christhood and Sonship with God— as it had created in Mary a new being and a Sonship of God.

31

Chapter 14

HIS REAL DOCTRINES AND MIRACLES

THE WHOLE PUBLIC life of Jesus, from the time of his baptism up to and including the Crucifixion, was an outer, objective manifestation of the series of initiations through which he had passed secretly— or more or less subjectively—during his years of preparation. This important fact is often overlooked by those who are analytical students of his mission and life work, and it is certainly slighted in emphasis by those who attempt to interpret his doctrines, teachings, activities, sufferings, trials, victories, and defeats.

I have intimated in many places, in the preceding chapters, that the fundamental mysticism of Christianity has been unwarrantedly neglected by modern Christianity and churchanity, but it is being reintroduced into Christianity by the foremost theologians and the clergy. At a recent conclave of one of the high Protestant churches of America and England, the statement was made by one of the foremost ecclesiastical authorities that the salvation of the Christian church today depended upon the proper emphasis of the mystical foundation of Christianity.

Pristine Christianity was intended to carry on the teachings and doctrines revealed by Jesus the Christ, and these were highly mystical though reduced to worldly parables. The apostles of Jesus, who were carefully selected by him because of their previous experience in life and their worthiness, were carefully initiated by him and spiritually developed during the secret conclaves which he held, and which never became a part of the public records of his life. The work that these apostles carried on, and which was later taken up by the leaders of the Christian church, was dual in nature. There was the secret or inner circle of students of Christianity, who were gradually developed in the mystical principles involved in the doctrines revealed by Jesus; and there was the outer circle which heard only the parables and preachments given to the multitudes by Jesus and amplified by his followers.

For many centuries after the life of Jesus the early Christian church was more of a secret mystery school than a public place or system of general religious worship. It was not until the conclaves of the church authorities in the 4th, 5th, 6th, and 7th centuries, that the present- day system of churchanity, separate from mystical Christianity, was adopted. And even so, the few in every land who were deemed worthy and properly qualified were permitted to enter the little-known inner circle and bask in the brilliant light of transcendental illumination. That the outer circle, with its churchanity, had a glorious work to do is unquestionable, and I do not mean to criticize the plans which permitted the outer work to grow with greater strength or to a more enlarged form than the work of the inner circle.

Even today the proportion of those who are ready to enter the inner circle is so small, as compared with those who are only partially ready for the broader and more general work of the outer circle, that it often seems like a hopeless task to make the inner circle sufficiently large to carry on the great work that must be carried on to retain the mystical elements of Christianity for future development. I cannot agree altogether with those who criticize the Church and claim that system and organization have eaten away the heart of Christianity, or that outer pomp and ceremony, structure and operations, have denied any place at all to the mystical work of the inner chamber. Spiritual development is a matter of evolution, and progressive evolution is rapid only with the few. The greatest work must be among the masses in order that the occasional one in every thousand persons may find the path that leads to the inner circle.

Before Jesus could begin his great work in life, and before he would lay the foundation of this work by the establishment of his personal school and personal council, composed of selected neophytes who would be his trusted apostles, he had to face once again the tests and trials of higher initiation. This time, however, he would not approach these things as a neophyte, but as the ordained Christ. And since his work would be in the objective world, so would his tests, trials, and initiatory experiences be of the objective world. For this reason, we see why it was that the first incident of his public career was his retirement into the silence for meditation.

In a previous part of this book I have referred to this principle of entering the silence and have commented upon the benefits of silent meditation. In the books of Matthew, Mark, and Luke, of the Christian Bible, we find reference to Jesus entering the silence, or going into the wilderness, whereas nothing is said of it in the Book of John. John was the most mystical of the writers of the New Testament, and his gospel emphasizes more of the mystical principles of Christianity than any of the others. His reason for skipping over the incidents of Jesus's meditation in the wilderness is probably because of its personal nature and because it had no bearing upon the work of Jesus with the public. Throughout the Christian Bible we find so many references in both the Old and New Testaments regarding those who went up on a mountain for illumination or for intimate contact with God or God's Consciousness. The proof that these references to mountains of inspiration or mountains of illumination have not been considered in their true mystical light is found in the fact that expeditions composed of scientists and ecclesiastical authorities have sought for many of these "mountains" in the Holy Land and have labored diligently to select the proper one to fit the various incidents described in the Bible. In many cases, the mountains selected have proved to be mere hills, much like thousands of others to be found in such a rolling country; and surprise has been expressed by a great many that such places should have been called mountains at all.

The truth of the matter is that going up onto a mountain for illumination is a symbolical, mystical statement, indicating no actual, physical mountain and referring to no physical height at all. We are surprised to find that the ancients who lived in lands where there were no mountains or even large hills referred, in their writings, to the illuminations which they received upon mountaintops. Even some of the early Christians inn Egypt spoke of the illumination which came to them out in the desert on the mountaintop.

Going up onto a mountain meant, in the mystical terminology of the G.W.B. and in all of the mystical writings of the avatars and masters of the past, the raising of one's inner spiritual self to a great height where cosmic contact, or Cosmic Consciousness, was definite and complete. We find that all such experiences in the Old Testament, including the one regarding Moses and the spiritual contact he made with God, were for the purpose of attaining spiritual illumination or the development and test of some spiritual principle. Logically, the very opposite of this expression was also true. Whenever one of the great mystics or masters of the past had to contact or come in contest with one of the earthly, nonspiritual phases of life and wrestle with a problem that was purely worldly, he went into the valley or into the wilderness, and not to the mountaintop.

Thus we see why the first incident of the life of Jesus, which concerned objective principles and earthly trials and tribulations, took him into the desert wilderness instead of onto a mountaintop. We read in the Christian writings that he spent forty days and forty nights in this wilderness. During this time he fasted and hungered, and in other ways suffered the conditions of the body and flesh.

It is interesting to note that the numbers seven and forty are the numbers mostly used in mystical literature, because they have a mystical significance. I will not take the time to recall to my readers the number of times the number seven is used in the Old and New Testament, beginning with the creation of the world and the number of days in the week, and the fact that the seventh day was made the holy day; for I am sure that a few minutes's reflection will bring to mind many such uses of this symbolical number.

The number forty is used so many times that its significance becomes apparent even to the casual student of the Bible. It is found very frequently in the most ancient of sacred writings in many lands. The Egyptians claimed that the body was not completely freed of the soul until after forty days of preparation. Moses abstained from bread and water for forty days and forty nights during his period of cosmic contact. Moses was on the mount for forty days and forty nights, and he was on Mount Sinai the second time for forty days and forty nights. Those who went to Canaan were forty days on their spiritual journey. It was prophesied that no foot of human or beast would pass through Egypt for forty years.

Elijah was forty days and forty nights on Mount Horeb, and the same number of days and nights on Mount Carmel. The children of Israel were in the hands of the Philistines for forty years, and for forty years the children of Israel ate manna. The people of Nineveh had to repent for forty days. We find that Saul, David, Solomon, and Joash reigned as kings for forty years. So we should not be surprised to find that Jesus went into the wilderness for forty days and forty nights.

We must also remember that both Moses and Elijah began their public ministrations by fasting for forty days and forty nights, and preparing for their final acts. In the case of Jesus, however, his first acts were to be those dealing with material, earthly affairs, while with Moses and Elijah they were to be of a spiritual nature, dealing with spiritual problems. Hence, Jesus went into the lowlands of a wilderness while Moses and Elijah went up on the mountaintop.

We find from the Christian accounts of the experiences of Jesus during his forty days in the wilderness that it was a period of temptation, and the story being told symbolically, the temptations of the earth are personified as coming from the person of Satan. The temptations, however, through which Jesus had to pass were symbolical of those presented to him during his initiation in Egypt, when he was being prepared for the ministry. According to the old records Jesus himself meditated upon what form of temptations the world would present to him during his ministry, and one by one these temptations were stated by himself as though being spoken by the "tempter." Then he reviewed the nature of the temptation, analyzed it carefully, and formulated what answer he would give and what attitude he would maintain throughout his life, if ever brought face to face with such temptations.

Therefore, the entire process was one of self-examination; and it is recorded that the ultimate result of the self-examination and a consideration of the conditions that Jesus would have to face brought him to the point where he realized that he would come to the final close of his career during a public attack upon his methods and life, culminating in his Crucifixion. Therefore, we understand why Jesus made prophetic reference a number of times to the sad close of his life, and why he anticipated and was more or less prepared for what actually occurred. In truth, he knew that he would not be the first of the avatars who had been crucified and who had been accused wrongly by the very people who would have benefited the most from the instructions and teachings offered.

In fact, we find that as soon as Jesus had completed his forty days of meditation and self-examination, and had outlined his plans for his ministry, he learned that John, who had baptized him, was already in prison because of his missionary work. So we know that Jesus was aware of the fate that awaited him, and yet it did not deter him nor discourage him, for all these things were tests of his sincerity.

So Jesus began to preach the doctrine of repentance. This doctrine was not unique with Jesus, but it was a new form of preachment for the public in Palestine. El-Moria in Egypt, centuries before, had introduced the doctrine of regeneration as the reward for repentance, and it had been a doctrine with the G.W.B. in all lands; but Jesus added an inspired hope to the hearts and minds of all— "The Kingdom of Heaven is at hand!"

Analyzing all of the doctrines introduced by Jesus, we find that each and every one of them had a mystical principle as its basis, and these mystical principles were natural, spiritual laws. Comparing the pristine doctrines of Christ and the general tone of his message to present-day Christian doctrines and messages, we find an outstanding difference. Jesus preached a message of hope which might be expressed in these words: "Believe in me and my teaching, love and act in love toward all and let hope be the soul of your deeds, for beyond this present existence there is a more perfect life to come. I know this, for I have come therefrom, and thither I will lead you. Aspiration alone will not serve you. To attain the more perfect life of the future, you must begin by realizing it now, first by finding it within yourselves, in the Kingdom of Heaven that is within, then afterwards finding it in humanity through the acts of love and charity."

Present-day doctrines preach a message of despair which must be phrased briefly in these words: "Ye are all children of evil, born in sin and living in sin, and in sin shall ye die. The Kingdom of Heaven is far from thee, and can never be attained except ye are born again and through regeneration become purified and saved from the sins which ye have inherited."

We can understand, then, why the multitudes of Palestine followed him and found peace and renewed life in his words. Nowhere in the records of the Order do we find that the miracles of Jesus nor the wonderful demonstrations of healing which he performed attracted as much attention or brought as much hope and happiness into the lives of the public as did his message. Those who are well acquainted with the principles involved rightfully feel that the present-day emphasis upon the miraculous healing of Jesus is a mistake, for in his time these things were but mere incidents and not the objective of his mission, nor the paramount benefit which he bestowed. His cordial message of "Come to me, all you that are weary and are carrying heavy burdens, and I will give you rest," was one which meant more to the multitudes than the raising of the dead or the healing of the sick. Think again of the contentions, the struggles, the bitter disappointments, the blasted hopes, and the peaceful aspirations of the people of Palestine at this time, and you will realize what such a message meant to them.

Jesus's famous Sermon on the Mount represents an image of the Kingdom of Heaven which he was already bringing into consciousness in the hearts of the people. Did he require them to do great fasting, make unusual sacrifices, or suffer public penance? None of these were recommended by Jesus; he merely said that all should lift up their eyes and attune their spirits with the new Kingdom. "Blessed are the poor in spirit; for theirs is the Kingdom of Heaven," was the consolation that he offered to the downtrodden and those who were forlorn and in despair. His presentation of the four Beatitudes—the marvelous power of humility, sorrow for others, the inner goodness of the heart, and hunger and thirst after righteousness— were the mystical doctrines or spiritual principles which he taught as being the Way to the Kingdom of Heaven. And like the sound of a mystic silver bell in the temples of old, resounded the pure, pristine principle of "Blessed are the pure in heart, for they shall see God!"

Even his doctrine of regeneration called for no material, physical sacrifice as demanded by others who had left the multitudes in despondency. "... no one can see the kingdom of God without being born from above," meant no difficult thing for those who understood the spiritual, mystical laws involved; for Jesus explained, "Very truly, I tell you, no one can enter the kingdom of God without being born of water and Spirit." These words are recorded in the Book of John; for John was careful to preserve the mystical statements of Jesus, knowing the importance of this part of the divine messages. Regeneration by water, rebirth through baptism, and awakening of the Divine Consciousness within through the Holy Spirit was the Way to the new Kingdom.

In the G.W.B. and in the Rosicrucian Order of today all of the doctrines, teachings, thoughts for meditation, and principles for experience are intended to enable the student to awaken that inner consciousness and permit the Holy Spirit to bring about the attunement which leads to the finding of the Holy Kingdom. With the coming of Cosmic Consciousness, through the awakening of the Holy Spirit, comes illumination of the mind, peace to the soul and body, power to the mental faculties, intuition, the healing touch, the ability to master and accomplish, and the prowess to overcome the earthly, material obstacles to success and happiness. These are the offerings of the Order in all lands, and freely are they offered and freely must they be accepted, in sincerity, and with an open mind. No material price can be placed upon these things, nor can they be commercialized in books and public manuscripts. For ages have the Rosicrucians preserved these teachings and carried on with the divine principles without bias and without price or prejudice. To the few who are worthy, these things are accessible. To those who are curious and demand a sign or a symbol, nothing is shown and nothing is given.

The miracles performed by Jesus were never supernatural in the sense that they extended beyond the limitations of natural law or found their manifestation through a unique application of an unusual law. To the mystics of old and to Jesus, the Master of these things, all laws were divine laws, all principles were godly, and there was nothing supernatural, nothing super divine, unique or extraordinary, in what he did. His power to perform miracles was dual: mental apprehension and comprehension of the laws involved, with the ability to apply them properly and direct their operation; and the divine within him which enabled him efficiently to direct the creative processes of the God Consciousness in his soul. Half of his power was a divine gift born in him; the other half, a power developed through study, training, and experience.

To some degree all men and women are born with the divine power to perform, and to some degree all men and women may attain the mental mastership necessary for the application of the divine power. Jesus himself is the authority for the statement that others could do the things which he did— even greater things. Great avatars before him had performed similar miracles, and even today there are those who heal and who raise those who are literally dead, through the divine power that is God's greatest gift to humanity.

Jesus did not teach that so-called death or transition was something which might be stayed, continually prevented, or completely eliminated from human life, but that it was an inevitable event in the life of all beings. In this we see a distinct contradiction of the unsound and unnatural doctrine that transition may be avoided and life made continuous in one body. "There is no death!" is true of the real part of humans, and of the physical part as well; but Jesus and his disciples taught that there is a change in all material things and that transition of the soul and body are manifestations of the spiritual law. However, disease and suffering are abnormal and preventable, and this Jesus demonstrated. Also, he taught how to live that the physical body might be free of suffering and the mind free of the tortures of sin. The Rosicrucians of today teach how we may live in harmony with natural law and avoid the suffering of the flesh and the sins of the body, so that we may dwell in peace and happiness until the hour of transition comes.

It is easily understood that the teachings and demonstrations of Jesus antagonized those of the orthodox faith. Jesus was a modernist in every sense of the word, and he came into the land of fundamentalists with doctrines and demonstrations of doctrines that were contrary to all that had been taught to and believed by the multitudes.

In my recent journey through Palestine I noted the contest between the various sects, and especially the determination of the strictly orthodox to adhere to the ancient customs and rites of their ancestors. It was quite evident that if Jesus came to Jerusalem today and preached once again as he did before, and made demonstrations of the truth of his teachings, he would be crucified again by incarceration, by rejection on the part of the strictly orthodox, and by ridicule on the part of the skeptics and doubters. Undoubtedly the same would result if he came to the Western world and right into the midst of those who are at present discussing the evolution of our thinking, and the advancement of our comprehension, which effects a change in our beliefs and faiths.

During the period of the public ministry of Jesus, he passed through four ancient, traditional stages of initiation as outlined centuries before by Pythagoras, which were: The first degree, or preparation, culminating in the Sermon on the Mount; the second degree, or purification, represented by the miracubus healings and the demonstrations of Christian mystical therapeutics; the third degree, or illumination, manifested by the raising of Lazarus; and the fourth degree, or spiritual vision, manifested by the transfiguration.

How these events and stages of his mission culminated, and what they meant to this great Master, I will present in the next and following chapters.

32

Chapter 15

THE TRUTH ABOUT THE CRUCIFIXION
WITHIN RECENT YEARS, one or two pamphlets have appeared, presenting what claims to be a story of the Crucifixion as recorded by an eyewitness. The story told
therein is very short and merely throws some light of a questionable nature on a few points of the story of the Crucifixion. The statements in that pamphlet which were worthy of consideration were taken from several reliable sources and fictitiously enlarged by an unknown author who was merely making his appeal to those who desire a surprising story.

The true story of the Crucifixion is recorded in a number of ancient writings, all of which are very dependable and consistent in their outline of the incidents. Even Judas left a brief outline of his connection with the affair and what he noted of it. His story merely substantiates some of the points contained in the other records. The principal and most complete outlines of the story are contained in the three manuscripts written by different scribes and preserved in the monasteries of Tibet, Egypt, and India.

It is generally believed by biblical students that the only record or story of the Crucifixion is that contained in the Christian Gospels. Critics of the Christian doctrines and biblical stories have often argued that they did not believe the story at all because they could find no verification or substantiation of it in other records or in the writings of contemporary historians. These persons seem to forget that at the time of the Crucifixion the event was one of paramount importance to the followers of Jesus and to the several sects, the members of which were associated with the work being done by Jesus and his apostles. The event was of little importance from a national point of view and from the point of view of the orthodox Jews and the powers of Rome.

For this reason, contemporary historians, writing of the broader and larger events of the day, did not look upon the crucifixion of a religious leader as an event of such national importance or such worldly consideration as to warrant a place in their writings. From our present-day point of view, the Crucifixion appears as one of the most important events in the history of civilization; but that is because time has given us the proper perspective, and the results of the Crucifixion have enlarged themselves into a worldwide effect that is still vital to the lives of men and women. Many events in recent years have passed by hardly noticed in the historical records and have since become of extreme importance. The assassination of one man in one country in Europe, in 1914, might have passed by with little comment in the newspapers, and certainly without any comment at all in the history of the nation, if the future developments associated with that event, or gradually resulting from it, had not quickly given it a place of worldwide importance, connected with one of the greatest wars in human history.

In the case of the Crucifixion of Jesus, the real importance of the event and the greater effect of it evolved very slowly, and only after many centuries had passed. Those who wrote about it while it was still fresh in their minds dealt with it, not as an event of worldwide importance, nor as an event that needed to be set forth in minute detail, but as an event that had its categorical place in the scheme of things associated with the purely religious activities of their sect. For this reason they recorded only those points which had a religious or spiritual significance, according to the individual writers personal opinion. Hence the difference in presentation of the story and the difference in emphasis of the various points involved. This explains the lack of details in the Gospels.

However, in the record of the writers who intended to preserve the complete story in the archives of the G.W.B. and its associated organizations, the matter was viewed as one that had an important connection with the series of events that had occurred in the history of the organization in ages past. The writers presented evidence in the relationship of this event with similar events substantiating the doctrinal teachings and traditions of the cosmic and spiritual laws as made manifest in the lives of every great avatar and every great leader of human evolution. In the opinion of these writers, many incidents connected with the Crucifixion were of extreme importance and were carefully recorded, while the same incidents were passed over as inconsequential by the writers of the records published in the Christian Bible.

Another reason for a considerable difference between the story as told by the Gospel writers and the story as told by the scribes of the G.W.B. lies in the fact that the writers of the Christian Gospels were writing for the purpose of establishing and maintaining certain doctrines and principles which were becoming the foundation of a new religious sect. Therefore, they had to adhere to the traditional story of the Crucifixion, as it had been officially outlined by the apostles and presented as the theological basis for the Christian foundation. Every incident of the Crucifixion inconsistent with these theological principles and foundation traditions had to be eliminated from their stories, not for the purpose of deception, but in order that those unprepared and not ready for the complete story would not be confused, or their attention distracted from the principal elements, by the presentation of mystical elements reserved only for the inner circle and the more advanced followers.

The emblem shown above is one of the oldest of the popular mystical signs and has been mistakenly attributed to the American Indians because it was found freely used in some of their mystical decorations. Recent research found it engraved among the very old symbols of the Mayans in Yucatan, where it was probably in use hundreds of years before the Christian era. It has also been found as one of the signs in the ancient Buddhist zodiacs and is a symbol in the Asoka inscriptions. It was the sectarian mark of the Jains and the distinctive badge of the sect of Xaca Japonicus. The earliest form of the cross found in the Christian catacombs is in this form. This symbol is one of the most sacred in use in the monasteries of Tibet by the G.W.B. In Christian symbolism this cross is supposed to represent two capital Gammas, crossed and reversed, and is used as the sign of "faith in the crucified."

From this the reader will understand that the complete story and the real facts of the Crucifixion were accessible to and known by the founders who established the early Christian church in the 4th to 7th centuries A.D. In fact, these founders had easier access to these records, and to many others now lost or hidden, than we of the present time, despite any connections we may have with the greatest and most complete existing library of secret manuscripts.

We know that the church authorities had access to these secret records, because in the council meetings of the early Christian church, and in the discussions that took place between the highest authorities of the early church, reference was made to certain portions of manuscripts and official records dealing with the Crucifixion and other incidents of the life of Jesus which are now concealed or have been destroyed. That many such records were destroyed is proved by the fact that at certain times in the past these various councils of the early church authorized the destruction of certain manuscripts which were discussed by them, because they decided that the existence of such records might embarrass them in the future. The official records of many of these councils contain long and lively discussions regarding these manuscripts and their contents; and we find that a number of eminent authorities in the early church seceded from the councils and brought the wrath of the early church upon their heads by their refusal to agree to the destruction of these important manuscripts and the plan to conceal certain known facts.

In previous chapters of this book I have referred to the statements of some of the church authorities that demonstrated how familiar they were with the secret or hidden details of the life of Jesus. Unquestionably many of these important records and manuscripts are today preserved in the Vatican at Rome, for it was the ambition of the church leaders during the 7th to 12th centuries to procure and take away from public or even private study, all books and manuscripts in the rare collections in Oriental lands which might contain statements differing from those established by them as the official traditions and doctrines of their church. We know, for instance, of one incident which took place during the Crusades to the Holy Land, at which time one magnificent library containing 20,000 rare manuscripts of historical importance, dealing mostly with religious matters, and especially with the affairs preceding and during the lifetime of Jesus, was destroyed completely—reduced to ashes after a selected few of the manuscripts were forwarded to Rome.

Fortunately for us, some very important manuscripts have survived all of the destructive processes, and it is from these that many incidents regarding the life of Jesus have been extracted for this book. The incidents of the Crucifixion, taken from these records, are especially illuminating, and because they are too long to be placed in any one volume, I find it necessary to select at this time merely the highlights from these records and piece them together in the following paragraphs.

First of all, we find that the Crucifixion of Jesus did not come about at the hands of the Jews as a protest against his teachings or as a punishment for his attempted leadership. The idea that the Jews persecuted and eventually crucified Jesus is a viewpoint adopted by the founders of the early Christian church, because it was consistent with the theological principles they wished to establish and with the traditions they wished to make the basis of their doctrines.

It is generally contended by Christian authorities that Jesus was an outcast among the Jews except for the few hundreds or thousands who constituted his followers; but there is no foundation for this idea in any of the incidents of his life, nor in the facts as we find them. While it is true that the Jews did not consider Jesus a Jew, but a Gentile, and many of them ridiculed the idea that anyone from Galilee or anyone who was believed to be a Nazarite could do anything that was good, nevertheless they would not have crucified him because he was a foreigner, nor even if they had considered him an "upstart" in their midst. The idea that he was destroying their religion or wrecking their church is not supported by any of the real facts. Jesus himself said, on more than one occasion, that he came not to destroy the law or the words of the prophets, nor to belittle the prophets and pull them down from the high place they held among the Jews, but to fulfill the predictions of the prophets and to support the laws they had established.

It has also been said that Jesus attempted to turn the faith of the Jews from their one God toward another, or a trinity of Gods, and for this reason brought condemnation upon his work. We find no foundation for this belief either; and when Jesus was asked as to what was the first commandment, he answered: "Hear, O Israel, the Lord our God is one, and thou shalt love the Lord thy God with all thy heart and all thy soul and all thy mind." Certainly that was consistent with the Jewish religious viewpoint and could not have been antagonistic. While it is true that he did criticize a few of the practices in the synagogue and did attempt to direct the thoughts of the people to higher ideals, this in itself would not have warranted the Jews to crucify Jesus, nor to do more than simply ignore him.

Jesus was no more radical than Isaiah had been and no more liberal in his orthodoxy than Micah. He did not attempt to establish a new sect or a new church of any kind, despite the statements of many Christians who think that Jesus himself established the first Christian church and started the first Christian movement toward the foundation of a separate and individual sect. Even if he had done so, this would have been no new thing in that land, for among the Jews there were various sects, some very old and some very new, such as the Pharisees, Sadducees, Essenes, Nazarites, Nazarenes, Kuthites, Boethusians, and many others. And yet not one of the founders of these various sects was ever punished by death.

Jesus may have proclaimed himself as a Messiah, much to the disgust of the strictly orthodox, but according to Jewish custom any member of the House of Judah might have believed it without being killed by the Jews for such a belief. He may have referred to himself, although we have no record of it, as the "unique and only begotten Son of God," but we doubt that the simple claim of being the "Son of God" would have antagonized them in any way; for all Jews believed that God was their "Father" and always prayed to God as their Heavenly Father, and referred to themselves as the Children of God. Such a conception of the Deity was common in Israel.

The one outstanding point in connection with the Crucifixion of Jesus is the use of the cross. That one thing tells the story that Rome had ordered his death, and that it was a Roman punishment and not a Jewish one, for the Jews would have stoned him, in their usual manner, had they desired to get rid of this man for any reason. The fact that his death was ordered in the Roman manner, and at the hands of those officially delegated to carry out the death sentence in a legal manner, indicates that the whole affair was not one of mob violence or religious persecution on the part of the Jews, but a sentence officially proclaimed at Rome.

We must remember that more important than the claim of the apostles or the disciples of Jesus that he was a Messiah and the Son of God, was the title being bestowed upon him by the enthusiastic followers who idolized him and, without discrimination or discretion, proclaimed him King of the Jews. This was a serious thing and the real reason for his Crucifixion.

The Jews were anxious to have a leader, whether he was the true Messiah or one anticipating or representing a Messiah to come. And if this self-appointed or truly ordained leader brought them a message of peace and happiness and performed miracles of healing, he would have been tolerated by the majority of the Jews if not by all of them. The restlessness among the Jews in Palestine and their hopes and plans to be freed from the yoke of Rome had caused Rome considerable anxiety in the past. Everywhere the spies of the Roman government were watching for the possible uprising of a rebellion and the selection of a leader that might start another war; and when the whisperings or even the open professions of the enthusiastic followers of Jesus proclaimed him the King of the Jews, it was a matter serious enough to be immediately reported to Rome and be given official attention.

Jesus was undoubtedly feared by Rome, according to many ancient records that deal with just this phase of the matter. His simple teachings were opposed to those taught as the official doctrines of the Romans. His preachments tended toward holy socialism, and the tyrannical imperialism of Rome could never harmonize with such teachings as this. The only offense that can be attributed to Jesus throughout his whole career was a political offense from the Roman point of view. The Roman standing army in Israel and the spies maintained by the Romans made it possible for that government to take stringent measures whenever there seemed to be a traitor in their midst or a possible uprising.

Caiaphas would appear to have been a spy for the Roman government if we are to judge by the secret reports that he made to Rome regarding the activities of Jesus. On the other hand, he may have been merely a personal enemy, for he certainly did do everything possible to keep Rome informed about Jesus and to make it difficult for Jesus to continue his work. Even though Caiaphas was an eminent leader of the Sanhedrin, he did not represent this body in the reports he made, nor in the attitude he assumed. It is even indicated that Caiaphas went so far as to present large sums of money for the purpose of procuring evidence and making sure that a warrant would be issued by Rome for the arrest and trial of Jesus. So we find in this man a greater enemy to Jesus and his work than Judas.

It appears from some of the ancient records that most of the contentions and revolts that became quite popular in Palestine at about this time were purposely attributed to Jesus, or more precisely to his followers. Gradually Rome became convinced that it could end the enormous expense to which it had been placed in constantly investigating and watching the Christ movement in Jerusalem, thus cutting short the trouble it had experienced in dealing with these matters by removing the leader of the so-called new political faction. Therefore, by the time Jesus entered Jerusalem for the purpose of carrying on the culminating phases of his work after a long and successful tour in the outlying sections, a warrant for his arrest was already in the hands of officials in Jerusalem. Owing to the fact that he arrived at the approaching festival period, it was deemed advisable not to interfere with the quietude and sacred peacefulness of the Jewish feast days. Caiaphas anticipated an uprising when the hour for the arrest came. Such an event would have been disastrous to the traditions of the church, would have upset the celebration of the feast pilgrims, and incidentally would have detracted from the very large financial harvest which always resulted when there were so many thousands of pilgrims in Jerusalem.

There are a number of references in the ancient records showing that an assassination of Jesus had not only been thought of, but had been planned by some of the hirelings of both the religious fanatics of Jerusalem and the local Roman authorities. It was decided, however, that such an act would be attributed to the Jews rather than the Romans, because the Romans had every reason and every power to proceed openly and have Jesus condemned as a political troublemaker.

The story of Judas as presented in the Christian version is a garbled one, modified in order to illustrate the fact that among the followers of Jesus, as with every great leader or avatar in the past, there was one who represented the evil forces and principles of the world, and who typified the untrustworthy element met with in all phases of life. The facts of the story are that the officials appointed to arrest Jesus realized that if they attempted to arrest him in public while he was preaching or performing his miracles, they would have to contend with a mob situation resulting in the use of arms and force, the destruction of life and property, and the creation of a condition not desired by either the Roman or Jewish people. Therefore, it was decided to arrest Jesus in private, when he was outside of the city and accompanied by but a few of his followers. Someone was needed, however, who could identify him at a distance in the white raiment which so many of the Essenes wore. Judas was willing to serve in this case for the bribe that was offered him, and in truth he did typify the element in life which the story in the Christian Bible presents.

That Jesus knew of the coming events, and that treachery and false reports were about to end his career, is evidenced not only in the Christian stories but in many of the private records. The soldiers representing the Roman government followed the directions of Judas and found Jesus in his usual environment in the Garden of Gethsemane where he was wont to hold secret consultations with Nicodemus, Mathaeli, Philopoldi, and Yousef of Arimathea. While the soldiers were arresting Jesus, Yousef of Arimathea made off hastily to inform others of what had occurred and to make immediate plans to aid Jesus. Pilate was consulted and he agreed to delay matters till after the feast days. He feared there had been some illegal trickery or action in what had occurred and that criticism would result, thus jeopardizing his own position. Reading between the lines of the various ancient stories, we cannot feel that Pilate was moved by any inner or outer sentiment in his dealings with Jesus that was impersonal or unselfish.

The warrant called for immediate trial, and Pilate found reason legally to delay matters without antagonizing the Roman authorities and yet serve his own purpose. There were those who called upon Pilate and represented themselves as Jews, while others represented themselves as supporters of the Roman government, who demanded that the order of the emperors prefect be carried out at once. The warrant was of a nature that called for the death sentence if the person arrested was found guilty as charged. It is recorded that the decisions of the minor judges and witnesses were reported to Pilate that very night, but there was not found in these decisions that testimony which Pilate believed was sufficient for him to permit immediate execution.

In some of the Christian stories there is an intimation that some persons in Pilate's household were followers of Jesus. We find no reason for this statement except that Pilate himself had had some absent healing conducted by Jesus, which had resulted in the cure of a diseased hand. But if all those who had been healed or helped by Jesus had been true followers of him, there would have been such a multitude of followers in Jerusalem that no one would have even dared to plan the Crucifixion, let alone carry it out. It is not uncommon for avatars to have the very arm that was once paralyzed and cured become the arm and the hand that smites them first. Pilate was pleading for delay, but pressure was being brought to bear and so he yielded.

The attempt to transfer the case to Galilee, because Jesus was not a Jew, and therefore bring it under the direction of Herod, who was attending the feast in Jerusalem, also failed. Herod himself was not in such a position of stability and so free of criticism that he dared to take part in an affair that he knew was a more serious matter than appeared on the surface. The intriguers, in the meantime, feared that

Jesus might slip out of their clutches, but no attempt was made by his followers to do otherwise than demand fair trial and sufficient delay to enable them to prepare their defense.

Jesus himself seemed to be unconcerned regarding the controversy among the higher magistrates, for it is recorded that during these very bitter hours he continued to give treatments, teach, and carry on with a peaceful mind. We must think of the majesty of such a mind that was able to do this, knowing, as Jesus knew, what was really in store for him. The followers of Jesus who were attempting to prepare some defense for him, or to secure his freedom, recalled the fact that it was customary on the occasion of such feasts to give life and liberty to some criminal, and this point was presented before the officials with the request that the multitude preferred Jesus as the one who should be the receiver of such a feast gift. Even this plan failed. Finally, Pilate turned Jesus over to the mob of accusers and personal enemies, and the process of scourging began as a preliminary to the Crucifixion. The manner in which the leaders of the mob exerted themselves at this time, as recorded in all the records, shows that the greatest enmity and ill feeling was felt on the part of a few of the Jews who were personal enemies.

However, the apostles and the Essenes were carrying on their plans silently and appealing to higher authorities to save the life of their Master. Those who knew what was being done in the form of appealing to the emperor for a reconsideration, and appealing to other authorities for intervention, could not understand why these things did not come to an issue more quickly. According to the records, a great many of the followers of Jesus thought that more trickery was being perpetrated, while those who knew realized that Jesus had advised them of the real nature of the Crucifixion, and how it would terminate, and what it meant to the great work of the secret organization. Therefore, there were two groups who watched the developments: one moved by anxiety lest each hour would produce no effect that would stay the proceedings, and the other group that knew intuitively, and perhaps from secret information given them, that all would not end as the others believed.

Nearly a week had elapsed since the warrant had been issued. Hour by hour passed until finally the body of Jesus was raised on the cross on Golgotha, a little hill just outside the city walls, that was so round and suggestive of the shape of a skull that it was called Golgotha. Here other condemned men had been crucified, as had been the custom of the Romans for many years. The cross had always been a device for Roman crucifixion and persecution, and to the Essenes it was an emblem of human suffering, tests, and trials; but the raising of this particular cross with its precious burden became at once a new symbol to the Brothers and Sisters in White Clothing and the secret organization. From that hour the cross had a new meaning in spiritual and mystical thought. The Jewish factions which had gathered round to witness the raising of the cross dispersed to prepare for the approach of the sabbath, and only the Gentiles and the members of the secret organizations remained there to watch and to protect the body of their Master.

Considerable comment has been made in recent years, and perhaps in many of the years gone by, concerning the words spoken by Jesus while on the cross. Those who have tried to argue that Jesus was not the great Master and Son of God as claimed by the apostles and the disciples refer to the words in the Book of Mark 15:34, which are given there, in one of the languages which Jesus spoke as "Eloi, Eloi, lema sabachthani?" which is translated in the Bible as meaning, "My God, my God, why have you forsaken me?" The Book of Matthew gives practically the same wording. However, the four books of Matthew, Mark, Luke, and John agree in saying that immediately after speaking these words, Jesus yielded up the ghost, or gave up the ghost.

These words spoken by Jesus and the statement that he gave up the ghost are highly significant in a mystical sense. It was the Holy Ghost which Jesus yielded up at that moment, and this was the same Holy Ghost that came into the womb of Mary and manifested the creative power of the Logos. It was the same Holy Ghost that descended upon Jesus at the time of his baptism and which infused him with the authority and power to be the living representative of the Logos on earth. At the time of yielding up the Holy Ghost, while on the cross, Jesus permitted the special power and authority to return to the Cosmic Consciousness and leave him as one who had completed his

mission and was no longer the living power of the Logos on earth. This is why Luke expresses the incident by having Jesus say, "Father, into your hands I commend my spirit," and John wrote that Jesus said, "It is finished."

Every mystic will understand that these references to giving up the Holy Ghost cannot possibly refer to the giving up of life, vitality, or vital consciousness. Those who have attempted, since the 5th century A.D., to advance the idea that Jesus actually died while still on the cross, or that his transition occurred at that time, attempt to use the term giving up the Holy Ghost as meaning giving up life and consciousness. If the Holy Ghost is to be considered in this particular instance as meaning vitality, life, and animation, then we must be consistent and interpret the term in the same way in every instance where it has been used in connection with the life of Jesus. Can we say then, that when Jesus was baptized and the Holy Ghost descended upon him, that it was life, vitality and consciousness, and that this was the beginning of his existence as a living being?

It is quite evident by the whole story of the baptism in the Christian Gospels that the descent of the Holy Ghost was the holy authority and divine power coming into the body of Jesus, or into his consciousness, completing his preparation and perfection of development as a divine Son of God, an avatar, and the living Christ. It was the reversal of this process—the Holy Ghost and the Christhood withdrawing into the spirit and consciousness of God— which occurred on the cross as the culmination of his brief mission and the end of his official Christhood.

We realize, now, that the words Eloi, Eloi, lema sabachthani? could not mean, "My God, my God, why have you forsaken me?" and that there is either some hidden meaning in this expression or the words have been misinterpreted. Going to our ancient records and the original version and transcriptions that are recorded in reliable archives, we find that the words written there are Heloi, Heloi, lema sabachthani? We find, then, that what Jesus said was, "My Temple of Helois, my

Brethren of Helois, why have you forsaken me?" and that he was referring to the brothers and sisters of the Temple at Helios where he had been

initiated. They were expected to prevent any unnecessary suffering and be ready to render any aid that was necessary. Just at this time, in the midst of his intense suffering, Jesus was not aware of all that was being done for him and probably looked upon the absence of so many of the brothers and sisters as a lack of attention at a crucial moment. It was at this moment that Jesus entered into the stage of transition from Divine Master to human Master, and the transition had its culmination in the Ascension as described in the next chapter. We see, therefore, that the problem regarding his last words on the cross resolves itself into a further indication of his real majesty and divine attunement. Just as the sun was casting its last rays over the horizon and the sky seemed to be darkening more rapidly and threatening a storm, which appeared highly significant to the faithful, a commotion was occurring in the palace of Pilate. A herald had arrived with a document bearing the private seal of Tiberius, and all were anxious to know its contents. This document instructed Pilate to cancel the warrant and to stay all proceedings until a complete investigation could be made by Cyrenius. In the meantime, Jesus was to be set at liberty until a full report could be made.

Pilate immediately sent a messenger to those who were in charge of the Crucifixion stating what had occurred, and he instructed that no further persecution or torture of the body was to be permitted. In fact, his instructions stated that if there was any life still in the body of Jesus, it was to be taken down from the cross and sent to a hospice to be cared for. This was the news anticipated by Nicodemus, Mathaeli, and Yousef of Arimathea, and of course it was unpleasant news to the intriguers, and especially the Covenanters.

The storm soon broke and delayed the removal of the body of Jesus for a few hours, but in that time food and drink were given him, and support was placed under his body to prevent it from pulling too greatly upon the nails which tortured his flesh. The few faithful ones noted with great anxiety that a somber stillness and a numbness was passing over the body, and that gradually Jesus lost consciousness. At the earliest possible moment, when the storm quieted, torches were brought and an examination of the body revealed that Jesus was not

dead. The blood flowing from the wounds proved that the body was not lifeless, and so the cross was immediately taken down and the body removed from it.

The body was then taken to a burial vault owned by Yousef of Arimathea, which had supposedly been built for the care of his family; being a wealthy man he made it an elaborate and well-constructed burial place. The body was placed in a special part of the tomb which had been prearranged for its reception, and physicians connected with the Essenian community were at hand to render every possible assistance in caring for the wounds.

The Essenes had secured permission for the use of this tomb as a burial place for Jesus, and the authorities had granted this permission in the belief that it was to be the permanent tomb of Jesus. Therefore, shortly after the body was placed in the tomb, some outer guards belonging to the organization announced the coming of the officials who were to inspect the tomb and approve of the burial. Jesus had just attained complete consciousness, and his wounds had been dressed sufficiently for the Essenes to wrap his body in clean white clothes, in preparation for a short sleep, when the officials reached the tomb. The officials were permitted to watch the closing of the tomb and affix their seals upon the stones and the door which closed it securely. Apparently everything of an official nature to make the tomb a permanent burial place had been done according to law, and yet according to our records, much was left undone because the Essenes had made sure that the officials did not go too far in the process of sealing and closing every means of entrance and exit.

The description of the tomb in the records from which I quote is not complete enough for us to understand thoroughly its form and structure, and we are not sure whether there were two doorways or only one. It appears, however, from all records, that a great stone was used to close up the doorway after the doors had been shut, for the purpose of hiding the doorway so that the burial place, which was in the side of a rock, would not be too apparent or attract too much attention. It was also recorded that Nicodemus was fearful that some trick might be played, as he realized there were those who knew of the trickery on the part of Caiaphas, and that the resentment of the

followers of Jesus might take the form of some plan to thwart the law. So he demanded that the sepulchre be watched for the satisfaction of Caiaphas and the law.

Late in the night the storm which had only partially ceased raged fiercely again throughout the whole valley of Judea, and thunder and lightning echoed and flashed in the mountains roundabout. According to the records, it was such an unusually severe storm that it cleared the streets of Jerusalem and the roads just outside of the walls of all pilgrims, and it even forced some of the guards and soldiers to take cover.

33

Chapter 16

THE SECRET FACTS OF THE RESURRECTION
SHORTLY BEFORE SUNRISE, Yousef of Arimathea and other Essenes who had been hiding nearby approached the tomb when the guards were trying to protect themselves from the rain by seeking shelter in some cattle houses at some distance. Using the means they had previously provided, and taking advantage of the laxity of the officials in sealing the doorway properly, they caused this great stone to be thrown over and the doorway to be opened. When they entered the tomb, they found Jesus resting easily and rapidly regaining strength and vitality. After an hour the storm ceased sufficiently for the Essenes to escort him from the tomb.

Jesus had used every one of the powers coming into his being, through the perfect attunement he had with the Cosmic, to restore strength and consciousness to every part of his body and to all of his highly developed faculties. Therefore, it was possible for the Essenes to place his body upon a colt and cover him with some heavy garments while they led the colt with its precious burden through the mild rain and deep darkness to a secluded place belonging to the organization, not far from the walls of the city.

In the Book of John in the Holy Bible, is revealed one of the interesting facts concerning the Crucifixion which appears in the ancient records from which I am quoting, and which incident is often overlooked by the most critical of the Bible students. It is that although it was a common practice to break the bones in the body of every crucified person and to cause their bodies to hang upon the cross for several days so there would be no possibility of the body remaining alive, nevertheless the body of Jesus was taken down without the bones being broken, even though the soldiers broke the bones of the two criminals that were upon the crosses close by.

This was not an oversight on the part of the soldiers by any means, for not only did they fulfill the law by breaking the bones of the two criminals, but they had been so accustomed to this procedure for many years that we cannot believe that after having performed their duty with the other two, they would forget the practice, momentarily, in the case of the third body upon the cross. The ancient records to which I have been referring state that when the soldiers were notified that the body must be taken down immediately because a release had come, and that everything must be done to permit Jesus to regain his consciousness and strength if he had not passed through transition, they realized that they were not to injure, torture, or in any way affect the ease and comfort of Jesus, but to relieve him as quickly as possible from the agony in which they found him.

It may be interesting to call attention to the fact that nowhere in the Gospels of Matthew, Mark, Luke, and John is the positive statement made as an observation of one of these disciples that Jesus died on the cross or that he was dead when they removed him from the cross and placed him in the tomb. In John 19:33 there is the statement that the soldiers believed Jesus to be dead, but John does not make a positive statement of his own, and when he continues by mentioning the spear thrust, we have no reason to believe it was more than a surface wound, while, on the other hand, the fact that blood and water flowed forth would indicate that Jesus was still alive. I know that in the Apostles's Creed used in the average Christian church, the statements therein refer to the fact that Jesus suffered and died on the cross, and it is commonly believed that the statements in this Apostles's Creed were taken from the statements made by the different apostles.

The truth of the matter is that the present-day Apostles's Creed went through a number of changes in the centuries after the Crucifixion at the various high councils of the church, and the first drafts of the creed, which I have before me, are considerably different from those later adopted. In the third of the five drafts of this creed, we find the statement that Jesus was "fastened to a cross, he rose the third day." In the first and original draft, the statement is that Jesus was crucified under Pontius Pilate and "on the third day brought to life from the dead." In the last draft, the wording was changed to read, "suffered under Pontius Pilate, was crucified, dead, and buried."

The statement in the early draft of the creed that Jesus rose from the dead should be associated with the wording in Luke 24:5, wherein the question is asked of those who were seeking for Jesus, "Why do you look for the living among the dead?" We must bear in mind that Jesus was placed in a tomb that was intended for the dead, and in an environment intended exclusively for the dead and surrounded by the so-called dead. In other words, the question might be reworded as follows: "If you are looking for Jesus, the everliving Son of God, why do you come to a cemetery and peer into tombs and sepulchres looking for him? Why do you expect to find a living person where only the dead may be found?" The early drafts of the Apostles's Creed clearly show that the idea meant to be conveyed was that after the Crucifixion, Jesus was temporarily placed in a tomb among the dead, and that he quickly rose from that place and out of that environment, and returned again to his place among the living.

There is absolutely no intimation in the early drafts of that creed, nor in any of the discussions which occurred in the high councils of the church when the creed passed through its many changes in the different centuries, that Jesus was believed to have died on the cross or in the tomb immediately after the Crucifixion. The creed was composed so long after the days of the apostles and the writing of the books of the Bible that it had to be invented and created like the many newer doctrines of Christianity. In the Roman Catholic Encyclopedia we find admission that many of the highest authorities state that the creed can be traced to no earlier period than the second half of the 5th century A.D., and there is the further admission that the idea that the apostles composed the creed on the day of the Pentecost is merely a legend dating back to the 6th century. We read also this interesting statement in the Roman Catholic Encyclopedia: "Modern apologists in defending the claim to Apostolicity (of the Apostles's Creed) extend it only to the old Roman form, and are somewhat hampered by the objection that if the

Roman form had been really held to be the inspired utterance of the Apostles, it would not have been modified at pleasure by various local churches, and in particular would never have been entirely supplanted by our existing form."

According to the Rosicrucian and other ancient records, various persons came to the tomb to see the body of Jesus after the sabbath was over. They brought spices, clean linens, and other things as was their custom in the case of any who had passed away, but they found the tomb open and Jesus gone. The storm and lightning, and perhaps a mild form of earthquake, had left much ruin and havoc in the cemetery. A number of tombstones were thrown over and a number of sepulchres were opened by stones rolling away or sliding down from their proper position.

The soldiers who were supposed to be on guard to watch and protect the body of Jesus, but who had slipped away into some sheltered place, were on hand bright and early to meet those who came to the tomb of Jesus, and they had a very ready explanation of what had occurred. They did not admit their own neglect, which would have caused them to be severely punished and imprisoned, but stated that during the height of the storm all of the tombs were opened by some miraculous power and that a great blinding light came down and surrounded the tomb of Jesus, and in this light they saw mysterious figures which escorted Jesus, who had returned to life. This story did not appear to the soldiers to be much different from hundreds of other stories being told about Jesus and his miracles, and about the manifestations of God's wrath and God's love in connection with many unusual things during the preceding nine years.

The public, and especially the followers of Jesus, were ready to accept the story that the soldiers told. Since Pilate realized that the body of Jesus had been saved and that the stories were only an explanation to satisfy the curious, and since Rome had authorized the release of Jesus, and therefore cared little regarding his present whereabouts, no investigation was conducted. Thus, the story of the soldiers and the followers became the accepted explanation.

The other incidents regarding the Resurrection, as told in the Christian Bible and in other sacred writings, may or may not be true in their minute details, for they are based upon testimony of various persons and are somewhat conflicting. Only one fact of interest is noted in the Rosicrucian records regarding the tomb of Jesus, and this is to the effect that during the first years after the Resurrection, the tomb of Yousef of Arimathea was used as a shrine by thousands who were followers of Jesus. The tomb was in a badly damaged condition, partly split open by a huge crack in the rock which sheltered it and a crack in some of the stone masonry that supported one side of it; the tomb had every appearance of having been struck by lightning during the terrible storm. If the storm did such damage as this to the Holy Sepulchre, and to the other tombs and burial places in the vicinity, we can easily understand why the soldiers conceived the story that they told and why it was so readily accepted.

As quickly as possible the Essenes escorted and conveyed Jesus to a home of one of their associates in Galilee. It was their intention to have Jesus rest and recuperate before escorting him to a place of secrecy and isolation for a time. Jesus recovered very rapidly so that he was able to walk part of the way on his journey. He was met by a few who knew him and who were surprised to find him still living. We have many traditional stories regarding his contact with his disciples and others during the time of his recuperation.

The appearance of Jesus in the midst of his disciples on various occasions during his period of recuperation constitutes in several cases, a mystical demonstration of the ability of the Master to project his personality and consciousness to places distant from his physical body. Such demonstrations of the higher spiritual laws as this were common not only to Jesus, but many of the eminent avatars of the past. In fact, some of his apostles and disciples and many of the sisters and brothers of the G.W.B. very often made themselves visible to others at distant points. We find in the present-day teachings of the Rosicrucians, in various lands, the simple laws which help men and women to attain that high degree of psychic development which enables them at will to project the psychic or soul consciousness to a distant point and become visible and even sensible to the higher faculties of persons who are likewise developed to the proper degree of receptivity.

The time was coming, however, for Jesus to close his public missionary work quite definitely and enter that stage of silent activity into which all great avatars of the past have entered, and which is always the goal of every messenger of the G.W.B. Jesus was devoting most of his time to teaching his disciples the doctrines and principles which they should present in their work with the public, thus preparing them for the missionary work they would have to continue after his retirement.

The great change that had come about in the personal appearance of Jesus after the Ascension of the Holy Ghost from his consciousness while he was on the cross caused a great many, who had been familiar with his physical appearance and spiritual aura, to fail to recognize him when they saw him clothed in different raiment and appearing as a simple Essene during his days at Galilee. The disciples knew that a still greater event in his life was imminent, and of course the eminent officers of the organization were already preparing for the final manifestation of his divine place among humans.

For forty days Jesus continued his close association with his disciples and apostles, and we find that this forty-day period is again significant and coincides with the other forty day periods mentioned in another part of this book. During these forty days Jesus attended several of the suppers or symbolical feasts which were typical of the Essenes and which later became one of the forms of ceremony in the Christian church. One of these, the so-called Last Supper, became important in Christian doctrines of Jesus's life; but there were many other such feasts thereafter in privacy not revealed in the Christian records, probably because they were not significant or attended by as large a number of his disciples as the one referred to.

So, on the fortieth day the apostles assembled, in accordance with instructions, on a mountaintop outside of the city of Jerusalem, where they would be separated from the multitude and out of sight of any passers-by. It was just at sunset that Jesus came into their midst and arranged them before him in a group forming a semicircle, facing the setting sun. He stood before them so that as they faced him they saw his magnificent figure outlined as a silhouette against the red and gold of the sky. He proceeded to explain to them the purpose of this unusual secret session and the real work that was to be accomplished by them in the future.

According to the records, he first announced that not one of them was to leave the circle or depart from the mountaintop until he had received from his Father in Heaven the Holy Ghost and the divine authority to carry on his work as an official apostle. In other words, he announced that apostolic power was about to come to them from a divine source and that they must not break the spell of cosmic attunement which he was about to establish until each one had experienced the influx of the Holy Ghost. In the light of what actually occurred, we can easily realize how important it was for Jesus to command them to remain where they were and not depart too quickly; for he knew that there would come a moment when each would believe that the strange session had ended and that there was no further need for remaining on the mountaintop.

Naturally, the apostles asked questions, and it appears that they sought to determine what form of activity they should adopt and just how their work would affect the establishment of the Kingdom of Heaven which Jesus had announced as imminent. But Jesus replied by rebuking them for their inquisitiveness at that moment and then assured them that in due season all would be explained to them. He further stated that after the Holy Ghost had come upon them, and they went out in the world to carry on their individual missions, they would be representing the great work in all parts of the world.

With further instructions regarding their first acts after they departed from the mount, Jesus directed each one to rise from his sitting position and fold his arms across the chest in the form of the Essenian salutation. Then, stepping some paces away from them, but directly in a line between them and the last edge of the setting sun, he lifted his hands and arms toward Heaven and prayed. While the apostles watched and listened, a great light surrounded Jesus and then a mist formed over his head and gradually enveloped him.

When the mist lifted and ascended toward the sky again, they saw that Jesus was gone and was no longer before them. In their astonishment, they looked toward one another as though each expected the other to make some explanation. A few of them were about to move from their assigned positions when one of them spoke and said, "Hold, for were we not warned to remain as we were until the coming of the Holy Ghost?" Realizing that the time for departure had not yet come, they remained standing, and in a few minutes there appeared before them two figures as faintly visible as though they were of a violet light.

One of these figures addressed the standing apostles, saying, "Gaze no longer into the mists in which your Master has ascended, for as he left you, so shall he come to you again and again; for his earthly mission is accomplished and he shall dwell in your hearts and in the hearts of those who love him and will henceforth direct the mission of his life through his messengers of light. Receive ye, therefore, from your Father which art in Heaven, the Holy Ghost and the Word, and by these ye shall have the power to teach and to demonstrate the spiritual laws of the Kingdom of Heaven, and the keys to the portals of the future." Then the figures disappeared as if dissolving before their eyes. The apostles then knew that they had been glorified by their Father in Heaven and that they had received the Holy Ghost.

In quietness and peace the apostles journeyed to their homes in Galilee to dwell among their brothers and sisters. That night Jesus appeared among the high priests in the monastery at Carmel and retired to the rooms that had been set aside for him as his sanctum. Thus the door of his public life was closed to humanity.

34

Chapter 17

THE UNKNOWN LIFE OF JESUS
ACCORDING TO THE stories in the Christian Bible, the life of Jesus the Christ ends or culminates with the Ascension.

Various other sacred books, originally forming the library of sacred writings from which the present books of the Bible were selected, contained accounts and incidents of the life of Jesus not presented in the selected ones, and for this reason they were rejected. These rejected books of the Bible, which constitute a separate volume, are used today by a great many ecclesiastical authorities because of the interesting light they throw upon many other important incidents of the life of Jesus and his apostles.

The Ascension, as described in the previous chapter of this book, was wholly a mystical and psychic event, and there is nothing in the original accounts of it to warrant the belief that Jesus arose physically or in his physical body in a cloud into the heavens. The words of Jesus that he would go unto his Father, or return to his Father in Heaven, most certainly did not mean to indicate that his physical body would rise, nor did he intend to intimate precisely when or how this return of his spiritual being would occur.

This important event in the life of Jesus must be viewed in the mystical and spiritual sense, the same as his statements regarding the necessity for being born again in order to enter the Kingdom of Heaven. He distinctly explained that in the case of rebirth through repentance, he did not refer to a rebirth of the physical body during the earthly lifetime of any individual. The idea of the Ascension has, however, become misunderstood as a spiritual doctrine and it has developed into a belief in the resurrection and ascension of the physical body. This misunderstanding, encouraged by theological support, is responsible for the rejection of many of the Christian doctrines on the part of those who cannot conceive of these things in a physical and material sense.

The description of the Ascension given in the books of Mark and Luke are slightly different, for in one we read that Jesus was received up into Heaven, and in the other we read that he was carried up into Heaven. In the Book of Acts, the wording is that he was taken up to Heaven and a cloud received him out of their sight. In carefully analyzing these three accounts we note that the cloud which surrounded him and "received him out of their sight" has a spiritual significance which all students of mysticism will appreciate. Among the work of the masters of Tibet, Egypt, and India today, and even in the work of such masters in the Western world, the formation of clouds or bodies of mist that can be called out of the invisible to surround a person, and thus shut one out from the sight of others, is a demonstration often performed to prove the operation of many cosmic and spiritual laws.

It is not my intention to intimate that the cloud which descended upon Jesus and shut him out of the sight of the disciples or apostles was of the same nature as that mystic cloud which the masters today draw around themselves when they wish to fade out of sight gradually and disappear temporarily. I believe that the disappearance of Jesus was unique and has not been duplicated by any of the great masters or avatars since his time; but I wish to call attention to the fact that disappearing in this sense or in this manner should not carry with it the idea that because the cloud or mist arose after Jesus had disappeared, that Jesus himself, either physically or spiritually, arose with the clouds into the Heavens. Not being able to see him after the clouds started to rise, it was natural for the disciples to assume that he was in the cloud. Later when they wrote their records, and knew that this incident actually ended his public appearance only, they stated their impressions as though Jesus had actually disappeared in the cloud, as they believed at the time.

We find, in going over the ancient records, that Krishna, who was crucified and saved from the dead, was also credited by his followers with having ascended into Heaven. The ancient description says that at the time of the ascension a great light enveloped him, and he disappeared in the light. They also assumed that Krishna returned with the light as it rose from the earth and returned to Heaven. The records also show that Buddhas last appearance was on the top of a rock on a mountain in the presence of his followers, when a great light surrounded him and he disappeared in the light. Buddhas followers claimed that he then rose to the celestial regions; and for several centuries after this occurrence, impressions in the rock were shown to pilgrims as being those of the feet of Buddha where he stood when the ascension occurred. Zoroaster, another one of the great avatars, was also credited in all the pre-Christian accounts with having ascended to Heaven at the end of his earthly career.

The Egyptians celebrated the resurrection and ascension of Adonis for many centuries preceding the Christian era. In fact, the festivals in honor of the resurrection and ascension of Adonis were observed in Alexandria, Egypt, the very cradle of Christianity, in the time of St. Cyrio, bishop of Alexandria, A.D. 412, and at Antioch, the ancient capital of the Greek kings of Syria, during the time of Emperor Julian,

A.D. 361-363.

Even the children of Israel worshiped Adonis under the Jewish designation of Tammuz, and there was an altar in his name in the Temple of the Lord in Jerusalem. Several of the Psalms of David were parts of the liturgical service employed in the worship of Tammuz, especially the 110th Psalm. On this point, Dr. Parkhurst, the eminent Jewish authority, says in his book called The Hebrew Lexicon: "I find myself obliged to refer Tammuz, as well as the Greek and Roman Hercules, to that class of idols which were originally designed to represent the promised Saviour (Christ Jesus), the desire of all nations. His other name, Adonis, is almost the very Hebrew word 'our Lord,' a well-known title of Christ."

At least twenty other ancient avatars and gods of the people are credited in the ancient writings with having risen from among the dead (not out of death) and having ascended into Heaven as the closing incident of their public careers. It is to be noted that in most cases there is no intimation that the disappearance of an avatar from public sight; and the ascension of his spirit to the invisible realm meant a bodily ascension into the heavens or a cessation of physical existence on the earth plane. We note that in the ancient teachings regarding the great avatars, the emphasis was always put upon the fact that the divine spirit or spiritual light of the avatar returned to God or to the celestial regions, after which the light of the world went out. These ancient peoples, whom Christianity called pagans, had no idea of intimating that the physical body rose or disappeared, except that it remained out of the sight of the public.

Contrary to this, we have the gradual development, in the Christian doctrines, of the idea of the Resurrection and the Ascension of the body in a physical form Such an idea was not in the original and early Christian doctrines, but was added in the later centuries, when so many other Christian doctrines were invented or made theologically necessary, as explained in an earlier part of this book. This change of interpretation of the Resurrection and Ascension has caused much of the argument in modern times against the acceptance of the Christian doctrines in their entirety.

The disappearance of Jesus from public sight, thus closing his public work and public mission as the Christ, was not the end of his existence on the earth plane in the physical body. This is definitely stated in so many ancient and reliable records that it is surprising that the founders of the Christian church attempted to make his ascension a physical fact and proclaim it the end of his earthly career. In many of the discussions of the church councils in the first centuries after Christ, there were frank admissions on the part of the greatest of the authorities that Jesus lived to be fifty, sixty, or even seventy years of age. In some of these early discussions, the matter of apostolic succession was taken up and seriously analyzed for many years; and during those discussions much evidence in the way of writings and the word-of-mouth traditions was submitted to show that after the Ascension Jesus had labored with his apostles.

It was not until the doctrine of the Resurrection of the body and the Ascension of the body in a physical sense appeared to be an important theological necessity that these early church leaders decided, in their high councils, to eliminate all references to the activities of Jesus after the Ascension, and to make the Ascension appear to be the culmination of his physical existence, as well as of his Christly mission.

The ancient records of the G.W.B. and other records in the Rosicrucian archives clearly show that after Jesus retired to the monastery at Carmel, he lived for many years. He then carried on secret sessions with his apostles and devoted himself, through meditation and prayer, to the formulation of doctrines and teachings which his apostles should give to the world.

The original twelve apostles of Jesus were all Gentiles and selected from among those who were living in Galilee. Perhaps it has never occurred to the average Christian student to look into the lives of the apostles and note that all of them were living in Galilee at the time of their selection to form the private council of the Christ movement. Of the twelve, all but three—Lebbeus, Paul, and Judas— were of Aryan blood and were members of the Essenian community. Lebbeus and Judas were of the Jewish race, but they had adopted the Gentile religion by becoming heretics and abandoning much of the Jewish doctrines. After the passing of Judas and others, the vacancies in the council of twelve apostles were filled by other Gentiles of the Essenian community selected by the council itself.

The council of apostles met at the monastery, and the members practically lived in the environs of the monastery because of the daily sessions that were held in what might be called the apostolic school or college. It was this college or school that was the basis for the later establishment of a similar college in the Roman church.

According to the records, Jesus appeared but once a week before most of the apostles. This was always on a sabbath when a ceremony of a mysterious nature was held, and all who were not away on missionary work indulged in a symbolic feast. During the other days of the week, sessions were held for the purpose of instructing the apostles in their work, and these were presided over by the several high priests of the monastery.

It is this phase of the work of Jesus with his selected apostles that constitutes the great unknown period of his life. Only a few outstanding facts are given in the records regarding the closing years of his life and his association with the apostles. We find that about ten days after the retirement of Jesus from public life his apostles were assembled at a place in Jerusalem for the purpose of establishing the first congregation of the movement which was to be organized and known as the Christine Church.

Jesus himself had no part in the foundation of this movement, for it appears in the records that the apostles anticipated only a public assembly for the purpose of continuing the Christ teachings. But so large a congregation assembled, and the power of the Holy Spirit became so manifest, that the enthusiasm of the men and women and the prayers and cries of the repenting ones attracted the attention of scoffers and others. Therefore, it was found advisable to organize the work of the apostles into a definite movement, having a definite name and a regular place for meeting. There is nothing in the records to show that Jesus agreed to this plan or gave it any consideration, since his contact with the public was ended and his interests were solely in instructing and guiding the apostles in their own personal development and comprehension of his teachings, so that they might be proficient in their work. Ever since the occasion of the Ascension, when the Holy Ghost came upon the apostles and granted to them the same authority to carry on his work as he had carried it on, Jesus considered the apostles his successors as public messengers. Whatever plans they made to facilitate and improve their work with the public seem to have received no comment from Jesus, so far as we can find in any of the records.

After a year had passed, the movement of the Christine Church developed to such an extent that it was organized in a wider sense so as to include an inner circle that was devoted exclusively to the preservation of the Christ teachings and the maintenance of certain traditions and symbols. It was at this time that the cross, as a Christian symbol, was adopted; but strange to say, it was not adopted with a crucified body upon it, but a rose.

The Essenes, as a part of the G.W.B., had always used the cross as a symbol. This device originated as a mystical or esoteric symbol in the days of Akhnaton, pharaoh of Egypt, who used the cross in his mystery schools as an emblem of the human body with arms outstretched, representing the physical body with its sufferings and the trials of earthly life. The cross at that time had not been used before for the purpose of crucifixion, but it was used in the mystical sense because the human body with arms outstretched suggested it, especially when facing the sun at sunrise in making the usual mystical, morning salutations; for at such a time the shadow of one's body thrown upon the sand is in the form of a cross. The fact that this shadow is but a passing thing, an unreal thing, and merely of temporary existence, suggests itself as emblematic of our physical body and physical existence. In many of the ancient writings of the mystery schools of Egypt, and even in some of the hieroglyphic writings on the walls of these mystery schools, the cross was carved or painted in connection with esoteric principles.

At a time between the adoption of the cross as a symbol of the physical body and the formation of the Christine Church, a rose was added to the cross as a second element in the mystical symbol. The rose was likened to the human soul, because of its gradual unfoldment, beautiful perfume, richness of color, and manifestation of maturity. By adding the rose to the cross, the esoteric meaning of the combined symbol was that the soul personality evolves and becomes rich in experience and manifestation through the sufferings, trials, tribulations, and incidents of the physical body and physical existence.

The rose was also placed upon a cross as a symbol of the Crucifixion, like unto the dove, the sun, and the serpent. The crucified rose became the official symbol of the Rosicrucians, but was used by the various branches of the Essenes and G.W.B. before its official adoption as a universal emblem. The emblem of the early Templars was a red rose on a cross, adopted by them because of its use by the Essenes. In some of the early mystical manuscripts, we find this rose referred to as the Nauruts, Natsir, or rose of Isuren, of Tanuil, or Sharon, or the Water Rose, the Lily, Padma, Pena, Lotus—crucified in the heavens for the salvation of humanity. Jesus the Christ was called The Rose, and the Rose of Sharon, or of Isuren. In this we see the relationship of the Rosicrucian emblem to early Christian mysticism.

Thus the rose and the cross became an emblem of soul expression through human, physical experience. We can see in this mystical symbology a beautiful reason for the combination of the rose and cross as the emblem for the Christine Church. Later in the history of Christianity, Jesus himself was called the Rose, the Rose of Sharon, the Beautiful Rose, and the Holy Rose; and the rose on the cross was interpreted by many to represent the soul of Jesus on the cross, in all of its beauty and maturity, uncrucified. It was not until many centuries later that the church authorities, in their high councils, established the cross with the crucified body upon it as an emblem of the Christine movement.

The inner circle of the Christine Church also formed itself into a militant organization for the preservation of its sacred symbol, the cross, and later adopted a name which, when translated into Latin, would read Militia Crucifera Evangelica. This militant organization, which was to include those who would be selected in every country to represent it and carry on its activities, was to protect its sacred emblem from being adopted by other unauthorized organizations, and especially to protect it from being misused and misrepresented in matters that were not truly according to the Christ principles. This militant organization finally included the Hospitalers, the Knights of the Cross, and similar organizations, which were carrying on humanitarian activities in the name of the cross and in the name of the Christ principles. For many centuries the organization remained a very secret and little-known body of several hundred individuals, controlling and directing the activities of a number of other allied organizations; and during the time of the Crusades for the redemption of the Holy Land from the control of the so-called infidels, the Militia directed and controlled the important activities of the armies.

It is interesting to note, also, that after many centuries had passed, the organization suddenly became a nonsectarian body of defenders of the Cross, through a convention called at Liineburg, Germany, on July 27, 1586, which was sponsored by Henry IV of France, Elizabeth of England, Frederick II of Denmark, and the potentates of many other lands. At this convention the ancient records of the organization were revealed, and the doctrines of the organization and of the Essenes and the G.W.B. were reviewed and adopted as the rules and regulations, teachings, and practices of the Militia. All these things were then compiled into one great book of almost 2,000 pages which was completed in the year 1604, and officially called the Naometria. The Militia became an important organization in the prevention of further wars and forms of persecution in the name of religion. Membership in the Militia eventually became an honor resulting from unusual and distinguished service rendered in behalf of the pure symbolism of the cross and in behalf of humanity's mystical and religious development.

Early in the formation of the inner circle by the apostles in Palestine, members thereof were delegated to go to various lands and spread the work of the newly formed church. Peter was sent into Jerusalem, Antioch, and Rome. The elder St. James worked also in Jerusalem. St. John, after some missionary work in Jerusalem, centered his activities in the establishment of a church at Ephesus. St. Paul aided, first at Antioch, and then at Iconium, Lystra, Derbe, Troas, Philippi, Thessalonica, Berea, Athens, Corinth, and other cities. The other apostles labored first as assistants in the new churches and then went off to other lands. The Christine Church thus had its foundation among the most advanced nations.

In the meantime Jesus outlined and perfected the doctrines and teachings which he had received through inspiration during the days of his Christhood, and in the confinement of his sanctum he outlined these teachings to the high priests and the apostles who came to see him from time to time. Most of these doctrines and teachings were preserved by the apostles and especially by the high priests of the G.W.B., and from these preserved writings the organization extracted many of the teachings which it now uses throughout the world. An outline of the secret teachings of Jesus, as revealed in his public and private sessions with his apostles, disciples, and officers of the G.W.B., constitutes a wonderful volume of the principles of metaphysics and spiritual law. Perhaps these will be given to the public in time, for they would prove of inestimable value to the student of Christianity and to the student of mysticism.

The ultimate passing or transition of the great Master Jesus is recorded in the ancient records as having occurred peacefully and in the presence of the sisters and brothers in the monastery at Carmel. His body remained in a tomb on the mount for several centuries, but it was finally removed to a secret sepulchre guarded and protected by his brothers and sisters.

Thus endeth the story of the Great Initiate—the Messiah and the Son of God— the AMEN of the world, Lord and Redeemer.

35

Appendix

SOME INTERESTING CRITICISMS
IMMEDIATELY FOLLOWING THE issuance of the first edition of this book and throughout the worldwide sale of the first and second editions, many letters were received by the author
making critical comments regarding the contents of this book. Many of these comments will be interesting to the reader. Naturally, it was expected that this new version of the old stories of the life of
Jesus, and the presentation of some hitherto unpublished facts regarding his life, would bring forth
many serious objections on the part of Christian orthodoxy and many critical comments from two
classes of persons— the defenders of the faith, and the careless students of Christian theology. It was
never believed by either the author or the publishers that any of the Christian priesthood or clergy
would approve of and endorse the book. Yet this very thing did happen in a great many cases.

One of the interesting facts revealed by the letters of criticism received, and by the critical comments
about the book published in various newspaper articles and magazine contributions, is that many
eminent Christian clergy who should not have attempted to criticize the book without first becoming well versed in Christian history rushed into print with their condemnations of the book and
centered their arguments in one sweeping rebuke. Taking all of these rebukes and melting them, so
to speak, into one mold, we find the following words typical of the expression used.

"The author of The Mystical Life of Jesus presents us with a unique story which challenges many of
the statements contained in the Gospel records, but absolutely fails to give any Christian authority
for a single challenging statement that he makes."

Other clergy have privately and publicly denounced the book with the statement that "the author
quotes no Christian records, nor any part of the Gospel records to substantiate the statements he
makes."

Such criticism of the book is unfair, or at least disqualified, for the book itself claims to be a version
different from that generally held by the Christian authorities relating to the life of Jesus, and common sense would tell one that an entirely different book with challenging statements in it could not
rest upon quotations taken from the Christian Bible or the Christian writings.

The author feels that if in writing about the life of Jesus he were limited to quotations from the
Christian histories and to statements made in the Christian Gospels, there would be no need of
writing another book, for the Christian faiths have given to the world as interesting and attractive
histories of Jesus as their inner light would permit. To merely re-quote the Gospels would be equivalent to attempting to paint the lily. If no facts had been discovered which were contrary to the statements in the Christian Gospels and no further facts found which were absent in the Christian

records, there would have been no need to prepare another book dealing with the life of this great Son of God.

It seems strange however, that these Christian clergy could find no other points upon which to base their sincere objections to the book. The various chapters of this book make many challenging statements which if untrue should have been pointed out by the critics of the book as falsehoods and as unsubstantiated statements, but which if true should have forced the orthodox Christians to admit that this new book contained newer light and newer knowledge.

Why, for instance, should all of these clerics in writing their condemnations of this book refuse to answer or explain away the statement that Jesus did not live in Nazareth and was not a Nazarene by virtue of his association with a city that did not exist in his lifetime?

Not one of the thousands of criticisms published about this book by the orthodox defenders of Christian records contains a single comment regarding this point. Yet, if the point raised about Nazareth in this book is true, it opens wide a very large door to a serious criticism of an important fundamental claim made in behalf of Jesus.

Another interesting point is the fact that none of these learned or unlearned orthodox critics attempted to show that the records contained in this book relating to the events of the unknown youth of Jesus were inconsistent, improbable, or of any importance. Yet to the thousands of persons who have read the book and valued it, the facts relating to the youth of Jesus were outstanding in importance because they cast a very important light upon the whole of the life of Jesus.

It is probably sufficient unto themselves for these critics to throw the book aside, as they say they have done, or confine it to the rubbish heap, as they unhesitatingly reveal to the author with the declaration that "the whole book is an unsupported and uncorroborated piece of fiction." Such an attitude has been assumed by the learned and wise ones throughout all of the ages in regard to every new revelation not only in the field of religion and philosophy, but in science. It was this attitude that caused the church to cast aside the words of warning and the sound advice given by those who became illumined with the new truths. Many of these were burned at the stake or condemned to eternal imprisonment, but later made saints. In all ages there have been those who refused to believe the new facts of life and have condemned the one who attempted to reveal them.

Among the many peculiar ideas advanced in some newspaper and magazine communications regarding the book is a typical one which appeared in the letter column of the New York Sun for August 15, 1929. In the letters on this page one gentleman wrote his criticism of this book and made the following comment:

"A letter appeared in your page recently in which it was stated that

H. Spencer Lewis had written a book on the life of Jesus from data contained in the archives of the Rosicrucian Order. It seems rather strange to me that after nearly two thousand years something should turn up that adds anything to our present knowledge on this subject."

This idea seemed to form the basis of the objection on the part of a great many readers of the book. Why, they asked, has it taken almost 2,000 years for such interesting light on the life of Jesus to find publication? Why, asked others, should we believe that at this late period in history anything new could be found regarding the life of Jesus after thousands of investigators or seekers have spent hundreds of years searching in vain for such matter?

Such questions and critical comments do not deserve extended answers nor explanations. One might say, why would the forty-niners who went to California from the East find any gold in the hills after the padres and the Indians and others had spent scores of years vainly hunting for gold? Why should astronomers be scanning the sky even at this very hour in the hope of finding new worlds or new planets after so many years of minute search that has seemingly revealed everything that is to be found? Why believe that there can be any light found that will add to the accumulation of human wisdom? And why, may we ask, assume that the matter published in this book is "a new and recent discovery of historical facts"?

Such a claim is not made for the book or the facts it contains. The facts contained in this book have been known to and preserved by eminent authors for hundreds of years, and we know that most of these facts have been called to the attention of prominent clergy of the world for several centuries, but these clerics refused to publish the facts, refused to add them to the old records, and refused to reveal the new facts in any form. But even if these facts had been discovered only recently and just brought to light for the first time in the history of the world, it would not be surprising, nor make the facts appear to be incompatible with truth. Excavations are being made in Egypt and in parts of the Orient today for the purpose of discovering new facts relating to human history and the advancement of philosophy and religion. Each year sees new light cast upon the lives of the people and the incidents of history relating to the periods covered in the Christian Bible.

Scores of newspaper clippings have been sent to me along with magazine accounts and other records showing that in various parts of the world research work is being carried on with the hope of finding new facts relating to the life of Jesus and the whole story of creation as contained in the Christian Bible. Expeditions composed of archeologists specializing in biblical research and of theologians devoted to the work of translating and making researches into the earliest scriptural records have gone forth into Palestine and the Near East at great expense, exclusively for the purpose of obtaining more light regarding the periods dealt with in the Christian Bible.

Within recent years such expeditions have brought to light many new tombs and burial places containing indisputable evidence of early Christian burial with certain writings, notations, dates, and other facts which have cast much light upon the life and work of Jesus and his followers in these countries.

History distinctly tells us that many books of sacred writings were rejected when the present Christian Bible was compiled. Many of these rejected books have been brought to light and are found to be of intense interest. More are being found and translated, and there is no reason to suppose that all of the facts relating to the life of Jesus have been uncovered by orthodox investigators or by others.

It is not strange that the Rosicrucian records have contained these facts for many centuries, and it is not true that the Rosicrucians have wilfully and deliberately concealed these facts, nor held secret the fact that they possessed ancient records of this kind; but up to recent years the best translators and workers on new variations of the Christian Bible and Christian history have refused to examine the Rosicrucian records or the records contained in the archives of India, Egypt, and other lands, on the basis of either prejudice or ecclesiastical condemnation.

Returning again to the statement made in the forepart of this appendix to the effect that the book has been endorsed by many eminent clergy, much to the surprise of the author and the publishers, the author feels that this is the proper place to express his appreciation to these many learned and broad minded theologians and Christian advocates who have written him and thanked him for this new history, and especially for the emphasis that had been given to the mystical side of the life of Jesus. And there are those Christian workers who have used chapters from this book in adult Sunday school lessons and in Bible class lectures over a large number of radio stations. In this wise the facts contained in the book have been brought to the attention of many thousands. A direct result of this has been a deeper and more careful reading and analysis of the pages of the Christian Bible.

The letters of appreciation, endorsement, and requests for the privilege of quoting from the book in classes and public lectures have been very pleasing to the author and the publishers, and their sole purpose in issuing this book has been to give these new facts to the world. And if these facts can be given without the necessity of further editions of this book, or the selling of the book, it will bring still greater joy and happiness to the author and publishers. The publishers have donated nearly 2,000 copies of the book to the largest libraries throughout North America so that millions may have the opportunity to read it. That it will continue to be condemned and criticized is taken for granted, but the criticism of truth cannot destroy it, and there are thousands of Christians in the world today who say that their faith has been strengthened by and through a better and more intimate, as well as more sympathetic, understanding of the mystical life of Jesus.

God-Man: The Word Made Flesh

God-Man: The Word Made Flesh

Few books are as bold—or as misunderstood—as God-Man: The Word Made Flesh. First published in the early 20th century, this work by George W. Carey and Inez Eudora Perry delivers an audacious synthesis of scripture, anatomy, and spiritual alchemy. At its core lies a radical proposition: that the story of Christ is not only symbolic of cosmic truth, but also a coded guide to the transmutation of the human body into a divine vessel.

Here, salvation is not belief—it's biology. The "Word made flesh" becomes literal, as Carey and Perry map biblical allegories onto the inner workings of the human body. Christ becomes the sacred oil or "Christos" produced in the brain and crucified at the base of the spine—awaiting resurrection through the disciplined raising of kundalini-like energy.

This is Christianity stripped of its external trappings and returned to the temple of the body. It fuses Hermeticism, astrology, and esoteric physiology into a singular vision: that the divine spark resides not only within us—but is us.

Placed last in this compilation, God-Man takes the mystical and initiatory themes of Steiner and Lewis to their deepest and most intimate conclusion. It doesn't just ask you to believe—it asks you to become.

Approach it with an open mind, and it may change how you read the Bible, view your body, and understand the real meaning of the phrase: The Kingdom of God is within you.

THE REVOLUTIONARY PLANET, URANOUS,

THE hour has struck that opens the door for a New Dispensation for man, and the standing prophecy, proclaimed, trumpet-tongued, down thru the ages, is
now being fulfilled.   The old order is dying "Amidst its
worshippers."

God's loosened thunders shake the world! Across the lurid sky the-war birds scream! Earth's millions die!

Fear and woe unutterable!

The fires of purification are lighted!

Into the cosmic melting pot has been cast hate, race prejudice, selfishness and the devils of greed
!

The towers of superstition and tyranny are falling!

The thrones and scepters of kings lie scattered and crushed along the highway of nations!

Pride has fallen from its insecure pinnacle of shame I

The rich are terror stricken!

"Their silver has been cast into the street!" "Their gold has been removed from them!"

"The merchants of the earth weep and mourn, for no man buyeth their merchandise I"

The churches are in panic! The liquor power rages I

The gambler is terror stricken !

The grafting politician seeks a hiding place and finds none I

The briber flees when "no man pursueth !"

The priest and preacher pray, but no help comes, for they, too, must be judged!

The harlot alone seems unafraid, BECAUSE SHE IS NOT A HYPOCRITE, and has heard the words, "The harlots will enter the kingdom before you I"

Mankind has gone to the limit of animalism I

THE SOUL WALKS FORTH, NAKED AND ASHAMED. IT IS HIGH NOON OF THE JUDGMENT DAY.

-Written in 1916.

REDEMPTION, THE ULTIMATE GOAL OF HUMANITY

TAOISM: "Man consisting of a trinity of spirit, mind and body, cometh forth from the Eternal, and after putting off desire re-enters the glory of Tao."

Brahmanism: "Man's inner self is one with the self of the Universe, and to that Universe and to that Unity it must return in the fullness of time."

Buddhism: "Man, fundamentally Divine, is held in the three worlds by desire. Purification from desire leads the man to Nirvana."

Hebrewism: "Man came into being through emanation from the will of the King, therefore is divine."

Egyptian: "Teaches the divinity of man, Osiris as his source."

Zoroastrianism: "Man is a spark of the universal flame to be ultimately united with its source."

Orphic: "Man has in him potentially the sum and sub stance of the Universe."

- Christian: "Man made in the image of God-Body, Soul and Spirit-a Trinity."

THE KINGDOM AT HAND

MAN is within one step of his ideal-the ultimate goal of his desires-that realm of freedom where he will rio longer be subject to law, but, being

"led by the spirit," will realize that he, himself, is an operator and attribute of the law.

Man is law in action. Will man now take the final step into complete liberty and become a god, or continue to eat of the husks of sJual concept and still cower beneath the lash of "precedent'and authority"?

There is no "salvation" or regeneration for Man, as long as he believes in vicarious atonement. The man who needs saving by that process is not worth the price.

Recognition of eternal unity will save Man from the idea that he needs saving, because it will reconcile him to his- place and mission in the Plan-the Great Necessity. It will reveal to him his true kinship to the causeless cause, the beginningless beginning, and he will know that he is an attribute of universal energy from which all forms, thoughts, motions, sounds, colors, and so-called "good and evil," proceed.

In the full light of this wisdom, man will not search for personal saviors, nor quibble about the meaning of the words of men who died tho1,1sands of years ago.

Jesus, Christ, Truth, Life-forever preaches the ser mon in the ear of man: "Lo I I am with you now." "He that confesseth not that Jesus Christ is come in the flesh, the same is an Anti-Christ."

Only the spiritually blind look for the "coming" of Truth, or Life, the Christ who is ever present, or for the "coming" of a kingdom which is already at hand. "When ye pray for a thing know that ye have it now."

If we accept a certain statement uttered, as an ultima tum, by some one who lived in the dim past, we may be called upon to reconcile the utterance with another opinion, spoken or written by the same person, which seems to contradict previous statements in which we have placed our trust.

These persons, bdng dead, cannot be asked for an ex planation in regard to the seeming contradiction. If they could, they might respond, as Walt Whitman did when a critic hinted that the "good gray poet" contradicted him self: "Do I contradict myself? Then I contradict my self. I am large, I contain multitudes."

We must consider the facts that the opinions uttered by men in past ages extend over a period of years, during which time empires rose and fell, and new concepts of life, due to planetary and zodiacal changes, obtained rec ognition. Thus radical changes occurred in the social, religious, scientific and industrial world.

Viewing the question in this light, need we wonder that the_seers and sages, saints and scientists of the past should sometimes contradict themselves?

Are we, today, so very consistent?

Do we not enact what we call "sacred laws," immedi ately violate them and carry the case to the court of last resort and get the "sacred" law repealed?

We have had high and low tariff, bimetalism and gold standard, and our great statesmen valiantly upheld the

·free coinage of silver in the year 1895, and in 1896 these same captains of finance declared through the public press that free coinage of silver would destroy civiliza tion, tear down the pillars of Hercules and wrench the stars from their cosmic thrones.

We have contradicted ourselves in our opinion of the earth's shape, the distance to the Sun, the origin and oper ation of electricity, the cause of light, the divisibility of elemental gases, the circulation of the blood, the reality of hell and the devil and other subjects too numerous to mention.

Then, shall we forever wrangle over the contradictory statements of dead men who wrought in their day as best they might with the light and data at their com mand, with no thought that people in future ages would war to the death or live with hate in their hearts for

[12]their fellows who differ with them on baptism, the size of Noah's ark, or whether a prophet swallowed a fish or a fish swallowed a prophet?

So much for the old world belief, that the Scriptures (writings) are records of men and women and places, geographical, historical, etc.

These wonderful statements are fables, parables, alle gories, dealing with the chemical, physiological, anatom ical and astrological operations of the HUMAN BODY, "Fearfully and /Wonderfully made."

"Great are the symbols of Being,

But that which is symboled is greater; Vast the create and beheld,

But vaster the llward Creator."-Richard Real/.

39

BOOKS REJECTED BY THE COUNCIL OF NICEA,

BOOKS of the Koran-Persia; Hebrew (Meaning Passover) ; Esther; Solomon; Egyptian Book of the Dead; Adam; Eve; Enoch; Seth; Seventh Book of Moses; St. Thomas (The Doubter); Nicodemus; Ptah

Hotep, the oldest book known; The Kabballah.

Again, the researches of such theological scholars as James Legge, L.L.D., first Professor of Chinese, at Ox ford University; Prof. Wm. Jennings, P.H.D., and Hon. Clement Allen of the Royal Asiatic Society, beside several hundred who might be named, embracing the leaders of thought along lines of "original sources," all agree that hundreds, if not thousands, of ancient manuscripts, tablets and carvings indubitably prove that all races of all people that have ever inhabited the earth have striven, as best they could, to leave records of the chemistry and physi ology of their own bodies.

Science, Egyptology, Inda-Iranian, Chinese, Japanese, Persian, or Sanskrit, all, all, forever strove to solve the riddle of the human body.

Seven hundred years B. C. we have the Shu King, China's oldest book; The Shih King, 600 B. C.; The Yi King, 1143 B. C.

Then came Confucius, 551-478 B. C.

The writings, statements, philosophy and symbols of these witnesses of the truth of being corroborates our 66 witnesses in every detail.

The writers of this book have in their possession a library of the ancient scriptures referred to above and know whereof they speak; but, as printing and book mak ing is well nigh prohibited by cost, we feel that we are not justified in lengthy quotations. Again, nothing really new can be added after the ne plus ultra statement, "There is no other way under heaven whereby ye may be

[14]saved except Jesus, Christed and crucified."

However, for the information of our readers we will give the table of contents of Vol. 14 of the Sacred Books and Early Literature of the East, entitled "The Great Rejected Books":

OLD TESTAMENT APOCRYPHA

The Books of Adam and Eve; The lives of Adam and Eve; The Appcalypse of Moses; The Slavonic Book of Eve.

The Writings Attributed to Enoch; The Great Prophetic Book of Enoch; The Lost Book of Noah.

The Apocalypse of Baruch; His Vision of Heaven.

The Story of Ahikar;

The Old Armenian Version; The New-found Ancient Book.

THE   NEW TESTAMENT APOCRYPHA

The Gospels of Christ's Childhood;

The Protevangelium, or Original Gospel of James; Gospel of Thomas the Doubter;

The Gospel of Pseudo-Matthew; An Arabic Gospel of the Infancy.

The Gospels of Nicodemus;

The Greek Gospel of Nicodemus; A Later Gospel;

The Harrowing of Hell; The Acts of Pilate;

The Letters of Pilate.

40

NAMES

NAMES will be explained without alphabetical order, the object being to show that the 66 books of the whole book (Holy Book), were 66 statements by 66 different writers about the same identical subject-the human body, its chemical operation and the planetary positions, impinging to create and bring into physical manifestation the visible universe.

ADAM: Red earth, or flow of spirit or energy, dammed up.

EVE: Mother of all the living; ether or pure spirit; Mother of God-Water; fluid; esse.

CAIN: What is gotten-acquisition, a spear, a smith; a worker.

ABEL: Transitoriness; breath; vapor; moisture (ab- sorbed-killed by Cain) .

SETH: Seed, seedling or germ. MAN: See Adam.

WoMAN: Wom(b)an, or womb in man (mankind); the regenerative womb or manger in the solar plexus. (See Bethlehem, house-of-bread).

Non: Flight; Cain absorbed (killed) Abel (moisture) and vegetation sprang up (shoot-movement) .

WIFE: Marriage of earth and water.

JOSHUA: Jehovah-in-salvation; son of Nun-fish. MosEs: Drawn from the water; fish.

ABRAM: High father, father of elevation. ABRAHAM: Father of a multitude.

AARON: Enlightened (Buddha-Third Eye).

HoR: Mountain, Mountain of Aaron, situated on the East side of the great valley of the Arabah, the high est and most conspicuous of the whole range of the sandstone mountains of Edom, having close beneath it on its East side, the mysterious city of Petra.

PETRA: Rock; Rock city, south of Jericho. EDOM: Red; Edom or Odumea-pituitary body.

JACOB: Circle; heel-catcher; lier-in-wait. (Applied to the 12 Zodiacal signs, in astrology; to the solar plexus, in physiology.)

LEAH: First wife of Jacob, represented in astrology by several of the Zodiacal signs, namely: Reuben, libra; Simeon, Scorpio; Levi, Sagittarius; Judah, Capricorn; Issachar, Gemini; Zebulum, Cancer, and Dinah, Leo. The name means, in Hebrew, wearied, weak, slow action, inferior. (See cut.)

RACHEL: .,. Second wife of Jacob: a ewe; Mother of Jo seph and Benjamin, represented in astrology by Vir go for Joseph; ijenjamin having a deeply esoteric significance. It represents the product.

BENJAMIN: Son of the right hand; son of my old age; called first, by his mother, "son of my sorrow." He was the only child to be born in Palestine-the Holy Land. In Smith's Bible Dictionary we find this, "The Ark was in Benjamin." To esoteric students this statement is significant. Plainly speaking, Ben jamin is the same as Jesus and refers to the seed or son that redeems.

PALESTINE: Land of sojourners; country of Israel or Holy Land.

ARARAT: Holy Land. ABBA: Father (God). ABSALOM: Father of Peace.

ADAH, ADAIAH, ADDI: Ornament, whom God has adorned: Refers to Pituitary body.

ADONAI: Lord.

ZoHELETH: THE STONE; serpent, the rolling stone; the serpent stone, the stone of the conduit.

G1LGAL: A circle or rolling away; the place where the 12 stones were set up, the place of the "Passover," "A hot depressed district," says Smith's Bible Dic tionary. Refers in anatomy to the 12th dorsal ver tebra, at which place the semi-lunar ganglion con nects. At this point the seed or ark enters Jordan or the spinal cord.

JORDAN: The descender; the flowing river. A river that has never been navigable, flowing into a sea that has never known a port. About 200 miles long, rising from the roots of Anti-Lebanon to the head of the Dead Sea. "The river of God"-see Smith's Bible Dictionary. In anatomy-the Spinal cord, the great nerve which is supplied with fluid from the claustrum in the cerebrum.

"The Jordan was crossed over by Joshua (Fish) , the son of Nun (fish)," Smith's Bible Dictionary. As Joshua and Jesus mean the same, we see by this that this is the place of the baptism of Jesus. See further reference to this.

Only two fords are mentioned in the Bible. These in anatomy are the end of the spinal cord at the 12th Dorsal vertebra, and at the base of the skull.

Smith also says that the true source of the Jordan is "Underground in Phiala (meaning vial or bowl), and on the right hand side." "It is from this 'cave' that the Jordan commences its course above ground." Compare this description with the anatomy of the head and its meaning becomes clear. Smith tells us that the upper part of the slope is alive with bursting fountains and gushing streams that find their way into the Jordan. These in Anatomy refer to the glands in the brain that connect with the spinal cord. Read in Smith's Bible Dictionary the wonderful de scription ,of this River.

GENESARETH: Gardens of the Prince; a crescent shaped (Moon-shaped) plain on the western shore of Lake Genesareth, which is also the Sea of Galilee. The Sea of Galilee is the semi-lunar ganglion thru which the seed or Jesus passes to reach the spinal cord. The Jordan enters in at the North and passes out at th·esouth. It abounds in fish.

DAUGHTER: Bath. Anything regarded as feminine. GALILEE: A circle or circuit.

NAZARETH: Shoot, sprout, twig.

CAPERNAUM: Village of Nahum (consolation). CANA: Place of reeds; Lungs.

JERICHO: Place of fragrance; Cerebellum.

41

JOURNEY OF JOSEPH AND MARY

THE MARVELOUS STORY OF THE JOURNEY OF JOSEPH AND MARY TO JERUSALEM TO PAY THEIR TAXES PHYSIOLOGICALLY EXPLAINED

ON EITHER side of the Thalamus, in the head, is a gland, known in physiology as the Pineal, on the posterior, and the Pituitary on the anterior side of the Thalamus.

The Pineal is cone shaped, and secretes a yellow or golden fluid. The Pituitary Body, opposite it, is ellipsoid in shape, and contains a whitish secretion, like milk.

The fluids that are found in both these bodies come from the same source, namely, the Claustrum, which means "barrier" or "cloister," and is referred to as cloister for the very good reason that a precious and holy thing is secreted or secluded there. Saint Claus, or Santa Claus, is another term for this precious fluid, which is indeed a holy gift in the body of each one of us.

The precious fluid which flows down from the Claus trum separates, part going into the Pineal gland and part to the Pituitary body, and these, being special laboratories of the head, differentiate the fluid from the Claustrum, and it takes on the colors above mentioned, and in the Pineal Gland becomes yellow and has electric properties. The Pituitary Body, having the milk-like fluid, has mag netic properties.

These two glands are the male and female, the Joseph and Mary of the physical body, and are the par ents of the spiritual son born in the solar plexus of each human being, commencing about the age of twelve.

This yellow and white material, which is the milk and honey referred to in the Bible, the children of Israel having been given the promise of a return to this land flowing with milk and honey, at last reaches the solar plexus via semi-lunar ganglia (see ch rt), the Bethlehem of the physical body. In He-brew, Bethlehem means "house" (Beth) of bread (lehem). "I am the bread of life," said the allegorical Jesus.

In the solar plexus is a thimble-shaped depression-a CAVE-or manger, and in this is deposited the psycho physical seed, or holy child, born of this immaculate con ception. This psycho-physical seed is also called "fish," as it has the odor of fish and is formed in the midst of the waters, the pure water. "Jesus is a fish in the midst of the waters"-St. Augustine. Before birth the human foetus floats, like a fish, in the fluids by which it is sur rounded. And as it is with the child formed on the generative plane, so it is with the spiritual child born in the solar-plexus-the Bethlehem. Joseph and Mary, by furnishing the material for the spiritual child which was to redeem the child or body formed in generation, paid the symbolical redemption money.

Holy Ghost-Greek for breath. The breath, descend ing the pneumo-gastric nerve into the solar center, enters the manger where Joseph and Mary are, and where is Jesus the Seed literally "conceived by the Holy Ghost."

42

MAN

"God hath made man upright; but they have sought out many inventions."

THERE is an automatic procedure within the human body, which, if not interfered with will do away with sickness, trouble, sorrow and death, as stated

in the Bible

Truly, mankind, or the natural man, seeks many ways and means to prevent the upright, perfect, automatic way from "accomplishing that whereunto it was sent."

The natural man forever seeks pleasurable sensation, wn1ch is at enmity with God. Physical sensation (the "Pleasures of sin for a season," or limited duration, re.:

£erred to by Paul, are under the law, or below the solar olexus, hence, "He that is led by the spirit is not under the J.:i.w."

The 21st letter of the Hebrew alphabet, "schin" or "shin," lacks one of the complete alphabet, "tav," the 22nd letter, meaning the "cross."

Herewith are given a few of the Greek and Hebrew

<:haracters that have been translated, "sin, or falling

<ihort." Hebrew: "asham, het, chet, hata, avon" (trans lated iniquity more than 200 times), means "Conceived in sin and brought forth in iniquity" (or sin), oesha or pasha.

In Greek we find this word written as "harmartia, proanartano, anamartetos, anomia, anomos, parabaimo." Any act, coming under the meaning of sin, retards

or prevents the automatic action of the seed, which, if not interfered with, lifts up a portion (one-tenth) of the life essence (oil or secretion) that constantly flows down the spinal cord (a "Strait and narrow way") and trans mutes it, thus increasing its power many fold and per petuating the body indefinitely, or until the Ego desires tc, dissolve it by rates of motion set in action by its inherent will.

If the allegories of Matthew, Mark, Luke and John, as well as Paul's Epistles and Acts of the Apostles teach any thing, they teach the mastery and transmutation of the human body by anyone who obeys the physiological guide book-the whole book-the Holy Bible.

But let the reader observe that each of the 66 books, as well as an almost countless number of ancient books of all races and languages, teach the same mathematical and physiological facts.

Man has turned the mighty power he possesses to every object and principle of force in the universe except himself, the greatest miracle of all. When man focuses his divine thinking lens upon himself, he will realize that he is an epitome of unlimited Cosmic Energy. Then the "Heavens will roll together as a scroll" and reveal the Real Man as 'the Lamb of God that taketh away the sins of the world."

43

IT: THE ETERNITY OF PERFECTION

A CHILD brought to its mother a piece of ice and asked: "What is this?" The mother answered, "it is ice."

Again the child asked, "What is there in ice?" The mother answered: "There is water in the ice."

The child desired to find the water in the ice, and it procured a hammer, pounded the piece of ice into little bits and the warm air soon changed all the ice to water. The child was grievously disappointed, for the ice that the child supposed contained water had disappeared.

And the child said, "Where is the ice that contained this water?"

And so it came to pass that the mother was compelled, by the child's persistent questions, to say, "ice is all water; there is no such thing as ice; that which we call ice is crystalized or frozen water."

The child understood.

A student brought to his teacher some water and asked, "What is water? What does it contain?"

The teacher answered, "Water contains oxygen and hydrogen," and then explained how the two gases might be separated and set free by heat.

The student boiled the water until all of the molecules of oxygen and hydrogen had been set free, but he was surprised to find that all of the water had disappeared.

Then the student asked of the teacher, "Where is the water that held the gases that have escaped?"

Then was the teacher compelled by the student's per sistent questions to answer, "Water itself is the product of oxygen and hydrogen. Water does not contain any thing other than these gases. In reality, there is no such substances or fluid as water; that which we name water is a rate of motion set in operation by the union of two

[23]parts of hydrogen with one part of oxygen and, of course, the phenomenon disappears when the union of the gases is broken."

The student understood.

A devout scientist presented himself before God and said, "Lord, what are these gases men call oxygen and hydrogen?"

The good Lord answered and said, "They are mole cules in the blood and body of the universe."

Then spake the scientist, "Lord, wilt thou tell me of the kind of molecules that compose Thy blood and body?" The Lord replied, "These same molecules, gases or principles, compose my blood and body; for I and the

universe are one and the same."

Once again the scientist said, "My Lord, may I ask, then, what is spirit and what is matter?"

And thus answered the Lord:

"As ice and water are one, and the gases and water are one, so is spirit and matter one. The different phases and manifestations cognized by man in the molecules of My body-that is, the universe-are caused by the Word; thus, they are My thoughts clothed with form."

Now the scientist felt bold, being redeemed from fear, and asked ' is my blood, then, identical with Thy blood in composition and Divine Essence?"

And the Lord said, "Yea, thou art one with the Father."

The scientist now understood and said:

"Now mine eyes are opened and I perceive that, when I eat, I partake of Thy body; when I drink, I drink of Thy blood; and when I breathe, I breathe Thy spirit."

So-called matter is Pure Intelligence and nothing else because there is not anything else.

Pure intelligence cannot progress or become better. There is nothing but Intelligence. Omnipresence, Omni potence, Omniscience must mean Intelligence; therefore these terms are all included in the word.

Let us adopt a short word that will express all that the above written words are intended to express, namely, the word IT. "I" stand for all-the eternal I. "T" stands for operation, manifestation, vibration, action or motion. The "I" in motion is "T," or Crossification, viz., the T-cross. We say, "IT" rains I "IT is cold I" "IT is all right I" What do we mean by "It?" Whoknows? Some say, "The weather!" Others, "Natural phenom ena!" Very well, then-what do we mean by "the weather," or "natural phenomena?" Why, just It, of course!

IT does not progress; it does not need to. IT forever manifests, operates, differentiates and presents different aspects or viewpoints of ITSELF. But these different phases are neither good, better nor best, neither bad nor worse-simply different shades and colorings of the One and Only Intelligence.

Every so-called thing, whether it be animal, vegetable or mineral, molecule or atom, ion or electron, is the result of the One Intelligence expressing itself in different rates of motion. Then what is Spirit?

Spirit means breath or life. Spirit, that which is breathed into man, must be intelligence, or man would not be intelligent. Non-intelligent substance, which is, of course, unthinkable, would not breathe into anything, nor make it intelligent if it did. Therefore, we see that Spirit, Intelligence and Matter are one and the same Esse in different rates of motion.

So-called molecules, atoms, electrons, know what to do. They know where and how to cohere, unite and operate to form a leaf or a flower. They know how to separate and distintegrate that same leaf or flower. These particles of omnipresent life build planets, suns and systems; they hurl the comet on its way across measureless deserts of star-dust and emboss its burning path.

From the materialistic and individual concept of life and its operations, it is pitiable and pathetic to view the wrecks along the shores of science. It is only when we view these apparently sad failures from the firm foothold of the unity of being and the operation of wisdom that we clearly see in these frictions and warring elements and temoorary defeats and victories the chemical operation of Eternal Spirit-operating with its own substance-its very self. It is only through the fires of transmutation that we are enabled to see that all life is one Eternal Life and therefore cannot be taken, injured, or destroyed.

The fitful, varying, changing beliefs of men in the tran sition stage from the sleep and dreams of materialism to the realization of the Oneness of Spirit show forth in a babel of words and theories, a few of which I shall briefly consider, beginning with the yet popular belief in Evolu tion:

The evolutionary concept has its starting point in the idea (a) that matter-so-called-is a something separate from mind, intelligence, or Spirit; (b) that this matter had a beginning; (c) that it contains within itself the desire to progress or improve; and, finally, that th race is progressing, becoming wiser, better, etc.

Against this assumption, I submit the proposition that the Universe-one verse-always existed without begin ning or ending and is and always has been absolutely per fect in all its varied manisfestations and operations.

A machine is no stronger than its weakest part. If the self-existing universe is weak or imperfect in any part, it must, of necessity, always have been so. Having all the knowledge there is-being all-it is unthinkable that there is any imperfection anywhere. Everything we see, feel, or taste, or in any manner sense, is perfect substance, con densed or manifested from perfect elements, but all differ in their notes, vibrations, or modes or rates of motion. A serpent is as perfect, therefore as good, as a man. With out feet, it outruns a man; with_out hands, it outclimbs the ape, and has been a symbol of wisdom through all the ages. Man is an evil thing to the serpent's consciousness. Neither are evil-nor good. They are different expres sions or variations of the "Play of the Infinite Will."

The brain of the jelly-fish is composed of the same ele ments, of the same substance as the brain of a man, merely of a different combination. Can man tell what the jelly fish is thinking, or why it moves and manifests its energy thus or so? How, then, is man wiser than the jelly-fish because his thoughts are of a different nature and operate to different ends?

Wisdom-all there is-simply operates, manifests, ex presses forms, or creates them, of, self-existing sub stance. As wisdom is without beginning or end, so are all its operations or manifestations without beginning or end.

Modern man is now taking his first lessons in con densing or materializing air, while through unnumbered ages the spider has performed the miracle without the necessity of first attending a school of chemistry. The modus operandi by which the spider forms his web from air is the desp'air of science. The wisdom of the ant or beaver strikes dumb all the believers in the Darwinian dream. The perfect co-operative commonwealth of the bees is still the unattained ideal of man.

Beneath the soil upon which falls the shadow of the throne of Menelik, tlie Abyssinian King, are layers and strata of buried civilizations, and astronomers in China mapped the Heavens, named the stars, calculated the eclipses and the return of comets ages before Moses led the Hebrews out of bondage, or the walls of Baalbeck cast a shade for the Arab and his camel.

The evidences and witnesses of the wisdom of men on earth hundreds of thousands of years ago confront the scientific investigator at every turn. Here the Rosseta Stone, and there the Inscribed Cylinder of Arioch or Statue of Gudea, King of Chaldea. Prophecies, inscribed on Cunieform tablets of Clay, foretelling the building of the Pyramids, are brought to light by the excavator; and the history of the Chinese Empire, running back in links of an unbroken chain for one hundred and fifty thousand years, forever refute the theory of the "Descent of Man I" Side by side with the anscient Asiatics, who knew all that we today know, dwelt the Crystal, the Cell, the Jelly-fish, the

Saurian, the Ape and the Cave-Man. Side by side with the masons, who could build arches of stone in ancient Yucatan that mock at the ravages of Time, lived and wrought the ant, operating in its co-operative common wealth of which man can still only dream. Side by side with the cave men and cannibals dwells the spider, whose operation in aerial elements is the despair of chemical investigators. And when Solomon's golden-spired temple illuminated the Holy City, or the tower of Babel grew toward the clouds, or the Mound Builders recorded their history in rock and soil, the eagle and the dove calmly floated in the air and wondered when men would evolve to their plane of science. They are wondering still.

Exponents of the evolutionary theory never tire in quot ing Professor Huxley. One who has not read the writings of this eminent scientist would be led to believe by the statements of his followers that he had positive views on the great question of force and matter. Following is an extract from a letter written by Professor Huxley to Charles Kingsley, under date of May 22nd, 1863, taken from the published letters of Huxley by his son, Leonard:

"I don't know whether Matter is anything distinct from Force. I don't know that atoms are anything but pure myths-'Cogito ergo sum' is to my mind a ridiculous piece of bad logic, all I can say at any time being 'Cogito.' The Latin form I hold to be preferable to the English 'I think,' because the latter asserts the existence of an Ego about which the bundle of phenomena at present address ing you knows nothing. I believe in Hamilton, Mansell and Herbert Spencer, so long as they are destructive, and laugh at their beards as soon as they try to spin their own cobwebs."

"Is this basis of ignorance broad enough for you? If you, theologian, can find as firm footing as 1, man of science, do on this foundation of minus naught-there will be naught to fear for our ever diverging. For you see, I am quite as ready to admit your doctrine that souls secrete bodies as I am the opposite one that bodies secrete souls-simply because I deny the possibility of obtaining any evidence as to the truth or falsehood of either hypo thesis. My fundamental axiom of speculative philosophy is that materialism and spiritualism are opposite poles of the same absurdity-the absurdity of imagining that we knew anything about either spirit or matter."

Huxley admitted that he did not know.

As the appetite craves new chemical combinations of food from day to day, so does mind crave new concepts of

infinite life. The word "Infinite" defines an endless dif ferentiation of concept.

If the Spiritual Consciousness-the "mighty Angel" that the clairvoyant seer, John the Revelator, saw descend ing out of the Heavens-shall carry away the pillars of material evolution, a Temple of Truth divinely fair will spring, Phoenix-like, to take its place. Eyes shall then be opened and ears unstopped. Man will then realize that the so-called lower forms of life are just as complex, won derful and difficult to form as the organism of man-that proto-plasm is1as wonderful in any other form as in the gray matter of the human brain, which is only another form of its expression-that the molecular composition of a jelly-fish puzzles the greatest chemist, and the wisdom of a beaver is enough to strike dumb all the believers in the Darwinian fairy -tale.

And has the dream of good and evil any better founda tion than has this one of material evolution? We are here to solve the problems of life, not to evade them; and, to name the mighty operations of Eternal Wisdom, good and evil is simply evading instead of solving.

The universal Principle, Spirit, or God, is impartial. Saint and Sinner are one in the Eternal Mind.   God, or Infinite Life is not in the least injured by so-called good or evil.   The Spiritual Ego is the interested party and must work out its own Salvation.   There is no point in the universe better, higher, or nearer God, or the centre, than any other point. All places are necessary, and no one is favored over any other.   As Huxley well said, "Good and evil are opposite poles of the same absurdity." Good must have evil for its opposite, if it exists at all. He who would realize Being must get rid of the concept of good, as well as the concept of evil. Good and evil are qualifications, and Being does not admit of qualification or grades.   It simply is.   The ideal we call good eternally exists, but its name is wisdom's operations.   Nothing is low or high, good or bad, except to that individual con cept which allows comparison. "Comparisons are odious." Physical Science, so-called, declares in its text-books that light travels from the sun to the earth in eight minutes a distance of about ninety-five million miles. To question this statement a few years ago meant ostracism from the circle of the elect who knew things. But today the icono clast stands at the gate of the temples of learning and batters at the walls with the hammer of Thor. Fear and trembling seize upon the votaries of material gods as they see evolution, progression, the theories of electricity, light and heat, good and evil, all cast into the crucible of truth for transmutation in the Divine Alchemy of Being, all dissolving as pieces of ice of different sizes and shapes change to water.

The present day chemist, as he begins to tread the soil where stood the ancient alchemist, tells us that light and heat are simply the rates of motion of a substance that does not travel from star to star or from sun to planet, but vibrates in its place at rates directed by the Eternal Word. This substance, aerial or etheric, does not travel

-it is everywhere present-the body of omnipresent being. .

Men now dare assert that there is no evidence that the sun is hot, but that there is evidence that the sun is the dynamo of the Solar System and so vibrates the etheric substance that light, heat, cold and gravitation are pro duced-not as entities separate from the universal ele ments, but as results or effects produced by different rates of motion of the molecules of the wire-molecular motion

-or of the air or etheric substance, as in wireless teleg raphy.

Another ancient belief, now obsolete, is the progression of man in a better state of existence after death or cess ation of bodily functions. This idea had its origin in the fallacy that there were grades of goodness in the Divine Mind, and that somehow we are not treated right during earth life, and that, in consequence, we must be rewarded by an easy berth "over there." But we now see quite clearly that the great cause of life and all its operations would be unjust to withhold from its sons and daughters for one moment anything that belonged to them. If the Cause ever does wrong, we see no reason why it should repent and do right. If the Cause ever failed in the least particular to give just dues, it m_ay do so a ain at any time. The "better state of existence" mentioned above can only come through wisdom obtained here and now; thus will man "work out his own salvation."

The time was, and not so very long ago, when the recognized scientist believed that there were about seven ty-four elements, indivisible, separate and distinct; but the alchemical iconoclast with his hammer of truth has pulverized the fallacy and remorselessly hammered and pounded the seventy-four faces into one countenance.

For a long time, hydrogen gas, the negative pole of water, was supposed to be indivisible beyond all question; but the present day chemist knows it .is only an expression of yet more subtle molecules back of which, "Standeth God within the shadow keeping watch above His own."

A post-mortem examination of some of the wrecks along the shores of the troubled sea of science discloses a belief that the Ego is an individual, who through knowl edge of its divine origin may draw unto itself all things it may desire I But as fast as the Sleepers awaken they see that each Ego is only "part of one stupendous whole" that does not draw unto its lf anything. That there is no law of attraction for the eternal substance is every where present and each one uses exactly that portion pre pared for him from everlasting unto everlasting.

When the continuity of life was first demonstrated be yond question those who caught the first dispatches from disincarnate spirits sprang forth from their beds of mate rial sleep and with half-opened eyes only saw the great truth through "a glass darkly." Then came a babel of words. They jabbered a jargon that needed translation to be understood. The ideas of progression in earth life that obtained among men was transplanted to the spirit realm and we were told by the votaries of spiritual phil osophy that men and women had great opportunities for progression after leaving the flesh. As the idea of a com mencement of the universe was a common belief among those asleep in material consciousness, being the corner stone of evolution, so the idea obtained that the individual had a commencement in the maternal human laboratory.

As these half-awakened individuals could not comprehend that an action contrary to their concept of good could possibly be caused by Infinite Intelligence they concluded that the so-called bad actions of men and women were prompted by evil earth-bound spirits. These people many of them also thought that the main object of the existence of Spirits in the Spirit realm was to gather infor mation about mines and stocks and bonds and lotteries and races and thus assist poor mortals to ret-rich-quick. It was supposed that these spirits were posted in regard to deeds and wills and knew when wealthy relatives would shuffle off the mortal coil or when undesirable wives or husbands would "pass out."

But at last the sun of Truth pierced the darkness and the jargon of selfishness changed to the "New Song." We now clearly see that each spirit is a part or attribute of the One Eternal Spirit-therefore has existed always and that the process of generation deals with flesh clothing, or mask for the spirit in which it performs a necessary part in the creative process. The word "person" is de rived from a Greek word, Persona, meaning mask.

We see that the phenomena we have called obsession by evil spirits is God's surgery or dynamic operation in His own temple quite as impossible for us to understand in our present environment as it is for the child to under stand the wisdom and necessity in the operation of the adept surgeon.

And, finally, we now see and realize fully that Eternal Wisdom without beginning or end of days does not prog ress before entering a temple of flesh, while it occupies it, or after it leaves it. All creative or formative proc esses may oroperly be termed operations of wisdom or Eternal Life.

In the unwalled temple of the Now, beneath its roofless dome there is no progression, but a constantly moving panorama forever presenting to consciousness new phases of the absolute.

The men and women who do things take hold of oppor tunities and material that they find all about them now, and operate with them, astonishing results following the efforts of all who recognize hat eternal force has use for them NOW to drry out the divine plan. We are all operators or workmen in the divine workshop, and the Divine Intelligence, the eternal IT, made no mistake in placing any of us here, but does insist that we recognize that NOW is the time and Here is the place to do our best. As the Great Cause does not need to first practice on lower forms in order at some future time to attain perfection, we must recognize and practice being in the present, instead of becoming in the future, for the Eternal Now is all the time there is.

"But," you1say, "your cience has taken away my God, and I know not where you have lain Him." On the contrary, I have brought you to the one true God, "which

was, and is, and evermore shall be."

The fifth verse of the last chapter of the book of Job reads as follows : ,

"I have heard of thee by the hearing of the ear; but now mine eye seeth thee."

The wonderful writings and scientific statements found in that Book of all books, the Christian Bible, were recorded at dates covering thousands of years by men and women who never heard of each other. Some of these teachers lived away back in the age when the Solar System was swinging through the zodiacal sign, Taurus; when Phallic worship prevailed; when the number six was understood as sex, and the creative or formative prin ciple operating through the sex functions was worshiped as the very Holy of Holies. Other teachers, who contrib uted to the knowledge of life and its operations contained in the Bible, lived in the age of Aries, a fire sign, when fire and sun were worshiped as the essence of God; and, as heat, the cause of the phenomenon called fire, cannot be seen, it was a reasonable thing to say that "no one can see God and live." So then, it depends upon the point of view one has of God, or the spirit of things, whether he says, "No one can see God and live," or says, "Now mine eye seeth thee I"

The writer of the book named Job must have lived more than eight thousand years ago, even before the Taurian age-symbolized by the Winged Bulls of Nineveh

-which was in the Gemini age, the age of perception and expression, being an air age.   Let it be understood that an age in this connection means twenty-two hundred years, the period for the Solar System to pass across one of the signs of the zodiac.   In an air age, Egos awaken to their divine heritage, and realize their Godhood.   The writer of Job, then, living in the Gemini or air age, could see God and live. Our Solar System has entered the sign Aquarius, another air sign, and the spiritualized elements so act upon our brain-cells that we are able to understand the teachers of a past air age, and also see God and live. Carlyle, the prince of literary critics, said "The book of Job is the most wonderful and beautiful literary produc tion ever given to the world."   Certainly the scientific truths of astrology and alchemy, and of the Spirit's oper ation in flesh, as set forth in that book, are without a parallel.   The letters J, 0, B, have an oc ult, scientific meaning, I and J are the same IOB meaning the same as JOB. I means the Eternal I. All the Hebrew letters were formed from I.   0 means the universe, without beginning or end, and B means Beth, a body, house, church, or temple; Therefore, GOD, or all, may be dis covered as seen in JOB or IOB. The word,

Job, has no reference to a person. The name, or letters of the word, symbolize principle, the same as wisdom, knowledge, in telligence, or Christ, or Buddha. We symbolize the prin ciples of our government in personalities, and picture them in the form of a man or woman, namely, Uncle Sam, or Columbia.   But we do more than that: we put words in their mouth and make them utter speech.   And shall we ignore these facts when dealing with the record of past ages?   One record plainly states that Jesus spake only

in parables.

But let us consider more closely the discovery of God. The numerical value of G.O.D., according to ancient Kabalia, is nine-the all of mathematics-no person is alluded to. If the statement, "I and the Father are one," is true, the "I" must be the Father manifested or ex pressed. As it is not possible to conceive of the Father exceot through expression, we must conclude that mani festation in some form of so-called matter is eternal the g-reat necessity-and has therefore always been.

It is quite reasonable to think that some oxygen and hydrogen has eternally existed in gaseous form, some in the combination that causes water and some in the con crete or concentrated form known as ice. Then upon the postulate that Spirit and matter-that is, bodily or mate rial expression-are one, it follows logically that matter, including the physical body or temple of man, is as neces sary to the Father-Mother principle while held in a given rate of activity or expression as this life essence is neces sary to matter, or the physical structure of man. I see oxygen and hydrogen when I look at the manifestation we call ice. When I see water, I know just how oxyger. and hydrogen appear when united. So when I look at any form of so-called matter, I know exactly how God appears at that particular time and place. I do not see the effect or works of Goc, bu I see God, and just as much of God, face to face, as I am capable of seeing or recognizing at a certain time.

Step by step, the scientific investigator is being led to the threshold of the awful, absolute Truth, that all matter, or substance, or energy or force-call it what you may is not only intelligent, but is Pure Intelligence itself. Atoms, molecules, electrons are but expressions of rates of motion of pure Mind, Thought, or Intelligence that man has personified and called God. Ice is not permeated with water, or controlled by water. Ice is water. Matter is not controlled by mind; mind and matter are one. A high vibration of mind does control, to a certain extent. a lower vibration of mind, as water, may carry a lump of ice here or there, water being a more positive rate of activity of the same thing. The particles, so-called, of matter know what to do. The atoms that compose a leaf know when to cohere and materialize a leaf, and they know how and wher. to disintegrate and dematerialize it: "Thou shalt have no other gods."

I hold in my hand that particular form of the one thing called a rose. Material thought says it is made by God, or that God is in the rose or back of it, or that God caused or created it; but when Spirit, the I Am, asks where is the God that created the rose, where has he betaken Himself, material belief is silent. But hold a moment I I have here a bud, a half-formed rose. If God makes a rose, He must continue the work to com pletion. Ah, speak softly I Look closely! The rose is now being made, and you say God is making it. Yes, you said God made this full-blown rose. Well, then, He is surely now at work on this half-blown rose. Bring on your spectroscope, your miscroscope I Quick, now, you chemist I Bring on your test-tubes, your acids and alkalis, your spectroscope and X-ray. Analyze, illuminate and magnify! Now we shall discover God. He is here at work before our eyes.

What do you see, chemist? What do you see, scientist? Ah I I know what you see. My experience in the realm of matter and of Spirit tell me what you see. 0 thou stupendous sex force-sex-days of creation, thou Father Mother Yahveh, thou divine male and female, thou eter nal positive and neg-ative dynamis I We now behold thee operating. Out from the chemicalizing mass of God's creative compounds, out of the quivering, vibrating sub stance, slowly comes forth the rose. But are you sure it is a rose? Hold a moment. What is a rose? Of what material is it formed? Ah I the chemist speaks-he of the crucibles and test-tubes and acids I Hear the chemist I

He says, "The rose is made from the universal sub stance," or "The rose is universal substance, in a certain rate of activity." Thanks I Blessed be the chemist! Universal-one verse-one substance-no other substance

-God is the rose, or the smile we call a rose-God is again manifested in the great Eternal IT, for which there is no other name.

Job did not say, "I see the thoughts of God," nor did he say, "I can fathom the mind of God." The plan can not be seen; but that which is planned-a planet-can be seen. One may see the substance of God without under standing the mind of God.

Let us hear Emerson on this stupendous, glorious theme:"The great idea baffies wit; Language falters under it;

It leaves the learned in the lurch- • Nor art, nor power, nor toil can find The measure of the Eter-nal Mind, Nor hymn, nor prayer, nor church."

0 thou ever-present Divine Mind and Substance I   We now fully realize our oneness with thee, and bathe and revel in thy glory. The mighty Angel of Reality has torn the veil of illusion, and we see the celestial City of Truth with wide-ope gates and the white light of Eternal Love forever upon its streets.

0 thou, in the shadow of sickness and trial, "Take up thy bed and walk; thy sins be forgiven thee."

A CHILD brought to its mother a piece of ice and a

S arah or Saria) (Abraham)

WHY was the letter "H" added to Sara and Abram? Heth (cheth) is the 8th letter of the Hebrew alphabet, and means "a field," something per

ceived, or that can be cultivated-in short, spiritual per ception.

In the story of Sarah and Abraham we find the marvel ous truth that age imposes no limit or bar rier to the birth of the "Incorruptible Seed" (Peter) for it is eternal life.

Sara, at the age of ninety, is told by an angel that she will give birth to a child. Abram, at the age of one hun dred, received information that he would be the father of an offspring.

Immediately following these revelations, the letter "H" was added to both names. See 16th and 17th chap ters of Genesis.

Abraham and Sarah now find Isaac, which in Hebrew means laughter or happiness.

"Thy seed shall be as the sands of the sea."

"Unto Abraham and hi seed was the promise given; and unto thy seed, which is Christ."-Paul.

Abraham, Isaac, Jacob, Noah, David, Solomon, Isaiah, etc., etc., are not historical characters. Pontius Pilate, Darius, Pharaoh, Herod, are names of ruling offices, or functions, not certain indi viduals, no dates being given to any so-called transaction in the Scriptures, or to any of Paul's Epis tles, nor to the Acts of the Apostles.

Pilate means "Dart; javelin; a giving up; death." Pontius means "Sea; the open sea."   "Marine." He-rod means "Heroic."

Pharaoh, "Rulership."

Darius, "Coercer, conservator" (see presidency, judge ship, etc.).

THE WORD OF GOD

IN the beginning was the word, and the word was with God, and the word was God."-John, 1st Chapter.

"W. 0. R. D." This combination of letters does not mean, in its first and original sense, voice, sound or speech. Physiologically speaking, it means a precious substance.

Therefore, as mankind must be "placed on their feet" physically before the same condition can exist mentally and spiritually, we must get down to fundamentals, and give the physiological meaning of W. 0. R. D.

The Hebrew alphabet consists of 22 letters, each letter having a concrete meaning. In the formation of Hebrew characters, letters were chosen, which, when combined, indicated plainly every phase of that idea which they wished to express.

Let us now take W. 0. R. D., dissect it, and understand the meaning of each letter.

There is no letter "W" in the Hebrew alphabet. That which they used to designate our letter "W" was VV (double V), which is also used in our modern French. Its meaning is "hook." The arm and legs are the hooks of the body.

VV, then, or double V, is the 18th letter of the Hebrew alphabet, and the characters which they used to express that letter, were written thus: TZADDI, almost unpro nouncable. This letter is also, as we write it, the eight eenth in our alphabet. Its number has a great significance. As the ninth letter of the Hebrew alphabet, "Teth," rep resents the equilibrium of the father and mother-the perfcet balance of the male and female, or positive and negative forces, as manifested in the perfected or com pleted human being, so the eighteenth letter, Tzaddi, or double V (VV), is the representation of the fall of spirit toward the material world-or the material body and its passions. In astronomy it corresponds with the zodiacal sign, Aquarius.

As the sixth letter of the alphabet, Va v, expresses the struggle between the passions and conscience, the antagon ism of ideas, so the eighteenth letter, VV, which is three times six or 666, represents the "beast" which we read of in Revelation, the Adam man. On the mental plane we use the expression He Phren, for this number, the lower mind, the material mind. In astronomy the affinity of this letter (6) is the bull (Taurus). Mankind, living wholly on the material plane, is hence a beast-a beast physically, mentally and emotionally. Animal on three planes. Thus in the Tarot we find that 18 represents "Antagonism."

Placing the two V's togther, one over the other, they represent the two arms and the two legs of the unregen erated man, as the upper V or triangle points downward. In the regenerated man the hands are folded together over the head in adoration of divinity, and thus the apex points upward.

In the lower triangle the same change takes place, the forces hitherto misused, going downward and outward are sent upward and returned to the "Holy of Holies," the triangle becomes closed at the bottom and opened upward.

The letter "W," then, or VV, represents the earthly or Adam man, the material body and the lower mind.

The letter "O," the sixteenth letter of the alphabet, written Ayin, in Hebrew, has somewhat the same mean ing as the first letter, but in a deeper sense alludes to a material building, an operation in the visible and material world. "The materialization of God, the Holy Spirit, the entrance of the Holy Spirit into the visible world," the Tarot tells us. Since God. One, is individual or undivided and undifferentiated, to manifest in the material plane, God or THAT must divide, must become two halves of the circle, must manifest as positive and negative, male and female, electricity and magnetism. From this we deduce the expression, "dual power" or "dual operation"

-"dual force." In astronomy this is represented by the sign Capricorn. These dual forces, operating within us, thus become the Goat, which "Bears away the sins of the world" (circle-material body).

In the average human being, this dual power is not operating in harmony. The action is unequal. If these two currents operated in harmony in the human body, the regenerated man would be manifested, the flesh would have become the WORD itself.

The letter "R" is the twentieth letter, written "Resh," and the symbolism of this letter is most wonderful. It represents the head of man and is, therefore, associated with the idea/of original and determined movement. It is the sign of motion itself, good, or bad, and expresses the renewal of things with regard to their innate power of motion. It corresponds to Saturn. "Resh" also sym bols rest. A ship may rest on water that is in motion.

The description of the inner meaning of this letter, in the Tarot, throws a flood of light upon it as used in its present position in W.O.R.D., as it has a deep esoteric significance. To quote: "A tomb opens in the earth, and a man, woman and child issue from it; their hands are joined in sign of adoration. How can the reawakening of nature under the influence of the WORD, be better expressed? We must admire the way in which the sym bol answers to the corresponding Hebrew hieroglyphic."

Comment on the above quotation is scarcely necessary, yet for the convenience of those not yet able to figure it out for themselves, let it be said, that the tomb, cave or manger, is the birth place of the seed, the WORD, the "Son of man" which redeems the Adam man, IF NOT INTERFERED WITH. "Under the influence of the Word," indeed, is the carnal man, "dead in trespass and sin," reborn to a new life.

The letter "D," the fourth in the Hebrew alphabet, as also in ours, is written "Daleth," and means the womb, or door, mouth. It denotes abundance springing from di vision. "Thus Daleth expresses a creation made by a being according to divine laws. It expresses domination of spirit over matter. The Tarot thus wonderfully inter prets its meaning: "In the Divine, Reflex of the Father, it is the will. In the Human, Reflex of Adam, it is power.

God-Man: The Word Made Flesh

In the Natural, Reflex of Natura naturans, it is the uni versal creative fluid, the soul of the Universe. In astron omy its affinity is Jupiter."

Summing this up we can see that the letter "D" stands for the solar plexus in the human body, as it is the reflec tion of the true sun (the Father), and the source of all things.

W.O.R.D., then, means this: The creation, according to divine laws, from the universal creative fluid, in the tomb, cave or manger of the earth (solar plexus), of that PERFECT ONE (SEED, fish, fruit, Jesus) Vishnu, Joshua, Moses, Horus, etc., etc., which has the power to spiritualize-regenerate the Adam man, so that he be comes the "Lord God from heaven"-the WORD MADE FLESH." "And the Word was made flesh and dwelt among us."-John 1:14.

We realize, then, that word does not refer to speech. The Hebrew letter which signifies speech is Phe, the seventeenth letter. It refers to the force which dispenses the essence of life, which gives it the means of perpetually renewing its creations after destruction. We can speak destructively and we have the power to speak construc tively.

The two letters "O" and "R" combined are used to specify a precious substance, originally ref erred to as "gold," for the ancients realized that the sun's rays, which they called "golden," precipitated in the human body and formed creative substance.

The Bible"tells us that "Man does not live by bread alone, but by every word (or seed) , that proceedeth out of the mouth of God," proving that, in order to truly live, we must save the precious substance. In anatomy, the passage way undernearth the sutures which leads down into the thalamus, is the mouth of God, for it is from the cerebrum, the upper brain, that the most wonderful "gift" to the human body comes. This represents the unseen "mouth." The visible mouth is the solar plexus.

We can turn to the pages of Gray's Anatomy, or any good medical dictionary, and examine carefully the illus tration of a 26-day old foetus. We see, then, that almost the entire body c'onsists of brain substance-in fact, it looks like an elongated brain. The upper brain, or Father-Mother substance, is what furnishes the material from which the body is made. Verily it is the Aloha, the beginning. Degenerates, and· people living in excesses, have become greatly deficient in this precious material, and the whole appearance of the body testifies to the dese cration of the temple.

Man can become regenerated, and thus save his soul, which is sown in corruption, so that it may be raised in corruption. /   ,

We can compare speech with the operations of the processes of the planets. "The heavens declare the glory of God, and the firmament showeth his handiwork.

"Day unto day u_ttereth speech, and night unto night showeth knowledge. •

"There is no speech or language where their voice is not heard."

The heavens, or the planets in the heavens, have their own particular influence, operation or speech, upon this planet of ours. We admit that the moon rules the tides, that without the sun we could not live, so why deny the influence of the other planets.

Thus we see, from the foregoing, that word, and voice or speech are two entirely different things, and that John meant the precious creative substance when he spoke of the "WORD."

"Now this is the parable. The SEED IS THE
WORD OF GOD."-Luke 8:11.

"Seed, word" and "God," are all synonyms of one and the same thing-the· wonderful creative substance, the universal esse, from which all things are brought forth, and in which all things are. The

Scriptures, or allegories and parables of the Bible, are the only writings that give us information as to what the Word of God is. There fore, in this book, we will quote what is written there in regard to it.

Seed is the cause, the nucleus of everything, therefore a seed is "the beginning." In the beginning was the WORD."

The fluid, oil, or marrow which flows down the spinal cord, comes from the upper brain, the Creator or Father, the "Most High," and is known in physiology as ovum, or generative seed-that life essence which creates the human form of corruptible flesh. In the Greek, from which the New Testament was translated, this marrow is called Christ, which is the Greek word for oil.

When this oil is refined, transmuted, lifted up, raised, it becomes so highly vitalized that it regenerates the body and "overcomes" the last enemy, death.

How can it be lifted up?

By lifting up the "Son of man," the seed, the word, the savior. The oil (Christ) in the spinal cord, is the salt which is mentioned in the Bible, and the savior is the seed, or Jesus.

The salt and the savior both come from the same source-the same place-the Father-the upper brain. In the Bible allegory the seed, Jesus, is made to say, "Without my Father I can do nothing." The material from the Father which forms the seed, has gone through a different process from that which forms the oil. The chemical formula of the oil is J.O.H.N., and Jesus was baptized or anointed of John, not by John, as it is incor rectly quoted. (See article on OIL).

If we lift up or raise the oil in the spinal cord, by the power of the seed, by saving it, it must be a physiological and chemical operation within the body of each of us.

Such is the·case.

There is no mystery, no marvel in all the universe that is greater than man himself. "Man know thyself" con fronts us, down through the ages, but only a few have paid attention to the voice of the Delphic oracle-only a few have looked within.

There is a wonderful "Strait and narrow way," a real strait, not straight, which extends from the upper brain, the cerebrum, to the end of the spinal cord, otherwise named Jordan, in the Bible. We find that the meaning of this in Hebrew is, descender or "River of God." The "Strait and narrow way is, indeed, the River of God, for it leads to the Father-the Most High-the upper brain.

As the Jordan edipties into the Dead Sea, so the spinal cord terminates in that section of the anatomy, which is designated, in the medical terminolgy as Sodom. Josephus refers to the region as the "Lake of Sodom," and in other writings we find it referred to as the "Sea of Lot," and "Lake Asphaltus."

The student of symbology can easily see thztt it is the slimy pool from which springs up the lotus, whose flower of a thousand petals blooms forth, reflecting in its golden heart the image of its creator.

The wondlrful pneumogastric nerve, rising in the floor or the fourth ventricle of the head, and connected with the cerebellum, crosses the spinal cord, or Jorcan, at the base of the Skull Golgotha, and sends numerous branches to throat, lungs, heai;t and stcmach, terminating in a plexus under the latter organ, which is named the androgynous brain, the stomach brain, or solar plexus. This wonderful nerve has six different physical functions, in addition to the deeply esoteric office of being the channel for the Holy Breath, or Holy Ghost, without which there would be no conception of the Holy Child, the WORD.

In Bible terminology the solar plexus also means man ger, cave, Bethlehem, for it is in the centre of this plexus of nerves that we find the thimble-shaped cavity or de pression from which issues forth the redeemer of the Adam man. In a dual sense it is the "house of bread," as it is the place where the divine bread or seed is formed, and it lies directly back of the house of material bread, the stomach. "Man shall not live by bread alone, but by every WORD (seed) that cometh from the mouth of God." Jesus was born in Bethlehem, and this word means in Hebrew "house (Beth) of bread (lehem)." See how wonderfully the Hebrew words expressed the true mean ing of the hidden truth. "I am the bread of life."

In the central part of the head is the wonderful cham ber or bed, called the "thalamus." Santee's Anatomy of the Brain and Spinal Cord" describes it thus: "It is the great ganglion of the inter-brain. The thalamus is an important sensory relay station. Its medial part is con cerned with smell and its lateral part with common sensation and taste. According to Head and Holmes, it is also an organ of consciousness for impulses of pain and temperature. The third ventricle separates the thalami from each other, except at the mid-point where they are joined by the MASSA INTERMEDIA. The thalamus is situated behind and medial to the corpus striatum, and projects backward over the mid-brain. Laterally it rests against the superior lamina·of the internal capsule, which separated it from the lentiform nucleus. The thalamus is shaped like an egg, with the small end directed forward.

It measures 4 cm. or about one and one-half inches in length and 2.5 cm. of one inch in width and thickness. It has an interior and posterior extremity and four surfaces; superior, inferior, medial and lateral."

The most striking statement in the above paragraph is, that the thalamus is egg-shaped, and we can readily see why there is so much reference made, in ancient religions, to the egg. For the thalamus with its adjacent append ages, when viewed in cross sections of the brain, looks ex actly like a beetle, the body egg shaped, and the "horns" of the lateral ventricle, typifying the horns of the beetle. In the scarabaeus of Egypt is exemplified the egg of im mortality, the light of the world. It is the chamber, the HOLY OF HOLIES, wherein is concealed the ark of the covenant. In the Egyptian Book of the Dead we find this referred to as the "Boat of Seker." Every religion, which has existed down through the ages, has told in its own terminology, the same story, the same physiological process taking place within the body of man.

On the posterior side of the thalamus we find the pineal body. It is a cone-shaped body, 6 mm (0.25 in.) high and 4 mm (0.17 in.) in diameter, joined to the roof of the third ventricle by a flattened stalk, the habenula. Santee tells us that "The interior of the pineal body is made up of closed follicles surrounded by ingrowths of connective tissue. The follicles are filled with epithelial cells mixed with calcareous (lime) matter, the brain-sand (acerculus cerebri). Calcareous deposits are found also

on the pineal stalk and along the choi-ioid plexuses,. The

function of the pineal body is unknown. Des Cartes facetiously suggesis that it is the abode of the spirit (the

sand of man."

The most significant statement in the above paragraph, to the esoteric student, is the reference to the calcareous deposit-the brain-sand. Now, indeed, do we find the words of the great occultist, Madame Helena Pretrovna Blavatsky, written nearly half a century ago, justified, proved true in the light of modern science. Who now dares to lightly cast aside the statements of seers and mystics recorded in secret and sacred doctrines, as unreliable and untrue?

The upper section of this pineal body is the optic, or eye, the "All-seeing Eye," it is the wonderful light of the candle, which "Gives light to the whole house."

This pineal body is the male spiritual organ. If you ask for proof as to "its being a male organ, you can find indubitable proof by referring to any good physiological chart or anatomy, for you will see that the lower portions of this organ has been given the names, "corpora quac rigemina," which means "four-fold bodies"-two nates (buttocks), and two testes (testicles). Thus we see, that in spite of our incredulence, even the scoffing scientist has unwittingly demonstrated the truth of occult investiga tions, in respect to this body.

In esoteric as well as physiological meaning, this is Joseph, meaning to increase, the father of Jesus, the seed, the redeemer. It is the organ through which the electrical forces of the body play. It is, in other words, one of the differentiators of THAT-the universal esse deposited, materialized, in the cerebrum, the upper brain. In the Medieval Hebrew, as quoted from the Sacred Books of the East, it is referred to as "The Crystalline Dew" from heaven, deposited in the cranium. The marvelous sym bology of our own Bible is duplicated in all the ancient Scriptures, in all the nations of the world. Some of this wonderful esse, this Father, flows down from the upper brain into the pineal body, where it is differentiated becomes masculine, positive, electrical, in quality and action.

On the other side of the thalamus is located the pituitary body, the feminine spiritual organ. It is a small, reddish, ellipsoid organ in a depression of the sphenoid bone, and is attached to the brain by a peduncle. It has two lobes, one of yellowish-gray and the other reddish gray color. It secretes a mucous or phlegm, and the latter substance is what gives it its name. It also receives its secretion from the Father, the universal ESSE, the undifferentiated substance from which all things are brought forth. Flowing into this gland it becomes magnetic, female, in its quality and action. It is the Mare, Mary, pure sea or water, the Mother of the Holy Child. The pineal gland is directly referred to in the Bible as Mount Penial, where Jacob wrestled with the Angel of the Lord. In Hebrew the word means "Face of God." It is indeed the face of God. The top of this gland being the eye. Where can the eye be located save in the face?

Connected with the pinal gland is a nerve called the "pingala" in secret writings. This nerve crosses the spinal cord at the base of the skull, in the medulla oblongata, and follows down the right side of the spinal cord to its end.

Likewise, connected with the pituitary body, is the nerve Ida, which crosses the spinal cord at the same place where the Pingala crosses, follows down the left side of the spinal cord to its base. Here the two nerves converge into the body through the semi-luna ganglion, where they merge into the solar plexus.

The divine esse which has been differentiated by entering these two glands has become Mary and Joseph, the mother and father of the holy child. This material, this actual substance, enters the solar plexus where it combines with the Holy Breath and the seed is born the bread is made which is intended to be eaten in the "Father's Kingdom."

The first seed is formed in the solar plexus of every individual, commencing at the age of twelve, which we have designated as the age of puberty. Thereafter, it is

formed every 29.½ days, this taking place in each indi

vidual at the time of the month when the moon is in the sign in which the sun was at the birth of the individual.

Herod, Pharabh, the passions, desires and emotions, seek to slay this Divine Babe.

Here we will quote the Sanscrit statement in regard to the danger always present for the seed, child, fruit or fish, as given in Vol. II of the Secret Doctrine, by H. P. Blavatsky:

"While Vaivasvata was engaged in devotion on the river bank, a FISH craves his protection from a bigger FISH. He saves it and places it in a jar (solar plexus) which, growing larger and larger, communicates to him the news of t;he forthcoming deluge. (Nate gold fish in jar).   .

"Vaivasvata Manu, the Son of Surya, the Sun, and the Savior of our race, is connected with the seed of life, both physically and spiritually."

The significance o,f the above is apparent.

In the Bible we find this statement: "Joseph shall have a double portion."

Joseph was one of the children of Jacob, which means "circle" in Hebrew. His name was afterwards changed to Israel, so that the sons of Jacob are also the sons of Israel. The signs of the Zodiac are also referred to as the children of Jacob, and when applied in physiology, refer to the solar plexus, and the twelve forces centered there. All the forces which enter the body of man are received in this part of the body, and are sent out from there. Joseph represents one of these divisions or centers, and this is one of his portions. The other is the pineal gland, that also being Joseph.

Thus all the so-called tribes referred to as Gad, Rheu ben, Levi, etc., etc., refer to the forces operative in the human body, and not to bodies of people.

We find, then, this seed, fruit, fish, bread and savior, born in the solar plexus.

We must lift up, save, or raise this seed. "If I be lifted up I will draw all men unto me."-John 12 :32.

It must be taken into the spinal cord or, in other words, be baptized of JOHN. It must be anointed with oil.

We find that there is oil present in the spinal cord. This subject will be dealt with elsewhere in this book. In the book of Joshua, we find the story of the Ark of the MOST HIGH GOD being taken by the Priests of the Twelve Tribes into the Jordan, and again, in the New Testament we find the identical story in the baptism of Jesus of John (oil), in the Jordan. The Hebrews told their story, in the Old Testament, and the Greeks gave theirs in the New Testament.

In Joshua's (fish in Hebrew) story we find that he commanded the sun and moon to stand still, while he slew his enemies. The semi-lunar ganglion, which is attached to the solar plexus, is identical with the moon. Nerves from this plexus extend to the lower parts of the body and, in fact, connect with the organs of generation. No wonder Joshua commanded these forces to be still so that the seed could pass into the Jordan in safety. For, we find that just below this passageway into the spinal cord is another, called the "fish-gate," which leads directly to the genitals. If the lower desires are not stilled this seed or fish will be "swallowed," killed by the generative fish.

When these lower forces are controlled, the High Priests of the body, the higher forces, are in command, and the seed is taken into the Jordan.

"At the time of the flood, when the Jordan overflowed its banks" and "stood up," was the Ark carried into the Jordan. This proves conclusively the exact location, physiologically, of the entrance into the spinal cord. For this portion of the cord is the broadest-it is where it "stands up," or contacts with that part of the anatomy termed Sodom and Gomorrah.

At the place where the ARK entered the "water," twelve men were chosen to set up stones, and the Bible tells us that "They are there to this day." These twelve stones correspond to the twelve Dorsal vertebrae, to each vertebra of which a nerve is attached that forms part of the solar plexus. These twelve nerves terminate in the solar plexus. They are the twelve priests whose services enabled the Ark to enter the "River of God."

The twelve forces, then, bore this ARK up out of the water.

They broke down the walls of Jericho and entered the city with the ARK of the MOST HIGH GOD.

In the New Testament story Jesus was baptized in the Jordan. Then, when the time came for His crucifixion, He went to the Garden of Gethsemene. In anatomy this is near the Medulla Oblongata, with the olives on either

side, a physiological fact, as any anatomy proves. There are two "pyramids," also, at this place.

In anatomy, Golgotha (place of the skull, in Hebrew) is the base of the skull, where the spinal cord enters the head. At this point is a double cross made by the Adi, the Pingala and the pneumogastric nerves. They are the St. George and St. Andrew crosses, with the form of a man displayed therein. Many very ancient Byzantine coins and frescoes show this deeply esoteric symbol. This same eight-pointed-star or combined crosses appears on amulets and seals of ancient Chaldea, Babylon, Assyria, Persia and India.

Can we any longer doubt that the ancient records told the same story as is found in our own Scriptures, and that it was all in regard to one thing, one process, the MASTERY OF THE BODY?

The seed, then, is crucified on the cross, it is raised in power, for nowhere does the crucifixion mean death.

We "cross" animals to improve the breed, the qualities. Crossed electric wires produce a more powerful current. By the process of crossing, or crucifixion, therefore, this seed took on added power, in fact, received the "illumination," which the seed had previously asked for "The hour has come. Father, glorify thy Son that thy Son may glorify thee."

At the moment of glorification or illumination, the seed did not say "My God, my God, why hast thou forsaken me." It is a gross mistranslation. It, moreover, is not at all in keeping with the tenor of the request, just previous to passing onto the cross. The correct translation of this exclamation, is "My God, my God, how thou dost glorify me." Does not this seem more in keeping with the calm and earnest request "Father, the hour has come, glorify thy Son that thy Son may glorify thee?"

Read John and note glory and glorify. John, or Ioannes, is ointment, or oil, here personified.

Glorify means to illuminate-to give light-glow ray. The passing of the seed over the crossed nerves, and its passage into the pineal gland does, in very truth, cause the illumination-the flash of light, the raising or illumi nation of consciousness of the individual in which this process is allowed to take place. For it is man that pre- vents its accomplishment.

After the crucifixion the "body" of Jesus is claimed by Joseph, and it is taken by him into his own tomb, where no man had ever been laid. This Joseph is the same Joseph-the father of Jesus, the pineal gland, for no other man, no seed had been absorbed by the gland prev iously, for this is the first seed that has been saved. In other words, the Son returns to the Father, the seed re turns to its source. The Father and the Son have become ONE.

No other explanation save a physiological one can make clear this statement of Jesus. "And greater things than I do, ye shall do, for I go unto my Father." The first seed that has been saved ap- parently makes this statement. When the first seed is saved, the entire body is changed. It vibrates at a higher rate, the fluids are purer. In 29 _½ days another seed is born, and the material from which this seed is formed is of a more refined substance, of greater power. Therefore, when it is crucified, is it not of greater power than the first seed? The third seed will also have been raised to the third power, and so on. The entire body is chanl!ed by the raising or saving of each seed. Paul says, "Ye are transformed by the renewing of your minds." The mind, the brain, is indeed renewed by each seed that is carried into the pineal gland, with the accompanying oil. "And the ransomed of the Lord shall return and come to Zion, with songs and everlasting joy."

This, then, is the process whereby the WORD, which is also GOD AND SEED, regenerated, transforms the Adam man, so that he becomes the "LORD GOD from heaven."

There are mariy direct references to the process, among which are the following:

Corinthians 11 :28, "_But let a man examine himself and
so eat of that bread and drink of that cup."

11:29, "For he that eateth and drinketh unworthily, eateth and drinketh damnation to himself, not discerning the Lord's body." Damn or damnation simply means to check or stop the "going on" or procedure.

Cor. 11 :30, "For this cause many are weak and sickly among you, and many sleep."

Acts I, "Ye men of Galilee, why stand ye gazing up into heaven? This same Jesus, which is taken up from you, into heaven, shall so come in like manner as ye have seen him go into heaven."

II John, 7th verse, "He that confesseth not that Jesus Christ is come in the flesh, the same is Anti-Christ."

John 3 :3, "Jesus answered and said unto him, verily, verily I say unto thee, except a man be born again, he cannot see the kingdom of heaven."

1st John 3 :9, "Whosoever is born of God doth not commit sin, for his seed remaineth in him, and he cannot sin because he is born of God."

Peter 1 :23, "Being born again, not of corruptible seed, but of incorruptible, by the WORD OF GOD, which liveth and abideth forever."

Luke 4 :4, "And Jesus answered him, saying, it is writ ten that man shall not live by bread alone, but by every WORD of God."

Galatians 3 :16, "Now to Abraham and his seed were these promises made, and to thy seed which is Christ."

Luke 8: 11, "Now the parable is this; the seed is the WORD OF GOD."

Colossians 1 :26-27, "Even the mystery which hath been hid from ages and generations, but now is made manifest to his saints. To whom God would make known what is the riches of the glory of this mystery among the Gentiles, which is CHRIST IN YOU, THE HOPE OF GLORY."

Deut. 28 :38, "Thou shalt carry much seed out into the field, and thou shalt gather but little in; for the locust shall consume it." Eating, devouring or gluttony. (See John the Baptist.)

Matthew 13 :27, "He answered and said unto them. He that soweth the good seed is the Son of man." (The Seed is the Son of Man.)

II Cor. 9 :10, "Now he that ministereth seed to the sower doth minister bread for your food, and multiply your seed sown, and increase the fruits of your righteous ness."

John 6 :58, "This is that bread which came down from heaven; not as your fathers did eat manna and are dead. He that eateth of this bread shall LIVE FOREVER." John 6:51, "I am the LIVING BREAD WHICH

CAME DOWN FROM HEAVEN. If any man eat of this bread he shall live forever; and the bread that I will give is my flesh, which I will give for the life of the world."   •

1st Cor. 15 :21, "For since by man came death, by man came also the resurrection of the dead."

Isaiah 45 :23, "The word is gone out of my mouth." Matthew 34:25, "My word shall not pass away."

John 17 :8, "I have given them the word thou gavest me."

Psalms 119 :130, "The entrance of thy word giveth light."

The phrase, "The truth in a nut shell," has a deep occult meaning.   "I am the truth."

"My WORD shall not return unto me void, but it shall accomplish that whereunto it was sent."

Acts 13 :26, "To you is the WORD of salvation sent."

Hebrews 2 :2, "The WORD of God is quick and powerful."

Hebrews 6 :5, "Have tasted the good WORD of God."

Peter 2 :2, "The sincere milk of the WORD."

Isaiah 30 :23, "Thou shalt be given the rain of thy seed, that thou shalt sow the ground withal; and bread of the increase of the earth and it shall be fat and plenteous."

Psalms 68 :11, "The Lord gave the WORD."

And yet Smitli's Bible Dictionary, in its seeming efforts to find the meaning of "WORD," fails to quote Luke 8 :11 "The SEED IS THE WORD OF GOD." Why

is it? Was it because the immortal statement proves beyond peradventure that the seed within us is the savior and not a man without? Error dies hard, but it always dies, and "Amid its worshippers."

.:;& .:;& .:;&

WHAT WAS THE "WORD OF THE LORD" THAT CAME SO OFTEN TO THE OLD-TIME PROPHETS?

„.,   "The Seed is the word"-Luke 8:11.

In all the statements in the Bible that refer to the "Word of the Lord," we find the same great truth told over and over again in the Hebrew Scriptures and trans lated "Word of the Lord"-the Seed.

"And the word of the Lord came to Jeremiah," or "Joel" or "Ezekiel" or "Hosea."

And thus it followed that after each seed had been saved, the Prophet foretold, admonished and preached truth to the world.

TRANSMUTATION-TURNING WATER INTO WINE

THE Lord of transmutation has ascended the throne of Aquarius to rule the world for 2160 years.

Aquarius, the fifth Son, Sun, of Jacob, circle, or to follow after, is Dan, Hebrew for Judge. Thus the day or time of judgment or understanding will have for its executor the revolutionary planet Uranus, or as it is in Greek, "Oranous." Uranus virtually means Son of Heaven.

This God is surely a suitable ruler for the zodiacal Sign Aquarius, the Man. "And then shall appear the Sign of the Son (Sun) of man in the heavens.'

The solar system now being in Aquarius we may expect, and as a matter of fact are experiencing, the prophecies of great astrologians as recorded in Matt. 24th, also Luke 21st.

In the Judgment Day, or time of knowledge, we are due to realize the process by which base metals are trans muted into gold.

The word gold comes from Or, a product of the Sun's rays or the breath of life.

Life or Spirit breathed into man precipitates brain cells and gray matter which create or build the fluids and structure of physical man.

Or is the seed or W or d-L or d, etc.

"In the beginning was the word * * * the word

was God."

God means power.

Thus the emanations from Sun, basic material, are changed to gold, and the process eternally proceeding is being recognized by man at the present day, due to the fact that the planet of gold, Oranous, is now ruling Earth and thereby bringing good judgment upon the people.

Both in Greek and Hebrew any fluid, air, or ether was called water until organized; then it was wine. The rain that falls on the ground and taken up into the organism of !r7e, vegetable or fruit is changed into wine, i. e., sap

or Jutce.

The parable of turning water into wine at the marriage at Cana in Galilee is a literal statement of a process taking place with every heart beat in the human organism.

Galilee means a circle of water or fluid-the circulatory system. Cana means a dividing place, the lungs or reeds, the tissue and, cells of the lungs.

Biochemists have shown that food does not form the organic part of blood, but simply furnishes the mineral base by setting free the inorganic or cell-salts contained in all foodstuff. The organic part, oil, fibrin, albumen, etc., contained in food is, burned or digested in the stomach and intestinal tract, to furnish motive power to operate the human machine and draw air into lungs, Cana, thence into arteries, i. e., air carriers. Therefore, it is clearly shown that air (spirit) unites with the minerals and forms blood, proving that the oil, albumen, etc., found in blood, is created every breath at the "marriage of Cana of Galilee."

Air was called water or the pure sea; viz.: Virgin

Mar-y. So we see how water is changed into wine-blood

-every moment.

In the new age, we will need perfect bodies to corre spond with the higher vibration, or motion of the new blood, for "old bottles (bodies), cannot contain the new wine."

Another allegorical statement, typifying the same truth reads, "And I saw a new Heaven and a New Earth,"i. e., new mind and new body.

Biochemistry may well say with Walt Whitman, "To the sick lying on their backs I bring help, and to the strong, upright man I bring more needed help." To be grouchy, cross, irritable, despondent, or easily discour aged, is prima facie evidence that the fluids of the stomach, liver, and brain are not vibrating at normal rate, the rate that results in equilibrium or health. Health cannot be qualified, i. e., poor health or good health. There must be either health or dishealth; ease or disease. We do not say poor ease or good ease. We say ease or dis-ease, viz., not at ease.

A sufficient amount of the cell-salts of the body properly combined taken as food-'-not simply to cure some ache, pain or exudation-forms blood that materializes in healthy fluids, flesh and bone tissue.

We should take the tissue cell-salts as one uses health foods, not simply to change health to health, but to keep the rate of blood vibration in the tone of health all the time.

Biochemistry is the sign-board pointing to the open country, to hills and green fields of health and the truth that shall set the seeking Ego free from poverty and disease.

Conservation and transmutation obtain in all the com mercial world. The force of falling water is transmuted into the product of the factories. Steam, the vibration of copper and carbon discs that turn night into day, the automobiles, "chariots that run like lightning and jostle each other in the streets," are the effects of the transmu tation of base or basic material.

On some fair tomorrow when the subtle vibrations of the Aquarian Age, directed by Oranous, shall have awak ened and called to action the millions of dormant cells of the wondrous brain, man will by the power of the lost word restored, conserve and transmute the mineral sub stance of his body, the soul, IO H N, and with the "product" the precious ointment-ail, Christ, triumph over the cross at Golgotha and ascend to the pineal gland that transmits the christed Son to the Optic Thal-amus, the all-seeing Eye of the chamber, and thus furnish "light to all that are in the house."

In these latter days our business world has been domi nated by a great oil trust, petroleum, mineral oil, petra stone, rock or mineral and oleum; oil was exploited, and then by the law of transmutation changed into gasoline. The transmutation of gasoline by the miracle of the "conservation of energy" causes the "ascension" of the air ship, and the pathway of the Eagle and the open road

of man lie parallel across the vaulted sky.

And when the Ego shall have triumphed over the car nal mind and transmuted the crude soul fluids into the gold of the "New Wine," it will ascend to the Father, the upper brain.

"And the temple needs no light of the Sun by day nor Moon by night, for the light of the Lard doth lighten it." The gospel miracle of turning water into wine is found only in John and appears as a companion piece to the multiplication of the loaves .and fishes.   The meaning of

miracle is: "To uncover a truth."

We are indebted to Lawrence Parmly Brown for much of the followi g: (See open Court, May, 1920.)

"This beginning of the signs (or 'miracles') Jesus did in Cana of Galilee, and manifested his glory; and his dis ciples believed on him." This is the first miracle of Jesus, according to John, jqst as the changing of the waters to blood was the first plague inflicted upon the Egyptians as one of the miracles of Moses. But the J ohannine mar riage-feast appears to have been recognized as a variant of the great feast of Rabbinical tradition, which is to in augurate the coming of the Messiah, and at which he shall drink wine made from the grapes that grew in Paradise during the six days of creation and were since preserved in Adam's cave (Buxdorf, Synod. Jud., p. 460). The Fo-pen-hing-tsi-king, a Chinese life of Gautama Buddha, relates that this last Buddha declared that when one of his predecessors attended a wedding in the city of J ambunada, he not only kept the foods and drinks miraculously undi minished during the feast, but caused the host's uninvited guests to come and partake of it, even as the host had silently wished (according to Lillie, Buddhism in Chris tianity, pp. 169, 170; Popular Life of Buddha, pp. 305, 306).

Compare Eucharistic bread and wine to the flesh and blood of Jesus in the Roman Catholic doctrine.

Words for "bread" are sometimes employed for all solid foods that are transmuted into the flesh or bodies of men, while water or (red) wine is conceived to be changed into blood: Wine is often called the "blood of grapes" or the "blood of the grape," as in the Old Testa ment (Gen. xlix. 11 ; Deut. xxxii. 14, etc.) ; and the juice of the grape is naturally conceived as having been transmuted from water by the heat of the sun, which is also the chief factor in the fermentation of wine.

In the Egyptian legend of Horus of Edfu, that god smites the enemies of Ra, and the latter says to the former: " 'Thou makest the water of Edfu (red with blood) like grapes, and thy heart is rejoiced thereat.' Hence the water of Edfu is called (the water of grapes)" (Sayce, Rel. dnc. Eg. and Bab., p. 220). In the De struction of Mankind, the deluge is poured out from seven thousand jars of human blood, representing the red color of the Nile waters shortly after the beginning of the inun dation (Records of the Past, VI, pp. 105-112).

The mythic marriage is primarily that of the sun (see Phredrus, I, /ab. 6), either with the earth or the moon whence, doubtless, the Athenians at one time celebrated marriages at the new moon (when she was in conjunction with the sun-Proclus ad Hesiod. Oper., 782). Prac

tically nothing is related of the Johannine bridegroom.

and there is no reference to the bride; but in the mythic view the bridegroom is a mere variant of Jesus (the figurative "bridegroom" of John iii. 29, cf. Mark. ii. 19, 20, etc.), while his mother and the bride are duplications of wider variation. Thus the Virgin Mary is often called the Rose of Sharon and Lily of Israel; epithets from Can ticles ii, where the bride is "a rose of Sharon and a lily of the valleys," who is brought by the bridegroom to "the banqueting-house"-literally "the house of wine," as in the Septuagint.

JOHN THE BAPTIST

JOHN, or Ioannes,. is the ointment, oil, that flows down the spinal cord from the reservoir of God sub stance in the upper brain, the "Most High," the heaved-up place, the Heave-n, within.   .

"VVe know .that we have in heaven a more enduring substance."-Paul.

The mysterious circumstances connected with the Bible story of John the Baptist and the information given in Smith's Bible Dictionary prove the wholly divine origin of that which was cal.led "John," but which means oil in Greek. John's father was said to be a priest of Ahia, or Abijah. This latter, in Hebrew, means "Whose father is Jehovah." Jehovah is the upper brain, the Most High -the "crystalline dew" referred to in Medieval Hebrew. Before the oil is raised by the seed, thus giving one tenth (tithe) to the Lord, it is called "natural" or "wild," "not cultivated," like wild flowers-"wild honey." So John was a wild man-a native. A parable? Most certainly I

"His food was locusts and wild honey."

The pineal gland and the pituitary body secret fluids called milk and honey in the Scriptures.

Locust means destructive, devourer-a glutton.

Deut. 28 :42: "All thy tree (tree of life and fruit seed) shall the locusts (sex desire) consume."

The reader will please remember that the Bible is Secret Doctrine, or that which is within and not without. History is a record of outward things.

John, the natural man, was an eater of the•fruit of the tree of life, with a girdle of camel's hair (from Gimel the 3rd letter of the Hebrew alphabet, which pertains to the external male organ). But John, like the prodigal son, changed his mind and is made to say, "One cometh after me (to get me) the latchet of whose shoes (pisces-the feet-fishes) I am not worthy to unloose."

Latchet and shoes are mblems of cover, or cup swaddling cloth. The oil in the seed, when born, is cov ered or protected by a crust of mineral salts, which, when anointed by being baptized in Jordan (John), is loosened ("He that saveth his life shall loosen it." See mistrans lation of Scripture) in order that the shell may fall apart when the seed, Jesus, goes over the cross, thus, "Father, remove the cup (cover or latchet) from me," in order that the precious material may ascend into the pineal gland.

THE PLAGUES OF EGYPT

THESE same locusts, sex appetite, gluttony, or de vourers, are and always have been the plagues, i. e., sickness and disease in all peoples in all ages.

And now, when evil doers wax worse and worse, a ma jority of human beings are deliberately and "with malice aforethought," committing suicide, through eating and drinking for pleasure, and indulging in sexual excesses on every plane, in every way known to carnal perverts.

Officers of the law tell us that licentiousness has surely reached its limit. The "Hand-writing on the Wall" appears. In proof of this allow us to quote the following by the great poet, Rabindranath Tagore, printed in the August 1st issue of the Los Angeles Examiner: "Paris, July 31.-I came from Asia expecting to find Europe a vale of tears, a desert of misery and grief. With ten million dead-10,000,000 stricken suddenly by shell or bullet from the roster of the earth, snatched from their firesides and their babies and the women whom they loved

-what should one visualize but a Europe draped in black, a Europe where the innocent laughter of a tiny child would seem a gross incongruity?

"Yet Europe weeps not. She has cast off her black, and is wearing her brightest colors, her most splendid plumes. Her men are already forgetting their slaught ered brothers in the incessant effort to profit from the abnormal financial conditions prevailing because of the war; her women-ah, her women I They are snatching flowers, bright red poppies, from the graves of their fallen husbands and sons, to wear them in their hair.

"Ten million dead-and naught but dust already I

Were these 10,000,000 the only sober, sane living people in Europe? Are those who are left only those consumed with avarice, selfishness and the desire to be amused at no matter what cost? Or is this Europe, which is dancing on its own coffin. a Europe gone stark mad?

"Paris, turn thine eyes to the south. There a templed city once stood, a living, breathing defiance to an inevitable death-a death that came sooner than it thought, and overwhelmed it. The name of that city was Babylon. Well named was Babylon! Well named also Paris, for call to mind the fate of her sister gods.

"They say to me: 'What strange man are you, to wish us eternal sadness? Would you have us grieve while we starve? Do you not know that work is impossible with a heavy heart and cannot you see that we have lightened our hearts in order to take up the burden our dead broth ers have left to us? What strange man are you?'

"I say to them: 'Europe, it seems to me that you are dancing more than you are working. Too many are living on the blood profits wrung from the slain.'

"They say to me: 'What do you want? We fought well-and we won.'

"I say to them: 'So did Babylon. Yet, though she won, she lost. Guard ye that you do not share her fate.' 11

49

THE GREAT PYRAMID AND THE SPHINX

IT is not an easy matter to get people to understand a subject to which they have given little or no thought whatever; but if one earnestly desires light on a rare and particular subject, as, for instance, the Great Pyramid

and the Sphini, deep concentration is bound to bring results, and the ideas that are the fruit of that "going into the silence;' may be similar to what others have given out and they may be dissimilar. If dissimilar, they may be offered to the earnest, esoteric student, as a working hypo thesis, to be accepted or rejected by him. In case he rejects, reason must be given in order that new light may be shed on the question.

Many scientists have personally studied the Great Pyramid and the Sphinx and made endless measurements. They have arrived, for the most part, at the same conclusion to which that great occultist, Madame Helena P. Blavatsky held, i. e., that "the measuring attainment of the Great Pyramid would indicate all the substance of measure of the heavens and the earth."

So much for that part, but there are other facts to be noted. It will be revealed-and no doubt within a comparatively short time, now-that there are many other secret chambers within this remarkable monument and that its true entrance is from the silent Sphinx. Verily it will not remain silent much longer. That celestial force which conquered the animal nature and resulted in a race of perfected human beings in a far distant Aquarian Age, enabled them to build monuments which would withstand the wear and tear of the ages and be a lode star and a beacon-light for fellow travelers along the same GREAT PATH-a path that is narrow and sharp as a razor; a path filled with stones that bruise and cut the feet. As one persists, the c,tones become fewer; green, velvet grass and beautiful flowers spring up beside the way, the heart of the aspirant is cheered and strengthened and he picks himself up again and yet again and goes on with eyes ever fixed on the flaming star in the distance. And these incomparable monuments show us what was done in past ages, what is being done now, and what will be accomplished by future generations until all humanity shall kneel at the feet of God-ultimate perfection for all of God's children-for we are all His.

In the King's chamber, which occupies the highest position therein, has been found an especially unique object, to which has been given many names, ranging from sar cophagus to corn-bin.   H. P. Blavatsky comments caustic ally on the denseness of those who ascribed the latter name to it, and says it is "a womb within a womb."   It is indeed a sacred chalice, the Holy Grail, and represents the pineal gland within the head of every human being. This receptacle within the King's chamber is forever un covered, waiting, patiently, for that precious treasure which is to rebuild the Sacred Temple.   It is the womb, the place of conception of the psycho-physical seed.   It is also the tomb of Joseph, the rock-hewn tomb, in which no man had ever lain, the place to which the seed returns. Humanity, as a whole, will, from now on, learn more and more about that wonderful process within the human

body, and more and more will their eyes become opened. Then, indeed, shall we not have definite assurance that the Great Pyramid will reveal to us the sacred Claustrum and the Door of Brahm?

The sarcophagus, then, was not intended by its per

£ected builders to contain a dead body, but a living one, living in the highest sense of the word. It is intended for a lasting memorial, an exemplification of that birth, life and transmutation of the Savior, the redeemer-the seed, within each human body.

Before entering the King's chamber we find ourselves in an ante-room, wherein "standing aU across the room from the floor to the ceiling" is the strange structure named the "granite leaf." It may well be that these four grooves correspond to the four eminences, the calliculi of the corpora quadrigemina in the mid-brain, the ante chamber of the head.

The King's Chamber and the Queen's Chamber stand in the same relation to each other as do the pineal gland and pituitary body. The King's chamber being placed the highest and likewise the pineal body. No wonder man has considered himself to be above woman. The Pyramid well, which connects the Queen's chamber with the subterranean grotto, corresponds in anatomy to the left sympathetic system, and the subterranean grotto is the sacral plexus, where the first crucifixion of the seed (Jesus) takes place. Without a doubt the future will reveal other nd more spacious rooms, corresponding to the organs of the body, and it is remarkable that the chambers which were first revealed to the eyes of hu manity stand for, and represent those organs within the human body which mankind is destroying in excesses.

It is no wonder that no trace of any lighting system has been revealed, for no system of lighting was needed. Those perfected builders enjoyed full use of the all-seeing Eye and were a light unto themselves the radiance from that inner eye giving light to all that was within the temple.

There was also great wisdom and forethought dis played in closing all the outlets of the Pyramid, all pas sageways-for those Great Ones knew that they were to be submerged, perhaps twice, before the impulse or spirit of the Aquarian Age would impel mankind to obey the inner urge and seek to solve the Pyramid mystery when he himself was beginning to seek and find the solution of the great and wondrous mystery within his own body. Hence passage ways were closed and kept free from the debris of ages.

In this Aquarian Age, this Sun-day of God, when the sign of the Son of man has appeared in the heavens, all things will stand revealed. Once again, in the course of the ages will mankind have reached the same goal which the builders of the Great Pyramid reached in that far re mote age of at least 50,000 years. And here and there are found a few whose eyes are beginning to be cleared, whose material vision is being purified, whose brain cells are beginning to vibrate to that harmony which, to the Ancient Ones, was sweet and thrilling music. And when this Aquarian Age shall reach its close, we, too, will be able to join in that great anthem of joy and sing the praises of the MOST HIGH-the God within us.

Humanity has been wandering many, many years in the wilderness, but the Promised Land, flow-inP. with milk and honey, is very, very near, and soon the 'Stone that the builders rejected will have become the head of the corner."

And in that day shall there be an altar to the Lord in the midst of the land of Egypt, and a pillar at the border thereof to the Lord."

-Isaiah 19:19.

. SAIAH in Hebrew means "Salvation of Jehovah." and

I   Jehovah means the whole body of man, but more especially does it mean the second man Adam, a

quickening spirit, the Lord God from heaven, the "I AM THE LORD THY GOD."

The geography of Upper Egypt and Lower Egypt resembles the anatomy of man's body. The solar plexus is the dividing line between the lower, ani-mal (Latin for bad life) or Adam-earthly man and the spiritual Ego residing in the heart-shaped cerebellum (see chart). "As a man thinketh in his heart so is he." The Ego thinks where it resides.

The salvation of the Ego is in the "midst of Egypt." etc.

In the archives of ancient Egypt, two crowns have

been found, one white, representing Upper Egypt, and the other red, representing Lower Egypt. Comment is un necessary.

The Great Pyramid is situated exactly on the geo graphical center between Upper and Lower Egypt. Thus it is "In the midst of Egypt as a whole and "on the bor ders thereof," of both sections.

The Pyramid of Cheops is an encyclopedia of physical science and astral lore. The science of numbers, weights, measures, astronomy, astrology and the secret mysteries of physiology are symboled in that incomparable monu ment. The history of Freemasonry is recorded there. Note on chart the descen-t of spinal cord, the pneumogas tric nerve, the two wonderful cords of nerves, Adi and Pingala and their relation to NUN, in Bethlehem, and you will find by the study of books on them that the pas- sage ways correspond to the inner man and typifies the mysterious Hiram Abiff by whose death the Word was lost and finally restored by his resurrection.

The Pyramid, the altar in the midst of Egypt, was reared by people who lived in some former Day of Judg ment, some past Aquarian Age, and who possessed wis dom that enabled them to solve the mystery of Christ hid in God-"The seed is the WORD of God."

$ $ $

FROM "THE GREAT PYRAMID JEEZAH"

By Louis P. McCARTY

"THE author believes that no man can study the Bible a great while, carefully and dispassionately noting its place in the world, its surroundings, its handings down, its prophetical bearings, not considered in detail, but in their large and comprehensive scope, with out coming to the conviction that a divine power and providence doth in some way hedge it about, and without coming to the conviction that this divine power is a conscious entity, just as we are; that he is, by his superiority, wisdom and power, continually and everywhere, intelli gently present as the immediate cause of each sequence in all the universe, however minute."

51

THE OPTIC THALAMUS

THE LAMP OR EYE

"THE THALAMUS," within which is the Optic, or eye, "is the great ganglion of the inter-brain. It is called the bed or chamber. It projects back

ward over the mid-brain. Laterally, it rests against the superior lamina of the internal capsule, which separates it from the lentiform nucleus. It is shaped like an egg, with the small end directed forward. It measures 4 cm. or about one and a half inches in length, and 2.5 cm. or one inch in width and thickness. It has an anterior and posterior extremity arid four surfaces."-Santee.

"The posterior surface (dorsal) of the mid-brain, though free, is entirely concealed by the cerebellar and cerebral hemispheres. It forms part of the floor of the transverse fissure of the cerebrum and is covered by pia mater. The lateral sulcus bounds it on each side. From the sulcus laterals it elevates abruptly toward the median line, where it presents a longitudinal groove. This pro duces two ridges which are subdivided by a transverse groove into FOUR EMINENCES (see article on The Great Pyramid and the Sphinx), the colliculi of the corpora quadrigemina. On either side, anterior and a little lateral to the quadrigeminal bodies, is the medial genicu late joined to the inferior quadrigeminal colliculus by an oblique ridge, called the brachium inferius. The nearly parallel longitudinal ridges below the corpora quadrige mina are formed by the brachia conjunctiva of the cere bellum. The bottom of the groove between them is formed by the superior medullary velum of Vieussens, when the trochlear nerve (fourth), is seen issuing.

Mid-Brain

Corpora quadrigernina and brachia.

Pedunculi

Tegrnenta.

Substantia nigra.

Bases pedunculi.

"The four colliculi of the corpora quadrigemina and the four brachia connecting them with the geniculate bodies constitute the quadrigeminal lamina, which forms the greater part of the posterior surface of the mid-brain. It is also called the tectum. This lamina rests upon the dorsum of the pedunculi cerebri. The lamina quadrige mina presents a small median triangle between the su perior colliculi and the habenula, called the subpineal triangle, in which the pineal body rests. The lamina is invested with pia mater."

All the above is taken from Santee's "Anatomy of the Brain and Spinal Cord." He is an authority on this subject.

"The ancients, from time immemorial, have considered the pine tree as the most sacred of all trees. The pineal gland or Corpus pineale, is shaped like the pine cone, and the ancient physiologist who gave it its name, must as suredly have understood its great esoteric function. It is 6 mm. (0.25 inches) high, and 4 mm. (0.17 inches) in diameter, joined to the roof of the third ventricle by a flat-teqed stalk, the habenula. It is also called epiphysis and conarium. It is small, reddish and the size of a pea. Its interior is made up of closed follicles surrounded by ingrowths of connective tissue. The follicles are filled with epithelial cells mixed with calcareous (lime) matter, the brain-sand (acervulus cerebri). Calcareous deposits are found also on the pineal stalk and along the choiroid plexuses."- Santee. This organ is Mars-Uranus in as tronomical correspondence.

Let us examine, for a moment.1. the wonderful term "pia mater."

What marvelous light floods the mind of the esoteric student when once the real meaning of this term becomes clear. Pia mater is Latin for "tender mother." It is the inner and most vascular (full of vessels) of the three membranes of the brain and spinal cord. The spinal fluid comes from the pia mater of the cerebrum, and this fluid, Santee tells us, "is more like tears and sweat, than serum." These fluids are both saline and alkaline, there being a large per cent of sodium chloride therein.

The wonderful pia mater, or tender mother, is the mother substance, the pure water, the Virgin Mary, the immaculate mother of all things. Most truly was Mary, the Mother of God, a spiritual as well as a physiological and chemical truth.

The Pituitary Body is given this name because it se cretes a mucus or phlegm. It is a small, red-dish, ellipsoid organ in a depression of the sphenoid bone, and attached to the brain by a pedun-cle. "It contains a viscid, jelly like material (pituita), which suggested the name. It is also called tl{e hypophysis. It consists of two lobes bound together by connective tissue, and in structure resem-bles the thyroid gland. The anterior lobe is hollowed out on its posterior surface (kidney-shaped) and receives the posterior lobe, the infundibulum, into the cavity. (The infundibulum is a funnel-shaped passage-a canal from this body (pituitary) to the third ventricle.) This body secretes a fluid that seems to stimulate the growth of con nective tissues and to be essential to sex development." Santee. This organ has a Mars-Neptune correspondence.

The pineal gland is the male spiritual organ-the elec tric body. Otherwise called "Joseph" in Bible terminol ogy. The Father of Jesus-the male element in the seed

-the source of the seed. To it, also, the seed, or Jesus, the Son, returns after his work is done. Joseph of Ari mathaea receives the body of J <;.sus and lays it in his own rock hewn tomb "wherein no man was ever laid before." The pineal gland becomes hard like a rock when the "brain-sand," the saved seed, is furnished it. When no material is being returned in tithes to the brain, the pineal body is flabby and pasty.

Let us examine, for a moment, those organs above the optic thalamus. In the article on Santa Claus, the Island of Reil and the claustrum have been described.

It is interesting to note that there are five different bodies lying in a perpendicular line directly beneath the suture, as follows : First, the Island of Reil; the claus trum ; the external capsule; the lentiform nucleus, and the internal capsule. Directly beneath the latter is the thalamus.

The internal capsule is a funnel-like group of nerve fibers which enter the cerebrum and are reinforced by a great number of additional fibers from the thalamus, which converge upward. The bell of this funnel opens upward and contains the lentiform nucleus.   L

"The lentiform nucleus occupies the cone like cavity of the internal capsule, by whose laminae it is separated from the ventricle.   IT RESEMBLES A BI-CONVEX LENS with a somewhat thickened anterior border, when viewed in horizontal section.   It is triangular in shape. The hypothenuse and base are formed, respectively, by the superior and inferior laminae of the internal capsule. The external capsule forms the perpendicular and separates the lentiform nucleus from the claustrum."-Santee. We can easily see, from the above description of the organs, that they are corelated and form the path from the thalamus to the "door of Brahma." It is through this channel that the attenuated, ethereal substance from without is conveyed to the inner eye. The rays, or vibrations, which converged along this pathway are, by means of the lentiform nucleus, the bi-convex lens in the cere

brum, focalized in the "ALL-SEEING EYE."

Wonder of all wonders is the head of man, within which the Adam-man and the God-man dwells-Taurus and Aries, the house and the temple.

"If a man cannot rule his own house, how can he take

care of the church (temple) of God?"

52

CENTRAL EYE

A nd the lamp thereof is the lamb."-Rev.

HE optic thalamus, the central eye, in the center of the head, is called both "lamp" and "lamb."

The thalamus ("chamber") is a mass of gray matter at the base of the cerebrum, projecting into and bounding the third ventricle.

The Hebrew letters, Lamed, Aleph, Mem and Beth mean, in their order, "overcoming," "father," "mother" and "house," or some materialized form.

While "p" in "lamp" gives a different meaning. P, from the seventeenth letter of the Hebrew alphabet, "pe" means "speech," or that which radiates or goes forth. In the Tarot it is referred to as "The force which dis penses the essence of life, which gives it the means of perpetually renewing its creations after destruction." One may speak destructively and then, having seen the light, is able to speak constructively.

Thus we see how it also means rays or light, etc., etc., hence LAMP.

The essence of life within us, the oil, is what feeds this lamp or causes it to give light-if it is carried up to the place where this lamp or candle, which the Bible refers to, is, which is the optic within the thalamus, referred to above.

"If thine eye be single ('free from defect'-Dictionary)
thy whole body will be full of light."

The outer eyes see only by reflection. The vibrations from the inner eye, optic, is conveyed along the optic nerves and produced, spectacular, on the ether.

Thus we, frequently, when trying to comprehend some thing, put our hand over our eyes for a moment and then exclaim, "Oh, yes, now I see."

"Behold the lamb of God which taketh away the sins of the world."

The seed is also referred to as the lamb, as it is neces sary for the seed or Jesus to be carried up into this part of the anatomy, in order that it may cause the optic to vibrate rapidly, and thus produce the illumination. "We shall be changed in the twinkling of an eye."

Exodus 15 :26, "If thou wilt diligently hearken to the voice of the Lord thy God, and wilt do that which is right in his sight, and wilt give ear to his commandments, and keep all his statutes, I will put none of these diseases upon thee, which I have brought upon the Egyptians; for I am the Lord that healeth thee.

Psalms 25 :1, "Unto thee O Lord, do I lift up my soul."

25:13, "His soul shall dwell at ease; and his seed shall inherit the earth."   •

Psalms 37 :1-5, "Fret not thyself because of evildoers, neither be thou envious against the workers of iniquity. "For they shall soon be cut down like the grass, and

wither as the green herb.

"Trust in the Lord and do good; so shalt thou dwell in the land, and verily thou shalt be fed.

"Delight thyself also in the Lord, and he shall give thee the desires of thine heart.

"Commit thy way unto the Lord; trust also in Him; and He shall bring it to pass.

"And He shall bring forth thy righteousness as the light, and thy judgment as the noonday.

"The steps of a good man are ordered by the Lord; and He delighteth in his way.

"Though he fall he shall not be utterly cast down, for the Lord upholdeth him with His hand.

"Depart from evil and do good and dwell forever more.

"Mark the per/ ect man and behold the upright; for the end of that man is peace."

Psalms 62: 1-2, "Truly my soul waiteth upon God; from Him cometh my salvation.

"He only is my rock and my salvation; He is my defense; I shall not be greatly moved."

I

Psalms 91, "He that dwelleth in the secret place of the Most High shall abide under the shadow of the Almighty. "He shall cover thee with His feathers and under His wings shalt thou trust; His truth shalt be thy shield and

buckler.

"Thou shalt not be afraid for the terror by night; nor for the arrow that flieth by day.

"Nor for the pestilence that walketh in darkness; nor for the destruction that wasteth by noon-day.

"There sh'all no evil befall thee.   Neither shall any plague come nigh thy dwelling.

"For he shall give his angels charge over thee, to keep thee in all thy ways."

Psalms 103 :5, ".Who satisfieth thy mouth with good things; so that thy youth is ren-ewed like the eagles."

Psalms 119 :105 NUN, "Thy word is a lamp unto my feet and a light unto my path."

Psalms 127 :1, "Except the Lord build the house, they labor in vain that build it."

Psalms 132 :11, "Of the fruit of thy body will I set upon thy throne."

St. Luke 12 :31, "But rather seek ye the Kingdom of God; and all these things shall be added to you."

53

THE PHYSIOLOGICAL STATEMENT

E XTRACTS FROM A PAPER BY PROF. SMILEY
(Lately of Cornell University)

HE sacral region of man's body, near the base of the spinal column, is a gland larger than a hen's egg, of spongy character, and into which is secreted, trom

the blood, a small amount of oil, at the same time that the blood throws out refuse into the bladder.

Exceedingly little has been known to physiologists about this gland, or about the purpose of the secretion, except that in elderly men it often becomes the seat of a disease called prostitis, and that in young men of dissolute habits the secretion becomes filthy.

This gland is known in the East as the Kundalini, and in the New Testament, Greek, as the Kardia.

It will be best to know it here by that name, rather than by the medical term. The oil in it will elsewhere be iden tified with the Greek psyche, and be so referred to herein.

The oil is subject to very varied degrees of consistency; from very thin, volatile oil that promptly evaporates when exposed to the air, to one having a good body, a truly fixed oil, that will form a permanent stain upon a piece of paper. In the most healthy, wise and vigorous men, it is a fixed oil. In the average kind of man to be met on the street, it is more or less volatile. In "rakes" it is very malodorus and may contain pus.

For its highest and purest condition when it is a fixed oil, colorless, odorless and tasteless or sweet, not really acid, nor really alkaline, we shall use the Greek term Chrism, or for short, by the root letters 9f the noun for oil, and of the verb, to oil-Chri-in Greek XPI.

It is necessity of nature that the oil, when purified or secreted in the Kardia shall usually make its way out again through the capillaries into the blood and so pass all over

I   .

the body, wherever the blood goes. It 1s, then, one of

the constituents of the blood. "The blood of Christ."

At the present day, boys fifteen years old and older, usually get more or less annoyed by nature's complaints of the congestion. Indeed, it appears in boys seven to four teen years old-a proof that this annoyance does not come from the seminal vesicles. Every cigarette smoker gets a certain relief from smoking, because the poisonous and narcotic effect of the tobacco deadens the voice of nature.

It has been proven that when this gland and its oil act properly, there is not only no desire for tobacco, but tobacco is then too repulsive to be tolerated for a moment. The BODY IS A LAMP. THIS OIL IS ITS

ILLUMINATING SUBSTANCE. WITHOUT IT THERE IS NO CONSCIOUSNESS. WHEN IT IS COMPLETELY EXHAUSTED, CONSCIOUS NESS CEASES AND DISINTEGRATION TAKES PLACE.

This oil is not only easily affected, but the effects are carried through the blood into the structure of the tissues of the brain and other parts.

In all ages of the world a small and select few have known how to multiply this life essence.

Of enormous importance is another fact regarding this oil. It is extremely affected by mental states, and by the states of consciousness. The oily milk of a nursing mother may be poisoned by a sudden fit of anger, so as to make her nursing babe sick. This is an effect of mind upon matter. A ferocious appetite can be destroyed in stantly by the reading of a telegram announcing the death of one's mother.

The physiological results of having plenty of good oil thus circulated constantly in the body we have demon strated to be:

First: Destruction o_f all semblance of nervousness, irritability, greed, fear and unrest.

Second: The perfection of digest on and assimilation.

Third: Restoration of impaired eyesight and hearing. Prevention of decay in the teeth.

Fourth: Full amount of the most enjoyable and restful sleep. Freedom from the use of all drugs. Much less food is desired or needed. There is no demand for stimulants.

Fifth: Neutralization of blood poisoning. Probable destruction of cancerous and all other blood diseases.

Sixth: Prompt and complete prevention of all kinds of self-abuse. Restoration from the effects of earlier in discretions.

Seventh: Immunity from colds and probably from all kinds of infectious diseases.

Eighth: Restoration of youthful vigor and prevention of all frailities of old age.

Ninth: In short-accomplishment of everything that unlimited vitality should be expected to produce.

54

THE WIVES AND CHILDREN OF JACOB OR ISRAEL

JACOB means "heel-catcher," hence circle. The name Jacob, or Jacob's ladder, is applied to the twelve signs of the Zodiac, and the sign Aries, the head, and Pisces, the feet, represent the point of contact, the place

where the circle joins.

In his dream Jacob saw the heavens open and God let down a ladder, and the angels (angles) of God descending and ascending upon it. God promised him that his seed should be as the dust of the earth, and in him all families of the earth should be blessed. God promised to be with him and to bring him again to the land whereon the promise was made.

On awakening from his sleep Jacob said, "This is none other but the house of God and this is the gate of heaven." The name of the place was called Bethel (House of the Sun). And Jacob promised to give one tenth of all that he should receive, unto the Lord. (See Tithes).

This story is one of the most remarkable and significant of all of the Biblical allegories, since it must be applied cosmically as well as microcosmically.   It represents the solar plexus in man-and the zodiac in the solar system. We can easily understand the meaning of Jacob's journey, and how, in process of time he came to l\1ount Peniel (pineal gland) where he wrestled with the angel of God, who blessed him and changed his name to Israel. He had then come again to the place from which he had started for he had again seen God face to face.   It means that the circle was complete-Jacob had caught hold of his

own heel.

The bread that he was to eat was the seed born or formed in the center of the circle-the solar plexus, and, of course, stands for the cosmic sun also, the savior of the world. This bread or seed was to become the savior of the Adam-man.

It is very evident that the "Old" Testament referred more especially to the cosmic processes; the "New" Testament to those same processes within man, since "as above, so below." There is nothing in the universe that is not within man.

Jacob was commanded to go and seek out Laban (white) and to marry one of his daughters. Therefore, the circle of the Zodiac proceeded to that part of the heavens called the "milky way," and Jacob came upon the daughters of Laban, tending the "flocks." He loved Rachel, for she was beautiful, and he agreed to serve seven years in order to possess her. When the time was up the "marriage" took place, but Jacob found that he had been given Leah, instead of the bride he so desired. The excuse that was given was that Leah was the eldest and hence must be married off first.

Rachel refers to the planet Venus and Leah to the planet Mars. We are told that Leah had "weak eyes," we know that Mars is called the "fiery-eyed." Venus represents love and beauty. Mars also stands for activity, and nothing could be accomplished on this earth by human beings, if there was no active force in mani festation.

Mars has been referred to principally as the planet of war, but we feel that it will not be long before the real nature of Mars will become known. Then will humanity realize that the same force that is manifested in war and brutality may be transmuted and used in numberless ways for the benefit of humanity. If mankind would use the same amount of force and energy in doing constructive, instead of destructive work, we would soon see Mars through rose-colored glasses, instead of those colored blood-red. Mars means activity, forcefulness, not necessarily war or bloodshed. Another great war has been prophtsied because very great activity of Mars is shown, astrologically; but the world is weary, sick unto death of war.

55

THE SOLAR PLEXUS

H OUSES of the Zodiac represented by the twelve children of Jacob (same as Israel). Benjamin, the thirteen, the Son of the Sun, is Jesus, the fish or seed. Hebrew, Persian and Syrian names of each house, month or sign.

HEBREW, PERSIAN OR SYRIAN DERIVATIONS QF THE MONJ'HS

	MONTH	SIGN
1st Month:	April, Aries	NISAN: March-April (New day, Passover, Exodus)
2nd Month:	May, Taurus	ZIF: April-May (Flower month, beauty)
3rd Month:	June, Gemini	SIVAN: May-June (Moon)
4th Month:	July, Cancer	TAMMUZ: June-July
5th Month:	August, Leo	AB: July-August
6th Month:	September, Virgo	ELUL: August-September (To glean the vine)

7th Month: October, Libra   ETHANIM: September-Octa-her (Perennial)

8th Month: November, Scorpio   BuL: October-November (Rain)

9th Month: December, SagittariusCHISLEU: November-Decem ber (From Aram, Mars, Orion)

10th Month: January, Capricorn TEBETH: December - Janu ary (Winter)

11th Month: February, Aquarius SEBAT: January-February 12th Month: March, Pisces ADAR: February-March

(Fire-God)

13th or Intercalary Month: VEADAR. (See article on Leap Year.)

As Leah and Rachel, or Mars and Venus, represent activity and love, they also stand for the median line of the Zodiac, for Libra and Aries are ruled by these two planets. Also, these two planets are represented in the head of man, Mars ruling Aries, the upper brain, the Almighty, the *creator* of all, and Venus ruling Taurus, as represented by the cerebellum. The head and the neck rule the body of man. The Adam-man, Taurus or Venus, rules it *if* he has become awakened, when he then becomes the Lord God from heaven, for God is Love. Activity works along wisdom's ways.

Aries and Taurus, represented by Gad and Asher, are the two "lost" tribes referred to by so-called Bible students. Lost tribes are not mentioned in the Bible text. They were never lost, but because they are not mentioned many times in connection with the other tribes, or children of Israel, they were *supposed* to have been lost. As they are located in the cerebrum and cerebellum, that part of the anatomy which is *separated* from the torso, we can easily understand the supposition that they were *lost.* Aries and Taurus are the two tribes that lay down the law to the other ten. If the individual lives in excess, saves no seed or oil, these two most important parts of the body *do* become "dead" in trespass and sin, and we say he died of "softening of the brain."

Leah and Rachel, then represent the divisions of the zodiac. From these two wives (and hand-maids) the children, or signs of the zodiac, were produced. These twelve are again divided into the seven and the five. "The seven representing the lunar forces, or seven pneu mata, being differentiations of the 'Great Breath' or 'World Mother,' and symbolized by the Moon. The signs are Cancer, Leo, Scorpio, Virgo, Libra, Sagittarius and *Capricorn.*"-*Pryse.*

"The five solar forces which pertain to the cerebro spinal system, called the five pranas, or vital airs, or life winds," are represented by Aries, Taurus, Gemini, Pisies and *Aquarius.*"-*Pryse.*

"The four divinities of the zodiac are represented by the Lion, the Bull, the Man and the *Eagle.*-*Pryse.*

The names of the children of Jacob, or Israel, are given on chart herewith. Benjamin, the only one born in the *promised land.* In Arabia, the blest, was Benjamin, the last and *thirteenth.*

The trials and tribulations of the children of Israel typify the struggle for self-mastery-the harmonizing of all the forces of the body.

The twelve dorsal vertebrae are also esoterically connected with each one of the nerves, ramifying to the solar plexus.

The Hebrew and Syrian names for the different months are also given on the chart.

The youngest child, Benjamin, at whose birth Rachel died, was the Beloved, the tender one, the little one, the ark which the Israelites carried with them on their great Journey.

Rachel died and her "grave is there to this day." Yea, verily in every human being-the seed-pod, the solar plexus center. (See article on Leap Year).

56

PROPHECIES FULFILLED

T HE 18th CHAPTER OF REVELATION-MATTHEW, 24th CHAPTER-LUKE, 21st CHAPTER

WE strongly urge our readers to very carefully read all contained in the above chapters, from the view point of astrology, physiology and chemistry.

The zodiacal sign, Aquarius, the man with the pitcher of water is the "sign of the Son of Man in the heavens." The monthly seed is the Son of Man in earth, the body.

The fifth son of Jacob (Genesis 29), named Dan, a judge, represents in astrology January 20th to February 22nd, which is the sign Aquarius, and through which the sun passes once yearly.

But the solar system entered that sign on its 2200 year cosmic circle in the year 1900.

As Dan is Hebrew for Judge, and Daniel for wisdom, or God's judgment, therefore, earth is now in the day or time of judgment.

The great revolutionary planet, Uranus (Ouranous in Greek), the son or sun of heaven, is the ruler of Aquarius and will be regnant for over 2000 years.

For a fulfilled prophecy of the destruction of the com petitive system' of commercialism and the destruction of gold and silver as mediums of exchange, see the 18th Chapter of Revelation. Also, see Russia.

Peter the Great was an Aquarian native, hence Russia will be (is) the first to establish a free Aquarian (wis dom) government.

All who oppose cosmic law are crushed.

"The stars in their course fought for" Russia.

And thus the prophecy, "A nation shall be born in a day" has been fulfilled.

KILLING THE FATTED CALF, OR KAPH

IT has been written, the origin of words and the application of the characters differ so widely that "confusion worse confounded" is the result in numberless cases.

The eleverith letter of the Hebrew alphabet is Kaph, a hollow and represents the human hand, a hollow or hal lowed place.

The cerebrum, upper brain, is hollowed and covers the cerebellum like a w_ing. The cerebellum is therefore a secret place where tlie Ego, or spiritual man; the "Second man Adam a quickening spirit," or "The Lord God·from heaven" dwells. (See 91st Psalm).

The upper brain, in the parable of the prodigal son, is represented as the Father, being the cause of and furnish ing the "Substance" to build and replenish the body.

The Ego is represented as saying to the Father, "Give me the portion of goods that falleth to me." Now this portion was the oil that flows do n the Ida and Pingala to form a seed, but the Ego, thinking on the carnal plane "wasted this substance in riotous living." The evil result that followed is likened to swine, husks, etc., etc.

As in the story of Hiram Abiff in Masonry, after the WORD was lost for a season ("The seed is the WORD"

-Luke) it was resurrected so in the prodigal son parable,

29 .¾ days passed, the material for another seed de scended and said, "I will arise and go to my Father."

When the seed comes forth out of the manger in Beth lehem (house of bread), "/ am the bread of life," a vibra tion of greater life is set up ("Life more abundant"), and it thrills the entire temple of God.

Now comes the astounding revelation:

The original meaning of "kill" is not to take life, neces sarily; it rather means to choke or squeeze. To choke a sponge, or squeeze water from it does not mean to take life, but if one's throat is squeezed or choked for a time and the breath ceases to enter the body, we say the person has been killed.

The gray matter of the upper brain vibrates high-is quickened when "one-tenth is returned to the Lord" and thus secretes more abundantly down to the magnetic, chemical center, the cerebellum called heart in Greek "As a man thinketh in his heart so is he."

So, then, the "Father killed the fatted kaph" for the Son, i. e., gave up life for the Ego. "Hallowed be thy name." The name is hollowed, viz., Kaph, a hollow.

The hollow of the knee is named Kaph and spelled calf. Probably it was applied to a young bovine, because of the peculiar hollow of the belly when the animal is very young. Here the reader is_referred to the 91st Psalm. In that marvelous allegory, or epic, the hollow of the "Most High" is represented as casting a shadow for the Ego in the "Secret place." (See cerebellum in chart).

"His feathers shall cover thee." Note the resemblance of the brain convolutions to feathers.

57

THE ANTI-CHRIST

PRIMITIVE Christians, the Essenes, fully realized and taught the great truth t at Christ was a sub stance, an oil or ointment contained especially in the Spinal Cord, consequently in all parts of the body, as every nerve in the body is directly or indirectly connected with the wonderful "River that flows out of Eden (the

upper brain) to water the garden."

The early Christians knew that the Scriptures, whether written in ancient Hebrew or the Greek, were allegories, parables or fables·based on the human body, "fearfully and wonderfully made."

These adepts knew that the secretion (gray matter creative) which issues (secretes), from the cerebrum, was the source and cause of the physical expression called man; and they knew that the "River of Jordan" was symbolized in the spinal cord and that the "Dead Sea" was used to symbolize the Sacred Plexus at the base of the spinal column where the Jordan (spinal cord) ends, typifying the entrance of Jordan into the Dead Sea.

The thick, oily and salty substance composing the Sacral Plexus, "Cauda Equina" (tail of the horse), may be likened unto crude Petroleum (Petra, mineral, or salt, and oleum-Latin for oil) and the thinner substance, oil or ointment in the spinal cord, may be compared with coal oil; and when this oil is carried·up and crosses the Ida and Pingala (two fluid nerves that end in a cross in medulla oblongata where it contacts the cerebellum (Gol gotha-the place of the skull)-this fluid is refined, as coal oil is refined, to produce gasoline-a higher rate of motion that causes the ascension of the airship.

When the oil (ointment) is crucified-(to crucify means to increase in power a thousand fold-not to kill) it remains two days and a half, (the moon's period in a sign) in the tomb (cerebellum) and on the third day ascends to the Pineal Gland that connects the cerebellum with the Optic Thalmus, the Central Eye in the Throne of God that is the chamber overtopped by the hollow (hallowed) ca used by the curve of the cerebrum (the "Most High" of the body) which is the "Temple of the Living God," the living, vital substance which is a precipi tation of the "Breath of Life" breathed into man therefore, the "Holy (whole) Ghost" or breath.

The Pineal Gland is the "Pinnacle of the Temple." The modus operandi by which the oil of the spinal cord reaches the Pineal Gland is described in what follows. "There is no name under Heaven whereby ye may be saved except Jesus Christed and then crucified" (correct

rendering of the Greek text).

Every twenty-nine and one-half days, when the moon is in the sign of the zodiac that the sun was in at the birth of the native, there is a seed, or Psycho-Physical germ born in the, or out of, the Solar Plexus (the Manger) and this seed is taken up by the nerves or branches of the Pneumo gastric nerve, and becom s the "Fruit of the Tree of Life," or the "Tree of good and evil"-viz.: good, if saved and "cast upon the waters" (circulation) to reach the Pineal Gland; and evil, if eaten or consumed in sexual expression on the physical plane, or by alcoholic drinks, or gluttony that causes ferment-acid and even alcohol in intestinal tract-thus-"No drunkard can inherit the Kingdom of Heaven" for acids and alcohol cut, or chem ically split, the oil that unite! with the mineral salts in the body and thus produces the monthly seed.

This seed, having the odor of fish, was called Jesus, from Ichtos (Greek for fish) and Nun (Hebrew for fish)-thus "Joshua the son of Nun,"-"I am the bread of life;" "I am the bread that came down from heaven;" "Give us this day our daily bread."

The fruit of the Tree of Life, therefore, is the "Fish bread" of which thou shalt not eat on the plane or animal or Adam (earth-dust of the earth plane) : but to "Him that overcometh will I give to eat of the fruit of the Tree of Life," because he saved it and it returned to him in the cerebellum, the home of the Spiritual mia,n, the Ego.

The cerebellum is heart-shaped and called the heart in Greek-thus "As a man thinketh in his heart so is he."

The bodily organ that men in their ignorance call heart is termed divider or pump in Greek and Hebrew. Our blood divider is not the button that we touch when we think, but it is the upper lobe of cerebellum that vibrates thought. The lower lobe is the animal (mortal) lobe that governs the animal world-that section of the body below the Solar Plexus, called lower Egypt-natural body kingdom of earth-Appollyon-the Devil (lived, spelled backward) Satan (Saturn governs the bowels), etc.

Fire and Brimstone (the lake of fire) comes from the fact that sulpliur (brimstone) is the prime factor in generating the rate of motion called heat, and overeating develops a surplus of sulphur.

During the first 300 years of the Christian era all that has been above written was understood by the real Christians, and about the end of that time the persecution of these Essenes by the priesthood became so marked that they met in secret and always made the sign of the fish.

About the year 325, Constantine, the pagan Roman Emperor, called the teachers of Christianity together at Nicea.

Constantine murdered his mother and boiled his wife in oil because they still held to the original doctrines of the Essenes. Constantine was told by the Priests of his time that there was no forgiveness for crimes such as his, except through a long series of incarnations; but the anti Christ sought to concoct a plan by which he hoped to cheat the Cosmic law.

And so it came to pass, after months of wrangling and fighting over the writings of the primitive Christians who clothed the wonders of the human body in oriental imagery, that the council, sometimes by a bare majority vote, decided which of the manuscripts were the "Word of God" and which were not.

The very important point in the minds of those ignor ant priests-whether or no an angel had wings-was decided in favor of wings by three majority. The minority contended that, as Jacob let down a ladder for angels to descend and ascend upon it was prima facie evidence that angels do not have wings.

Just think, for a moment, upon the colossal ignorance of these priests who did not know that Jacob in Hebrew means "heel catcher" or circle, and that ladder referred to the influence of the signs of the zodiac upon the earth; and as one sign rising every two hours forms a circle every twenty-four hours (the four and twenty Elders of Revelation) the outer stars of the rising suns (sons) '.' catching on" to the last sons (suns) of the sign ascend ing.

But now we come to the anti-Christ:

The council of Nicea, dominated by Constantine, voted that the symbols of the human body were persons; that Jesus was a certain historical man, a contention utterly and indubitably without foundation, in fact, and that all who believed (?) the story would be saved and forgiven here and now. The idea appealed to Constan tine as an easy way out of his troubled mind and so the scheme of salvation by the actual blood of a real man or god was engrafted in the world.

Constantine and his dupes saw that the only way to perpetuate the infamy was to keep the world in ignorance of the operation of the Cosmic Law, so they changed "Times and seasons."

The date that they made the sun enter Aries was March 21st. Why? March 21st should be the first day of Aries, the head; April 19th should be the first day of Taurus, the neck, and so on through the twelve signs; but these designing schemers knew that by thus suppressing the truth the people might come to realize what was meant by "The heavens declare the glory of God."

Again: the moon, in its monthly round of 29¼ days

enters the outer stars (or suns) of a constellation two and one-half days before it enters the central suns of the constellations that are known as the Signs of the Zodiac or the "Circle of Beasts." But even unto this day the whole anti-Christ world (so-called "Christian") except the astrologers, go by almanacs that make the moon enter a sign of the zodiac two and one-half days before it does enter it and thus perpetuate the lie of the pagan Constantine, the anti-Christ.

58

WHAT SO-CALLED CHRISTIANS SAY, AND THE ANSWER

"Christ was a man, born of a woman."

"We believe in Jesus, we expect to die and then•be saved." "Jesus is greater than man." "Only Jesus was conceived of the Holy Ghost."

"We will go to heaven when we die." •,

"The earth will be destroyed." "I believe in Jesus."

"I am born of God."

"Jesus Christ is a man, a Savior that died and went away and will come again."

Jesus was born, conceived of the Holy Ghost (Ghost is "breath" in Greek-the whole breath, or air breathed in.

"He that believeth in me shall never die." Death is an enemy to be overcome."

"All that I do ye can do." "Know ye not that the Holy Ghost dwelleth in you?"

"The Kingdom of Heaven is within you."   "Thy will be done in earth as it is in Heaven." "The earth endureth forever." "These signs shall follow those who believe in me," etc., etc. "He that is born of God will not sin, for his seed remaineth in him."

"He that confesseth not that Jesus Christ is come in the ftesh (your flesh), the same is an Anti-Christ. That means, one opposed to the truth that there is a seed born in you from the Christ (oil) in you. "And unto thee and thy seed, which is Christ."-Pau/.

For more evidence that Jesus and Christ are in your flesh see 1st Epistle of John-4th Chapter, 2nd and 3rd verses.

The Greek and Hebrew texts of our Scriptures plainly teach that Jesus and Christ, John and baptism, crucifixion and ascension, the triumph of the Ego over the "Enemy death" are in the substance and potentialities of the body; and that these fluids can and will save the physical body, if conserved and not consumed (or wasted) in sexual or animal desire.

All of whatever name or religious denomination who teach a contrary doctrine agree with Constantine who appeared in the "Latter days" of the Pure Christian Practice.

Who is the anti-Christ? Look at a world of ruins.

Does a good tree bring forth evil fruit?

The so-called teachers of, and believers in Christian ity believe as Constantine and his priests, that Christ is "out in the desert" of the Judean hills-out on Calvary. Do they ever look for the meaning of Calvary in Greek? Calvary means a skull, and Golgotha-the place of the skull, exactly where the seed is crucified.

One-half of the combatants in the world's Armaged don have been praying, as Constantine prayed, "for God's help for Christ's sake." The other half pray to the same imaginary God and Christ out in "The desert" of their own ignorance for "peace and victory."

Return and come unto the God and Christ within you,

oh I ye deluded ones, and the bugles will all sing truce along the iron front of war and the "Ransomed of the Lord will return to Zion with songs and everlasting joy upon their faces."

59

THE RIB-LAH THAT MADE THE WOM(B)MAN

FOR the Lord hath created a new thing in the earth. A woman shall compass a man."-Jere miah 31;22.

"And she brought forth a man child." See Revelation 12th, Chapters 1 to 6.

"Rib-lah, the eastern boundary of Israel." It was between Shepham and the Sea of Chinnereth (Gennes aret)".-Smith's Bible Dictionary. This was the place of the "Holy Fountain."

"But when the fullness of time was come, God sent forth his Son, made of a woman, made under the law."

-Galatians 4;4.

The children of Israel (warriors of God-see Smith's Bible Dictionary), are the thirteen seeds. (See Jacob's Children-name changed to Israel) .

There is no historical Land of Israel. The name is found first in the Secret or Sacred writings which pertain to the inner functions of the human body-purely chem ical and physiological.

Sacred-from "sacral," refers to the lower part of the spinal column.

Secret, from secretion, gray matter or oil from the upper brain, the fountain of life, the "Secret place of the Most High"-the heaved up place, the heaven within us.

N, the fourteenth letter of the Hebrew alphabet, added to heave, makes it heaven, because the seed, the fish which N, Nun, the fourteenth letter represents, on being carried to the pineal gland regenerates the in dividual, and the upper brain becomes a manifested heaven. This seed "Seeks the kingdom of heaven."

There is probably no definite trace of the semi-lunar ganglion, two half moon-shaped ganglion near the suprarenal glands, situated near the kidneys, that connect the spinal cord at the twelfth dorsal vertebra with the solar plexus, in the body of an infant, yet it is quite probable, if not certain, that the vestigal form, power and potency is implanted there at birth.

When the boy or girl reaches "about twelve," the semilunar and the manger (or nun) in Bethlehem is in full function, and hence Jeremiah's declaration.

It is evident that the fluids, creative, omnipotent, flow ing "Out of Eden to water the garden" (Gen. 2:10), creates a new thing in the earth-the body, about that age, using the rib-lah to make the woman or worn (b) an, or womb in mankind-male or female.

This womb does compass circle a man (child-seed), "The seed is the Son of man." Again, "Know ye not that the Son of man hath power in earth to forgive sin?" Analysis of "man," according to the Jewish Kaballah, reveals the fact that M, the thirteenth letter of the alpha bet, means woman, mother, and is written thus, "mem."

A, the first letter-Aleph, means father or male strength or forces.

Nun, the fourteenth letter of the alphabet, means fruit, son, child, savior that redeems, therefore, man is mother, first (or Mary), then father, then son-redeemer, hence destined to be ultimately saved.

The sun and moon (see Joshua commanding the sun to stand still) and the pneumogastric or vagus nerve, the spinal cord and all that portion of the body above the median line, the "Middle wall of partition," is exactly the same in man and woman, and the functions in the "king dom," in each body, enables them, separately and alone, to "work out their own salvation, or secretions. (See Joseph and Mary), the pineal gland and pituitary body, both in one human organism, thus; "In my kingdom (saith the seed), there is no marrying nor giving in marriage."

Note: Rib-lah, the eastern boundary of Israel: The

back is called the East, front, West; feet, South (down South), head, North (up north) , hence the semilunar g-an,zlion is East of Israel, the regenerative womb in man. See chart.

According to Hindu secret writings, God took a rib out of the female to make the male. Literally speaking, this idea would be much more reasonable than a literal rendering of the passage in Genesis.

"A woman hid a little leaven in a bag of meal and it leavened the whole lump."

Woman, or the womb in man, the upper or regenerative womb. Leaven, or yeast, the seed that comes forth from the womb in man, expands or causes the oil in the spinal cord (the "bag of meal"), to multiply. See loaves and fishes in the gospel. Also "Give one-tenth (tithes) to the Lord."

No wonder David-the Seed-is made to say of the man whose delight is in God: "And in thy law will I meditate day and night.

60

THE BRIDGE OF LIFE

A "Conceived in sin and brought forth in iniquity."
NOISELESS, patient spider,
I mark'd, where, on a little promontory, it stood, isolated;
Mark'd how, to explore the vacant, vast surrounding,
It launch'd forth filament, filament, filament, out of itself; Ever unreeling them-ever tirelessly speeding them.
"And you, 0 my soul, where you stand,
Surrounded, surrounded, in measureless oceans of space,
Ceaselessly musing, venturing, throwing-seeking the spheres, to connect them ;
Till the bridge you will need, be form'd-till the ductile anchor hold;
Till thegossamer thread you fling, catch somewhere, 0 my soul."
-Walt Whitman.
"O Man of Earth, watch well the steps thou findest, Spread out before thy feet by cosmic plan;
Do thy soul's best, with body and with mind,
To pay thy debt, and bridge this Karmic Span."
-Edith F. A. U. Painton.

The statement of Holy Writ, that "man is conceived in sin and brought forth in iniquity" has a three-fold mean ing, viz., chemical, physiological and astrological. The real meaning in the original is, that the hum n embryo remains nine months in the female laboratory, thus fall ing short three months of completing a solar or soul year. It also represents the journey of the ego from the moon to earth, or conception. Twelve, which represents the circle and stands for completion.

The word sin comes from Schin, the twenty-first letter of the Hebrew alphabet, and means to fall short of com pleteness, or understanding, wisdom. In the Tarot sym bol, S, or Sin, is represented by the "Blind Fool," one lacking in wisdom, "Brought forth in iniquity" is merely a repetition of the words "born in sin." Iniquity and inequity or unequal, ean the same. The ancient He brews called Moon, Sin, because it gave light only part of the time.

To acquire wisdom that will enable the Ego in flesh to build a bridge across the three-month gap, or space between the point of conception and birth, is the one real problem that confronts the ego on the material plane of expression. The alchemists, seers and astrolo ians of all ages have wrestled with this problem in their ceaseless endeavors to unravel the great mystery of man's dominion over flesh. Whether it be the chemist seeking new com pounds, the physiologist searching and testing the fluids of the fearfully and wonderfully made body of man, the alchemist probing for the Elixir of Life-the lchor of the Gods or the astrologian pulling and adjusting the etheric wires that criss-cross the spaces in an earnest desire to make good and sane the statement "The wise man rules his stars,"- all, all are seeking to span the awful space that yawns between the neophyte and the Promised Land of imlmortality in the body, where "in my flesh I shall see God," and when and where he can truly say with the regenerated Job, "I have heard of thee by the hearing of the ear, but now mine eye seeth thee." Man must work out his own salvation.

The bridge to be built across the three-months space must have a mineral base or rock foundation. "Thou art Peter (petra, stone, or mineral) , on thee will I build my church," etc. Church is from the second Hebrew letter, Beth, a house temple, or church. The human body is a house, temple, or church for the Soul which may be lost or saved by the higher self or spiritual ego residing in the cerebellum the "Secret Place of the Most High." "Know ye not that your bodies are the temple (church) of God?"

There are twelve inorganic mineral cell-salts in the human body, and these minerals (stones in the temple) correspond in vibration to the twelve signs of the Zodiac. During the nine m;onths of gestation the embryo receives and appropriates the creative energies of nine of these salts, leaving three to be supplied after the parting of the umbilical cord. Take for example a native born February 22nd, with the Sun's entry into Pisces: The embryo, having begun its journey at the gate of Gemini and nego tiated the nine gestatory signs, his blood vibration at birth is thus deficient in the qualities of Pisces, Aries and Taurus, as also in the chemical dynamics of phosphate of iron, phosphate of potassium and sulphate of sodium- the mineral bases respectively of the signs of this uncom pleted quadrant. In so far as his circulatory system may receive these needed builders, the health will be balanced and life prolonged.

The chemical union of these cell-salts with organic matter, such as oil, fibrin, albumen, etc., forms the various tissues of the body and administers to the physiological needs as represented by the Bridge, that the multiple cells may respond more harmoniously and completely to the magic touch of the Divine energy, just as the tones of a musical instrument are made the more melodious through a properly skilled manipulation. And as bridge building in a mechanical sense depends upon the plans and specifications of a competent civil engineer, so does the Bridge of Life depend upon the astrologian to chart and compass the way.

Our diagram indicates at a glance the chemical for mula that appertain respectively to the zodiacal divisions, but to give a clearer conception as regards their specific qualities and physiological action in relation to the various signs, reference may be had to the following compend: The coming of Christ and the end of the world has been preached from every street corner for several years, and thousands are pledging themselves to try to live as

Christ lived or according to their concept of His life.

No great movement of the people ever occurs without a scientific cause.

The Optic Thalamus, meaning "light of the chamber,"

is the inner or third eye, situated in the center of the head: It connects the pineal gland and the pituitary body. The optic nerve starts from this "eye single."   "If thine eye be single, thy whole body will be full of light." The optic thalamus is the Aries planet and when fully developed through physical regeneration it lifts the initi ate up from the Kingdom of Earth, animal desire below the solar plexus, to the pineal gland that connects the cerebellum, the temple of the Spiritual Ego, with the optic thalamus, the third eye.

By this regenerative process millions of dormant cells of the brain are resurrected and set in operation, and then man no longer "sees through a glass darkly," but with the Eye of spiritual understanding.

We venture to predict that the planet corresponding to the optic thalamus will soon be located in the heavens. "The new; order cometh."   Mars must be dethroned as ruler of the brain of man.

To those who object to linking chemistry with astrol ogy, the' writer has this to say:

The Cosmic Law is not in the least disturbed by nega tive statements of the ignorant individual. Those inves tigators of natural phenomena, who delve deeply to find Truth, pay little heed to the babbler who says, "I can't understand how the zodiacal signs can have any relation to the cell-salts of the human body." The sole reason that he "cannot understanc" is because he never tried to understand.

A little earnest, patient study will open the understand ing of any one possessed of ordinary intelligence and make plain the great truth that the UN/verse is what the word implies, i.e., one verse.

It logically follows that all parts of one thing are sus ceptible to the operation of any part.

The human body is an epitome of the cosmos.

Each sign of the Zodiac is represented by the twelve functions of the body and the position of the Sun at birth.

Therefore, the cell-salt corresponding with the Sign of the Zodiac and function of the body is consumed more rapidly than other salts and needs an extra amount to supply the deficiency caused by the Sun's influence at that particular time.

In ancient lore Aries was known as the "Lamb of Gad," or God, which represents the head or brain. The brain controls and directs the body and mind of man. The brain itself, however, is a receiver operated upon by celestial influences or angles (angels) and must operate according to the directing force or intelligence of its source of power.

Man has been deficient in understanding because his brain receiver did not vibrate to certain subtle influences. The dynamic cells in the gray matter of the nerves were not finely attuned and did not respond-hence sin, or falling short of understanding.

From the teachings of the Chemistry of Life we find that the basis of the brain or neyve fluid is a certain mineral salt known as potassium phosphate, or Kali Phos.

.A deficiency in this brain constituent means "sin," or a falling short of judgment or proper comprehension. With the advent of the Aries Lord, God, or planet, cell salts are rapidly coming to the fore as the basis of all healing. Kali phosphate is the greatest healing agent known to man, because it is the chemical base of material expression and understanding.

The cell-salts of the human organism are now being prepared for use, while poisonous drugs are being dis carded everywhere. Kali phosphate is the especial birth salt for those born between March 21 and April 19.

These people are brain workers, earnest, executive and

?etermined-thus do they rapidly use up the brain vital- 1zers.

The Aries gems are amethyst and diamond.

In Bible alchemy Aries represents Gad, the seventh son of Jacob, and means "armed and prepared"-thus it is said when in trouble or danger, "keep your head."

In the symbolism of the New Testam nt, Aries corres ponds with the disciple Thomas. Aries people are natural doubters until they figure a thing out for them selves.

The astronomer, by the unerring law of mathematics applied to space, proportion, and the so far discovered wheels and cogs of the uni-machine, can tell where a cer tain planet must be located before the telescope has veri fied the prediction. So the astro-biochemist knows there must of necessity be a blood mineral and tissue builder to correspond with each of the duodenary segments that con stitutes the circle of the Zodiac.

Not through quarantine, nor disinfectants, nor boards of health, will man·reach the long-sought plane of physical well-being; nor by denials of disease will bodily regenera tion be wrought; nor by dieting or fasting or "Fletcher izing" or suggesting, will the Elixir of Life and the Philosopher's Stone be found. The Mercury of the Sages and the "hidden manna" are not constituents of health foods. Victims of salt baths and massage are bald before their time, and the alcohol, steam and Turkish bath fiends die young. Only when m;an's body is made chemically perfect will the mind be able perfectly to ex press itself.

And_,.the secret of this chemical perfectionment is the sum total of the requirements involved in this zodiacal Bridge. The rock-Peter, or Petra-must be completed before the etheric wires that span the gulf between birth forward to the sidereal point of conception can vibrate in such harmony as to sustain the traveller on this "magical bridge of three piers," or the three zodiacal signs through which the material body must successfully function before it may hope to lift the veil of Isis.

The Bridge of Life, a symbol of physical re-genesis, has been exploited in song, drama, and story. Paracel sus, Pythagoras, Lycurgus, Valentin, Wagner, and a long and unbroken line of the Illuminati, from time immem orial have chanted their epics in unison with this "riddle of the Sphinx," across the scroll of which is written, "Solve me, or die."

Of all the multiple adepts or masters that have kept the lights burning above the Three Piers of the magical Bridge, none has more clearly and beautifully written thereof than did the great astrologian poet, Isaiah:

"Then the eyes of the blind shall be opened, and the ears of the deaf shall be unstopped. Then shall the lame man leap as a hart, and the tongue of the dumb shall sing; for in the wilderness shall waters break out, and streams in the desert. And the glowing sand shall become a pool, and the thirsty ground springs of water; in the habitation of jackals, where they lay, shall be grass with reeds and rushes. And a hiqhway shall be there, and a way and it shall be called, The way of holiness; the unclean shall not pass over it, but it shall be for the re deemed; the wayfaring men, yet fools, shall not err therein."

Here we have the last step on the physical plane that breaks down the "middle wall of partition."-Pau/. Then the Ego is enabled to regenerate by saving the Word of God-the Seed-and thus render further m carnations unnecessary.

61

VOL. IV, SACRED BOOKS OF THE EAST

Extracts from Sepher D'tzenioutha, or the book of concealed mystery-medieval Hebrew

, , THE Book of Concealed Mystery" is the book of the ,equilibrium of balance.

In His form (in the form,' of the Ancient One) existeth the equilibrium.

It is incomprehensible, it is unseen.

The head, which is incomprehensible, is secret in secret.

But it has been formed and prepared in the likeness of a cranium and is filled with crystalline dew.

His skin is of ether, clear and congealed.

His hair is as most fine wool, floating though the balanced equilibrium.

His eye is ever open and sleepeth not, for it continually keepeth watch. And the appearance of the lower is according to the aspect of the higher light.

Therein are His two nostrils like mighty galleries, whence His spirit rusheth forth over all. The creative spirit-the "breath of life."

The crystalline dew is the creative lux, or Aur, AVR proceeding from the Limitless One."

Now the author of the "Sepher Dtzenioutha" descend eth to the inferior paths, leaving out Macroprosopus, and examineth the name IHV, YDO HE VAU. In this are represented father and mother and Microprosopus. And first occurreth the supernal I, YOD (the symbol of the father), which is crowned with crown of the more Ancient One (that is, whose highest apex denoteth the highest crown, or Macroprosopus; or, according to another read ing of the passage, "which is surrounded by the secret things"-that is, by the influence or beard of Macropo sopus, which covereth both the father and the mother). It is that membrane of the supernal brain which, on account of its excellency, both shineth and is concealed."

"In the cranium:" (or skull), Begolgoltha, or in Gol gotha. In the New Testament it is worthy of note that Jesus Christ (the Son) is said to be crucified at Golgotha (the skull) ; while here, in the Kabbalah, Mircoproso pus (the Son) as the T etragrammation, is said to be ex tended in the form of a cross, thus-in Golgotha (the skull).

"And amid the insupportable brilliance of that mighty light, as it were, the likeness of a head appeareth. (That is! the highest crown is found in M acroprosopus) .

"And above him is the plenteous dew, diverse with two-fold color. (Like as in Macroprosopus it is white alone, so here it is white and red, on account of the judgments).

"It is written in Isa. XXXIII.20: 'Thine eyes shall behold Jerusalem at peace, even thy habitation.'

"The 'peaceful habitation' is the Ancient One, who is hidden and concealed.

"Macroprosopus is only the COMMENCEMENT OF THE MANIFESTED DEITY.

"And when a man wisheth to utter his prayers rightly before his Lord and his lips move themselves in this manner, his invocations, rising upward from him, for the purpose of magnifying the majesty of his Lord, unto the place of abundance of pure water where the depth·of that fountain riseth and floweth forth (that is under standing emanating from wisdom)) ; then (that fountain floweth forth plentifully, and) spreadeth abroad, so as to send down the influx from the Highest, downward from that place of abundance of water, into paths singly and conjointly, even unto the last path; in order that her bountiful grace may be derived into all from the highest downward."

62

SANTA CLAUS

All down the ages there have been stories of fairies, gnomes, mermaids, naiads and fabled characters galore. The ancient Norsemen, Dutch, Huns and all the oriental races, possess literature prolific with allegories, parables and fables built around the wonders and physical

and chemical operations of the human body.

The birth of the monthly seed is the basis of the Mother Goose Stories and similar tales in all lands.

Santa Claus, or Saint Nicholas, the patron saint of sea farers, virgins and children, is the bearer of gifts to children on Christmas eve.

Of all festivals celebrated all over the known world, that held in honor of Santa Claus ranks as first in the hearts of all humanity, old as well as young. This in itself is a most significant fact. •

It is time that the truth in regard to this age long custom be made known to the world, time that its real and true significance be understood. Then will it be truly celebrated, for it will have become an inward process, as well as an outward observation.

Parents, from time immemorial, have explained to their children that the presents which they found in their stockings, when they jumped eagerly from their beds in the morning, were placed there by a mysterious person called "Santa Claus." No one saw him come, no one saw him leave, but he left unmistakable evidence of his visit.

Some children ask many questions in regard to this mysterious "person," and when they become too insistent the ingenuity of parents is sorely taxed to give satisfactory answers. There comes a time, however, when they must have the Santa Claus "myth" explained to them, and it is then that their deep childlike trust and confidence in their parents receives its first shock. Thereafter they commence to doubt their parents, to question their veracity, and many tears have been shed, because, after all Santa was not a "really, truly person."

THERE IS A SANTA CLAUS, IT IS A PHYSIO

LOGICAL FACT, and IT does "SECRETE" the most holy and wonderful "gift" or substance in the body of every individual. Those who understand it-who receive it in the right spirit-have "Become as little children."

"As above, so below." As in the Macrocosm-the universe, so in the microcosm-man.

Can anyone think for one moment that the parables, fables, allegories and myths that have come down to us through the ages have no basic foundation? They, as well as the fast days and feast days are founded on great esoteric truths. Otherwise they would have ceased to be.

The Great Hierarchy that rules the Universe see to it that nothing is forgotten that needs to be remembered. Santa Claus, or Saint Claus, is derived from the same root word as "claustrum," from which "cloister" is also derived.   Claustrum means a barrier, a covered place, se clusion. Cloister is referred to as a place of seclusion, and more especially as a place of seclusion for something

holy, something dedicated to divinity.

There is a Saint Claus, or Claustrum within the cere brum, and whoever gave it that name knew why they did so.

The suture of the skull is the point where the bones meet. We can very easily see this place on the head of infants, as the sections are not then drawn closely to gether, and the vibrations of the brain can be both seen and felt.

In Sanscrit this is called "The Door of Brahm," for it is the apperture through which the Ego, or Spirit leaves the body. It is also the chim:ney of Santa Claus.

The vertebrae as a whole is called the "stick of Brahm."

Directly underneath the "door of Brahm" is a tri angular shaped body named in physiology the "Island of Reil." This is the place where "John" was when "he" looked back and saw the wonderful vision of the regen erated man in the "Isle of Patmos" This island is the central lobe of the cerebrum, and is also called the Pole;

hence, the Island of Reil is the North Pole of the body, and is, as we well know, the imperishable, sacred land. In Santee's anatomy of the brain and spinal cord, we find that this island is "situated in the medial wall of the lateral fissure of the cerebrum, between the frontal, parietal and temporal lobes,   whose   growth,   after   the   fifth   month   in   utero,   gradually   covers   it over.   At the end of the first year of extrauterine life, it is entirely concealed by temporal, parietal and frontal parts of the operculum"

-cover or lid. Thus we see that Mother Nature has taken great pains to conceal this sacred center.

Underneath this island, and directly in a line with the Optic Thalamus lies the Claustrum, but separated from it by yet three other bodies.

The claustrum is thin sheet of isolated gray matter, found just medial to the Island of Reil. Santee says it "is a sheet of peculiar gray substance, and is made up of fusiform (spindle shaped) cellbodies." It is from this claustrum that contains yellow substance within its outer grayish exterior, that the wonderful, priceless OIL is formed that flows down into the olivary fasciculus, "de scending with the rubro-spinal tract through the reticular formation in the pons and medulla to the lateral column of the spinal cord. It terminates in the gray matter of the spinal cord, probably giving off collaterals to cor responding nuclei in the brain stem."-Santee. This is the OIL, the precious gift of which the Bible speaks, "Thou anointest my head with oil."

And not only is there oil manufactured within this

·special laboratory of the brain, but there is actually an olive tree, which bears actual olives-so named in any anatomy. The two olives are two infinitesimal eminences on either side of the medulla, with the Pyramid between. They are one-half inch in length. It is found well de veloped only in the higher mammals. They are RELAY (Santee) stations between the cerebrum and the cere beHum and between the spinal cord and the cerebellum.

This oil is the most sacred substance in the body-it is the quintessence of gold-the "Gold of Ophir"-most truly a rare gift. Globules of oil are found in the vital fluid, the semen, and when the prodigal son has wasted his substance, he finds that it takes a long time to replace the deficiency and make good the looted bank account.

This wonderful oil is the secret work of the immaculate Virgin, Mary (or Mare) 'represented by the sign Virgo. In chemistry we find that sulphate of potassium is the mineral salt, which, uniting with sulphur and oxygen, manufactures the oil. We find that this salt also crystal lizes out from the mother-liquors of sea water and salt springs. People born under the sign Virgo, if they have become deficient in this salt suffer from dryness of the skin, and baldness. We can also understand why draining of the vital fluid-living in excesses, will also produce baldness. If there were no oil in the body, the skin would become harsh and dry.

The story of the wise virgins who had their lamps trimmed and filled with oil is given to emphasize the necessity for the presence of oil in the body, for they cannot go out to meet the "bridegroom" unless their lamps are burning. "The lamb is the lamp thereof."

The olives, which contain the oil, are the reservoirs the relay stations, of course, which furnish the oil for the lamp, the pineal gland, at the top of which is the flame or eye. When the Kundalini, the serpent fire that lies con cealed within the sacral plexus is awakened, burns up the dross within the spinal cord, and reaches the conarium, it sets fire to this oil and thus lights the "perpetual lamp," which "Gives the light to the whole house."

Santa Claus is thus the giver of the supreme gift in the human body, the oil.for the perpetual lamp-the gold of Ophir, the quintessence of richness..

A total lack of oil in the body will, in itself, cause death.

Santa Claus brings his gifts when the Christ-mass is celebrated.

The Greek characters that stand for Christ are X PI, and the word itself (Christ) means oil, in Greek. The seed is the bread of life, and when anointed with oil (Christed and crucified) become the Christ-mass-the bread, eaten in the Father's Kingdom.

Thus we now clearly understand the meaning of Santa Claus and his Christmas visit with gifts to the children.

63

LEAP YEAR

LEVITICUS 19 :23, 24, 25: "And when ye shall come into the land, and shall have planted all man ner of trees for food, then ye shall count the fruit

thereof as uncircumcised; three years shall it be as uncir cumcised unto you; it shall not be eaten of.

"But in the fourth year all the fruit thereof shall be holy to praise the Lord withal.

"And in the fifth year shall ye eat of the fruit thereof that it may yield unto you the increase thereof: I am the Lord, your God."

Deuteronomy 14 :22 to 24: "Thou shalt truly tithe all the increase of thy seed that the field bringeth forth year by year.

"And thou shalt eat before the Lord thy God, in the place which he shall choose to place his name there, the tithe of thy corn, of thy wine and of thine oil and the firstlings of thy flocks; that thou mayest learn to fear the Lord thy God always." •

We find that in one year there are twelve moons and a fraction equal to just about one-third. Therefore, it would require just three years to make an extra moon or month. This is where "Leap Year" comes in, as at that time there was great rejoicing, for at the end of three years all the tithes were gathered and laid up within the gates. This represents the seed of the field, one seed being saved every month, and at the end of the three years, if all seeds have been saved, there would be thirty six and, with the extra month added, would make a total of thirty-seven seeds. As seven represents or stands for the conqueror, we can easily see that there is some special significance in this 37th seed, and also a great significance to the fourth year. The seed born at this time must have some special function to perform in the physiological economy and must be the seed which begins to lay the foundation of the temple. For the seeds that are saved for three years complete a certain process in the body (if all are saved during that time) ; so that, with the beginning of the fourth year a special and most wonderful process begins. It is probable that the thirty-six seeds have been carried into the blood and completed the cir cuit of the body, producing a very great change therein, so that, when the three year process is completed, the thirty-seventh seed, or conqueror, is born and is the cause of very great rejoicing, as then the results of the three years, the tithes, are "collected within the gates"- taken to the Holy of Holies and used to lay the foundation of that sacred place.

I Kings 7 :13 and 14: "And King Solomon sent and fetched Hiram out of Tyre.

"He was a widow's son of the tribe of Naphtali."

Naphtali refers to the Pisces sign and, of course, means fish. Therefore, Solomon used the fish, or seed born in the sign Pisces, to commence the building of his temple. As in Leap Year we add one day to February, making 29, we utilize this day or man (seed) for a special work, in the human body, every fourth year, in the Pisces month.

There are thirteen full moons every fourth year.

64

REVELATION OF HERMES

The Ne Plus Ultra Statement on Physical Regeneration," by Para celsus, written at a time and in an age when concealment of deep esoteric truths was made necessary because of persecution by its enemies. Para celsus has reserved the last line for the revealment as well as the con cealment of the /great key.

, 'THE Book of Revelation of Hermes, interpreted

)Y Theophrasyus Paracelsus, concerning the Su f>reme Secret of the World."

"Hermes, Plato, Aristotle and other philosophers, flourishing at different times, who have intro-duced· the Arts, and more especially have explored the secrets of in ferior creation, all these have ea-gerly sought a means whereby man's body might be preserved from decay and become endued with immortality. That there is one 1hing which may postpone decay, renew youth and prolong short human life.

Therefore, the above philosophers and many others have sought this ONE THING with great labor and have found that which preserves the human body from corruption and prolongs life itself, with respect to other elements, as it were like the heavens; from which they understood that the heavens are a substance above the Four Elements. And just as the heavens with respect to the other elements are held to be the fifth substance (for they are indestructible, stable, and suffer no foreign ad mixture), so also this ONE THING (compared to the forces of our body) is an indestructible essence, drying up all the superfluities of our bodies, and has been philosoph ically called by the above mentioned name. It is neither hot and dry like fire, nor cold and moist like water, nor warm and moist like air, nor dry and cold like earth. But it is a skillful, perfect equation of all the elements, a right commanding of natural forces, a most particular union of spiritual virtues and an indissolu-ble uniting of body and soul. It is the purest and noblest substance of an indestructible body, which cannot be destroyed nor harmed by the eliements, and produced by art. With this Aristotle prepared an apple (Fruit-seed, Authors) prolonging life by its scent, when he, fifteen days before his death, could neither eat nor drink on account of his old age. This spiritual Essence, or ONE THING, was revealed from above to Adam (man), and was greatly desired by the Holy Fathers; this also Hermes and Aristotle call the truth without lies, the most sure of all things certain; the secret of all secrets. It is the last and highest thing to be sought under the heavens. (Nate by authors: "There is only ONE WAY under heaven, whereby ye may be saved-Jesus, Christed and crucified.")

"A wondrous closing and finish of philosophical work, by which are discovered the dews of heaven and the fast ness of earth. What the mouth of man cannot utter is all found in this spirit. As Morienus says: 'He who has this has all things and wants no other aid,' for in it are all temporal happiness, bodily health and earthly fortune. It is the spirit of the fifth substance, a fount of all joys (beneath the rays of the Moon), the supporter of Heaven and Earth, the mover of Sea and Wind, the outpourer of Rain, upholding the strength of all things and an excellent irit above heavenly and other spirits, giving Health, Joy, Peace, Love; driving away Hatred and Sorrow, bringing in Joy; expelling all Evil, quickly healing all dis eases, destroying poverty and misery, leading to all good things, preventing all evil words and thoughts; giving man his heart's desire ('Seek ye first the Kingdom of God and His righteousness and all things shall be added unto you'-Bible), bringing to the pious, earthly honor and long life, but to the wicked who misuse it, eternal punish ment.

"This is the Spirit of Truth, which the world cannot comprehend without the interposition of the Holy Ghost, or without the instruction of those who knew it. The same is of a mysterious nature, wondrous streng_!h and boundless power. The saints from the beginning of the world have desired to behold its face for it heals all dead and living bodies.

Here Christ ism witness that I lie not, for all heavenly influences are united and combined therein. This essence also reveals all treasures in earth and sea, converts all metallic bodies into gold, and there is nothing like unto it under heaven. This Spirit is the secret, hidden from the beginning, yet granted by God to a few holy men for the revealing of these riches to His glory-dwelling in fiery form in the air, and leading earth with itself to heaven, while from its body there flows whole rivers of living water./ This Spirit flies through the midst of the heavens like a morning mist, leads its burning fire into the water and has its shining realm in the heavens. And although" these writings may be regarded as false by the reader, yet to the initiated they are true and possible, when the hidden sense is properly understood. For God is wonderful in His works and His wisdom is without end. This Spirit in its fiery form is called a Sandaraca, in the aerial a Kyorick, in the watery an Azoth, in the earthly Alcohouh and Aliocosoph. Hence they are de ceived by these names, who, without instruction, think to find this Spirit of Life in things foreign to our art. For, although this Spirit which we seek, on account of its quali ties, is called by these names, yet the same is not in these bodies and cannot be in them. For a refined Spirit can not appear except in a body suitable to its nature. And, by however many names it may be called, let no one imagine that there be different spirits, for, say what one will, there is but one Spirit working everywhere and in all things. That is the spirit which, when rising, illumi nates the heavens, when setting incorporates the purity of earth, and when brooding has embraced the waters. This spirit is named Raphael, the Angel of God, the subtlest and purest, whom the others all obey as their king.

Through the same, Moses made the golden vesse_s in the Ark, and King Solomon did many beautiful works to the honor of God. Therewith Moses built the Taber nacle, Noah the Ark, Solomon the Temple. By this Ezra restored the Law and Miriam, Moses' sister, was hos pitable. Abraham, Isaac and Jacob and other righteous men have had life-long abundance and riches, and all the

saints possessing it have therewith praised God. For it is the best of all things, because, of all things mortal that man can desire in this world, nothing can compare with it, and in it alone is truth. Hence it is called the STONE and Spirit of Truth; its praises cannot be sufficiently ex pressed.

0, unfathomable abyss of God's wisdom, which thus hath united and comprised in the virtue and power of One Spirit the qualities of all existing bodies. 0, unspeakable honor and boundless joy granted to mortal man; for the destructible things of nature are restored by virtue of said Spirit. 0, mystery of mysteries, most secret of all secret things, and healing and medicine of all things. Thou last discovery in earthly natures, last best gift to Patriarchs and Sages, greatly desired by the whole world. 0, what a wondrous and laudable spirit is purity in which stand all joy, riches, fruitfulness of life, and art of all arts, a power, which to Initiates grants all material joys. 0, de sirable knowledge lovely above all things beneath the circle of the Moon, by which nature is strengthened, and heart and limbs are renewed, blooming youth is preserved, old age driven away, weakness destroyed, beauty and its perfection preserved and abundance insured in all things to men.   0, thou Spiritual substance, lovely above all things.   0, thou wondrous power, strengthening all the world. 0, thou invincible virtue, highest of all that is, although despised by the ignorant, yet held by the wise in great praise, honor and glory, that proceeding from humors' wakest the dead, expellest diseases and restorest the voice of the dying.   0, thou treasure of treasures, mystery of mysteries, .called by Avicenna "An unspeak able substance," the purest and most perfect soul of the world, than which is nothing more costly under heaven, unfathomable in nature and power, wonderful in virtue and works, having no equal among creatures, possessing the virtues of all bodies under heaven.   For from it flows the water of life, the OIL AND HONEY of eternal healing, and thus hath it nourished them with honey and water from the rock. Therefore, saith Morienus: "He who hath it the same hath all things."   Blessed art thou,

Lord God of our fathers, in that thou hast given the prophets this knowledge and understanding that they have hidden these things (lest they should be discovered by the blind and those drowned in worldly godlessness) by which the wise and the pious have praised thee.

"Oh, you doubtful man, you Peter of little faith, who are moved by each wind and sink easily. You are your self the cause of all your diseases, because your faith is so little and feeble, and your own evil thoughts are your enemies. Moreover, you have hidden within yourself a magnet which attracts those influences which correspond to your will, and this celestial magnet is of such power that for more than a hundred, or even thousands of miles, it attracts that which you desire out of the four elements."

Moral: Purify your desires. Save the seed.

"Matter and force are one and originate from the same cause."

"True knowledge consists in a direct recognition of TRUTH, and is taught by nature herself."

"The highest aspect of alchemy is the regeneration of man in the Spirit of God from the material elements of his physical body. The physical body itself is the greatest of mysteries, because in it are contained, in a condensed, solidified and corporeal state, the very essences which go to make up the substance of the material man, and this is the secret of the "Philosopher's Stone." The sign in which the true alchemist works is the cross, because man, standing erect among his brothers of the animal kingdom, roots with his material elements in the earth, penetrates with his soul through the elementary forces of nature to suffer and die, but his head reaches above the animal creation into the pure atmosphere of heaven."

"All the powers of the universe are potentially con tained in man, and man's physical body and all his organs are nothing else but products and representatives of the powers of nature.   What is the human body but a con stellation of the same powers that formed the stars in the sky?   He who knows what Iron is, knows the attributes of Mars. He who knows Mars, knows the qualities of iron. What would become of your heart if there were . no sun in the universe? To grasp the invisible elements, to attract them by their material corresponder.ces, to control, purify and transform them by the living power of the Spirit-this is true alchemy."

"Faith is a luminous star that leads the honest seeker into tLe mysteries of natare. You must seek your point of gravity with God ('Seek ye first the Kingdom of God') and put your trust into an honest, divine, sincere, pure and strong faith, a,nd cling to it with your whole heart, soul, sense and thought, full of love and confidence. If you have such a faith, God will not withhold his Truth from you, but He will reveal His works to you, credibly, visibly and consolingly. This means that by the power of God acting within you and opening your own inner senses, God will reveal His works within yourself; so that His wisdom being born within, you may recognize through you, and you with it, the truth in all nature."

"Nature is the universal Mother of all and, if you are in harmony with her, if the mirror of your mind has not been made blind by the cobwebs of speculations and mis conceptions and erroneous theories she will hold up before you a mirror in which you will see the truth. But he who is not true to himself will not see the truth as it is taught by nature, and it is far easier to study a number of books and to learn by heart a number of scientific theories than to ennoble ones own character to such an extent as to enter into perfect harmony with nature and be able to see the truth."

"Those living in vice are unworthy of it. Therefore is

this Art to be shown to all God-fearing persons, because it cannot be bought with a price. I testify before God that I lie not, although it appears impossible to focls that no one hath hitherto explored Nature so deeply. The Almighty be praised for having created this Art-the seed) and for revealing it to God-fearing men. Amen ! And thus is fulfilled this precious and excellent work, called the revealing of the Occult Spirit, in which be hidden the secrets and mysteries of the world. But this Spirit is one genius, one divine, wonderful and lordly power. For it embraces the whole world and overcomes the elements. TO OUR TRISMEGISTUS SPA GYRUS, JESUS CHRIST, BE PRAISE AND GLORY IMMORTAL. AMEN!"

65

EXTRACTS FROM THE SECRET DOCTRINE

By Madam H. P. Blavatsky, the Greatest Occultist of the 20th Century
,'SEED OFLIFE, FISH: While Vaivasvata was engaged in devotion on the river bank, a FISH craves his protection from a bigger fish. He saves

it and places it in a jar (solar plexus) which, growing larger and larger, it communicates to him the news of the forthcoming deluge."

"Vaivasvata Manu, the Son of Surya, the Sun and Savior of our race, is connected with the SEED OF LIFE,• both physically and spiritually."

"For them the passage entrance and the Sarcophagus in the King's Chamber meant regeneration, not gener tion. It was the most solemn symbol, a HOLY OF HOLIES, indeed, wherein were created Immortal Hiero phants and Sons of God."

Page 63, Vol. III: " 'The first man is of the earth, earthy; the second (inner-our higher) man is the Lord from heaven * * * Behold, I show you a mystery.'

-Bible. Thus says Paul, mentioning the dual and trini tarian man for the better comprehension of the non initiated. But this is not all, for the Delphic injunction has to be fulfilled; man must know himself in order to become a perfect adept. How few can acquire the knowl edge, however, not merely in its inner, mystical, but even in its literal sense, for there are two meanings in this command of the Oracle. This is the doctrine of Buddha and the Bodhisattvas pure and simple."

SATAN: "Many names hath God given him (Satan), names of mystery, secret and terrible."

"The adversary, because matter opposeth Spirit, and time accuseth even the saints of the Lord."

"For Satan is the magistrate of the Justice of God (Karma). He beareth the balance and the sword."

"For to him are committed WEIGHT AND MEAS URE AND NUMBER."

Hades, or the Limbo of Illusion, of which theology makes a region bordering on hell, IS SIMPLY OUR GLOBE, the earth, and thus Satan is called "the angel of the manifested worlds."

It is Satan who is the God of our planet and the ONLY GOD, and this without any metaphorical illusion to its wickedness and depravity.   For he is one with the Logos. "The Gnostics wei;e right, then, in calling the Jewish God an 'Angel of Matter,' or he who breathed (con scious) life into Adam, and whose planet was Saturn. 'I create good and I create evil, I the Lord God create all these things.' "-Bible, Isaiah.

"When the church, then, curses Satan, -it curses the Kos mic reflection of God. It anathematizes God made mani fest in Matter, or in the objective; it maledicts God, or the ever-incomprehensible

Wisdom, revealing itself as Light and Shadow, Good and Evil in Nature, in the only manner comprehensible to the limited intellect of man."

"It was by Kriyashakti, that mysterious and divine power, latent in the WILL of every man, which if not called to life, QUICKENED AND DEVELOPED BY YOGA TRAINING, remains dormant in 999,999 men out of a million, and so gets atrophied."

"It is this mysterious· POWER OF THOUGHT, which enables it to produce external, perceptible, pheno menal results by its own inherent energy. The ancients held that any idea will manifest itself externally, if one's attention and will is deeply concentrated upon it."

"Mystically Jesus was held to be man-woman."

"The ship or ARK-Navis-in short, being the sym bol of the female generative principle, is typified in the heavens by the moon and on earth by the womb; both being the vessels and bearers of the SEEDS of life and being, which the SUN, or Vishnu, the male principle (SON), vivifies and fructifies."

"Water is the symbol of the FEMALE ELEMENT everywhere: Mater, from which comes the letter 'M' is derived pictorially from MMM, a water hieroglyph."

"The human Ego is neither Atman nor Buddhi, but
the Higher Manas."

"MAN NOT CREATED FROM NOTHING: Very
soon the day will dawn, when the world will have to choose whether it will accept the miraculous creation of man (and Kosmos) out of NOTHING, according to the dead letter of Genesis, or a first man born from a fantastic link, absolutely 'missing,' so far-the common ancestor of man, and of the 'true ape.'   Between these TWO FALLACIES, Occult philosophy steps in.   It teaches that the first human stock was projected by higher and semi-divine beings out of their own essences."
(See Prov erbs quoted elsewhere.)

"Man's (mankind) symbol is the cube unfolded and 6 becoming 7, or .the 3 crossways (the female) and 4 vertically; and this' is man, the culmination of the deity on earth, whose body is the cross of flesh, ON, THROUGH AND IN WHICH HE IS EVER CRU CIFYING AND PUTTING TO DEATH THE DI VINE LOGOS, HIS HIGHER SELF."

"A few years longer and this system (numerical and geometrical keys) will kill out the dead-letter reading of the Bible, as it will that of all the other exoteric faiths, by showing the dogmas in their real naked meaning. And then this undeniable meaning, however incomplete, will unveil the mystery of Being, and will, moreover, entirely change the modern scientific systems of Anthropology, Ethnology and especially that of Chronology."

"The glyph of Pharaoh's daughter (woman) and the Nile (the great deep and water) and the baby boy found floating therein in the ark of rushes, was not primarily composed for, or even by Moses. It was anticipated in the fragments found on the Babylonian titles, in the story of King Sargon, who lived far earlier than Moses."

66

WHY REINCARNATE?

It is taken for granted that we, spiritual Egos, reincarnate for the sole purpose of obtaining knowledge that will enable us to triumph over matter.

If this statement is a true presentation of the great mystery of flesh and blood, it is indubitable evidence that we failed to obtain the wisdom that we are seeking in all the past incarnations and experience in flesh and blood.

Nowhere in sacred, or secret script, do we find a line indicating that any definite number of incarnations are required for spiritual man, or the "I AM" before the realization comes as expressed in the language of the allegorical Master, "I can lay my body down and I can take it up again," and again, "All the things that I do ye can do and greater things shall ye do." The time to do this great work is now.· "Now is the accepted TIME. Now is the day of Salvation."

It is most encouraging to those who seek the Kingdom of the Real to find in the physiological and chemical writings of the Bible, that the process of attainment of this tremendous truth is so plainly set forth in both Old and New Testaments, that the "wayfaring man, though he be a fool," may understand.

There is but "One way whereby ye may be saved." Jesus, the monthly seed, christened in the waters of

Jordan, the marrow or oil of the spinal cord, and crucified (refined or transmuted) by crossing the nerves of regener ation at the junction of the medulla and cerebellum at the base of the skull, Golgotha, where the christened or christed seed is crucified, or crossified, in the regenerative process.

Matthew 19th Chapter: "Ye which have followed me in the regeneration, when the Son of man shall sit in the throne of his glory, ye also shall sit upon twelve thrones judging the Twelve Tribes of Israel." Son of man refers to the seed, of which there are twelve and one-third born yearly, here represented by the Twelve Disciples of Jesus. Israel also means the seeds "Warriors of God" and the twelve thrones are typical of the twelve bodily functions

mastered by the regenerated seeds.

"The Kingdom of Heaven," "The Temple of God," "Work out your own salvation," and the multiple epi grams of sacred symbolism are no longer meaningless phrases to be mouthed, parrot-like, but they are coming to be realized as the thunder-lipped speech from the Infinite One.

Out of the chemicalizing mass of God's creative com pounds,..w.-e may see outlines of a new life, a new heaven and a new earth traced on the murky background of grime and dust and,battle smoke.

Earth's catyclism, the world war, has rent the veil of illusion, and many have come forth from the grave, and with the eye behind the eyes behold the "Real."

Within the "Temple, not made with hands," there dwells the spiritual Ego-a Son of the living God, preach ing in the wilderness of doubt and error, "Now is the accepted time, now is the day of salvation and now the Kinrrdom of Heaven is at hand."

"There is a spirit in man and the wisdom of the Almighty giveth it understanding."

THE LAKE OF HELL-FIRE AND BRIMSTONE

THE lower portion of the torso, bowels, etc., is called "hell," a "grave or lake," many times in the Scrip tures. Sulphur is a product of brimstone. There is more or less sulphur in all food-stuffs. Over eating results in an over supply of sulphur, i. e., brimstone. Over eat ing causes acidity. A portion of the food, failing to di gest, ferments, and acid results. The acid, uniting with sulphur causes heat, fire, fever; hence hell, fire and brim

stone are chemical statements.

The vital force, or fluids of the body, is the Soul that is injured, devitalized, destroyed in the poisons of the intestinal tract called Egypt and Sodom.

Thus can a man lose his soul in hell, fire and brim stone, here and now.

But, "As by man came death into the world, so by man came also the resurrection of the dead," seed.•

"Let the wicked man forsake his ways" (cease to eat of the fruit of the tree of life) , "and return unto the Lord who will abundantly pardon," and thus save his soul. All who bodily die lose their soul, for, says Job, "As the soul of a beast goeth downward, at death, so doth the soul of man."

Certainly, for "The wages of sin (ignorance) is death."

But the soul is not the spiritual Ego, and man is body, soul and spirit. When the "spirit in man" receives the "wisdom of the Almighty" and understands, it is then able to lift up and transmute the soul fluids and disinte grate both fluid and flesh, as the ascension of the seed Jesus, or Elisha, or Enoch are made to show, in the fables and parables.

"All that I do ye may do."

PHYSICAL REGENERATION

THE inner eye-"the eye behind the eye"-just above and attached to the pineal gland by delicate electric wires, or nerves, is called Optic Thalamus, and
means "Ligh't, or Eye of the chamber."

In the Greek, it means "The light of the World." "The Candlestick," "Wise Virgins," "The Temple Needs no light of the Sun," "If thine eyes be Single, Thy Whole Body shall be Full of Light," and other texts in the New Testament' refer to the single eye or Optic.

Let us now search for the oil that feeds this wonderful lamp, the All-Seeing Eye.

Christ Jesus is made to say "I Am the Light of the World." The word "world" comes from "whirl," to turn as a wheel, to gyrate, etc.

The human body is a certain rate of activity, motion or whirl, i. e., world, and light of the world and the temple that needs no light of sun or moon refer to the body "Temple of God," when there is "oil in the lamp."

Error is not sanctified by age. It behooves every lover of truth to cast aside prejudice and dogma and find truth. Until we know the meaning of the words "Jesus" and

"Christ" we will not understand the Bible which was written in Greek and Hebrew and translated and retrans lated all down through the centuries.

Constantine was told by the priests of his time that there was no forgiveness of crimes like those he was guilty of and so this Roman Emperor devised the elan of salvation in order that the blood of the innocent Jesus (or Christ) might save him from eternal damna tion. An easy way out for this monster, and all the other blood-smeared tyrants, Kings, Emperors and Napoleons of finance, competition and war, from Pharaoh to the present-day rulers.

The word Jesus is from Ichthos, Greek for fish. The word "Christ" means a substance of oil consistency, an ointment or smear. Varnish or paints are used to pre serve or save wood or paper or cloth-hence they become Saviors.

At about the age of twelve, Jesus was found in the temple arguing with the doctors or teachers. The word "doctor" is from Latin "docere," to teach.

Every month in the life of every man or woman, after puberty, when the moon is in the sign that the sun was in at the birth of the individual, there is a psycho-physical seed or 'Son of Man" born in the Solar Plexus or the pneumo-gastric plexus which in the ancient text was called the "House of Bread."

Bethlehem, from Beth, a house, and lehem, bread. "Cast thy bread upon the waters and it shall return to thee after many days." Waters are the blood and nerve fluids of the body that carries the fish on its "Divine Jour ney" to regenerate, save and redeem man. Nazareth means to cook. Nazarene means cooked. Cook means to prepare. Any materialized thing is bread, Nazareth, mass, maso, or dough. Thus the Catholic Mass. Also Mas-on. It will now be made plain why the Masons and Catholics are not in agreement, for our letter N is an abbreviation of the 14th letter of the Hebrew alphabet, Nun, a fish. By addnig N to Maso, the riddle of cooked or prepared fish was made so plain that the priesthood strenuously objected, and thus developed friction between the church and Ma-sonry.

The disciples were fishermen. The early Christians used a fish as their secret symbol. Money to pay taxes was taken from the mouth of a fish. Bread and fish were increased until twelve baskets full were left, etc. God prepared a fish to swallow Jonah. Jonah means dove. Dove means peace-the germ descending from the gray matter of the brain (see baptism of John). The storm means sex desire. The life seed was thus saved. "He that is born of God cannot sin (or fall short of knowl edge) for his seed (fish) remaineth in him."-John. The age of puberty is about twelve. Up to that age, a child does not understand moral responsibility. "The first born" means the first seed or fish. Pharaoh, sex desire always tries to destroy the first born.

Before we explain the baptism in Jordan and the chris tening and the crucifixion, etc., let us briefly explain Moses, Joshua, Nile, Pharaoh and the children of Israel.

Egypt means the dark lower part of the body. That part of the body below the Solar Plexus is Egypt, or the Kingdom of Earth. All above the center constitutes the Kingdom of 'Heaven. ("The Kingdom of Heaven is within you.") The Manger, or Bethlehem, is the cen ter, or the balance.

Nile, Moses and Pharaoh's daughter, all refer to gen eration. (See overflow of Nile). It rises in the moun tains of the moon. Moses means "drawn from the water." Fish are drawn from water. "There are two fishes in our sea"-Vaughn. See Sign of Pisces, two fishes.

"Joshua the Son of Nun." Nun is Hebrew for fish. Moses was the physical or generative fish.

Moses' laws were on the physical plane.

Joshua means "God of Salvation," and salvation comes from saliva or salivation. Sal is salt which Saves. "If the salt loses its Savor" i. e. Savior, wherewith shall it be salted?" Saliva saves the body by di-gesting (or pre paring) the food. Saliva is a smear or ointment, and so Joshua compares with Christ as Moses compares with Jesus. Moses died on Mt. Nebo. Nebo means under standing. Joshua took the place left vacant by the death of Moses. Jesus was haptized of John in Jordan-the fluids, Christ-substance of the spinal cord and became "my beloved Son in whom I am well pleased." The word "John" IO H N NE S means "Soul" or "fluids of the body" and not the Ego or Spiritual Man. So when the body dies, the fluids die-thus man loses his soul when he loses his body. To prevent the loss of soul and flesh is the mission of the Son, or Seed, of God, or the Son of man.

But the question will be asked-what or where is the

source or origin of this seed or redeeming Son? We answer: "Ether, Spirit or God."

Esse, Universal intelligence, or It may be used. It breathes into man the breath of life. This elixir is carried through lungs into arteries, or air carriers, where it unites with the inorganic cell-salts, materializes (cooked) and forms granules, and is then deposited as flesh and bone. The study of

Astrology, Biology and Biochemistry, added to Physiology, will lead one into the great Alchem ical laboratory of the "Fearfully and wonderfully made" human temple-the temple made without sound of saw

or hammer.

Before the Neophyte can fully realize the power of the Divine Eye within his own brain, he must understand the meaning of Or especially in its relation to Word and Jordan.

Or is gold, not metal, but the "precious substance" the seed. Dan is Hebrew for Judge, therefore the Crea tive Power operating through the precious substance pro duces Judgment, the man of good judgment or wisdom.

The upper brain is the reservoir of this Or and is the gray matter or "Precious Ointment" or Christ.

"In the beginning was the Word and the Word was

God. All things were (or is) created by it" etc., etc.

The "Lost Word" is a symbol of the generative or animal thought eating the fruit of the Tree of Life thus destroying or losing the gold, "or," of the body.

Hiram means "high born," or the seed destined to reach the pineal gland and "Single Eye."

Tyre means a rock. By the conservation and trans mutation of the sex substance the pineal gland becomes firm and hard and is, in the fable, called rock (Tyre). "The wise man built his house, Beth or body, upon a rock." So here we have the explanation of Hiram Abiff. Abiff is derived from the word Abid-month.

Hiram Abiff (there are some who will understand) was resurrected during the delay caused by searching for his body: in other words a month passed and another seed was born which the candi- date for initiation is ad monished not to slay.

The upper brain furnishes all that man contains, or is. Jesus was not a Savior until he was Christed of John in the Jordan. Then he became the "Beloved Son."

Why was the baptism necessary? Because there are two fish, one was Jesus the Carpenter, the man. The other, the Christed Jesus, the Son of God. The Christ substance gave the electric or mag- netic power to the seed to cross the nerves at Galgotha without disintegrating or dying. I

To crucify, means to add to or increase a thousand fold. When electric wires are crossed, they set on fire all inflammable substances near them. When the Christed seed crossed the nerve at Galgotha, the vail of the temple was rent and there ,was an earthquake, and the dead came forth, i. e., the gen- erative cells of the body were quick ened or regenerated.

The crucifixion or crossing of the life-seed gives power to vibrate the pineal gland at a rate that causes the "light of the chamber" to fill the "whole body with light" and send its vibration out along the optic nerve to the physical eye and thus heal the blind.

69

THIRTEEN, THE OPERATION OF WISDOM

THE number thirteen is unlucky for ignorance only.

All so-called laws of nature may be reduced to thirteen.

The origin of words and their application vary widely. Thus the origin of twelve is circle or completeness, or without break or sin; that is complete. All operations that produce something may be called twelve, being com plete in order to produce, the product is therefore thir teen. Thus all machines or factories symbol twelve and the product thirteen.

THE ZODIAC

There are twelve constellations, the central suns of which constitute the signs of the Zodiac.

One sign rises every two hours, or so appears to our sense, because the rotation of earth causes the phenom enon, and the earth, or sun, makes thirteen.

THE HUMAN BODY

There are twelve functions of the human body and the seed, or psycho-physical germ, born in the solar plexus every 29¾ days. So then there are twelve moons and a fraction in 365 days. The pneumo gastric nr.rve, vagus nerve, that comes down from cerebellum across (a cross) the medulla oblongata branches out at the lungs (pneumo) and at the stomach (gastric), and is called "The Tree of Life" (thirteen letters), also pneumo gastric (thirteen letters).

There are twelve mineral salts in the blood and blood

. itself-the product-thirteen.

DAVID'S THIRTEEN SONS

1st Chr., 14th ch., 3d ver. "And David took more wives and concubines at Jerusalem; and David begat more sons and daughters."

Here follows the names of thirteen children.

THIRTEEN CHILDREN OF JACOB

The 29th and 30th chapters of Genesis record the birth of eleven sons and one daughter, Dinah. The 35th chap ter records the birth of Benjamin, the 12th son and 13th child.

Jacob, in Hebrew, is circle, or to follow after, also represented in Hebrew symbology by a circle of men, each one with h'and holding the heel of the one in front, and thus describing a circle.

The origin of the allegory is founded in the rotation of earth and the apparent rising of one of the Signs of the Zodiac every two hours, making twelve, and the earth itself thirteen. •

The esoteric meaning is based in the marvelous oper ation of the wonderfully made human body. All of the parables, fables or allegories of the human organism are related to 13.

Moses, Joshua, Jesus, Christ and all the characters of the Scriptures are symbols of the psycho-physical seed that is born in, or out of the solar "manger" in the center of the body.

Twelve symbols a circle, in Hebrew, meaning complete. The product of twelve is thirteen. Galilee is a circle. The Sea of Galilee, circle of water, or fluid, hence circulation of the blood and fluids of the body. So Jacob may be applied to the body.

Rachel means Ewe, or Mary, Eve or the manger (solar plexus) where Mary and Jesus were found. There is no U in the Hebrew alphabet, hence no double U.   So V is the letter, or double V-hence EVE or EVVE-i. e., Rachel. The solar plexus is symboled by many names in the Bible, all female, whether they refer to a man or a woman, because it gives birth to the seed.   This won drous redeeming seed is exactly the same in male and female and plays no part in generation, but is the "Plan of Salvation" whereby the child "born in sin" may be redeemed and saved. Thus, "In my Kingdom (regenera tion) there is no marrying," etc.

For key to Benjamin, the entire chapter, Genesis 35th, should be studied carefully in the light of the new reve lations.

Sixth verse, 35th chapter: "So Jacob came to Luz, the same is Bethel" (or Beth-lehem), house of bread, the solar plexus. "He built there an altar (same as "man ger" or plexus,-womb) and called the place "El-beth el," (God's house of God) because there God was re vealed, etc.

Sixteenth verse: "And they journeyed from Bethel and there was some distance to come to Eprath" (fruit, posterity, Bethlehem, seed).

Here Rachael "had hard labor" and gave birth to Ben oni and died. Ben-oni means "child of my sorrow," but Jacob called him Ben-Ja-min, "Son of my right hand."

Sixteenth to twentieth verse: "And Rachael died and was buried in the way to Ephrath (the same is Bethle hem). "And Jacob set up a pillar upon her grave; "The same is the pillar of Rachael's grave unto this day." The solar plexus, chamber or manger is the pillar.

The death of Rachael, the mother, simply means that thirteen completes the number of seeds born during the thirteen moon months. See chapter on The Passover.

Great latitude must be given to writers of parables, fables and allegories.

Genesis, 35th chapter, 10th vers:!: "And God said unto him, thy name is Jacob (the circle), thy name shall not be called any more Jacob, but Israel shall be thy name."

Israel here clearly points to the seeds, thirteen, one every moon, that cross Jordan. Twelfth verse, 35th chapter: "And to thy seed after thee will I give the land."

Jacob (circle) means complete operation; and thirteen the seed, Israel, the product.

JOSHUA AND JERICHO

In the book of Joshua (Son of Nun), a fish-born in the solar plexus twelve times in 365 days and a fraction, see Leap Year, it is recorded that the host marched around the walls of Jericho once daily for six days and seven times on the seventh-thirteen.

Jericho, captured by the British troops, 1917, is situ ated thirteen miles outside the walls of Jerusalem.

JESUS AND THE TWELVE DISCIPLES

Before the crucifixion of Jesus, the seed, fish, there were twelve Disciples or workers and Jesus was the thir teenth. After the crucifixion, which means to increase in power, (note the increase in power of the electric current when the wires are crossed), Paul was added to the twelve Apostles. Paul is made to say: "I was born out of time."

The meaning of Paul is small or the "still small voice," as P is from the-Hebrew letter Pe, to speak, or the mouth. S is from the 21st letter of the Hebrew alphabet, Schin, meaning falling short of completeness as there are 22 letters in the Hebrew alphabet. So the allegory makes the allegorical character Saul before conversion, or re generation, and Paul, the preacher, after the transmuta tion.

There are no dates to the so-called Epistles of Paul. Neither are there dates to any of the writings-scrip tures-gathered by the Council of Nicara under the Pa gan Emperor, Constantine. No one knows when they were written.

THE UNITED STATES AND THIRTEEN

The thirteenth degree of the Zodiacal Sign Cancer was rising July 4th, 1776, when the Declaration of Independ ence was signed. Cancer represents the breast and is therefore the mother sign, or woman. M is from Mem, the thirteen letter of the Hebrew alphabet, and means woman. The United States plays the part of mother to all peoples and gathers them under her protecting care. We commenced our individuality as a nation with thirteen states.

In 1782 the obverse side of the United States Seal was made and contained thirteen stars, thirteen stripes, and an eagle with a quiver containing thirteen arrowheads in one talon and an olive branch with thirteen leaves in the other. And the motto "E pluribus unum" contains thir- teen letters.

About this time, 1782, an unknown man appeared in Philadelphia and offered the drawing of a seal (see cut) which he suggested be added as the reverse side. This man declared that the seal would be adopted in the Year 1921, the digits of which equal thirteen, and that the eagle would no more be used.

Strange to say the stranger's seal was adopted, but has not come into prominence until within the past three or four years.

The reverse side of the United States Seal shows part of the pyramid of Egypt, the base of which covers thir teen acres.

There are thirteen steps or terraces. The motto over the pyramid, "Annuit Creptis," contains thirteen letters and is Latin for "Prosper us in our undertaking."

Our solar system has passed out of the water sign Pisces, and thus occurred the "end of the world"-thir teen letters.

So our great fleet of planets and flag ship Sun is now in the air or spiritual sign Aquarius.

In the allegory of the suns or sons of Jacob (see Gene sis 29), the fifth son born was Dan, a judge, thus Daniel

-"Judge appointed by God," as El is face of God in Hebrew.

The first son or sun was Reuben or Libra, the loins, therefore the fifth would be the legs, or Aquarius, sign of man, where the solar system is now and where it will remain for over 2000 years.

Day means an indefinite period of time-thus we say Napoleon's day or Lincoln's day. Therefore, t is plain to be seen that we are now in the "Day of Judgment," thirteen letters.

Woodrow Wilson---13 letters. He landed in France,

both trips to Europe, on the 13th. American soldiers crossed the Rhine the 13th. Gen. Pershing was born on the 13th.

The League of Nations is printed on thirteen pages. Every 4th year there are 13 moons.

Every year there are 12 moons and a fraction, thus

leap year-1,920, two new moons, July 1st and 30th.

70

DANIEL IN THE LIONS' DEN

THE word Dan, in Hebrew, means a judge. Daniel, judgment or God's judge. El or iel, in Hebrew, represents the supreme ruler or God. God and good are synonymous, i.e. Daniel-good judgment or wisdom.

The word Darius, traced to its root, simply means an office, same as Presidency, and whoever fills the office is for the time called Darius.

Medes is from media, the middle, and is represented in the body by solar plexus.

Persia, the East, Persians, people of the East.

In scripture allegories East always means the back; West, the front; North-up, or the head; South, down the feet.

There is a wide difference between the original meaning of a word and the multiple applications of a word. For instance, lamb, dove, hog, wolf, eagle and names of all birds and animals represent ideas or principles that have been applied to different species of animal forms on the hypothesis that these names fitted some peculiar trait or habit of the animal or reptile to which they gave the appellation.

Lion means strength and is used to designate the "King of beasts" or animals. The part of the human body be low the solar plexus is referred to in the Scriptures (physiological writings) as Kingdom of Earth, hades, lower Egypt and the seat of sex desire (Pharaoh) or the animal passions, appetites, etc.

Ani: breath or soul.

Mal: bad, or imperfect, hence malformation, malnutri tion, bad breath or soul (unregenerated substance), or the Animal man.

The "Lion's Den" is used in the fable to typify the ani mal functions that were regenerated by wisdom or good judgment-Daniel.

The following definitions will assist the reader to more fully realize the esoteric meaning of words in scripture:

DANIEL-]udgment.

BELSHAZZAR-Bel, Belia! or Be-elzebub, has formed a king.

BELTSHAZZAR-A maintainer or Prince. (This title was given to Daniel after his regeneration as shown by the letter T from Tav, the 22nd letter of the Hebrew alphabet meaning cross, where the redeemer (seed) is crucified. "There is no name under heaven whereby ye may be saved except Jesus, the seed, Christ-ed and cruci fied."

NEBUCHADNEZZAR-From Nebo-understanding. A protector against misfortune.

ELAM-Unlimited duration.

A-BEDNEGO-Servant of Nego, i.e., understanding. MESHACH-Guests of Sha, the Son-god.

SHADRACH-Royal or rejoicing in the way.

(Thus it is made clear why Shadrach, Meshach and A-bednego were not consumed in the fiery furnace. They are principles, eternal verities that are not affected by physical expressions and can, therefore, complete the ini tiation of the Ego.)

In the 8th chapter of Daniel, verses 1 and 2, we find the words "Shushan the palace which is in the province (or country) of Elam; and I was by the river Ulai."

ELAM-Eternity.

SHUSHAN-From Susanna, a lily (known as the Capi tol of Elam), real meaning, the product of divine mind.

ULAI-From Hebrew Pehlvi, meaning pure water.

Daniel was "By the river Ulai." Ulai here refers to the spinal cord. The marrow, or oil, in this channel is pure crystal in color.

"And he showed me a river of water of life, bright as crystal, proceeding out of the throne of God and the Lamb, in the midst of the street thereof. And on this side of the river and on that was the Tree of Life bearing twelve manner of fruits yielding its fruit every month; and the leaves of the tree were for the healing of the nations."

Month is from Moon (Moonth) and there are twelve and one-third moons in the Solar year.

Leaves are effects of a tree.

The monthly seed (fruit) when saved, not "eaten," heals disease and sin.

"Moses lifted up the serpent in the wilderness," the

body.

Moses, the first born, the seed, desired to regenerate the blood and lead it to the promised land, thus he lifted up the animal•forces, sex desire, here symboled as the ser pent (see the temptation of Adam and Eve)   . . . So shall the "Son, or Seed, of Man be lifted up," etc., etc. that is put on the cross in order to reach the pineal gland. "If I be lifted up, I will draw all men unto me." I will draw all other seed unto me.   Study the etymology of "men." Also read "The tree in the midst of the garden

bore fruit every month and its leaves were healing."

The Commandment to not eat of the fruit of this tree was not (is not) heeded by the race and death is the re sult.

The serpent said "Eat, thou shalt not die," but sex desire was a liar from the beginning.

A noted Professor of Greek in one of our universities

says that the translation of many New Testament texts from Greek are radically wrong. For in-stance, "He that saveth his life shall lose it, and he that loseth his life, for my sake, shall find it," should read: "He that saveth his seed-life-shall loosen it (set it free), and he that loosens it, shall find it," which means that this "Bread cast upon the waters" shall redeem him. Galilee means a circle of wa-ter-the fluids of the body.

Jesus walking on the water is a symbol of the seed, or fish, on its journey. Peter, from petra (stone) is a sym bol of physical or material thought which was rescued by the fish, Savior.

The Optic Thalamus, or light in the room, is called "The Lamb of God that taketh away the sins of the world."   The Hebrew letters Lamed, Aleph, Mem and Beth form the word Lamb, meaning innocence or purity. Sin is from the Hebrew letter Schin, meaning to fall short of knowl-edge.   Sin does not mean wrong or crime, but one may commit a crime and do wrong through lack of knowledge.   Paul said: "I die daily"   .   .   .   I am
the chief of sinners." Revelation: "And the lamp thereof is the Lamb." The word "Lamb" ends with B, which means a house or body of some kind. Now, the optic or central single eye is a body, like the outer eye ball, therefore, a beth. This is called lamb by the ancient poet.

Lamp ending with P, which means speech or sending forth or radiating, is from Pe, the 17th let-ter of the He brew alphabet, and was used to express light or knowl edge emanating or going forth from this eye or "Lamb of God."

"As a man thinketh in his heart, so is he."

The cerebellum is heart-shaped, and in the Greek is known as the heart. The organ that divides blood was called the "Dividing Pump." The seat of thought is the Cerebellum. Our thoughts shape our lives. If we think continually below the solar plexus in the Kingdom of Earth; if we dwell in thoughts of material pleasures, we become animal and materialistic. If we really desire the Kingdom of Heaven, we must think of the process that will enable us to realize it.

When Jesus·was born, they put him in "swaddling clothes." Now the psychic germ (fish) is com-posed of the concentrated essence of life and is covered by a gos samer capsule for protection. If this swaddling cloth is broken, the "precious ointment" is lost, i.e. it disinte grates and corrupts the blood.

In order to save this germ of life, man must remember that as a man thinketh, so is he. While men must abstain
entirely from sexual contact, he must also realize that "He who looketh on a woman to lust after her, hath com mitted adultery with her in his heart."

By constant prayer do we attain the Kingdom, for Jesus said "With man it is impossible; but with God all things are possible."

Envy, hatred, ambition, covetousness, will destroy the capsule that contains the seed and thus corrupt the blood, as surely as sexual contact. Alcohol in all its deceptive forms is the arch foe to this life-seed and seeks by every means known to the enemy of man to destroy it. "No drunkard shall in-herit the Kingdom of Heaven" because alcohol destroys the redeeming substance that enables man to understand or think in his heart the thoughts of the Spirit. Alcohol cuts the capsule that holds the Esse born every month in Bethlehem. Alcohol eats the fruit of the tree of life.

Gluttony is another enemy to regeneration. All excess of food, all that is not burnt up in the fur-nace-the stom ach and intestinal tract, all that is not properly digested, ferments and ptoduces acid which develops alcohol.

Auto-intoxication is common among those who overeat.

Most everyone overeats.

The furnace, stomach and digestive tract becomes a distillery when the surplus food ferments, and thus be comes Babylon, the home of unclean birds and beasts which pander to carnal mind.   Here we have the reason why sickness was considered Sin by the ancients.   "To heal the sick and cast out devils" is the mission of the seed. "He that is born of God cannot sin, or be sick, for his seed remaineth in him." "The blood of Christ clean seth from all sin," therefore from all disease.   Here is the physiological explanation   When the Christed sub stance, the ointment from the river of Jordan, the oil in the spinal cord, reaches the pineal gland, it vibrates to a rate that causes new blood-the new wine. This is the blood of Christ that heals all infirmities.   Unless so called Christians repent of their sins, the doom of the church is at hand, "M ene, mene teckel upharsin" is writ ten on the wall.

Here are the words that define a Christian: "These signs shall follow those who believe; they shall lay hands on the sick and they shall recover. They shall cast out devils and raise the dead. All the things that I do, ye shall do and greater things shall ye do."

If there be one Christian on earth today, let him stand forth and prove himself worthy. "He that overcometh, I will give to eat of the fruit of the tree of life." To overcome a habit is to cease to do it. When the earthly man is controlled by the spiritual man-the Lord God he ceases to eat of the fruit, th,it is, waste it. This fruit

is then carried up to the brain and "Eaten in the Father's Kingdom." "And the last enemy to be overcome is death." We overcome death by ceasing to die, and in no other way. "He that believeth in me, shall not perish." Those who die are sinners, and therefore are not Chris tians, for Christ Jesus was (is) without sin. "The wages of Sin is death." Repent, forsake evil, take up thy Cross, call upon the Lord and He will abundantly pardon. "And the ransomed of the Lord shall return and come to Zion." When the sexual functions are used for the propagation of human bodies, there is no condemnation or sin. Moth erhood is holy, pure, divine. But motherhood forced is crime. Unwilling motherhood has created the spirit of war and murder and well-nigh destroyed the race. Sexual union for pleasure alone is the broad road that leads to death. "And there shall be no more Curse"-Revela tion. The word "Curse" has no reference to an oath. Curse means friction, to grind. The statement "Then Peter began to curse and swear" . . . And immedi ately the cock crew," when understood physiologically, fully explains the meaning of curse. Sexual commerce for the birth of children where the parents sacrifice them selves for their offspring's sake, or total abstinence, is written with a pen of flame on all the pages of ancient Scriptures and modern biology.

"And I saw a woman clothed with the Sun, having the Moon under her feet and twelve stars upon her head." The Sun is the Seed, the "Son of Man," the product of her own body, saved and lifted up. The Moon refers to the generative life. Twelve stars are the twelve func tions, typified by twelve zodiacal signs, which she has mas tered through physical regeneration.

"When thou prayest, enter into thy closet and pray to thy Father in secret, and he shall reward thee openly."

The word Secret is derived from Secretions. The upper brain, the Cerebrum, contains the secretions, gray matter, creative or that which creates, builds and supplies all the life force of the human temple,-Soul of Man's (Solomon's temple). Hence God, the Creator, dwells in you. The cerebellum is his throne. Prayer or desires expressed by man in the cerebellum for righteousness is answered in the cerebrum. Thus by prayer to God within, and in no other way, can man overcome the ad versary or the "carnal mind .which is at enmity to God."

All so-called sex reform that tolerates union of sexes, may be answered by:

"There is a way that Seemeth right to man,

The end of which is death."

"In my Kingdom there is no marrying nor giving in marriage, But they are as the

Angels in Heaven."

No page of the wonders of the human body-the tem ple of the, living God-is more divinely sci- entific than the parable that follows:

"The foolish man built his house on the sand And the rain washed,it away."

"The wise man built his house on a rock

And it stood the storms, for it was builded upon a rock."

The Bible is a compilation of astronomical, physiolog ical and anatomical symbols, allegories and parables.

In the technical terms of modern chemistry and physi ology the above text is explained as follows: Sand and cement form rock or stone. Sand alone, without some medium-cement-is unstable, simply "shifting sand."

The Pineal gland, the dynamo that runs the organism of man, is composed of sand plus a ce- ment, an ointment, a smear, found, as has been explained, in the spinal cord, also to some extent, in all parts of the body. When this cement is wasted, as the Prodigal Son wasted his sub stance in riotous living, there being a deficiency of this precious oil, the pineal gland becomes pasty, and does not vibrate at a rate that vitalizes the blood and tissue at the health and strength rate, and the house, beth or body, falls.

In the common slang of the hour, we say: "He lacks the sand," or "grit."

The mineral salts of blood were called sand or salt by the Greeks. The cell-salts that are found in the pineal gland are chiefly potassium phosphate, the base of the gray matter of the brain, and lime, but all of the 12 inor ganic salts are represented. In Revelation, the pineal gland is called "the white stone." In Biochemistry, the phosphate of potassium is given as the birth salt of Aries people.

Those who build their house upon a rock are they who conserve the substance that unites with the sand-cell salts-and thus form the rock upon which a body may be built that will be free from sin and sickness.

The mission of Jesus, the Christ, was to triumph over death and the grave, over matter, and trans- mute his body and also materialize at will. He not only succeeded in doing this, but stated most em- phatically that all the things that he did, we may do also.

Did he proclaim the truth? Answer, thou of little faith!

"Rock of Ages, cleft for me, Let me hide myself in thee."

71

NOAH, THE ARK AND THE ANIMALS

EW theologians are there, of to-day, who insist on a literal interpretation of the biblical story of the flood, Noah and the ark.

There are known to be 1656 species of mammals; 6266 species of birds; 642 of reptiles; 20 of oxen; 27 species of goats; 48 species of antelopes; insects, fish, turtles and creeping things on land and sea innumerable.

There is not a bit of geological evidence that the earth was ever totally sub"rnerged. But, going to the root of the words Noah, ark, Ararat, etc., it is quite easy to read the riddle of the allegory.

Noah is Hebrew for rest. Ararat simply means a mount or elevation. In English we say hill, mound, peak, mountain, etc. So in both Greek and Hebrew we find Nebo, Pisgah, Ararat, pinnacle of the temple, Zion, Gib eon, used to typify brain and pineal gland.

Ark, or boat, is used to symbol the seed (fish or Moses) born in the solar-plexus to be carried 1.,1p through the regenerative process to the pineal gland. Moses was found in an ark and the ark of the covenant was carried by the children of Israel (see Jacob s 13 children) through the wilderness and across Jordan, where the "waters stood up at the City of Adam."

Adam means earth or sand. At the source of the spinal cord there is a body called medulla oblongata. Medulla means marrow or thick oil or ointment. This oblong body (oblongata in Latin) is a bed of mineral salts of the body and marrow. This precious oil (Christ) is received there by secretions from the cerebrum, the upper brain-the "Most High."

This oil flows down the spinal cord to the Caudia Equina, and this is a symbol of the Jordan and Dead Sea of Palestine.

Jordan means the "Descender" or oil flowing down.

Witness: Dove or dive-to descend. Dove, i.e., a diver

-"The Spirit of God descended like a dove, and a voice said, 'This is my Son,' " etc.

This occurred af Jer the baptism of Jesus, the seed, in Jordan, the oil or Christ.

The animals taken up to Ararat, the pineal gland, or "Pinnacle of the temple," simply means the transmutation of animal desires and propensities by saving the ark (seed) and crucifying it at Golgotha where it Crosses Jordan in medulla, the "Place of the Skull."

Woman the 4th Dimension.

The solar system has entered the "Sign of the Son of Man,"where it will remain for over 2000 years. In as trology this sign is symboled as "The Water Bearer," while in Bible Alchemy it is represented by Dan, the fifth son of Jacob, and means "judgment,11 or "he that judges."

From these statements it is easy to realize that all that is taking place in the world to-day is but a "working out" or a summing up of all that has been taking place for cen turies.

The world is awakening, the old order is passing, worn-out traditions that are no longer applica ble to pres ent conditions must be replaced by new.

Radical and fundamental changes stare us in the face on all sides. Science, philosophy, religion, bodies politic and social-all are being shaken from their very founda tions-to be rebuilt anew.

There is no equilibrium, no balance, no harmony, no equality, anywhere.

Nowhere do we see a better illustration of this unbal anced condition of the world than in man's attitude toward woman. For some time, now, this viewpoint has been gradually changing and Aquarian vibrations, or, in other words, the vibratory influence of the planets, have made condi tions possible for this change.

Woman is at last coming into her own.

Co-equal with man I Mighty strides toward the regen eration of the human race will now be made.

With equilibrium of forces now possible world har mony shall grow apace.

All these truths can be mathematically expressed.

Four (4) means realization-one and three (1 plus 3) equals four.

Woman or mother comes from the Hebrew word Mem-M (womb, man, water, Mary-same meaning in all).

"I saw a woman clothed with the Son, the moon (from month-menses) under her flfet. She con trolled the twelve functions of the body. The Son signifies "Sun" or "Son of Man," the seed or prod uct of her own life, saved and lifted up. The Moon refers to the generative life. Twelve stars are the twelve functions, typified by the twelve zodiacal signs which she has mastered through physical re generation.

•

Having been upon the cross, or having crossed over, the seed is Christed; and in the man or woman seeking to regenerate or "save," the seed is saved, it then enters the Optic Thalamus, the eye of the chamber, which "giveth light to all that are in the house," that is, to the twelve functions that are in the body, represented by the twelve signs of the zodiac.

Woman regenerated-"clothed with the Sun"-is the Queen of Sheba, in Bible symbology, and is represented by the number seven (7).

Then woman is Queen of 7. Sheba is seven in He brew, and Solomon's temple (soul-of-man) is the physical body where the Queen of Sheba found so many wonders.

Queen of seven what?

Man is only three (3) dimensions. Dimension means line.

The human body as well as the universe are geomet rical figures, a fact which the old philosophers well knew, for they said that sound and number governed the laws of creation.

Man is proved to be a three dimensional creature by physiology; and woman is the fourth dimen sion, by the same means of proof.

In the thirty-first chapter of Jeremiah, twenty-second verse, we read: "A woman shall compass a man."

Mathematically, a woman can encompass a man.

Man cannot compass a woman, for he is only a three line creature, while she is four. Therefore, four is able to compass, or contain within its radius, three.

Woman may be represented by the square (four lines). Man may be represented by the triangle (three lines). Three and four do not balance, and never have. There has not been universal harmony or balance between them, for man has never considered woman his equal until very

recently.   .

But man is "coming off his high horse," and the scales will soon balance.

All down the ages man has considered himself the "lord of all creation." The "spare rib" which he so con descendingly parted with in the so-called "beginning" un balanced him entirely. He considered himself superior to woman and has continued to do so to the "end of the world," or "whorl of activity"-the activity or manifestation of the solar system in the last or previous sign, that representing the water age.

During the water age man conquered the water-inventions pertaining to water were perfected, etc., etc.

To return to the mathematical equation of man and woman:

The three dimensions or lines of man that can be shown on a physiological chart are the creative centers of the brain, the solar plexus and the sex organs . Woman also possesses the creative centers of brain, solar plexus and sex organs; but she also possesses another, and in a way the most wonderful of all-the breast that nourishes infant man. This is the fourth dimension or line. These imaginary lines are at equal distances from each other.

Work this out for yourselves on the chart and you will never forget it.

In the triangle drawn to represent man we find the eye,

also. This is a well-known Masonic symbol.

See "The Rib-lah that made the Wom(b)an."

72

TRANSLATIONS OF SCRIPTURE

H e that saveth his life shall lose it."-Mark 8 :35.

THE above sentence does not ring true and is not logical.

A Greek professor recently went to Oxford, England, for the sole purpose of looking into the Greek text in regard to this seeming inconsistency. (Also Luke 16:9. See below.)

The discovery was made that the letter N (from nun, mean-ing a fish), was omitted, also the letter 0, and that a correct translation reads: "He that saveth_his life shall loosen it," etc.

The seed, in the fable, or Jesus, said: "I am the way, the truth and the !if e," etc. Therefore, he that saveth his life (Seed) shall loosen it so that it may enter the "Strait and narrow way," etc. This strait is the Spinal Cord. As has already been written, "I am the bread of life." Again, "Cast thy bread upon the waters"-i. e.,

the strait. Cast thy bread upon the water exactly harmo nizes with "Loosen it."

Luke 16 :9: "And I say unto you, make unto your selves friends of the mammon of unrighteous-ness; that when ye fail they may receive you into everlasting habita tions."

Literally the statement would nullify all the teaching of Jesus, and it is simply amazing that the so-called Chris tian world has so largely ignored it. However, a few critics from the orthodox ranks, not being at all satisfied with the rendering, have tried, in various ways, to recon cile the paradox, and to that end several pamphlets may be found in the theological departments of our colleges and universities.

Here is the explanation by a Greek scholar:

"Make unto your self other friends than those who worship the mammon of unrighteousness," etc.

Accenting the New Testament error, without question accounts for the great anxiety shown by churches of all denominations to secure the financial support of the wealthy, whether they be vital Christians, in belief, or nominally so. Proof of which may be seen in the end of the world, or age, nominally dominated by so-called Christianity.

Many worshipers of the mammon of unrighteousness exhibited much more horror over the de-struction of costly cathedrals by the Huns than they did at the rape of women and slaughter of chil-dren by the Germans in Belgium, or murders by the sinking of the Lusitania.

Nothing can survive this "Day of Judgment" except it be founded upon the Truth, which liveth and reigneth forevermore.

73

JOSHUA COMMANDS THE SUN AND MOON
TO STAND STILL

IN Physiological Chart the solar plexus, a round body of tissue ganglion, may be plainly seen. Attached to the SUN (center) is a body called semi-lunar gan
glion (half moon), which is attached to the vertebra and spinal cord.   A median line (across the center of body) will divide these organs, half above the line, half below. The upper halves of the sun and moon vibrate for spir itual man and the lower half for natural, or animal man.

"There is a natural and a spiritual body."-Paul.

Now Joshua, the seed, on its way to the pineal gland is made to say, "Sun, stand thou still on Gibeon."

Gibeon means a mound or elevation. So the seed (Joshua, a fish), commands the animal vibration of solar (sun) plexus to stand still, i.e., cease to continue to domi nate the spiritual forces, "while I slay my enemies" that is, the animal blood that predominates in carnal thought.

"And thou moon in the valley of Ajalon."

Ajalon means a "valley in Bethlehem," says a Bible dictionary.

Bethlehem-the house of bread: the seed is the bread.

Whoever conquers sex desire commands the sun and moon to stand still.

Who can do this?

"With man it is impossible, but with God all things are possible." Matt. 19th chapter.

Therefore, all can succeed by asking help from the "Most High."

. A cloud of witnesses may be found to substantiate the statement made above that the sun and moori in the Joshua story refer to the solar plexus and semi-lunar gan glion.

Eph. in Hebrew is prefix to many words meaning the centre or middle. It is defined in Smith's Bible Diction ary under the name Eph-ah, as "First in order of the sons of Midian, i. e., strife or contention between Michael and Apollyon occurs in the center of the body where the ani mal continually fights the upper force that seeks tq lift up and regenerate the animal or natural man.

Ephah also means weight (measure or balance, Libra, the scales).

Again, E-phes-dammin, "boundary of animal blood." "I fought with wild beasts at Ephesus."-Paul.

Ephesians are the children of Ephesus, the solar plexus, therefore the seed. Paul the still small voice, or intuition, redeeming (lifting up).

The seeds constitute Paul's Epistle to the Ephesians.

Once more: "Eph-raim is joined to his idols; let him alone."

This epigram defines the physical man, "Dead in tres pass and sin"-one who cannot be awakened by reason ing with him.

74

GLOSSARY

THE MEANING OF GLORY

GLORY is derived from glow and ray-to illumine, to light.

Prof. Smiley, formerly teacher of Greek in Cor nell University, writes: "The body is a lamp and this oil (referring to the oil descending the spinal cord) is its illuminating fluid."

Prof. Smiley also says: "This oil, in Greek, is from the root letters X. P. !.-Chrism or Chri"-Greek for oil, or Christ. •• "The Christ in you, the hope (substance) of glory," or light.-Paul.

But, says Paul, "If ye have only hoped Christ, ye are

of all men most miserable."   Why?

For "Unless Christ be raised our preaching is vain." The only way to raise THIS oil is by the seed entering the spinal cord and lifting up the oil. "If I (Jesus, the seed) be lifted up, I will draw all men (se-men, or oil) unto me."

Thus is the command, "Give one-tenth (tithe) unto the Lord," obeyed.

"The entrance of thy word giveth light"; "The seed is the WORD."-Luke.

John, Johannes, or Ioannes, means OIL, also an oint ment, and "Came to bear witness of that light." St. John 1 :6.

Again-"That the Father may be glorified in the Son." John 14:13.

"Father, the hour has come; glorify thy Son, that thy Son may glorify thee."

Lip service cannot glow-ray or glorify God, but the seed "which is Christ" (Paul), saved and lifted up, car ries illuminating oil to the Father, enters the optic in the thalamus and giveth light. "And the temple needs rio other light."

We feel sure that those who desire the whole truth in regard to the real meaning of "glory" and "glorify". will esteem it their duty and privilege to read St. John, and especially verses 22 and 24 of the 17th Chapter; also 19th verse of the 21st Chapter.   .

The word Saint means a perfect person, or one who realizes that Perfection even as the Father is perfect. According to the teachings of Scripture, the Only way that perfection can be attained is by saving the seed and thus be "Born of God."

The ancient painters painted a halo or a "nimbus of gold-colored light," as Walt Whitman sang, about the head of the Madonna, the infant Jesus and many of the saints and prophets. Hence we infer that the idea of an illuminating oil prevailed all down the ages. •

The Greek epic of the vestal Virgins keeping the fire or light forever burning and the wise virgins with lamps filled with oil, bear witness to the cosmic belief that there is a substance in man that enlightens and redeems, if not destroyed by animal forces.

OUR' EVER-PRESENT HELP

"For who maketh thee to differ from another? And what hast thou that thou didst not receive? Now if thou didst receive it, why dost thou glory, as if thou hadst not received it?"

"What I Know ye not that your body is the temple of the Holy Ghost which is in you, which ye have of God, and ye are not your own?"

"For ye are bought with a price," etc. See "Give one tenth to the Lord," etc.

"Is not my help in me? And is wisdom driven quite from me?" Job 6 :13.

"Send the help from the sanctuary, and strengthen thee out of Zion." (See explanation of these terms in glossary.)

"Our soul waiteth for the Lord; he is our help and our shield."

"God is our refuge and strength, a very present help in trouble."   •

"I will lift up mine eyes unto the hills, or mountains, from whence cometh my help." "Mount of the Lord," the upper brain, "Most High."

THE TEMPLE OF GOD

"Know ye not that ye are the temple of God and that the spirit of God dwelleth in you? If any man defile the temple of God, him shall God destroy; for the temple of God is holy, which temple ye are." Man defiles the temple by .preventing the seed (the word) from going up, or returning to the upper brain, the cerebrum. In short, he eats of the fruit of the tree of life, and there fore it cannot arise or return to the Kingdom, the optic thalamus, ana become the "Light in the chamber," where it may "Cleanse from all sin."

He that overcometh (does not eat or destroy the seed, allows it "to remain in him") "I will give to eat of the tree of life in the "Father's Kingdom." See Lord's Supper.   •

The tree of life is the Vagus nerve (pneumogastric) and its branches. (See article on Vagus nerve.)

Whose branches, or nerves, are called Nazareth, which is Greek for shoot, sprout or twigs-little branches; hence, "Jesus of Nazareth, whom thou persecuteth."

Jesus, the seed, thus speaks to Saul, who, after con version, no longer used "S" (Schin or sin), but substi tuted "P," speech or "going forth, radiating," and thus became Paul the preacher.

Paul means "small" and refers to the seed itself. After the crucifixion of Jesus (the seed) , the parable makes another seed take the place of the first-born, and thus says, "I was born out of time."

SAUL OF TARSUS

Tarsus means "foot." Pisces, the fishes, are repre sented by the feet. In regard to "small," read the par- able of the "mustard seed."   .

"IN   MY KINGDOM,,

"He that is born in thy house shall not be thine heir, but he that cometh forth out of thine own bowels shall be thine heir."

"She that is desolate hath many more children than she that hath an husband."

Here is proof that in the regeneration, that is, the plan of salvation above the solar plexus, there is no marrying nor giving in marriage, for male and female are the same.   Both have the same manger or WOMB, in man, both the same Ida and Pingala, or Joseph and Mary; and the same pneumogastric nerve that brings down the same Holy Ghost-breath-that conceives the seed, Jesus. Hence, Peter reads thus: "Born not of corruptible seed but of incorruptible; the Word of God." So, then, male and female in the new order MUST WORK OUT THEIR OWN SALVATION, the sav

ing seed that is in each separate body.

No sex reform, no physical contact-"Thou shalt not touch it"-Genesis; no effort to "climb up some other way" is tolerated, in the GREAT TEXT BOOK OF PHYSIOLOGY, THE HOLY BIBLE, or whole book.

THE BELOVED CATHOLIC PRIEST

Father John A. Ryan lays it down as "a fundamental ethical principle" that sexual intercourse for any other object than procreation is unnatural and "a perversion of the generative faculty on exactly the same moral level as the practice of the solitary vice."

"THE TREE OF LIFE"

The branches of the Vagus, or pneumogastric nerve, which extend to lungs and stomach, are called the "Tree of Life."

The oil or substance that flows down the plexus of nerves that branch off from the main nerve is deposited in the manger (the nun) or mouth of the fish, and forms a seed or fruit of the tree. This seed, being formed of the Esse of God, is called the Son of God, also the Son of Man that has "Power in earth (the body) to forgive sins. This seed says, "I am the way, the truth and the life"-hence the "Tree of Life."

THE ONLY CAUSE OF OLD AGE

Youth, strength and health depend entirely upon the automatic action of the blood which deposits the ma terial (itself) formed from the Esse, or substance called air, the breath of God, and the residue (ashes) of food, the mineral salts, and deposits it in the upper chamber, the cerebrum (Most High), the hallowed or hollowed place. (See fatted calf or Kaph.)

The secretions descending from this fat, oil the place of the secretions, build and sustain the entire bodily struc ture. But, if a certain amount, "one-tenth," is not re turned, the reservoir becomes depleted day by day until the deficiency, or sin (i.e., falling short) causes weak ness, decrepitude, etc., which we, in our ignorance, have called "old age."

The Bible tells the cause and the remedy, thus: "The wages of sin is death."

But, "His delight is in the law of the Lord," then: "He shall be like a tree planted by the river of waters that bringeth forth its fruit in its season; but his leaf also shall not wither, and whatsoever he doeth shall prosper." .

There is one' cause of old age and one only: wasting the LIFE FORCE, the gray matter of the brain, the SEED, the WORD of God, which, if saved, results in "THE WORD MADE FLESH."

When people say unto you, "Lo l here," or "Lo I there

is the cause of old age," believe them not, for the cause of old age is within YOU.

SAMSON OR SAM SUN

The letter S in Hebrew is the 15th of the alphabet, and symbolizes the great dragon, the Great Dragon of the Threshold. In Hebrew it is Samech. The stomach is also symbolical of this letter.

Here, also, is the Solar Plexus, the Sun Center or Son. Likewise, the physical power of the mind is centered here, the desire for Ani mal vibration, the "things thy soul lusteth after."

Samson, in Smith's Bible Dictionary, also means "Sun like, strong, distinguished."

Gaza simply means the "strong," or "strong city." Delilah means "weak, feeble," or "to pine with desire,"

and the symbolism is wrought into the form of a woman that tempted Samson, to destroy his strength by yielding to desire, or Delilah.

After sufficient time had elapsed in which material for a new seed could descend (as in the case of Hiram Abiff, in Freemasonry), Samson, through prayer, was able to save the seed, and was then spiritually strong, thus giving him strength to tear down the Strong City of Gaza, or "Carry away the pillars of Gaza."

The reader is urged to study carefully the 13th Chapter of Judges to the 16th.

The story of the birth of Jesus and the warnings and prophecies concerning Samson are almost identical. He is even called "A Nazarite," which means, in Hebrew, "One consecrated to God."

In the story of Samson we read how he went down to, Etam. In Smith's Bible Dictionary we find that, in Hebrew, Etam means "A place of ravenous beasts." In this place was a high cliff or lofty rock which led down into a chasm or cleft where Samson went. Going down into this chasm, or place of ravenous beasts, is represented in Physiology by the vital fluid in the spinal cord going down into the seminal vesicles.

ISAIAH 31 :7

"For in that day every man shall cast away his idols of silver and his idols of gold, which your own hands have made unto you for a sin."

ISAIAH 28 :7-8

"But they also have erred through wine, and through strong drink are out of the way; the priest and the prophet have erred through strong drink, they are swallowed up of wine, they are out of the way through strong drink; they err in vision, they stumble in judgment. For all tables are full of vomit and filthiness, so that there is no place clean."

REVELATION, 22D CHAPTER, VERSES 1, 2

"And he showed me a pure river of water (spinal cord) flowing out of the throne of God (brain), and the Lamb (optic thalamus). "In the midst of the street of it and on either side of the river (both sides) was there the tree of life (pneumogastric nerve), which bare twelve manner of fruits, and yielded her fruit every month (seed every moon), and the leaves of the tree were (are) for the healing of the nations"-people.

The Indians, in their legend of the "Four trines within the Grand Symbol," call the solar plexus the "seed pod."

"BETWEEN TWO THIEVES"

The words "thief" and "steal" both mean "to operate in secret." Many things may be done in secret that are good, thus: "Give thine alms in secret"; "Let not thy left hand know what thy right hand doeth."

There is a wide difference between the original mean ing of words and their common application.

The pineal gland and pituitary body secrete the positive and negative substance along nerves that cross in the medulla, and the seed is crucified between them, and the oil set free ascends to the pineal gland which is made to say: "Lord, remember me when thou cometh into thy kingdom."

Now, as th·e·fluids of the two glands had united and were ascending up the one on the "Right hand of the Father," the central eye, it would naturally say, "This day (now) shalt thou be with me in paradise."

He who spoke and he who replied were one and the same.

"MY YOKE IS EASY AND MY BURDEN IS LIGHT"

YoKE: To cross or bind. Oxen were yoked about the neck.

The nerves from the pituitary and pineal gland unite, and are thus bound together or yoked in the medulla oblongata ("Place of the Skull") and form a Cross.

In regeneration, when the seed crosses in the regular, automatic manner as the plan of salvation designed that

it should, the cervical, or neck, functions properly, and the soreness and uneasy feeling so prevalent in all who lead the animal or carnal life, which is "At enmity to God," or the spiritual life, often experience, and complain of, as every physician will testify.

Burden simply means that which is carried, not neces sarily something heavy or tiresome.

The seed (any of the characters in Scripture) absorbs and carries the precious oil that flows down the spinal cord-the "strait," up to the cross (yoke), where the "Cup" (cover of minerals) is "removed," which frees the precious oil. This illuminating substance then enters the optic and "Giveth light to all that are in the house," or the chamber, the thalamus.

Thus does the redeeming seed truly say, "My burden is light," or illumination.

Paul bears witness thus: "The Christ (oil) in you, the hope of glory"-Glow-ray. Also, "Unless Christ be raised then is our preaching vain."

DORMANT BRAIN CELLS

In every brain there are countless dormant brain cells, waiting for the coming of the Air Age, the Bridegroom or the recognition of the "Christ in the flesh," that will quicken them into activity-i.e., resurrect them.

Everywhere there is evidence of the awakening of dormant brain cells. Spiritual phenomena, multiple per sonality, mental telepathy and kindred manifestations are explainable upon the hypothesis that dormant brain cells may be made to bloom and thus operate according to new concepts.

We know that there are many millions of dormant brain cells in the cerebrum, especially in the "Most High" portion, the seat of spiritual faculties; or, we may say, the key, which, when touched with the vital fluid set free, "Cast on the waters" and "Lifted up" through the process of physical regeneration, completes the at-one-ment with the Ego, whose indwelling place is the cerebellum. And then the statement, "I and the Father are One," becomes living thunder and flaming light from Sinai, instead of a popular epigram with no vital meaning.

The dormant brain cells may be likened to a flower yet in the bud; but when the substance that is required for their completion reaches them, the modus operandi of the plan of salvation, the buds open, or unfold, and then vibrate at the rate that causes the realization of the New Birth-the "Birth from above."

"He that is born of God will not sin, for his seed

remaineth in him."

And thus spake Paul: "We shall be changed in the twinkling of an Eye"-not eyes-but the optic thalamus, the "single," or perfected eye. See chart.

CHILDREN

Child means young, not aged.

"Children of Israel, or "warriors of God." See Smith's Bible Dictionary. There is not now, nor was there ever a geographical, historical land or nation called Israel. The name originated in secret or sacred books which are not historical or outward, but secret or inward.

The seeds that were saved every 29¼ days were called

the "warriors of God."

"Suffer little children to come unto me, and forbid them not, for of such is the kingdom of heaven."

The seed is small.

"The kingdom of heaven is likened unto a mustard seed." •

The seed of all seeds, Jesus, the first seed, asks that other seeds might also be saved, for the seeds, saved and raised to the pineal gland, return to the heaven from which they came.

"Whosoever shall not receive the kingdom of God as a little child, he shall not enter therein."

The lion (animal force) (see Daniel in the lion's den) and the lamb (innocence, or spiritual con-cept) make at-one-ment (shall lie down together), and "A little child (seed) shall lead them," which means that the seed will carry up one-tenth of the descending fluid in the spinal cord (the great strait) to the Father, thus giving tithes to the Lord.

THE PSALMS OF DAVID

David is "Beloved of God"-psalm, "Praise, or hymn."

David is the seed, speaking, praising the source of its being and asking continually that its enemy, the carnal man, be destroyed.

"And David said to Gad, I am in a great strait, let me fall into the hands of the Lord and not in the hands of man."

The hands of man refers to the first man, Adam, or ani-mal desire. The strait is the spinal cord-"The strait and narrow way that leads to life eternal."

Gad refers to the tribe of Aries, the ram-the head ruled by the brain substance-the OR, the Lord, or "Lord God from heaven."

"Jonathan-the praise of Jehovah." T, or Tav, in Hebrew, means a cross.

H, from Heth, means spiritual perception.

So Jonathan is a symbol of John, the baptizing fluid (oil) that descends from the upper brain that has been lifted by the seed (David), just as John, in the New Testament, was lifted up by Jesus after the baptism. "HE   THAT   RULETH   HIS   OWN SPIRIT

(SELF) IS GREATER THAN HE THAT TAKETH A CITY"

"If a man cannot rule his own house, how can he take care of the church of God?"

The Ego resides in and operates from the cerebellum, a house or beth, and is in direct commu-nication with the upper brain, the FATHER, not only by means of the connective tissue partition of ganglia, but also by the wondrous lever, the pineal gland, the "Root and the stem of Jesse." Jesse means "a traveler from Bethlehem" the very same as Jesus, the seed.

The pneumogastric nerve also commences in the me dulla oblongata, against the cerebellum, and reaches down to the plexus, branches, in Bethlehem.

The thoughts of the Ego in its home in the cerebellum (called "heart" by the Greeks-"As a man thinketh in his heart so is he") may operate in the lower or Adam man, or in the "Lord God from heaven" realm.

This operation is·clearly and startlingly set forth in the ancient, thrice-told parable of the prodigal son, who thought it best to take his portion or substance and waste, or "eat it," in riotous living. The Ego thus ate of the fruit or bread of the tree of life, so that he did not rule or master himself. The natural sequence to this failure is a deficiency or wasting away of the gray matter of the brain, for the seed that should lift up one-tenth (tithe) every 29 _½ days has been eaten in Egypt and Sodom, "Where our Lord was also crucified." "For he that eateth and drinketh unworthily, eateth and drin-keth dam nation to himself, not discerning the Lord's body."

In order to be able to take care of the house of God "Your body is the temple (house or church) of God," one must return a portion to the brain in the "Only way whereby he may be saved, Jesus Christed and crucified" the seed carried up the "Strait and narrow way," and cross-ified at the "place of the skull."

"AND ENOCH WALKED WITH GOD AND WAS N:OT, FOR GOD TOOK HIM"

"Enoch" is·Hebrew for initiation, and "Hebrew" means to Passover.   (See "Crossing Jordan," or "Crucifixion.") "Elijah went up in a chariot of fire."   Elijah means

the same as Jesus.

"Elijah's mantle fell on Elisha." Elisha represents the material for the next seed. "Mantle" means the same as cover or cup; "Father, remove this cup from me."

"The latchet of whose shoes I am not worthy to un loose." Mantle, cup, latchet, and shoes all refer to some thing that covers.

The record states that when Jesus was born he was "Put in swaddling clothes," or covered. The mineral salts in the medulla oblongata, through which the pineal and pituitary fluids flow on the way down the Ida and Pingala nerves, carry enough of the mineral salts to form the crust or seed that protects the "Precious Oint ment" that is finally released when the seed goes over the crossed Ida and Pingala, at Golgotha. Hence, "Father remove this cup (cover) from me."

Again, the "mantle that fell on Elisha" was this same cup or swaddling cloth that is represented by "As I go so will I come again." Who? This same Jesus, or "Elisha-Elijah.

"I am the resurrection and the life."

Moses represents the seed, also, found in an ark.

"To Abraham and his seed was the promise given, and to thy seed, which is Christ."-Paul.

"Whom do men say that I the Son of man am?

"And they said, Some say that thou are John the Bap tist, some Elias, and others, Jeremiah, or one of the prophets"-i.e., resurrected seeds.

God-Man: The Word Made Flesh

OM MANI PADME HUM

The Jewel in the Lotus

The lotus flower is the cerebrum, whose convolutions or petals receive all vibrations from without and are transmitted to the mechanism within, there to be trans lated into terms of the senses. Dew-drops from the boundless sea of the Virgin Mary, the tender mother, glisten on its perfumed petals, while they reflect the golden glory of the spiritual sun.

Countless thousands of these wondrous petals lie tightly closed in the cerebrum of the average person. Sad to relate, there are many, many people in whom the lotus petals have atrophied, died and decayed. Then the asy lum or the institution for the feeble minded claims them.

The Optic within the Thalamus is the heart, the fair jewel within the lotus bud. It is the stone the builders rejected.

The spinal cord is the stem of the lotus, a filament from which reaches down into the slime of the asphalt bed.

The Kundalini fire within the sacred plexus is the Bride of the Lot-us, Lot's wife who looked back and became a pillar of salt.

As the dark and slimy bed conceals the quintessence of richness which fertilizes the lotus, and causes it to bud, so the vibrations from the sun above impinge upon this wonderful bud, and the force from above and the force from beneath, meeting in that wondrous heart of the lotus, causes all those beautiful petals to unfold, and lo I its heart lies bare to the universe.

And thus in you and I, when that quintessence of rich ness is kept within the body-when it is not "wasted in riotous living"-ascends the spinal cord, rising ever higher and higher until at last it reaches the heart of the lotus, the optic thalamus, vivifying it, revealing it, a glow ing, scintillating jewel reflecting the light of the Logos Himself and its petals wide open to receive vibrations which translate into the music of the spheres-and once again a lotus has bloomed.

When a human lotus blooms it is said that all nature thrills with gladness and thanksgiving.

THE HUMAN AUTOMOBILE

Man never invented anything.   There is no new

thing.

Within the "Fearfully and wonderfully made" human machine are the vestigial multiple forms conceived in the Infinite Mind, the prototypes of all things; and when the "Spirit in m n," the Ego, receives understanding from the "wisdom of the Almighty," it operates on the canvas of life before it, the plane of expression and form, shapes machines, and the factories of a transient commercialism which serve their day like a child's toy, then go into the discard and dis"appear. One day the coach and four-in hand, the next day the locomotive. Then man springs upon an automobile and drives it until the axles blaze and the spaces shrivel behind him.

Tomorrow he leaves earth behind and climbs the etheric terraces, peering into the unknown as if searching for the portals of some Celestial City.

The cerebellum is the chauffeur's seat, the pineal gland the lever, the cerebrum the gasoline tank (woe be to him who is out of oil}, the solar plexus is the speedometer, and the spinal cord is the passageway from the oil tank. The individual can run his automobile carefully, wisely,

at just the right speed, and with common sense. He can lose control and try to climb a telegraph pole, or go over an embankment. If he or she is a careful driver and looks to the well-being of his machine, he would be care ful to have his steering gear in perfect order. If he found his machine had a hole in the gas tank and that the gas was being' wasted, he would hasten to have it repaired. Does he • ever even think of the oil tank in his own body?

THE HUMAN THERMOMETER

The spinal cord may be likened to a thermometer. The lower part of the vertebrae, the Dead Sea, or the Lake of Asphaltum (Cauda Equina) is the congealed mercury or quicksilver, which may be refined (melted) or raised by heat.

When seeds have been saved so that that body becomes purified, the rate of its vibration has been changed, and at the proper time the wonderful Kundalini, the serpent fire, is released and rises to the top of the cord, going into the head and out through the door of Brahm-which is between the su- tures. The mercury thus rises to the 33rd degree and goes over the top, reaching the shade or shadow of the Most High; 3 times 3 equals 9; thus 90 degrees in the shade.

THE PNEUMOGASTRIC OR VAGUS NERVE OR TREE AND HOLY GHOST

This wonderful nerve is the largest bundle of nerve fibers in the body. It is truly a Tree of Life, and its branches distribute the Holy Breath, essence, or Ghost, to lungs and solar plexus.

The breath, speaking from the natural body, is the air breathed into the lungs via the branches of trachea (Greek for rough), commonly termed wind-pipe.

For further information about the breath or air see "Turning water into wine." But the office of the pneu mogastric tree is to conduct and properly distribute the "Holy Ghost," the highly refined substance, a first potency of the breath that "God breathed into man."

When this breath is breathed into the body, about the age of twelve, and unites with the two dif- ferent potencies of creative ".substance" that descends from the "Most High," via the pineal gland, Joseph (or increase), and also through the pituitary gland, Mar-y (pure fluid-water) that have de- scended the two wonder nerves, extensions of pineal gland and pituitary body, one on each side of the spinal cord, and cross this great Strait between the 12th dorsal vertebra, "in Egypt where our Lord was also crucified" ; thence united, they go up to the semi lunar ganglio, a little space (see chart), thence into the manger in Bethlehem. Here the Divine Drama is en acted and "Jesus is con- ceived of the Holy Ghost"-the whole breath, coming down the pneumogastric tree or nerve.

Pneumo means breath. Breath in Greek is ghost.

I

THE SON OF MAN

"Know ye not that the Son of man hath power in earth to forgive sins?"

Who is the Son of man?

"The seed (or word) is the Son of man."

Again, Revelation 19 :13-"And his name is called the WORD OF GOD."

REGENERATION

"Ye who' have followed (disciple is a follower) me in the regeneration. "Read entire chapter of Matthew 19. "Sell or exchange what thou hast and give to the poor." Return one-tenth of the de- scending substance to the poor pineal gla,nd, the central eye and the upper brain that is slowly but surely wasting away-therefore get

ting poorer every day. Matt. 19.

How can this poverty be prevented? See Matt. 19. "With man• (carnal or Adam-of earth, earthy), it is impossible, but with God all things are possible."

How shall we come in touch with God and realize our power-i.e., to be perfect, even as our Father in heaven 1s perfect?

Answer: "When ye pray for anything, know that ye have it now."

This means that we recognize that all things exist now and that the upper brain, the Most High, the great reser voir of "enduring substance" (Paul) will give to the Ego, who resides in the cerebellum (see chart), whatso ever it asks, because the Ego RECOGNIZED the reality of the "Secret place of the MOST HIGH."

There are four brains in the human body. The cere brum, the cerebellum, the medulla oblongata, and the solar plexus.

The Pingala nerve corresponds to the right sympathetic system; the Ida, to the left sympathetic system.

Sushumna passes from the terminus of the spinal cord to the top of the cranium.

"The spino-olivary fasciculus is a small tract, triangular in section, which runs on the surface of the cord and just lateral to the anterior roots of the spinal nerves. This is connected with the Dorsal Spino-cerebellar Fasciculus.

The latter conveys non-sensory sympathetic impulses re ceived from the viscera. In the dorsal part of this nerve is a small strand of fibers called the spinal vestibular tract which rises in the lumbar-sacral region of the cord." Santee. We can easily see the connection between these nerves. The olivary of course has to do with the dis tribution of the oil and we know that the sacral ganglion is con-nected with the genitals.

"Fibers of the cerebrum concerned with the higher psy chic functions of the brain become medullated gradually, year after year, keeping pace with the mental develop ment, and the process of medullation is not completed until late in life."-Kaes.

There is a central canal within the spinal cord. That which is within this canal is of a substance more like steam or gas than anything else.

"AS A MAN THINKETH IN HIS HEART SO IS HE"

THOUGHT is the creative power in the universe. Universal intelligence,   operating as thought, sprang' forth, "Spirit-sandalled and shod," at the

appointed time and in the appointed place, and Lo! the planet e,arth, man's sorrowful star, be-came manifest.

Earth is man's sorrowful star for the reason that only by means of trouble and pain does human-ity learn its lessons. '

Spirit, manifesting on earth, uses earth as a negative pole, in order that the personality may grow. The min eral, vegetable and animal kingdoms use earth in much the same way. The earth is one plane of manifestation.

How can a man think in his heart?

The organ that divides blood was called by the ancients "dividing pump"-not heart. The real heart is the cere bellum and was so named by the Greeks and is the seat of thought.

Madame Blavatsky says, in the Secret Doctrine, that the cerebellum contains all, being the seat of intelligence. The thinker, the individual or "man who never dies," has his home, therefore, in the cerebellum, under the

shadow of the Almighty.

Read what the writer of the 91st Psalm has to say about this: "He that dwelleth in the secret place of the Most High shall abide under the shadow of the Al mighty."

Secret (secretion, oil or ointment) place of the Most High-is that place where the secretion of oil or ointment is found. In the Bible we see so many references to oil anointing, secret, secretions, etc.

This plainly shows that the place of the Most High is the cerebrum, that portion of the anatomy of man whence comes the oil or ointment-the precious substance that fructifies the brain of man and causes it to develop; it is that which nourishes the brain.

The abiding place of the Ego is "Under the shadow of the Almighty," since the cerebrum extends entirely over and around it.

And again the Psalmist says:

"He will cover thee with his pinions

and under his wings shalt thou take refuge."

The feathery convolutions which are plainly shown in the upper brain may be well compared to the feathers of a bird. The "Voice of the Silence" speaks of the Ego resting "Under the wings of the Great Bird."

The upper brain is composed of highly specialized sub stance. It is a reservoir of God's creative compounds. It is that God-making material-the Kingdom of Heaven wherein all is found.

"Seek ye first the Kingdom of Heaven and all things shall be added unto you."

"The Kingdom of Heaven is within you." Heaven means "heaved up"-a high place.

The cerebrum is, then, the kingdom of heaven, for it is within us. By seeking it we draw from it the precious oil or ointment which shall nourish the brain and therefore cause it to grow and ex-pand.

Certain parts of the brain cells are dormant. They are in a certain slow rate of motion or activity, and, therefore, answer to vibrations of their kind.

Let us suppose, for example, that little cell in the brain is composed of spirallae, spirals of nerves, seven sets of which can be seen by the trained occultist.

In a person of low intelligence only three or four of these spirallae will be found to be active, while the man who is already working along the line of regeneration living the life of self-sacrifice, will show five and six in active operation.

The higher and more lofty the quality of the thought, the finer or higher the vibration. Just as the vibration of the ether strikes upon the tympanum of the ear and pro duces sound-so are the spirallae of the brain cells oper ated upon by the fingers of the heavenly man, when the Kingdom is sought.

Thought, then, is a vibration, and as a·man thinks so does he vibrate his brain cells.

How many people really think?

The war has done more to wake people up and set them to thinking than anything else ever could have done. It has started that process, in many people-it has forced them to think.

Thought is a particular development of ideas, some thing entirely apart from the "hit-or-miss," "ramshackle" process w ich was supposed to be thought. .

Let us begin to think; let us choose the material from which we shall build our temples-the temple of the "Liv ing God."

The process that the average man calls thought is not consecutive thinking. God hasten the day when people will realize that all that is, has been or will be, is the re sult of thought.

Thought is both creative and destructive.

Not only are we making our bodies now, but we are making those which we shall wear in the future. .

By the future I mean when the individual is reincar nated.

A great thinker has said: "Know this mighty fact, the soul is but the fruitage of thought tinctured and tarnished with the emotions, passions and desires of the flesh.11

First, as regards the physical body. Thought selects the food by which the body is nourished. The cells of the body are being constantly destroyed and rebuilt. The purest food possible to obtain will construct a pure body. Vegetables, fruits and grains are of much finer construc tion than flesh, and hence can vibrate to much higher rates of motion.

Flesh is decaying animal matter and is detrimental to the highest development of man. Much flesh eating thor oughly coarsens the body, and the marks of his calling are stamped on the face of the butcher.

Another example is that of a man who drinks. Alco hol brings about exactly the same result. The body can not respond to any of the higher vibrations.

Just as surely as the note you strike on the piano must produce a certain tone, just so surely will your body answer to the same rate of vibration around it that it vibrates to in itself.

The high cost of flesh food during the war has been a blessing in disguise, for it was the only means whereby people could be brought to realize that they could still live if they never ate meat. Then, after a time, they will begin to realize that they can enjoy much better health without it.

If you wished to do a fine, delicate piece of work, you would not use coarse or unwieldy instruments in doing it.

Just as true is it that the vehicle of the spirit-Solo mon's Temple-must be delicately and finely constructed.

The body must be kept scrupulously clean and be given sufficient exercise.

If your body is not satisfactory to you, it is because you have indulged in thoughts that have marred its con struction.

It is never too late to do something toward the recon

struction and regeneration of the body.

Start NOW.

The physical man is made up of twelve divisions, i. e., bone man, muscular man, nerve man, etc.   These are all constructed with a certain cell salt or mineral as a base for each man or division of the body, see "Relation of the Mineral Salts of the Blood to the Signs of the Zodiac." Each cell of the body is a living, throbbing intelligence.

Each cell actually reaches out and grasps from out the water of life-'that living stream of blood that is the life of the body-just the material it needs in its construction. "The quality of the force·called into action in any king

dom determines the quality of the offspring."

You are directly responsible for each thought that occupies your brain.

The soul is the thought man and the emotional man that occupies the physical bodies resembles it in form and feature. We do not here refer to the Spiritual Ego.

If, then, our thoughts build our bodies, what thoughts are the cell lives of the body filled with? We must natur ally see that they are, in vast numbers, filled with thoughts of fear, strife and blood. Fears of microbes, disease, poverty, the neighbors, the weather, the night air, the dark, burglars, etc., etc.

Eternal strife for wealth, position and power, for ma terial benefits. Benefits, so-called.

All this brings about war-the cell life gorged with blood, calling for the blood of its brothers.

Is not the cause of the war clear?

Do not thoughts pollute the very air? Is it not true that our thoughts affect those around us? What about the cells th:h we throw off from our bodies every minute

-cells that we have built and that are impregnated with our thoughts?

What is the matter with the people in the world? For there is nothing the matter with the world itself.

Each cell, then, that we throw off from our bodies, hour by hour and day by day, bears the stamp of our thoughts upon it. These go to make up the record of our lives, which those whose eyes are opened can read. In occultism this is called the Akashic record.

Then each man is the recording angel.

"Like attracts like." Birds of a feather flock to gether." These are trite sayings.

We see, then, that the cellular construction and fineness of the tissues of the physical man is de-termined by the character of the thoughts we store away in them.

The prodigal son wasted his substance in riotous living. His thoughts were turned toward the indulgence of the lower passions, like the rich young man who went away sorrowful because he had many possessions. Therefore the precious substance, the oil or ointment, the elixir of life, was sold for a mess of pottage. The seed, Jesus, or Christ, was not saved. If his thoughts had been pure and clean, the seed would have reached the cerebellum and would have increased in power a thousand fold. They then would have become the anointed of the Lord would have received the oil or oin-ment. The prodigal would then have become the son "in whom the Father was well pleased."

When the thoughts of the disciple are purified from every undesirable thought-then he be-comes the son of the Master for his thought flows like a river through the consciousness of his Lord.

His body has become transfigured, for each seed has become crucified and Christed. Each cell of his body has thrown off all its impurities and has become white in the blood of the lamb, for the blood of the lamb is as a crystal stream.

The process of regeneration causes the white corpuscles of the blood to overcome the preponderance of red, or Mars corpuscles.

Therefore the flesh becomes transparent-and he man ifests more and more of the Father-he is no longer man-but has become a God.

Paul says: "Now, then, are we the sons of God." "All things I have done ye can do, and greater."

As we go on living the regenerative life, the time comes when we no longer respond to any law within the physical realm, for all physical matter has been cast off from the body. "It is sown a material and is raised (because the seed has been raised-the rate of vibration has been raised) a spiritual body, and the Kingdom of Heaven has been attained.

"HE THAT OVERCOMETH"

The above sentence occurs nine times in Revelation.

To overcome a vice or habit means to cease to do it. In the Scriptures overcome is used to symbol the triumph of the Ego over sex or animal desire. It means the con quering of the carnal mind.

REVELATION 2, 7-"He that hath an ear, let him hear

what the Spirit saith unto the churches; To him that overcometh will I give to eat of the tree of life, which is in the midst of the paradise of God."

REVELATION 2, 11-"He that hath an ear, let him hear what the Spirit saith unto the churches; He that overcometh shall not be hurt of the second death." REVELATION 2, 17-"He that hath an ear, let him hear what the Spirit saith unto the churches; To him that overcometh will I give to eat of the hidden manna,

and I will give him a white stone, and in the stone a new name written, which no man knoweth saving he that receiveth it."

REVELATION _2, 26, 27-"And he. that overcometh, and keepeth my works unto the end, to him will I give power over the nations." "And he shall rule them with a rod of iron; as the vessels of a potter shall they be broken to shivers; even as I received of my Father. And I will give him the morning star."

REVELATION 3, 5-"He that overcometh, the same shall

be clothed in white raiment; and I will .not blot out his name out of the book of life, but I will confess his name before my Father, and before his angels."

REVELATION 3, 12-"Him that overcometh will I make a pillar in the temple of my God, and he shall go no more out: and I will write upon him the name of my God, and the name of the city of my God, which is new Jerusalem, which cometh down out of heaven from my God: and I will write upon him my new name."

REVELATION 3, 21-"To him that overcometh will I grant to sit with me in my throne, even as I also overcame, and am set down with my Father in his throne."

REVELATION 21, 7-"He that overcometh shall inherit all things ; and I will be his God, and he shall be my son."

EXTRACT FROM "DISCOURSES FROM THE SPIRIT-WORLD

IT IS thought that Stephen Olin was First President of Wesleyan University.

"The inhabitants of the earth may look forward with joyful assurance that the time is approaching when heaven shall be manifest on earth in the glorious harmo nies that will everywhere greet the eye and cheer the heart. As certain as the revolutions of time move for ward, SO SURELY WILL THE DIVINE GLORY BE VISIBLY DISPLAYED AND ALL NATIONS SHALL BEHOLD AND ENJOY THE BLESSED NESS OF CELESTIAL ILLUMINATION. Such

being the future and happy result that awaits the earth and its inhabitants, how important, fellow mortal, is your duty to hasten on the grand consummation. Arise from your inactivity and dullness and move forward in obedi ence to the laws of your being. Let no excuse prevent the utmost development of your whole nature. Exercise all the powers of your mind and body with reference to the harmonial unfolding of yourself. Do what you can to assist others in the great work of spiritual and physical development. Learn from the volume of inspiration in the universe without, and let your spirit look within for still higher manifestations and more refined enjoyments.

CONSUMMATION 1927
HE reyolutionary planet Uranus will have com pleted·his seven years' journey through Pisces, and entered the sign Aries, representing the upper brain,
in January, 1927.
The stars in their course
Are nearing the dawn of peace. The purpling mountain-tops
Of human love appear. Look! Listen!
Above the battle's din you may hear The anthem of "Peace on earth." Good will to men is in the air.
Out from the curling mists of the Pacific Sea That twist and twine
Like things alive;
From the glory of the upclimbing clouds Of the morning, that spill their jewels On the grass and flowers ;
In the liquid notes of the shuttle-throated mocking bird That pours its rippling prayers
Into the ears of Deity;
F.rom the clean-trunked eucalypti,
From orange blossoms and pendant pepper bough; From the sweet-faced little children;
From the hearts of earnest men; From the souls of women-mothers; From the planetary angles
And rising constellations; From the heavenly hosts that "Declare the glory of God";
From the inner sanctuary of cosmic law Wemay hear the song of Peace.
Peace comes!
Reach forth thy hands, brothers, sisters, Welcome thy Savior-Peace.
Offend her not I
Bow to the radiant queen I
We are so weary-
Yea, sick unto death-of war. Our Healer comes-
The Great Physician.
Let all rejoice and be glad.
Let us join the song, Peace unto Thee!

From the Seven Sacred Centers of regenerate human bodies; from the Secret Places of the Most High, where immortal Egos sit enthroned in the wondrous brain of man-the new Jerusalem-is heard the Divine Anthem. The music of the Spheres, out and out in realms of Cosmic Law, now becomes audible, and choruses with the redeemed and glorified earth.

Flowers bloom fresh in her footsteps;

The folds of her white garments are like "trailing clouds of glory." The co-operative commonwealth of humanity looms behind her. The bugles all sing truce along the.iron front of war.

Ironclads rust.

Airships climb and climb into the ether,

As if seeking the portals of the Celestial City. The trenches are covered with grass.

Vines clamber over arsenals, Flowers bloom on deserted forts.

Soldiers become men at home, field, shop, firesides, Women love and children play.

"The ransomed of the Lord return And come to Zion---

With everlasting joy upon their heads." And all over and about

The air is full of the scent of flowers, And the trickling fall of fountains,

And free men and women have started on the Great Adventure To find God.

"And I saw a New Heaven and a New Earth,"

The old has passed away and the sun of righteousness arises with Healing in its beams.

THE END